BUILDING SOCIAL WORLDS

WYSE Series in Social Anthropology

Editors:
James Laidlaw, William Wyse Professor of Social Anthropology, University of Cambridge, and Fellow of King's College, Cambridge
Joel Robbins, Sigrid Rausing Professor of Social Anthropology, University of Cambridge, and Fellow of Trinity College, Cambridge

Social Anthropology is a vibrant discipline of relevance to many areas – economics, politics, business, humanities, health and public policy. This series, published in association with the Cambridge William Wyse Chair in Social Anthropology, focuses on key interventions in Social Anthropology, and is based on innovative theory and research of relevance to contemporary social issues and debates. Former holders of the William Wyse Chair have included Meyer Fortes, Jack Goody, Ernest Gellner and Marilyn Strathern, all of whom have advanced the frontiers of the discipline. This series intends to develop and foster that tradition.

Recent titles:

Volume 17
Building Social Worlds: Thinking Forwards with Esther Newcomb Goody
Edited by Barbara Bodenhorn, Alicia Fentiman and Mary Goody

Volume 16
Asian Lives in Anthropological Perspective: Essays on Morality, Achievement and Modernity
Susan Bayly

Volume 15
An Anthropology of Intellectual Exchange: Interactions, Transactions and Ethics in Asia and Beyond
Edited by Jacob Copeman, Nicholas J. Long, Lam Minh Chau, Joanna Cook and Magnus Marsden

Volume 14
Against Better Judgment: Akrasia in Anthropological Perspectives
Edited by Patrick McKearney and Nicholas H.A. Evans

Volume 13
New Perspectives on Moral Change: Anthropologists and Philosophers Engage with Transformations of Life Worlds
Edited by Cecilie Eriksen and Nora Hämäläinen

Volume 12
Where Is the Good in the World? Ethical Life between Social Theory and Philosophy
Edited by David Henig, Anna Strhan and Joel Robbins

Volume 11
Making Better Lives: Hope, Freedom and Home-Making among People Sleeping Rough in Paris
Johannes Lenhard

Volume 10
Selfishness and Selflessness: New Approaches to Understanding Morality
Edited by Linda L. Layne

For a full volume listing, please see the series page on our website:
https://www.berghahnbooks.com/series/wyse

BUILDING SOCIAL WORLDS

Thinking Forwards with Esther Newcomb Goody

Edited by

Barbara Bodenhorn, Alicia Fentiman and Mary Goody

berghahn
NEW YORK · OXFORD
www.berghahnbooks.com

First published in 2025 by
Berghahn Books
www.berghahnbooks.com

Library of Congress Cataloging-in-Publication Data
A C.I.P. cataloging record is available from the Library of Congress
Library of Congress Cataloging in Publication Control Number:
2024052544

British Library Cataloguing in Publication Data
A catalogue record for this book is available from the British Library

ISBN 978-1-80539-952-0 hardback
ISBN 978-1-80539-953-7 epub
ISBN 978-1-80539-954-4 web pdf

https://doi.org/10.3167//9781805399520

For Esther

Esther Newcomb Goody, 1980s. © Goody Family Archive.

Contents

List of Illustrations   ix

Acknowledgements   xi

Introduction. Going Against the Grain, Again   1
BARBARA BODENHORN, ALICIA FENTIMAN AND MARY GOODY

Chapter 1. Sisters into Wives, Wives into Sisters   51
MARILYN STRATHERN

Chapter 2. Fragments of Intimacy and the Reassembling of Relations   66
BARBARA BODENHORN

**Chapter 3. The Visible Invisibilities of the Circulation of Women in
the Ottoman Mediterranean and Their Implications**   80
PAUL SANT CASSIA

**Chapter 4. The Circulation of Women and Children – and Everybody
Else – Half a Century Later**   104
LYNNE BRYDON

**Chapter 5. Video, Voice and Vygotsky: Narratives of Learning among
the Konkomba of Northern Ghana**   122
ALICIA FENTIMAN

**Chapter 6. Lessons in Milking and Lessons in Maths: A Case Study
of Andean Children in Colombia**   140
CATALINA LASERNA

**Chapter 7. Singing the Names: Custom and Chronology in Mamprusi
Drum Histories**   170
SUSAN DRUCKER BROWN

**Chapter 8. 'One Snake is the Biggest in the Pond': Linguistic Fragments
from Mambila Funerals as Evidence for Religious Change**   189
DAVID ZEITLYN

**Chapter 9. Childrearing through Social Interaction on Rossel Island,
Papua New Guinea**   199
PENELOPE BROWN AND MARISA CASILLAS

Conclusion   222
FELICIA KAFUI ETSEY

Afterword   236
JOHN KEITH HART

Appendix I. Esther N. Goody: Unpublished Notes   243

Appendix II. Jean La Fontaine: A Memory of Esther Goody   255

Appendix III. Interview with Suzanne Hoelgaard   258

Appendix IV. Selected Tributes   269

Appendix V. Esther N. Goody: Bibliography   284

Index   291

Biographical images follow pages 117–121

Illustrations

Figures

0.1. Ted and Esther Newcomb in Bennington, USA, ca. 1937.
© Goody Family Archive (photograph Mary Shipherd Newcomb).   2

0.2. Picnic with friends in the Lot, southwest France, ca. 1973.
© Goody Family Archive.   4

0.3. Early fieldwork: album page showing Esther Goody and Christine
Muir documenting the Bole Damba festival, northern Ghana, 1965.
© Esther Newcomb Goody Archive (photographs Jack Goody).   6

0.4. Boys' Drawing V: one of the ambiguous Thematic Apperception Test
figures drawn by Anna Craven and used by Goody in the Kpembe
study, 1970. © Esther Newcomb Goody Archive. Published in
Esther N. Goody, *Parenthood and Social Reproduction: Fostering
and Occupational Roles in West Africa*, 1982, Cambridge
University Press, reproduced with permission.   10

0.5. Fieldwork album double page: weaving sheds in Daboya, northern
Ghana, 1974. © Esther Newcomb Goody Archive.   16

0.6. Daboya strip-woven cloth worn by Pontali *wura* (chief), 1965.
© Esther Newcomb Goody Archive.   19

0.7. Daboya strip-woven cloth worn by chiefs' followers at Bole Damba
(carrying a chief's chair inside), 1965. © Esther Newcomb Goody
Archive.   21

0.8. Fieldwork among the Gujarati community in Leicester, 1980s.
© Esther Newcomb Goody Archive.   22

0.9. 'Local Language Initial Literacy' project class, northern Ghana,
2000s. © Esther Newcomb Goody Archive.   31

0.10. Esther Goody's last visit to Ghana in 2011; on the veranda of her
Bole home with her friend and collaborator Fati Mumuni (left),
Fati's older sister with her daughter and baby, and a friend from
Bolgatanga. © Esther Newcomb Goody Archive (photograph
Stephen Aboagye).   35

5.1. Children and young adults carrying sand for building
construction, Kachilinde Village, Kpandai, Ghana, April 1992.
© Alicia Fentiman.   127

5.2. Konkomba women and children at the farm peeling cassava,
Kachilinde Village, Kpandai, Ghana, March 1992.
© Alicia Fentiman.   129

5.3. Sei Hoeing/Tiny kitchens: Esther Goody's Baale fieldwork video
stills, ca. 1990. © Esther Newcomb Goody Archive.   134

6.1. The village of San Juan and surrounding landscape, Department
of El Cauca, Colombia, 1978. © Catalina Laserna.   141

6.2. A four-year-old son observes and assists his mother making
cheese in the village of San Juan, El Cauca, Colombia, May 1978.
© Catalina Laserna.   144

6.3. *Minga* (community labour): weeding the school garden in the
village of San Juan, El Cauca, Colombia, April 1978.
© Catalina Laserna.   149

7.1. Mamprusi performer, musician and drummer during the
installation of a chief, Nalerigu, northern Ghana, 1956.
© Estate of Susan Drucker Brown.   178

7.2. 'The *Nayiiri*'s court in Nalerigu', aquatint etching by Susan
Drucker Brown, ca. 2010. © Estate of Susan Drucker Brown.   185

Acknowledgements

The editors would like to express our appreciation of the Department of Social Anthropology at the University of Cambridge for its support of the conference which generated this volume, and to thank all those who attended and participated in the meeting. We thank especially all those who have contributed to this present work, both through the conference and subsequently. Marion Berghahn and Tom Bonnington at Berghahn Books were steadfast in their patience and support for the project as it evolved. The editors also extend their special gratitude to Marilyn Strathern, who kindly provided guidance on the project, reviewed many papers and offered us constructive feedback. Penelope Brown, Michael Cole, Ziba Mir-Hosseini, David Olson and Frances Pine provided important editorial advice, while David Anderson, JoAnne Bennett, Jean La Fontaine and Suzanne Hoelgaard gave generously of their recollections. The keen professional eye of Xavier Ribas was invaluable for our photographic content and Benjamin P. Macias efficiently and thoughtfully indexed the manuscript with a very tight deadline. We also thank the friends and colleagues who allowed us to include their tributes in honour of Esther; they include Francesca Bray and A.F. (Sandy) Robertson, Lynne Brydon, Stephen Levinson and Penelope Brown, Leslie Casely-Hayford, Magdeleine (Marie) Chatry-Komarek, Michael, Sheila and Jennifer Cole, Paola Filippucci, Chris Hann, Ziba Mir-Hosseini, Fati Mumuni, David Olson and Marilyn Strathern. In addition we would like to thank L.M. (Mick) Brown, Magdeleine Chatry-Komarek, Edith Esch, Patricia Owens for their kind assistance; Rachel and Tony McMahon for their encouragement and discussion. We gratefully acknowledge the significant contribution made by Suzanne Hoelgaard and the late Kusum Gopal who initiated the idea of honouring Esther Goody through a publication, and our debt to the late Susan Drucker Brown for her profound knowledge of Esther's life and work. Sadly, Kusum, Esther and Susan all passed away while the book was being produced. It is a source of particular pleasure that Esther herself took great delight in the project, but a matter of great sadness that she did not see its conclusion. We trust that the completed volume is a fitting memorial to her passionate contribution to scholarship.

Esther and colleagues in the garden at Adams Road, Cambridge, 2012. Left to right: Esther Goody, Susan Drucker Brown, Kusum Gopal, Ziba Mir-Hosseini, Alicia Fentiman. © Suzanne Hoelgaard.

Introduction
Going Against the Grain, Again

Barbara Bodenhorn, Alicia Fentiman and Mary Goody

This volume is a celebration of Esther Newcomb Goody's legacy, a ground-breaking anthropologist in many ways. Although she worked in Ghana for decades, she also promoted the importance of conducting fieldwork at home. Her anthropological commitment to dedicated and detailed fieldwork never prevented her from drawing on – and collaborating with – sociolinguists, developmental psychologists, and educators, among others. She was a boundary-crosser in many senses, something we explore in the pages below. The conference that provided the impetus for the present volume was testament to her ongoing footprint.[1] The chapters to come explore that footprint, bringing it into view through each author's own current work. To set the intellectual context, we offer here an overview of Esther Goody's life and an exploration of some of the key themes that inform her works. We finish with a brief consideration of the chapters themselves, each of which invites readers to explore some of the ways in which contemporary anthropologists continue to engage with her ideas.

Esther Newcomb Goody: Setting the Scene

A Brief Biographical Sketch

Esther, the eldest of three siblings, was born in Cleveland, Ohio in 1932 to Mary (née Shipherd) and Theodore Newcomb; she always emphasized the Newcomb part of her name, largely because of the close relationship with her father, who was a pioneering social psychologist.[2] The intellectual footprint of that relationship remains visible throughout a great deal of her work.

Newcomb's university teaching posts took his family from the American Midwest to New England and back again. His daughter's favourite school memory was a one-room schoolhouse in Bennington, Vermont, where she

Figure 0.1. Ted and Esther Newcomb in Bennington, USA, ca. 1937. © Goody Family Archive (photograph Mary Shipherd Newcomb).

flourished under the impact of hands-on learning in small groups of mixed-age students. She would appreciate the dynamics of this form of teaching as she encountered them in many contexts throughout her career. With Newcomb's move to the University of Michigan in 1941, the family settled in Ann Arbor where Esther finished her schooling. It was during these years that her father's research showed her that intellectual work was not just theoretical but applied.

As an undergraduate, Esther studied sociology and psychology at Antioch College, during which time the family spent six months in London. Here Esther audited classes at the London School of Economics and University College London, her first taste of British social anthropology. She was subsequently impressed by Meyer Fortes when he visited the United States, and in 1954 seized the opportunity to start postgraduate study at the Cambridge University department he headed. There Fortes assigned her Jack Goody as a supervisor. She accompanied the latter to Ghana in 1956 where she began her own research and they married during that time. Completing her PhD in 1961, she joined New Hall College (now Murray Edwards) in 1966, was made a Cambridge University Lecturer with the Department of Anthroplogy in 1972 and became Reader in Social Cognition in 1997.[3]

In between, and overlapping with, spells of Ghanaian fieldwork, Jack and Esther Goody had two daughters, and moved to a very beautiful house in Adams Road, Cambridge.[4] This became the centre of all kinds of sociality: informal supervisions conducted in the kitchen while children and dinner preparations competed for attention; lively meals attended by visiting scholars, faculty and graduate students; and offers of a place to stay when graduate students regularly ran out of resources at the end of their writing up period.[5] The family would spend August in a rural hamlet near Figeac in southwest France. This was a haven where serious writing took place, although many visitors appeared here too. Open doors, available beds, meals and talk shared after the day's work continued term-time conviviality in a more relaxed setting.[6]

Goody's open-handedness was by no means limited to her academic world. Felicia Kafui Etsey, a Ghanaian colleague and a contributor to this volume, speaks of Goody often paying for children's education in Ghana (see Conclusion). Goody consistently displayed a profound generosity of spirit; she knew that her capacity for reaching out across intellectual, cultural and socio-economic frontiers enriched her life as well as the lives of others.

Academic Themes

Although Esther Goody's publication list is extensive, we will focus here on a subsample of seminal works that we believe resonate with the contributors' chapters. We set out the recurring fascinations she felt for her research, and explore the implications she thought that research might have for the conduct of social life.[7]

Figure 0.2. Picnic with friends in the Lot, southwest France, ca. 1973. © Goody Family Archive.

A number of intellectual themes attracted Goody's repeated attention: the performativity of kinship; the psychological effects of fostering, adoption and movement (both individual and collective), particularly on children; the intersection between the things people say and do; and the profoundly social nature of teaching and learning. These all informed what she called 'the puzzles' that framed her research.[8] The different manifestations of these puzzles over her career illustrate how consistent was her practical as well as intellectual engagement with social life, even as we note the trajectories that that engagement took over time.

Esther Goody was clearly Meyer Fortes' student in her commitment to the accuracy of her ethnographic detail and to the careful documentation at all levels of what it was she was trying to do. And like Fortes, who drew on his own background in psychology to analyse his material, she took tools from other disciplines to unravel some of the puzzles she was confronting in the field.

Thus, despite her training in conventional anthropological methods, Goody often worked against the grain of mid-twentieth-century thinking regarding the 'proper' subject of anthropology. At a time when 'that's psychologizing' was a criticism, she continued to draw on the tools that she had developed through social psychology, cognitive psychology, linguistics and sociolinguistics for her analysis. And at a time when 'applied' anthropology was considered a poor cousin to 'theory', Goody was steady in drawing attention to the policy implications of her findings (see, e.g., Goody 1966).

The Performativity of Kinship

Relations through Circulation in Time and Space

From 1956 to 1957, Goody conducted extensive ethnographic research in Ghana focusing on kinship and domestic organisation in Gonja communities.[9] This was submitted in 1961 as her doctoral dissertation *Kinship, Marriage and the Developmental Cycle among the Gonja of Northern Ghana*. Supplemented by further fieldwork carried out between 1964 and 1966, Goody's first major work on kinship was published in 1973 as *Contexts of Kinship: An Essay in the Family Sociology of the Gonja of Northern Ghana*.

Her research extended Meyer Fortes' examination of the fluidity of kinship residence patterns over time. In his 1958 article, Fortes showed that female-headed households were not anomalous, but rather tended to occur at specific points in both men's and women's lives. Out of this material emerged the model he labelled 'the developmental cycle of domestic groups'.[10] By pushing the Fortesian concept of the developmental cycle, and by considering both human and social capital, Goody showed how Gonja women moved between residences during their adult lives. As in many groups, Gonja women had the

Figure 0.3. Early fieldwork: album page showing Esther Goody and Christine Muir documenting the Bole Damba festival, northern Ghana, 1965. © Esther Newcomb Goody Archive (photographs Jack Goody).

G 969 Bole Damba '65 Early am
in front of BW's lembu after all
night dancing, Mbowura & Mpotasibi
Bole Mboz W T Seripe Mboz W(r) on
thier chairs.

G 971 Bole Damba '65
Early am after all night dancing
B. Wura at back with his Mpotasibi
Nazbewura, spearholder etc.

option of returning to their natal kin if, for whatever reason, their marriages ended. In addition, however, Goody found that even during marriage these women might alternate between their roles as wives and as sisters. In a similar way, she noted that the common practices surrounding fosterage and apprenticeship meant that children too moved between households and between kin caregivers without permanently rupturing their relations with their natal parents. In both cases, then, what we find is a form of constant rather than periodic movement. The dual orientation towards both maternal and paternal kin was key throughout a person's life, and Goody's detailed analysis of this bilateral kinship structure helped to shed light on the significance of such patterned movement in Gonja society. Like Fortes, Goody provided an in-depth analysis of residence at various levels, including the household, the compound and between villages. In addition, however, she emphasized kinship institutions such as fostering, terminal separation and the ousting of widows as significant factors influencing movement. These practices, which not only permitted rupture and continuity but also were underpinned by the principal of oscillation, contributed fundamentally to Goody's understanding of kinship as processual as well as structural. Women's repeated movement between marital and natal homes, Goody argued, should not be considered a sign of marital weakness (as suggested in models of the 'matrilineal puzzle') but of sibling codependence alongside spousal responsibility. She thus posited the notion of an alternative development cycle that would incorporate this ongoing fluidity of movement. The shifting nature of siblingship in the context of marriage is the focus of Marilyn Strathern's chapter in this volume, as we discuss below.

Before the publication of *Contexts of Kinship*, Esther Goody co-authored 'The Circulation of Women and Children in Northern Ghana' with Jack Goody (1967), a comparative study of kinship structures and movement among Gonja and LoWiilli, two groups with very different political structures: the Gonja had created a relatively hierarchical, stratified state whereas the LoWiilli were organized as an acephalous society.[11]

In contrast to the spatial mobility among Gonja already mentioned, both LoWiilli women and children were more constricted in their movement. This ensured continuity of agricultural labour and was institutionalized through high bridewealth, low rates of divorce, very little kinship fostering (except in crisis), and widow inheritance or levirate. Significantly, the same factors impinge on the movement of women and children in other acephalous societies of northern Ghana such as Tallensi and Konkomba. Of note here is the extent to which this material runs against the grain of assumptions that acephalous political organization is uniformly more egalitarian than hierarchical polities.

Several chapters in the present volume extend Goody's focus on these mobile kinship strategies. Marilyn Strathern starts from Goody's analysis of Gonja sibling relations to explore important differences in brother/sister relationships in nineteenth-century middle-class England. Strathern high-lights the difference between the enduring value of male–female kinned relationships exhibited in Goody's Gonja data, and the greater emphasis on fears of permanent rupture expressed in the English material.

Paul Sant Cassia also compares Goody's work on surrogacy to his historical analysis of circulation in the eastern Mediterranean, both of preadolescent males through the Ottoman 'child levy' and of women moving between religious groups through intermarriage and religious conversion.

In her account of fluid childcare arrangements among the Avatime of southern Ghana, Lynne Brydon acknowledges Goody's significant influence on her own research but expands her focus to encompass globalized kinship relations in a twenty-first-century context.

Barbara Bodenhorn's chapter uses the lens of commemorative practices in the United States to explore the fragmentable nature not only of parenthood but of childhood. In doing so, she examines the traumatic nature of rupture, and the potential for new relations to emerge from it.

The Performativity of Parenting

i) *The Kpembe Study*

Even before her doctoral work was published, Goody produced a 'preliminary report' on fostering in the *Ghana Journal of Sociology* (1966: passim) , that is, for a Ghanaian audience. In it she drew explicit attention to what she considered 'unhelpful' barriers between models of 'traditional' and 'modern' family practices, which often underpinned social welfare measures both in Ghana and the UK. As a means to break down such barriers, she proposed an examination of the complex fostering strategies she had found to be so ubiquitous in Ghana. Subsequently she produced a further document for the UK Social Science Research Council (1970a) outlining several issues that would continue to be key for her throughout her career; in the Kpembe Study, a comparison of fostered and non-fostered children in eastern Gonja, Goody analysed Ghanaian material to examine UK assumptions about the impact of fostering.[12] In the UK at the time it was taken as given that the psychological consequences of fostering could make children feel abandoned and vulnerable, and therefore that fostering should not be a first choice in long-term care planning. In the United States it was also considered to be second best to adoption because, as a temporary measure, it was thought that children might get confused about where their home was and who was meant to care for them.[13] Thus at the time of Goody's report, in both the US and the UK, the notion of fostering was already constituted as a somewhat useful but not quite satisfactory solution to children's needs for care.

It was striking to Goody that among Gonja families, fosterage was the norm, not the exception, and it was positively valued. Her research question, then, was whether there was any evidence that Gonja children might nevertheless be

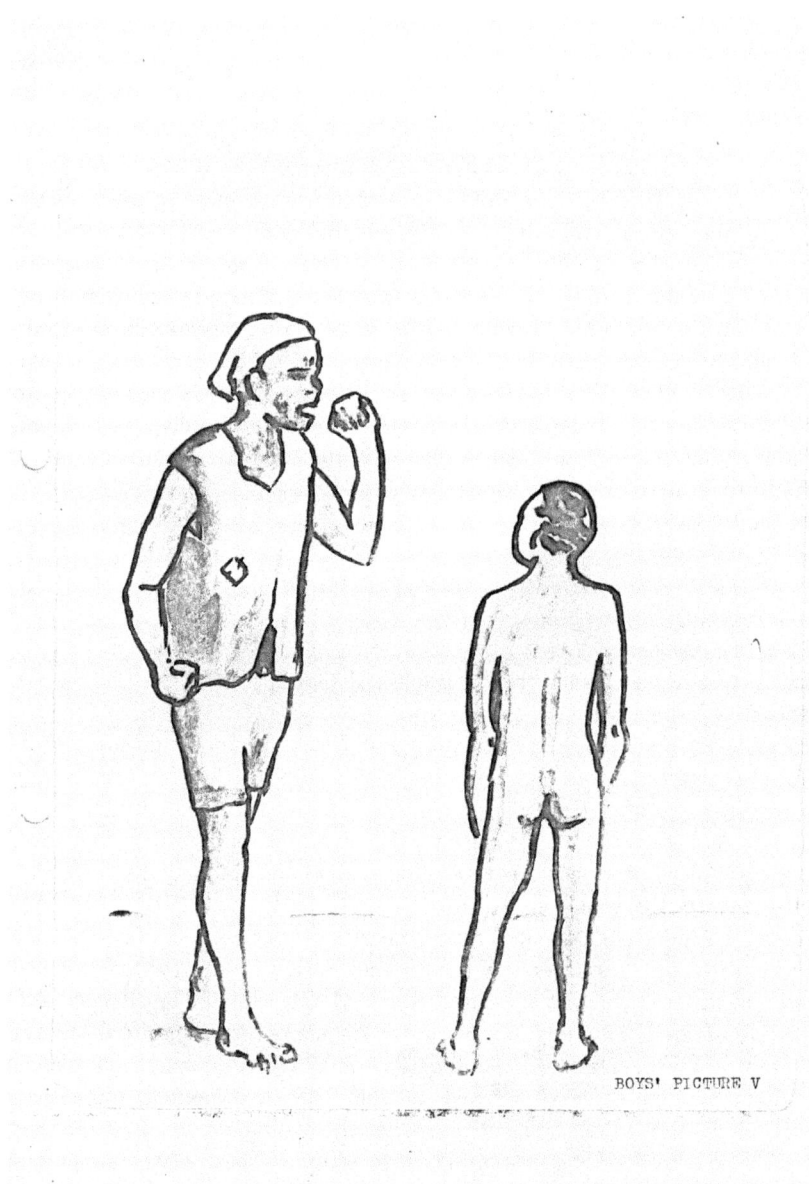

Figure 0.4. Boys' Drawing V: one of the ambiguous Thematic Apperception Test figures drawn by Anna Craven and used by Goody in the Kpembe study, 1970. © Esther Newcomb Goody Archive. Published in Esther N. Goody, *Parenthood and Social Reproduction: Fostering and Occupational Roles in West Africa*, 1982, by Cambridge University Press, reproduced with permission.

negatively impacted by the experience. As a dedicated sociologist, anthropologist and psychologist, Goody designed her own TATs (Thematic Apperception Tests);[14] these presented culturally appropriate-but-ambiguous scenarios between adults and children, about which children were asked to tell stories.[15] Goody used her knowledge of Gonja storytelling genres to produce a fine-grained analysis that went beyond the words themselves. The stories were then coded for perceptions of aggression, the imputation of motivation, and for evidence of unease. This first phase – exploring emotional states – drew almost entirely on the tools of social psychology, but the results were interpreted with a Geertzian commitment to thick description. She then added life history interviews with parents, children, teachers and community members, which provided further grounds for understanding the relationship between narrative form, cultural context and the shape of these young people's lives. The overall research programme thus strongly incorporated both qualitative and quantitative techniques of psychology and social anthropology.

Goody's findings revealed no statistically significant differences between the two groups, although there was a slight tendency for some fostered children – both boys and girls – to show more independence than children reared by their own parents (Goody 1982a: 87).[16] This supported her initial hypothesis that the two sets of children were substantially the same (ibid.: 57).

We felt it important to spend time with this relatively unknown study because of the ways it sets the stage for engaging with the corpus of Esther Goody's subsequent work. What invites attention at the outset is the extent to which Goody's research questions developed from her experiences, which themselves were self-consciously considered in a comparative way. The categories she examined were emergent rather than imposed. Her tools were interdisciplinary, and her thinking was as applied as it was theoretical. She was not simply trying to understand fosterage as a cultural institution; she was seeking to understand what sort of effects these strategies might have on children's well-being.

ii) *The Fracturability of Parenthood*
We have already noted how Goody saw that the daily lives of Gonja women and children could involve regular movement between sets of kinsmen. From the beginning she began to develop her core anthropological ideas about the nature of parental responsibility and parental being as both fragmentable and processual – set out in a series of publications between 1971 and 1982.[17] For Bodenhorn, 'Forms of Pro-parenthood' (Goody 1971a) was seminal. With its focus on how parenthood can be fragmented, negotiated and modified, this article resonates with much of the anthropology of kinship and personhood as it has taken shape from the critiques of postmodernism through to the first decades of the twenty-first century.[18] Briefly, Goody suggested that parenting encompasses different kinds of responsibilities – begetting, bearing, bringing up, training, and introducing into the social world. In the UK, a child's legal parents are assumed to be responsible for doing all these things, whereas in

Ghana they are not. In Ghana the 'personing' of parenthood, Goody argued, is neither assumed to be a biological given, nor necessarily invested in a single physical entity. A parent's job is to make sure that their children are mentored by the people who are best placed to realize each of the parenting tasks. That West African views of parenting approved this form of delegation did not imply a loss of primary parental responsibility. Although 'crisis fosterage' is an accepted strategy for dealing with unexpected and short-term events across many cultures, Goody was most interested in the extent to which 'purposive fosterage' (her term) was in fact the norm amongst her Gonja interlocutors (Goody 1975a: 1).

This strategy was seen as having important advantages for children, parents and foster parents. Many Gonja parents felt, for instance, that a child would show more respect to a foster parent and therefore get a more effective moral training from them. Carers would also benefit: a mother's brother could teach his foster son the ways of the mother's family, for instance, or a father's sister could have a foster daughter to help her in the house. These kinsfolk in fact traditionally had special rights to foster (as did the mother's mother), claims a parent could not easily refuse (see Goody 1975a: 140–41; 1982a: 180f.).[19] Parents benefitted from strengthened links between adult siblings scattered to different villages, reinforced through reciprocal duties of help and support. Such fosterage could also act as future insurance. A daughter fostered out to a mother's brother, for instance, would be in place when the mother returned in old age to live with her brother, and available to care for her (1975a: 139). Furthermore, it was important for Gonja children to know their parents' natal villages and extended family: most children grew up in groups of 'siblings' that included some fostered cousins, so the bonds between branches of the family were recreated in each generation (Goody 1973: 107; 1989: 240).

Purposive fosterage is also a strategy to place children where they will have education, training and an introduction into society. In Goody's experience, this became increasingly pertinent during the second half of the twentieth century as life was becoming more urban and the division of labour was becoming more complex; these practices were then adapted to meet new needs. The training aspect of parental responsibility informed Goody's engagement with apprenticeship in Ghana, a topic to which we will return.

iii) *Expanding the Focus: West African Families in London*
In the 1966 article mentioned above, Goody was already drawing attention to the challenges being faced by young West African couples when they came to the UK to study. Between 1970 and 1972, she and Christine Muir conducted a study in London of 295 West African couples with at least one child, of whom half had placed their children with English foster families (Muir and Goody 1972: 334–35). In a series of co-authored articles (Muir and Goody 1972; Goody and Muir Groothues 1977, 1979, 1982), they connected what they had been learning in Ghana with what they were also seeing in London.[20] They

worked intensively with twenty student parents from Nigeria and Ghana, all struggling to complete their studies while working to support the family. The striking difference in the student parenting strategies in London, Muir and Goody noted, was the age at which children were fostered out. The customary practice in West Africa was not to send children away before the age of five or six. That half of the student couples left their youngsters with English foster parents, many before their first birthday, the authors suggested, was a recognizable adaptation of the accepted West African strategy of reaching out for support and of ensuring their children were in a positive and advantageous situation. In this case the arrangement brought familiarity with English language and culture, something the parents assumed would benefit their children upon their return home; the students were thus being good parents in unfamiliar and challenging circumstances (Muir and Goody 1972: 333ff.).

In this new situation, fosterage was seen as a coping strategy, but one that was not problem-free. In 1975, Goody published 'Delegation of Parental Roles in West Africa and the West Indies', which elucidated further the dilemmas of these student parents.[21] Just as patterns of fostering within West Africa varied from place to place, and adapted over time in response to different situations, the pattern in London adapted to the particular challenges facing student parent immigrants: living isolated from relatives and friends, they had to make do with little money, whilst both parents tried to work and study (Muir and Goody 1972: 333ff; Goody 1975a: 148).

In the extended kin networks studied by Goody in West Africa, fostered children maintained frequent contact with the birth parents and remained embedded in a wide fabric of familial relationships; fostering reinforced existing secondary ties, rather than creating new primary ones. In London the conditions and their implications were very different. We have already noted the striking difference in the age at which children were fostered out. In addition, they were being sent to live with strangers. While the children were with the English families, both birth parents and children had to manage without the supporting cultural and kinship context that strengthened fostering relations in West Africa. In London, the customary parental contact was often restricted; the children were not getting an introduction into their own language and culture, or even to the food they would normally eat within the family (Muir and Goody c. 1971: 18).[22] As Goody notes, parents struggling to fill multiple roles 'were often distressed to have to part with their very young children' (1975a: 148). Nonetheless, for some this worked reasonably well. Others, however, encountered unexpected institutional barriers when they wanted to reunite with their children. They found their parental rights challenged because it was assumed by Social Services and the courts that they had abandoned their offspring, not that they had been taking care of them (Goody 1966, 1982a, 1984a).

In 'The Quest for Education', Goody and Muir Groothues (1977, 1982: 217–18) explore the case of a Ghanaian couple who placed their three-month-old daughter with English foster parents. The foster couple repeatedly pressed for adoption; the birth parents repeatedly and forcefully claimed their parental rights.[23] When the parents wanted to return to Ghana with their daughter, the foster family went to court to sue for custody where the judge sided with them, declaring that the birth parents should not be allowed to 'tear away' the child from the people who had cared for her so long.

This lack of fit between the people with the authority to judge what proper care is and the parents themselves can impact families drastically. Esther Goody was emphatically drawing attention to something that marginalized groups experience the world over, namely that those in power often override the moral universes of the people being judged.[24]

It is important to appreciate that Goody was acutely aware of the stumbling blocks in these arrangements, and was by no means suggesting that the foster-age would be fine as long as Social Services did not intervene. She understood that these patterns of fosterage indicated relations between the fosterers and the fosterees which were never static. In this we hear echoes of Fortes' aware-ness that social analysis requires a recognition of flux, whether that be cyclical or in response to much broader social, political and economic changes that frame the conditions in which actors make their decisions. Goody's continuing relevance regarding these issues was evident in a 2022 conference held in Paris, 'Parenthood in Africa after E.N. Goody', which took her work as the starting point for in-depth discussions.[25]

Esther Goody acted as scientific advisor to the UK Department of Health and Social Security (DHSS) from 1973 to 1985, during which time she spear-headed a great deal of research, and interacted with policymakers.[26] She was clearly one of the pioneers of doing anthropology 'at home', at the forefront of establishing anthropology in the community, and one of the first to bring cul-tural practices and official policy into mutual view. She published 'Can Anthropology Contribute to Social Policy?' in 1984. The legacy of that multiple commitment is evident in the work of many of her students.[27]

Knowledge Transmission: Apprenticeship and Questions

While in Ghana, Goody became intrigued by the possible connections between the fostering practices she found among so many Gonja parents and their con-sequences. The Kpembe Study, already discussed, explored these issues, but she also examined institutionalized fostering for the transmission of knowledge, asking not only what children were learning, but how they were learning it, and with whom. Through the lens of apprenticeship, she turned her attention more directly to language and communication as a function of social process (1975b), which in turn had implications for her understanding of learning (1989).

On Apprenticeship as Historical Process: Continuity and Adaptation

From the 1960s, Goody encountered fluid teaching dynamics across a wide range of skills throughout West Africa, most enacted through kinned relationships (1982a: 250–59; 1989: 241–43).[28] Her work on fosterage in northern Ghana led her to engage in a series of comparative studies in three southern Ghanaian communities in 1964 and 1965, where she became increasingly interested in the learning of specialist skills (1982a, chapters 6 and 8: passim). More in the south than in the north of Ghana, Great Britain's colonial presence introduced an increasingly complex division of labour as well as changes to the nature of 'work' – and, after the Second World War and Independence, a rapid multiplication of occupations. With these developments, 'apprenticeship took on added importance both for education and employment' (1982a: 196). Parents customarily sent their children to kin in order to learn specific traditional crafts, such as iron-working, goldsmithing, or weaving. With the introduction of 'Western' skills, such as those of auto mechanics, electricians and photographers, Goody noted a gradual shift to include new kinds of non-kin experts, who were incorporated into what she called 'apprentice fosterage'.[29] Such an apprentice lived with the master's family where they were fed, clothed and trained; in return they gave labour and lifelong respect and support to the teacher – evoking a parental relationship (1982a: 195–98; 2006a: 254).

Apprenticeship as a Pedagogical Mode: Learning to Weave

In the mid-1970s, Goody turned her attention more specifically to weaving, a craft of particular importance in Gonja. She was fascinated by this, and found in the transmission of weaving skills in Daboya, the epicentre of Gonja dyeing and weaving, a special form of apprenticeship. This was a major economic activity for men who worked in large extended family businesses. There were seven stages in the life of a weaver through which young men moved from unskilled, to semi-skilled, to highly skilled status over many years. A young apprentice or bobbin boy would be assigned or choose a master to work with from within the extended kin-group; as he became more skilled he would take on more responsibilities while still working as a dependent weaver. Once trained he would work for his father, and over time become a master weaver himself, organizing the labour of his own sons and apprentices (1982b: 70–77). For Goody, the developmental cycle of the weaving enterprise thus showed the fluidity of family dynamics – repeated shifting of responsibilities between members and across generations.

To learn more about the Daboya weaving industry as an example of institutionalized informal education, and to gain firsthand knowledge of the learning dynamic, Goody apprenticed herself to a master weaver in Bakarambasipe, Daboya, for three months in 1974 (see Appendix I for her personal account of this).

Figure 0.5. Fieldwork album double page: weaving sheds in Daboya, northern Ghana, 1974. © Esther Newcomb Goody Archive.

Bobbin boys winding weft in farla
Bobbin boy untangling weft thread for bobbin winding
'Weaver' sitting in front of mosque porch
Independent weaver weaving (Old Loom Shed - ?Gbadulae)

Introducing the Theme of Questions

The mode of learning here was primarily watching and doing alongside more advanced experts, not necessarily through explicit teaching. It was striking, Goody noted later (1989: 253), that apprenticeship studies seldom mentioned teaching as such. For her, this was a vivid example of learning in what Vygotsky terms a 'zone of proximal development' – a concept referring to the space between what a learner can do on their own and what they can do when working jointly with an experienced practitioner (Vygotsky 1978: 84–91; Cole 1985: 154–59; Goody 1989: 235–36; Rogoff 1990). She also drew on Bruner's notion of 'scaffolding' (in Wood, Bruner and Ross 1976) in which adult experts structure a student's activity gradually to extend their ability (see also Fentiman in this volume).[30]

Goody was curious about 'how the organization of production was related to the teaching process on the one hand, and to the authority of close kinsmen and of the head of the kin group ... on the other' (1982b: 51). As she began to weave, she had difficulties with the loom, but noticed that the students around her were not asking the master any questions. Although her first impulse was to ask for help, she took on the same discipline herself and spent her three-month apprenticeship without asking questions. This made her think. Twentieth-century anglophone pedagogical practices generally expect students to ask questions to clarify what the teacher is saying. Questions are also perceived as a way of signalling students' attentive interest to teachers. Goody realized she was experiencing completely different dynamics, not only about what questions are for, but also what they indicate about social relations, what sorts of social information they reveal, and what the consequences of posing them are.

Goody began to consider how questions not only seek information but also carry what she called 'a control valence'. As she discussed in an overview of apprenticeship, it was 'not possible either in action or in analysis completely to separate the information and control messages of a question. Unless they are carefully constructed and managed, questions tend to appear to claim authority' (Goody 1989: 252). Therefore, she argued, even simple information questions from a student would inevitably be heard as a challenge to the master; 'Hence, it is safer not to ask questions' (ibid.). This interest in status and control in hierarchical societies and in deference between junior and senior members continued, informing Goody's subsequent project on authority roles and learning.

Disseminating Results

In 1975 Goody was invited to give the Malinowski Memorial Lecture, entitled 'On Asking Questions'. Here she argued that analysts must consider first the

Figure 0.6. Daboya strip-woven cloth worn by Pontali *wura* (chief), 1965.
© Esther Newcomb Goody Archive.

mode of questions, and the relations between the people doing the questioning and the people being questioned and deciding whether or not to respond. She created a circle or grid of opposites. One set of opposites was defined as 'purely informational' versus 'purely rhetorical', and the other juxtaposed questions indicating deference with those indicating a command. With this grid, she considered the different modes through which these elements can combine, and then explored how the inter-actors involved were both embroiled in and shaped the nature of those relations.

Man (the Journal of the Royal Anthropological Institute, now *JRAI*), which usually publishes the Malinowski Lectures, refused to publish hers, saying it was not 'appropriate to anthropology' as the editor considered it to be too much like linguistics.[31] Ironically, within a few years, Cambridge University Press published it as a chapter in Goody's edited volume *Questions and Politeness: Strategies in Social Interaction* (1978b).[32] As many readers will know, this chapter has become one of the most frequently cited works in Goody's corpus.

In 1992 Esther and Jack Goody published a paper in the journal *Africa* on 'Creating a Text: Alternative Interpretations of Gonja Drum History'. In it they analysed both how drums may be held to speak themselves as well as accompanying chants that are delivered in 'deep Gonja' (1992: 267). In the present volume, Susan Drucker Brown's chapter on Mamprusi kingship in northern Ghana also illustrates how the *lungsi* (the king's drummers) and praise singers use musical phrases in their performances that echo the form of questions. Both are examining 'deep history' – the connection of present chiefs to a long line of chiefly titles – but whereas the Goodys' primary focus is the ambiguity involved in interpretation, Drucker Brown spends more time looking at the relationship between the Mamprusi kings and the drummers.

Both Drucker Brown and David Zeitlyn expand on aspects of the power dynamics of call and response that underlie Goody's understanding of questions and answers. In Chapter 8, Zeitlyn examines a Mambila burial rite in Cameroon, revealing how sociolinguistic nuances illustrate the conflict between traditional burial rites on the one hand and Christian practices on the other. His Goody-inspired analysis shows how one might learn to understand the semiotics of the event without asking explicit questions.

Thus again we see Esther Goody's thinking as organically emergent. From her recognition of fostering out as integral to kinship practices she argued that it should be seen as a form of parental support and not as evidence of parental failure. Once Goody saw apprenticeship fostering as a parental life-preparation strategy, she then began to explore how this embodied the transmission of knowledge, both through teaching and learning. Finally 'school fosterage', she suggested, placed children with others who could help to optimize their schooling and hence their status.[33] In short, this body of work expands a more general understanding of fosterage beyond the scope of kinship, just as her understanding of questions and politeness broadens the analytical frame beyond the domain of language.

Figure 0.7. Daboya strip-woven cloth worn by chiefs' followers at Bole Damba (carrying a chief's chair inside), 1965. © Esther Newcomb Goody Archive.

Figure 0.8. Fieldwork among the Gujarati community in Leicester, 1980s. © Esther Newcomb Goody Archive.

In parallel with her work in Ghana and with West Africans in the United Kingdom, Goody spent time in India in 1977 looking at kinship, caste, and the transmission of craft skills in Gujarat.[34] This laid the foundation for further research in the UK throughout the 1980s among Gujarati Barber sub-caste families in Leicester, exploring continuity and change in the culturally informed practices of this migrant community as well.[35]

As Goody continued working with multicultural families, she also published two books drawing on her research on learning and apprenticeship in different ways. *Parenthood and Social Reproduction: Fostering and Occupational Roles in West Africa* (1982a) brought together a number of her related studies, including several we have touched on here, while *From Craft to Industry: The Ethnography of Proto-industrial Cloth Production* (1982c) was an edited volume that included her own study of the Daboya weavers.[36]

Goody's apprenticeship work remains a source of intellectual stimulation. Jean Lave, well known for her own work on apprenticeship in West Africa as an example of complex 'situated learning' (1977; Lave and Wenger 1991), has recently returned to the topic in *Learning and Everyday Life: Access, Participation and Changing Practice* (2019). She re-examines contemporary apprenticeship and devotes considerable discussion to Goody's detailed study of weaving. In the present volume, Goody's views on learning are expanded in both Alicia Fentiman's chapter on informal education among the Konkomba of northern Ghana, and in Catalina Laserna's comparison of informal and formal learning in the Colombian Andes.

Of Might and Right: Accounting for Sexual Herrschaft

One of the consequences of Goody's twelve years of research with the Department of Health and Social Security was her growing awareness of domestic violence throughout the UK.[37] In the early 1980s she was invited to give a paper at a Max Planck Institute (Göttingen) conference in Bad Homburg on 'Herrschaft and Social Praxis'. She used her experiences of domestic violence to write 'Why Must Might be Right? Observations on Sexual Herrschaft'. Unable to present the paper herself, a colleague read it for her at the meeting where it created considerable controversy. Goody then sent the text to a US colleague asking for clarification regarding the nature of the outcry. They responded that the paper was 'harmful to the feminist cause; it must not be published' (Appendix I). She ultimately published the piece in a number of places (Goody 1986, 1987, 1991a, 1997a); nonetheless this was the second time in a decade that she had been told that a subject of profound interest to her was not considered acceptable for publication.

Our reading of the argument is that Goody makes the non-controversial observation that, globally, more men beat up women than the reverse. What struck her as needing explanation was the extent to which this act of physical domination was so frequently accompanied by a need, on the part of the men, to be perceived as being right in that decision to castigate. She was *not* arguing that 'Might is Right', rather that this should not be understood as a pure act of physical domination, but one that the perpetrator needs to be seen as justified. Drawing on cross-cultural material, Goody noted how frequently the women in question had to be defined as being 'bad' in some way. She was thus analysing this as a set of sociological phenomena, not making an apology for domestic violence.[38]

The editors are not well placed to understand why this argument in itself appeared so threatening. Nonetheless, we think there is a profoundly important question at stake here: to what extent are anthropologists committed to the free flow of information and to the exploration of ideas and intelligent discussion where participants are not necessarily in agreement with each other? That question, we suggest, is as relevant for anthropology in the early twenty-first century as it was at the end of the twentieth.

The title of our introduction – 'Going Against the Grain, Again' – should now be clear. Esther Goody simply kept on doing what was most interesting to her: she kept on making the connections that she felt were important, and she was not worried about whether it was popular, whether it was timely, or whether it was cutting edge. She just said, 'this is a puzzle, let me see what I think about that'.

Social Intelligence

The developmental psychologist David Olson recently noted that Esther Goody 'was among the first to point out that language was not only cognitive but also and primarily social, a way of managing relations among people'.[39]

During the 1990s, Esther Goody continued to expand her collaborative network and developed two grand projects, both of which drew together her thinking about language, learning and communication as fundamentally informed by social process. Although always grounded in solid ethnographic observation, her arguments about the origins of social intelligence formed the most theoretically abstract work of her career. At the same time, her commitment to the Authority and Learning project in northern Ghana and the related Local Language Initial Learning pilot, while theoretically informed, was probably the most ambitious of her applied endeavours.

On Language and Human Intelligence as Fundamentally Social

In the spring of 1990, Goody organized a workshop on 'Some implications of a social origin of human intelligence' at the Wissenschaftskolleg zu Berlin. The wide range of participants included, amongst others, Richard Byrne (primate studies), Stephen Levinson and Penelope Brown (psycho-anthropological linguistics), social psychologist David Good, sociologist Thomas Luckmann and social anthropologist Michael Carrithers.[40] From their several perspectives, all were committed to bringing together the cognitive, the communicative, and the social.

Goody had been excited by Nicholas Humphrey's 1976 paper 'The Social Function of Intellect', which the author gave her while she was writing the introduction to *Questions and Politeness*. By the time of the Berlin workshop, the hypothesis that social life was a major factor in the evolution of intelligence was well established. Under discussion here was the place of language in this process: what happens to the model of primate social intelligence if the social beings have human language? The participants spent a week discussing the working papers Goody had provided, each from their disciplinary perspective. As linguist Edith Esch recently commented, 'For Esther, interaction was indeed crucial and new ideas and new knowledge were the result of dialogue between people' – something, according to Esch, that Goody was adept in facilitating.[41]

In the resulting edited volume, *Social Intelligence and Interaction: Expressions and Implications of the Social Bias in Human Intelligence*, Goody (1995a) sets out her argument for recognizing the social contexts that not only foster but enable the evolution of human language, and with it, human intelligence. Drawing on what she had learned from her studies of the social organization of Gonja greeting rituals (1972) and of questioning in apprenticeship relationships (1978b, 1982b) as well as on the work of her Berlin colleagues, she explored the strategic nature of human communication that enables deception as well as cooperation, underpins persuasion, fosters reflection, and contributes to the interpretation of intent. The tool-like nature of these communicative strategies, she suggested, are not only a function of lived experience but also further cognitive development. Each 'becomes an element in ... cognitive and strategy modelling' (1995a: 25).

Contributors explored how communicative acts enable negotiating as well as managing meaning. What Goody designated 'anticipatory interactive planning' (or AIP) – the ability to imagine others' possible alternative responses – relies on the complex analysis of intentions for its efficacy but is itself subject to multiple social processes. These tools – such as the deployment of irony amongst Tzeltal women discussed by Penelope Brown (1995) – can be marshalled to signal solidarity, to express hostility, or to maintain ambiguity. Echoing Goody, Brown emphasized that her material supported the notion that 'human thinking is systematically biased in the direction of interactive thinking' (ibid.: 153).

Recordings of naturally occurring conversational sequences were analysed by several contributors (see the chapters in *Social Intelligence and Interaction* by Brown, Streeck, and Drew) to reveal patterns of continuous mutual coordination and adaptation of gesture and speech between speakers. This echoed Goody's understanding of language as both dependent on and producing social interaction and process. Goody was committed to an exploration of spoken language from this angle, which was a relatively new position for British anthropologists at the time.[42]

David Good had taught a joint course with Esther Goody in Social Anthropology and Social Psychology during the 1980s at Cambridge University. In his 2014 presentation, Good revisited the Berlin workshop discussions and explored some of the ways in which those early interdisciplinary conversations had shifted the contemporary intellectual landscape concerning human intelligence. The then widely accepted model of 'Machiavellian intelligence', made famous by Byrne and Whiten (1988), emphasized competition over cooperation, and relied heavily on 'chess model' assumptions of planning and the anticipation of future contexts. Humans are notoriously bad at sustained planning, Good noted, and future contexts are unknowable. Affirming Goody's stress on dialogic negotiations of meaning, he was thus more attracted to notions of interaction and experimentation as not only expressions of human intelligence, but profoundly central to its development. Good described how, despite divergent starting points, workshop discussions converged over the week, shifting 'contra the Machiavellian intelligence view, and heading off into a new direction' (Good 2014).

Beyond the Berlin Workshop

Two papers following the publication of *Social Intelligence and Interaction* allowed Goody to expand the themes underpinning the Berlin workshop. The first of these appeared in Whiten and Byrne's 1997 edited volume updating the Machiavellian intelligence model. Goody was the only contributor to consider the effect of the emergence of language on the evolution of human social intelligence. She proposed that as proto-language gradually emerged, it 'provided a new tool for cooperation at the same time that it can only be used through cooperation' (Goody 1997b: 366). Goody thus argued that the emergence of spoken communication not only required joint attention but also produced the collaborative development of shared meanings over time, progressively augmenting social intelligence.[43]

In the same year, Goody's delivery of the biennial Radcliffe-Brown Lecture (published in 1998) allowed her to continue to unpack her thoughts on how AIP and language may have contributed to the emergence of 'roles and rules' in social interaction. Social roles operate as a shared 'lexicon' of cultural formats, so that the patterning of relations becomes public, and builds social structure through collaboration and exchange. Her intellectual links with earlier scholars are evident in the lecture; in particular, she acknowledged her debt to Meyer Fortes and his identification of the dynamic relationship between roles and rules in the emergence of human society.[44] Reading Radcliffe-Brown's accounts of joking relationships through the lens of her own fieldwork experiences, Goody showed how social roles and the accountability they entailed were being used in the management of social interaction. These patterned behaviours, she suggested, made contingent responses more predictable, and social intelligence more effective (Goody 1998).

Even while engaging with these earlier anthropologists, Goody drew on the multidisciplinary work of her contemporaries, often still under debate, such as William Foley's *Anthropological Linguistics* (1997), and the application of Conversational Analysis. Productive interdisciplinarity was still far from the norm, although questions of multi-, inter- and transdisciplinarity attracted increasing amounts of methodological debate throughout the 1990s. Goody herself did not engage in those debates but simply continued to embark on cross-disciplinary conversations. The *Social Intelligence* volume, with its wide set of multidisciplinary contributors, has had a lasting impact on an equally wide-ranging readership.

From Pragmatics to Politics: Education Styles, Learning Efficacy and Policy

Some of Goody's most politicized writing comes in a little pamphlet called 'The Roles of Knowledge and Policy in Contributions of Research on Education to Development' (2002). She begins:

> The challenge for social anthropological research that is most relevant to the 21st Century lies in the politicization of both the policy and the practice of the problems we study. This politicization occurs at all levels: international, national and local. Sometimes it is crystal clear and publicly proclaimed; sometimes it is hidden behind the closed portals of international agencies and ministerial offices. Very often the actual outcomes of [such] policies are unintended consequences of implent[ation] … in the real world of constrained resources, ethnic tensions and powerful entrenched interests. (Goody 2002: 1)

Her article discussed the fine line that one draws between taking an engaged position and maintaining analytical distance. But Goody also exhorted anthropologists to make visible the ubiquity of the politicization of policy and practice. It was written during the period of her final longitudinal research on learning in northern Ghana that led her to engage substantially with officials, to examine the politicization of issues affecting children's literacy, and to explore the practical effects of government policy. We turn now to look at this major project, which occupied Goody into her late seventies.

The Authority and Learning Project: Patterns of Learning in Four Northern Ghanaian Societies

As with so much of her research, Goody's project on 'Authority and Learning in Northern Ghana', which ran from 1990 to 2011, emerged from pre-existing work on apprenticeship and questions, already discussed, and from her extensive experience of northern Ghanaian communities with very different authority structures. Hierarchical societies such as the Gonja had highly for-malized systems, and their relationships stressed respect, deference and obedi-ence. More 'egalitarian' groups, such as the acephalous Birifor, discouraged attempts to exercise authority over others and prized individual autonomy, as well as making collective decisions about community matters (Goody 2006b: 2).[45] These marked differences offered a comparative framework for asking whether and how interpersonal interaction styles might systematically affect the performance of teaching and the dynamics of learning.

Two things in particular had caught her attention. She had witnessed much successful and enthusiastic learning by children in the midst of everyday activi-ties, but when it came to learning in school, many dropped out; few who did finish primary school had even basic literacy (Kraft et al. 1995: 65; Goody and Bennett 2001: 182).[46] She was curious about why children suddenly 'failed' when learning moved into the classroom.

Secondly, she was struck by comments from local teachers that children from the acephalous societies quite often did better in school than those from the more stratified states. This seemed counterintuitive, since the latter have a Muslim literate tradition. Yet it was children from the historically non-literate, mostly rural, acephalous groups that, according to these teachers, more often progressed through school and went on to take up literacy-based positions as bureaucrats, teachers and office staff, both regionally and in the capital Accra (Goody 1994: 1; Draft Report ca. 2005: 1). Goody's hypothesis was that hierar-chical social structures might generate dynamics that inhibit effective learning in school. Conversely, she was curious as to what it was about interaction in acephalous societies that might support learning.

The resulting research included a four-way comparison between formal (school) and informal (home and community) learning contexts, and between learning styles in hierarchical and acephalous societies. Goody received a series of major grants for its different stages, and as a consequence of the project, she also engaged on the ground with associates in Ghana to work on education reform, involving collaboration with local, professional, governmental and international parties.

Studying Informal Education:
Ethnographic Examples from Northern Ghana

The first phase of the project (1990–92) used video recordings to create a close ethnographic study of informal learning in two acephalous communities (Birifor and Konkomba), and two hierarchical groups (Gonja and Wala), docu-menting how children learnt adult skills in domestic, work and ritual settings.[47] These recordings showed children in acephalous communities learning skills through adult-structured (scaffolded) work and by role modelling, with elabo-rate autonomous peer role-play being especially important (Goody 1993:

passim).[48] Goody proposed that such learning was incremental and social; children learned skills by participating in the basic activities of their world. In the hierarchical communities on the other hand, scaffolding and modelling were less evident and little peer role-play practicing adult roles was found (Goody 1996a: 1; 2009: 3–4).[49]

Goody's research officers at this time were Alicia Fentiman and JoAnne Bennett. Fentiman's chapter here on 'Video, Voice and Vygotsky' draws on her own work with Konkomba to explore this phase of the research, with particular attention to the methodological implications of the video techniques, which were still unconventional at the time. Her data resonated strongly with Goody's Birifor material already discussed. (See figures 5.1, 5.2, 5.3)

Catalina Laserna's chapter in this volume gives another vivid example of scaffolded informal learning in her description of a mother–daughter milking lesson in rural Colombia. The everyday context provides what Laserna describes as 'free contextual scaffolding' both to the novice learner trying to master the milking chore and to the expert milker demonstrating the necessary skills.

Penelope Brown and Marisa Casillas also examine day-to-day social exchanges in Chapter 9, extending Goody's study of how children learn social roles and practice prosociality, or 'behaviour carried out for the benefit of others' (Goody 1991b: 106). Their video recordings of children's interactions on Rossel Island (Papua New Guinea) demonstrate vividly the processes of scaffolding and modelling that Goody (1993) describes. Here it is not adults who teach, but older ('expert') children who are responsible for ensuring the younger ones know what is considered safe and healthy behaviour.

Learning in Schools and the Local Languages Initial Literacy Pilot

The second phase was designed to look at formal learning in schools in the same communities, but the project encountered obstacles almost immediately. Goody and her research officers found that the schools were scarcely functioning.[50] This was at least in part due to the huge disparities between the urban south and the more rural and remote north of the country (Goody 2006a: 257–60). The advent of formal education in Ghana and the historical differences between north and south are well documented (see, e.g., Foster 1965; Thomas 1974; Bening 1990). Educational statistics at the time of Goody's research showed that the north lagged behind the south in terms of enrolment, gender ratios, and completion of basic education.[51] Goody noted this mismatch in her contribution to Kraft et al.'s nationwide survey of Ghana's educational system.[52] As Kraft and colleagues noted (1995: 5–13), factors contributing to classroom failure included a lack of resources and teaching materials, a shortage of trained teachers, teacher absenteeism, low enrolment and general despair. All of this was made worse by delayed salaries for teachers, the borrowing of schoolchildren by teachers for free farm labour, and a lack of dialogue between teachers and communities. The single most significant factor, however, was the language barrier (Kraft et al. 1995: 62; Goody 2002: 5 and 10, footnote 5).

Ghana is a country boasting more than eighty distinct languages; the government-trained teachers mostly came from the south and therefore differed both in language and culture to their northern students.[53] English was generally used as the medium of instruction as if it were a common language, but whilst the southern urban elite spoke English at home and were largely bilingual, most northern children did not understand English at all and so could not follow or learn effectively (Goody and Bennett 2001: 183; Goody 2002: 15–16).

Thus, Goody found classes poorly attended or not taking place at all. Where classrooms *were* functioning, children were unengaged and did not seem to understand much of what was going on. As in many places around the world, children born into one language were being taught in another from the first day, with no recognition that they had to learn a new language in order to participate. However, much research demonstrates that if children can start learning in their own language, further language learning builds on their native literacy and goes much more smoothly.[54] At the time, this had not yet been studied on the ground in northern Ghana. In response, Goody set up a pilot project to teach children to read in their own language over a number of years, looking at the effect on subsequent English (second language) literacy and success in other subjects (Goody 2002: 5–17).

From its inception in 1993, the Local Languages Initial Literacy (LLIL) project involved Goody in collaborations with local vernacular speakers in each community who could be trained to teach, and with education and language experts who advised on training teachers and creating teaching materials.[55] One of these, Felicia Kafui Etsey of Cape Coast University, discusses Goody's project, its context and impact, in her conclusion to this volume. Etsey refers in particular to the 'language wars' or conflicting public attitudes, and the concrete problems created by the lack of vernacular teachers and materials, which hampered the early years teaching of local languages.[56]

In 1996 and 1998, district and national education officials trying to improve school practice asked Goody to provide concrete evidence of the benefits of first language literacy. The results of the formal comparisons she carried out showed that children learning to read in their mother tongue had an advantage over those in the Government Education Service (GES) schools: they could read better in both mother tongue and English by the end of primary school, and were ahead in other basic subjects also (Goody and Bennett 2001: 184–86; Goody 2002: 6–9). Student attendance and enthusiasm throughout primary school also increased dramatically for those attending LLIL project classes.[57]

Despite the clearly demonstrated advantage brought by mother-tongue initial teaching, it continued, and still continues, to be irregularly and often ineffectually implemented. Later Goody would comment, 'If there was a "finding" from this work it was that decisions about education at the national

Figure 0.9. 'Local Language Initial Literacy' project class, northern Ghana, 2000s. © Esther Newcomb Goody Archive.

level reflect political and economic constraints and bureaucratic rivalries before they consider factors relating to effective teaching and learning' (Draft Report ca. 2005: 3). Nevertheless, as Etsey shows, the LLIL project contributed to laying the groundwork for other literacy interventions, and forms part of an ongoing effort in this field.[58] Goody's paper 'Where Might GES Literacy Teaching Go after NALAP?' (2011) tackled what a national literacy programme would need in order to be successful in the long term.[59]

Returning to the Question: Modes of Relation and Comparing Learning

i)   Considering Classroom Interaction
Even while setting up the LLIL pilot project, Goody's wider aim was to establish effective classrooms and to enable a close study of learning patterns as originally planned (Goody and Bennett 2001: 182–84). The literacy pilot therefore worked with classrooms in two 'egalitarian' and two hierarchical communities, to mirror the first phase of research on informal learning.[60] Video recording was again used systematically to document class sessions, with the children often working in small groups, which Goody and her teachers had found greatly improved their proactive learning (Goody 2006b: 3–4).

The data gathered showed that in the egalitarian settings, it was more likely that the teaching style was 'discussion-oriented' and the mode of dialogue 'open', whereas in the hierarchical systems the teaching style was more likely to be 'controlling-didactic' and dialogue 'closed' (Goody 2009: passim).[61] In the former, students were encouraged to explore on their own terms; they were not criticized if they did not repeat what the teacher had said, or if they gave an answer the teacher was not expecting. In the more controlling classrooms those things did happen. Yearly test results showed that in egalitarian classrooms (that is, where teacher and pupils were both from 'egalitarian' societies) children had a slight advantage over pupils in hierarchical classrooms in terms of how much they were learning (Goody 1996a: 6–7).[62] This supported the anecdotal observations by local teachers that had initially triggered Goody's curiosity.

The classroom dynamic reflected the larger social ethos. In the egalitarian societies the children were incorporated into social life; they were needed to help with farming and domestic work, and their contribution was recognized. They were encouraged to try out adult activities, as Goody saw in her observations of informal learning. Thus, when they came into school, they already had the sense they might have something to contribute, setting up teacher–pupil relationships that encouraged active engagement and initiative. This was in stark contrast to the more static pattern common in the hierarchical classrooms, where questioning and deviation from set routines of rote learning were not encouraged.

In this volume, Brown and Casillas's comparison of Rossel Island child socialization with that of Mexican Tzeltal children shows widely varying modes of dialogue and interaction, echoing some of the differences Goody had identified in northern Ghanaian classrooms. The authors underline the need for a fine-grained typology that can distinguish the similarities and differences of multiple interactional styles.

ii) In and Out of School: Extensions and Developments
Goody continued to explore the nature of these dynamics over the ensuing years of the project through observing the classrooms she had helped to set up, initially deepening her study of the relation between local patterns of informal learning and primary school learning (see Goody 1997c). Here, she was particularly struck by the parallels between mathematics learning and literacy struggles, where in both cases clear ability in the home and community context was followed by an almost complete lack of understanding at school. In addition to her attention to the benefits of learning to read in one's mother tongue, she wanted to understand how abilities in informally learnt 'street' or 'market' numeracy might support mathematics as taught in the classroom.[63]

In a grant report to the Spencer Foundation, Goody began with the observation that informal community-based learning seemed 'no fail' – virtually everyone learnt the relevant skills. This was in stark contrast to national tests of school-based skills, where in 1995 only 5 per cent of final year primary school students reached the 'mastery' level in English literacy, and only 2 per cent of them achieved mastery in arithmetic (ibid.: 1).

During this phase of her research, Goody spent her time documenting activities that required local methods of market calculation and/or explanation, and encouraging children to create analogous problems in school. She identified several potential stumbling blocks to a straightforward transfer of local skills to classroom arithmetic achievement. Although children could calculate rapidly and accurately, they also learnt to operate with ambiguity. Prices might refer to containers of differing sizes and, importantly, both prices and costs might be affected by the social relations involved (ibid.: 2–4). Arithmetic, on other hand, is based on assumptions of standard measurements that produce predictable outcomes. Goody admitted that she was uncertain how best to bridge those divides in order to demystify the problems presented to students in class (ibid.: 4).

In her 2011 conference paper comparing reading and maths learning, Goody describes how, despite their best efforts to teach students how to calculate profit and loss using local market-based examples, she and her teacher colleagues were consistently unsuccessful. Goody ends her paper with more questions than answers.

In Chapter 6 of this volume, Laserna also explores this question; her comparison marks a shift from meaningful and located tasks on the ground (milking) to apparently abstract concepts with no contextual scaffolding (mathematics) in the classroom.

As well as spending time working on practical and policy aspects of supporting mother-tongue teaching across government primary schools, including the development of classroom materials in different languages (see, e.g., Goody 2006b: 18–19; Chatry-Komarek 2003: 76–77),[64] Goody continued to probe the original puzzle of how effective learning was related to the modes of authority used in different classrooms (Goody 2006a), fine-tuning this by close study of the dialogue between teachers and pupils in the classroom and its impact on learning (2009).

Goody's twenty-year project on authority and learning took an enormous amount of commitment, time, attention, and network-building with Ghanaian colleagues on the ground, as well as with those working in international aid and development.[65] Goody advocated for initial first language literacy at many levels, and emphasized what she saw as dialogue's crucial role in effective teaching. She met with government education officials, contributed research findings to government, non-profit and academic bodies, was in touch with donors such as the World Bank and Overseas Development Administration about her findings, and argued to all concerned for the importance of improved teacher training, both in relation to teaching in pupils' first language and the use of more interactive methods.

When both Goody's funding and health faltered in 2009, she was obliged to return from the field, making visits to Ghana in 2010 and for the last time in 2011, to foster continuity in the schools, tie up loose ends and celebrate her local teachers' achievements with them. She was 79. Provisional research conclusions were drawn in reports (1994, 1996a, 1997c, 2006b, 2009) and conference papers (including 1996b, 2011a), but beyond key articles in 1993, 2001 and 2002 the results of the Authority and Learning study remain unpublished.[66] After her return to Cambridge she continued to work at her desk every day, but at the time of her death she had not made a final analysis of the project's video records. A large amount of this raw data is held in the Esther Newcomb Goody Archive, still awaiting analytic attention.[67]

Dialogue and the Evolution of Spoken Communication

Goody continued to explore the sorts of exchanges involved in learning and what makes it effective. She felt that the proto-findings of her final fieldwork could have wider relevance to the problems for minorities in schools in many societies. This included the benefits of teaching basic literacy in a child's first language, the productiveness of small-group interactive learning and the positive influence of reciprocal modes of dialogue for facilitating productive teacher–pupil relations (Goody 2006b: 4 and 15).

She was increasingly interested in the dynamics and implications of dialogue itself, and remained convinced that the possibility of building jointly constructed meaning through dialogue made it central to processes of

Figure 0.10. Esther Goody's last visit to Ghana in 2011; on the veranda of her Bole home with her friend and collaborator Fati Mumuni (left), Fati's older sister with her daughter and baby; and a friend from Bolgatanga. © Esther Newcomb Goody Archive (photograph Stephen Aboagye).

developmental and evolutionary cognitive shifts. She drafted the outlines of a book on 'Learning to Learn', and of another on dialogue.[68]

This fascination with dialogue also fed back into Goody's ongoing curiosity around how spoken language developed; she focused her inquiry again on the role of human speech in relation to human sociality (e.g. 2012). This final riddle revisited the various kinds of puzzles that had engaged her for the better part of sixty years. Goody started, as always, by looking at the ways in which social life is interaction. She began with 'the dyad' which, for her, was about communication, and communication was about dialogue. In 'About the Curious Power of Dialogue' (published posthumously in 2019), Goody argued that what we need is a paradigm shift. She felt that a model of human interaction beginning with a theory of mind might be going down the wrong road. If we start from a theory of *interaction*, asking how those interactions may shape human thought, we have the tools to move away from internalizing to externalizing these processes and to consider how that might have had an evolutionary route (ibid.: 134). Esther would be pleased to see how this is increasingly reflected in current models of enactive social cognition (see, e.g., Gallagher 2020; Hipólito and van Es 2022).

In 'The Uses and Abuses of Anthropology in Science', Michelle Rosaldo (1980: 389) countered the claim that anthropology lacked information about women with the assertion: 'we don't need more data, what we need are different questions'. That resonates strongly with what Esther Newcomb Goody did all of her life – to ponder 'if we asked it *this* way, would we be able to come out with something new and different and productive?'

The Order of the Chapters

Esther Goody's work is brought into twenty-first-century focus through contributions by scholars actively engaged across the range of her intellectual explorations. The chapters are roughly ordered between a focus on kinship in its various aspects, and themes concerned with communication, literacy and learning.

In Chapter 1, Marilyn Strathern uses Goody's analysis of enduring Gonja sibling relations as a lens to explore the emotional weight of brother–sister relationships in nineteenth-century middle-class England. She calls particular attention to the feelings of abandonment that English men expressed when their sisters married and left the natal home. In this way she contrasts Gonja assumptions of continuing sibling solidarity with fears of rupture in England.

In Chapter 2, Barbara Bodenhorn stretches Goody's notion of the fracturability of parental relations to include the complex personhood of children, reflecting on how they may move between the boundaries of life and death in sometimes unexpected ways. She asks what sorts of partibility may be reflected when 'angel babies' take on a profound emotional life for middle-class parents in Northeastern United States, and when paperclips collected by children in

Tennessee to commemorate the Holocaust seem capable of generating new relationships.

The following two chapters revisit Goody's work on the movement of women and children. Taking a historical perspective in Chapter 3, Paul Sant Cassia expands the study of human circulation with his focus on the Mediterranean from the late fourteenth to the early seventeenth centuries. He explores the movement of women through marriage and conversion; in addition, he examines the status shifts of young boys taken through child levy to become privileged members of Ottoman households, and compares this with Ghanaian surrogacy. By contrast, in Chapter 4, Lynne Brydon updates Goody's analysis with her rich twenty-first-century account of Avatime (southern Ghanaian) movement. Like Goody, Brydon has developed long-term relations in the field, which underpin her account of how Avatime forms of mobility have been modified to reflect changes, not only in global economic processes but also – more fundamentally – in ideas of 'home'.

At this point, the volume shifts focus towards the communicative/pedagogical aspects of Goody's research. In Chapter 5, Alicia Fentiman focuses on informal learning amongst Konkomba of northern Ghana. The work reflects a collaboration with Esther Goody, making innovative use of what was, between 1989 and 1992, revolutionary video technology. This enabled a fine-grained comparative analysis of children's learning experiences with the data recorded. In the subsequent chapter, Catalina Laserna builds on Goody by contrasting Andean children's responses to an informal mother–daughter milking lesson with the more structured dynamics of mathematics instruction in the classroom. Her findings support Goody's own emphasis on the importance of community context for rendering learning activities both meaningful and valuable, something Laserna labels 'free contextual scaffolding'.

Chapters 7 and 8 both attend to communicative aspects of ritual action. In Chapter 7, Susan Drucker Brown opens her paper by acknowledging the importance of Goody's contribution to *Questions and Politeness*. Her close attention to the speech performed by Mamprusi (northern Ghanaian) drummers reveals both the intricate power relationships in these communication exchanges and how they contribute to the maintenance of social stability. In her description of such praise drumming as part of chiefly installation, she pays equal attention to what the drummers are saying and, crucially, the protocols that govern their performance. Communication is clearly not restricted to words, and, just as clearly, is framed through politeness. She thus elaborates Goody's view on the social effects of language and dialogue, including an awareness of their importance in building consensus around social roles and rules. In addition, she departs from Goody in her exploration of how these drummers capture a collective memory for past and present kingship. Like Goody and Brydon (mentioned above), Drucker Brown reveals the influence of Meyer Fortes in her commitment to detailed ethnographic description. In Chapter 8, David Zeitlyn provides a Goody-inspired analysis that unpacks conflicting local attitudes to Cameroonian Mambila burial rituals through attention to sociolinguistic nuance that illuminates social change. In this, he expands on Goody's depiction of the power dynamics embedded in systems of call and response. His is the only chapter in this volume that examines religious debates as a factor in these ritual performances.

In Chapter 9, Penelope Brown and Marisa Casillas extend Goody's study of children's informal learning – including the importance of recognizing the role of older children in teaching their youngers proper social responsibilities. They too deploy detailed video analysis of day-to-day social exchanges to produce a comparative examination of these relations. In this, they bring several of the volume's themes together through applying a psycholinguistic perspective to their analysis of children's learning. By combining Tzeltal (Mexico) and Papua New Guinea material, they highlight both the benefits and the challenges of fine-grained cross-cultural analysis.

Felicia Kafui Etsey contributes the concluding ethnographic chapter with a personal account, not only of Esther Goody's commitment to literacy and first language learning in Ghana, but also of the 'language wars' that have punctuated these efforts. Her words provide vivid testimony to the strength of the long-standing collaborations that Goody developed with her colleagues in the places she worked.

John Keith Hart's Afterword skillfully embeds Esther's multiple intellectual-social projects in a sweeping account of the development of critical ideas that have shaped social inquiry since the seventeenth century. For Hart, Goody's great contribution to social anthropology was to bring together social psychology as it originated in the United States, and a British ethnographic focus, especially on kinship and marriage. That dual focus, Hart concludes, will be increasingly important for twenty-first-century social analysis, underscoring Esther Newcomb Goody's position as a cutting-edge thinker.

Barbara Bodenhorn is an Emeritus Fellow of Pembroke College, Cambridge. She has worked in Arctic Alaska since 1980 and in the Sierra Norte of Oaxaca since 2004, with a current focus on young people's environmental knowledge. Recent books include *Risky Futures*, edited with Olga Ulturgasheva (Berghahn Books 2022).

Alicia Fentiman is a social anthropologist who conducted her PhD under the supervision of Esther Goody at the Department of Social Anthropology, University of Cambridge. She has worked extensively in the field of international development in sub-Saharan Africa. She has also worked as a consultant and a senior researcher at the Faculty of Education, University of Cambridge.

Mary Goody is an artist and researcher, currently working on links between sculpture-making and embodied empathy as a doctoral student at Goldsmiths, University of London. As Esther Goody's daughters, she and her sister Rachel provided editorial and secretarial support to their mother during the latter years of her life.

Notes

1. The conference was held in the Department of Social Anthropology at Cambridge University on 1 November 2014. Participants included some twenty former students and colleagues.
2. Amongst other activities, Theodore Newcomb led the seminal Bennington College Study on the influence of college experience on political and social beliefs (Newcomb 1943); he founded the doctoral programme in Social Psychology at the University of Michigan, and the Institute for Social Research grew out of his collaborations. Mary Newcomb's artistic and socially engaged qualities also reappear in Goody's work and interests.
3. During her lifelong association with Cambridge University, Goody also taught at Newnham College from 1961–63, and was one of the founding members of Lucy Cavendish College in 1965. Her fellowship at New Hall/Murray Edwards continued for 33 years, until she became an Emeritus Fellow in 1999. See tributes by Paola Filippucci and Marilyn Strathern in Appendix IV for further details of her university engagements and activities.
4. The young family spent most of two years in Ghana between 1964 and 1966, where Esther Goody combined fieldwork with motherhood under challenging conditions. In Cambridge, they first lived in two tiny adjoining cottages in Shelly Row, where supervisions and entertaining already combined with family life (as Susan Drucker Brown recollected at Goody's funeral). Jack's first family sometimes joined them there and for holidays, so that Esther was often busy as mother and stepmother to Jeremy, Joanna and Jane as well as Mary and Rachel.
5. For personal accounts of the time by former students and colleagues, see Appendix IV.
6. See Appendix II, where Jean La Fontaine refers to their time together in France.
7. Appendix V provides a fuller bibliography.
8. See Appendix I for Esther's own account of how puzzles helped to frame her research.
9. Gonja was once an important state in what is modern-day Ghana. At the time of Goody's fieldwork it was a weakly centralized state divided into two administrative districts in the country's northern region. The 1960 census recorded 118,229 Gonja residents, organized in three major social categories: the ruling estate, Muslims and commoners. Economic life was largely organized around trading and farming (Goody 1973).
10. See also Fortes 1949.
11. An acephalous society is one without titular heads. Comparison between hierarchical and acephalous social organization was an area of interest running through Goody's research.
12. The manuscript report is archived in the Haddon Library, Cambridge University, and the Social Science Research Council Archives, London; the Kpembe study is also the subject of Chapter 3 of *Parenthood and Social Reproduction* (1982a).
13. This was, for instance, the explicit position of Alaska's Division of Youth Services during Bodenhorn's tenure at the Iñupiaq Community of the Arctic Slope in the 1980s. See also Bodenhorn 2013.
14. Thematic Apperception Tests are figures that the viewer is invited to interpret with the assumption that their ambiguity will elicit underlying states of mind.
15. The appendices of the Kpembe Study manuscript present the raw data showing how the research was designed and carried out, including all of the figures and the stories that the children told about them.
16. There was also some evidence that, as adults, fostered children were somewhat more likely to be successful economically or to hold office (Goody 1982a).
17. See for instance Goody 1971b, 1973, 1975a. *Parenthood and Social Reproduction* (1982a) brought together a number of Goody's studies on this subject. She continued to develop her arguments in later papers (e.g. 1984a, 1999).

18. See, e.g., Weiner 1979; Bodenhorn 1990; Carsten 1995; Astuti 1998; Weston (1995) 2013; Strathern 2018.

19. If kin claimed these rights when a child reached five or six they would act as parents until that child was ready to marry; the young person would often then return close to their parental home. Goody noted that the shift in southern Ghana of more parents proactively asking kin to take a child was relatively recent at the time of her early fieldwork (1982a: 177–80).

20. The London study was supported by the Social Science Research Council. Goody and Muir Groothues wrote further publications connecting West African and Anglo domestic and child-rearing practices with reference to education (1977) and marital stress (1979). Initially Goody's field assistant in northern Ghana, Muir trained in social anthropology and psychology, becoming Children's Officer for Southwark, and subsequently working in adoption and child psychology research at the Institute of Psychiatry.

21. Goody was curious about the different responses of these two groups to the similar stresses of isolation and poverty, and of combining child-rearing with study and work; the West Indians used daily minders who were themselves generally from the West Indies, but did not foster out children.

22. Jimi Famurewa discusses this in the *Guardian* (2022a), and his book *Settlers* (2022b).

23. Her father wrote: 'I must make it clear to you that [Ann] belongs to us and nothing can separate us and the baby, not all the riches in the world...' (quoted from High Court transcript in Goody and Muir Groothues 1982: 217; Goody 1984a: 277).

24. See, for example, David Case on Native Alaskans and American laws (Case and Voluck 2012); Bodenhorn (1988, 1997) for Arctic Alaska. When discussing the judge's decision, for instance, Goody notes that the 'acceptable' solution to childcare needs under such circumstances in the UK is for the wife to stop working and become a full-time mother (1975a: 148; 1982a: 227). Goody goes on to explain why that is not an option for these students, either economically or culturally, even though the act of giving up their very young children pains them.

25. 'La Parentalité des Anthropologues: Avant et Après Esther N. Goody' (English title 'Parenthood in Africa after E.N. Goody') was organized by Yazid Ben Hounet and Marie-Luce Gélard with the support of the École des Hautes Études en Sciences Sociales and other institutions, and took place in Paris on 16 March 2022. A 2022 issue of *Journal des Africanistes* was published as a result.

26. Beyond Goody's work with the UK DHSS, she was also a member of the Joint Working Party on Transmitted Deprivation organized by the Social Science Research Council and the DHSS between 1973 and 1982. In addition, she was a member of the Chief Scientist's Research Council and the Personal Social Services Research Unit.

27. See, for example: Bodenhorn's report to the Iñupiaq History and Culture Commission (1988) on tensions around land tenure, the court system, education, and alcohol; Bodenhorn with Elsa Lee (2022); Fentiman's work on cultural constraints to the education and health of children in Ghana (1999, 2001); Kusum Gopal's work on reproductive policies (2007); Suzanne Hoelgaard's work on international adoption policy (1988a/b, 1998); Ziba Mir-Hosseini's work on being a 'Native Anthropologist' (2010), as well as the politics of divorce law in Iran (2012); and Marilyn Strathern's public policy work in Papua New Guinea (e.g. 1972, 1975a/b, 2000) and the UK (1993a/b, 2011).

28. During Goody's Ghanaian fieldwork she also reviewed others' research across several West African societies: Azu (1974) on Ga; Cohen (1967, 1971) on Kanuri; Hill (1972) and M.G. Smith (1955) on Hausa; Lallemand (1976) and Skinner (1961, 1964) on Mossi; and Oppong (1973) on Dagomba. On Yoruba apprenticeship she found excellent Nigerian data in the work of: Callaway (1964, 1973), Koll (1969), Lloyd (1953) and Peil (1970, 1978). See Goody 1982a: chapters 5 and 8.

29. Goody discusses apprenticeship fosterage as a form of training, particularly for high-status occupations in 'the traditional states' (1982a: 127). Here she is talking about the

expansion of the practice as an adaptation to new conditions: '...training by non-kin has become very much more common within the past few decades in Ghana and Nigeria, particularly in the cities' (ibid.: 188).

30. Goody also cited Lave (1977), Greenfield and Lave (1982) as making the point that 'Learning in the "zone of proximal development" is built into apprenticeship' (Goody 1989: 253).

31. Penelope Brown has commented that this was a specifically British resistance, and that no US anthropology journal of the time would have considered it outside the realm of the discipline (personal communication with the editors, 31 August 2022).

32. The title was changed for publication in *Questions and Politeness*, to 'Towards a Theory of Questions'.

33. Goody talks about children being sent to non-kin to be close to a primary or secondary school. This was especially prevalent in northern Ghana, where the number of schools was limited. She also gives examples of children being sent to live with schoolteachers, or religious teachers, who could provide a literate environment to support their studies (Goody 1989: 242).

34. In *From Craft to Industry*, Goody explores the specialized skills of Gujarati cloth production (1982d: 5–6). Otherwise she did not publish directly on this material; but see Jack Goody and Esther N. Goody (1990: 160–78) for a discussion of Gujarati marriage and family.

35. Goody made extensive fieldnotes on almost a decade of close engagement with the Gujarati community in Leicester, but as far as the editors have been able to ascertain she did not publish on this fieldwork.

36. *Parenthood and Social Reproduction* won the Amaury Talbot Prize for the outstanding book published in 1982 on African Anthropology.

37. Goody notes that during this time 'we commissioned research on domestic violence and then held a conference bringing together people working with women's shelters, doctors, social workers and the police' (Appendix I).

38. This argument resonates with Goody's (1970b) exploration of witchcraft as gendered practice in West Africa, where male witches were thought to exercise 'legitimate' power. For a woman to be defined as a witch, on the other hand, was a label that could justify violence against her.

39. Personal communication to Mary Goody (26 June 2020).

40. The participants in the workshop all contributed to the published volume (Goody 1995a).

41. Esch continued 'I think the [1995] book is evidence that the whole seminar, thanks to Esther's own social intelligence, helped a … generation of intellectuals on the rise in their respective fields to focus and sharpen their thinking together and cooperatively. There is no better compliment one might make to a thinker like Esther' (Correspondence with Mary Goody, 17 February 2021).

42. American anthropologists such as John Gumperz and Dell Hymes had analysed natural conversation data from the 1960s; Goody referred her students to this material.

43. Goody also mentions the historical resistance to the study of the evolution of spoken language, perceived as dangerously speculative from the 1860s onwards, and reinforced by twentieth-century linguistic theory such as Chomsky's (Goody 1997b). Her determination to follow her sense of its importance in human social and cognitive development is another example of her readiness to be 'unfashionable' in following her intellectual intuition. Today this field of study is much more accepted.

44. Goody dedicated the written version of this lecture to Fortes, citing his influence and his 1983 *Rules and the Emergence of Society*.

45. Goody often used 'egalitarian' in inverted commas in her written reports and articles.

46. Yearly national testing of children finishing primary school showed that only 5 per cent in 1995 and 6 per cent in 1996 reached the expected level in English at this age.

47. Video data are included in Berghahn Book's online publication of this volume. Goody, Fentiman and Bennett coded these records for specific verbal and non-verbal behaviours, and for settings, activities, and types of dialogue.

48. Peer role play happened away from adult activities, following an 'egalitarian' model: each girl had her own cooking fire, or each boy his own patch of farm, but close together in small groups so they could help one another (see Goody 1993: 489; Fentiman in this volume).

49. Goody had already discussed how, in the more centralized hierarchical polities, increasing job specialization was leading to dissociation between what children saw around them and skills to be learnt for adult economic activities (1989). In the relatively unchanging acephalous farming communities, on the other hand, opportunities for adult role learning were plentiful.

50. Fentiman remained a research officer until late 1992, and Bennett until 1997. After this Goody gathered the data alone.

51. See, for instance, UNESCO 1990; Ministry of Education, Ghana 1990; UNICEF 1991.

52. This was a major survey of Ghanaian education to which Goody contributed the section on the north of the country (contributors were listed collectively under 'Study Team'). It detailed the contemporary situation in schools, and the consistently poor literacy and numeracy results in many areas.

53. Ghanaian government policy for most of the time since independence has been to teach the first three years of primary school in local languages, then transition to English. However, mixed messages about policy from different governments, and many obstacles on the ground, meant the policy was rarely implemented.

54. See Bodenhorn 1997 for Alaska; Cummins 1984 on immigrant children in Canada; Ezzaki, Spratt and Wagner 1987 on Morocco; Fentiman, Wyse and Vikiru 2010 on sub-Saharan Africa; UNICEF 2016 on eastern and southern Africa; and UNESCO 1953, 2003 more generally.

55. Among others, Kurt Komarek and Magdeleine (Marie) Chatry-Komarek of the German Agency for International Cooperation gave key assistance with a tutor training workshop and instruction on composing and using local language workbooks, which was pivotal to Goody's project. Coming out of her extensive experience of working with teachers in several African countries on the design of mother-tongue teaching materials and the training of teacher-training tutors, Chatry-Komarek's (2003) book made teaching methods and suggestions available to local teachers. Goody contributed a foreword, and Chatry-Komarek cites examples from their rich correspondence (ibid.: 76–77).

56. On the conflicting attitudes around language of instruction, see Goody 2006a: 257–60; also see Chatry-Komarek (2003: 41–53) discussing the subject for teachers' reference.

57. 'These L1 readers consistently top district-wide testing in English, maths and science' (Goody, Draft Report ca. 2005).

58. For example, the National Literacy Acceleration Programme (NALAP) was developed by a collaboration of Ghanaian and international consultants from 2007, and put into practice from 2010. Among those involved, Rosekrans, Sherris and Chatry-Komarek (2012) describe this programme and the conditions of its creation, while Etsey's conclusion here discusses its evolution and continuation by different forms of intervention up until 2022.

59. This paper was circulated in 2011 to education officials and colleagues in Ghana, and to a 2014 conference on 'Language, Learning and Literacy in Africa: Practical and Policy Aspects of Effectively Implementing Bilingual Primary School Literacy Programmes', organized by Alicia Fentiman at Cambridge University. The interdisciplinary conference focused on educational research providing empirical data to inform policy and practice. It also reunited colleagues from Goody's work on LLIL and NALAP (Felicia Kafui Etsey, and Kurt and Magdeleine Komarek all attended).

60. Fierce fighting amongst Konkomba meant that it was no longer possible to work there, so the participant acephalous communities were Birifor and Dagaaba. Where possible, one rural and one more urban school was recruited in each region.

61. 'Open' dialogue allows for unscripted exchange, the questioning of patterned responses and the establishing of new shared meanings, while 'closed' dialogue has a particularly fixed routinized patterning that does not allow for deviation (Goody 2006b: 5–9; 2009: 4ff.).

62. In her reports (1996a: 7; 2006: 14), Goody discussed reasons why these results were not easy to evaluate, including variations between school conditions, and the young age of the children – factors that encouraged her to move towards analysis of comparative description. She carried out yearly testing throughout, but did not rely on the results for her assessment.

63. She notes this in her first year report to the Spencer Foundation (Goody 1997c), which had supported her comparative research in formal learning.

64. This aspect of the work was largely funded by USAID, the US Agency for International Development.

65. See Goody 2006b, 2009, and Etsey's chapter in this volume, for more on Goody's collaborations.

66. She made sure copies of relevant parts of her formal reports reached and were discussed with the director general of education and the director of basic education in Accra, the three district directors of education she had worked with in northern Ghana, and also with colleagues in faculties of education at the universities of Legon and Cape Coast. In her final report from the field she cited a book being drafted on 'A Social Anthropology of Education', based on detailed case studies for several different ethnographic kinds of education system, and a further possible volume on why countries fail to adopt recognized research results to improve education (Goody 2009: 15).

67. The Esther Newcomb Goody Archive is housed at the Centre of African Studies, Cambridge University.

68. Goody's notes on these planned publications are held in the Esther Newcomb Goody Archive.

References

Astuti, Rita. 1998. "'It's a Boy", "It's a Girl!'": Reflections on Sex and Gender in Madagascar and Beyond', in Michael Lambek and Andrew Strathern (eds), *Bodies and Persons: Comparative Perspectives from Africa and Melanesia*. Cambridge: Cambridge University Press, pp. 29–52.

Azu, Diana Gladys. 1974. *The Ga Family and Social Change*. Leiden: African Studies Centre.

Ben Hounet, Yazid. 2022. 'La Parentalité Après Esther N. Goody', *Journal des Africanistes* 92(1).

Bening, R. Bagulo. 1990. *A History of Education in Northern Ghana, 1907–1976*. Accra: Ghana Universities Press.

Bodenhorn, Barbara. 1988. 'Documenting Family Relationships in Changing Times', Volume 2 (Family Stresses). Unpublished report produced for the North Slope Borough Iñupiaq History, Language and Culture Commission. Archived at the Tuzzy Library (Utqiagvik); University of Alaska (Fairbanks); Scott Polar Institute (Cambridge); and McGill University (Montreal).

――――. 1990. "'I'm Not the Great Hunter; My Wife Is": Iñupiat and Anthropological Models of Gender', *Etudes/Inuit/Studies* 14(1–2): 55–74.

————. 1997. '"People Who Are Like Our Books": Reading and Teaching on the North Slope of Alaska', *Arctic Anthropology* 34(1): 117–34.

————. 2013. 'On the Road Again: Movement, Marriage, Mestizaje and the Race of Kinship', in Fenella Cannell and Susie McKinnon (eds), *Vital Relations: Modernity and the Persistent Life of Kinship*. Santa Fe, NM: SAR Press, pp. 131–54.

Bodenhorn, Barbara, and Elsa Lee. 2022. 'What Animates Place for Children? A Comparative Analysis', *Anthropology & Education Quarterly* 53(2): 112–29.

Brown, Penelope. 1995. 'Politeness Strategies and the Attribution of Intentions: The Case of Tzeltal Irony', in Esther N. Goody (ed.), *Social Intelligence and Interaction: Expressions and Implications of the Social Bias in Human Intelligence*. Cambridge: Cambridge University Press, pp. 153–74.

Byrne, Richard W., and Andrew Whiten (eds). 1988. *Machiavellian Intelligence: Social Expertise and the Evolution of Intellect in Monkeys, Apes and Humans*. Oxford: Oxford University Press.

Callaway, Archibald. 1964. 'Nigeria's Indigenous Education: The Apprenticeship System', *ODU: University of Ife Journal of African Studies* 1: 1–18.

————. 1973. *Nigerian Enterprise and the Employment of Youth*. Nigerian Institute of Social and Economic Research, Monograph 2. University of Ibadan.

Carsten, Janet. 1995. 'The Substance of Kinship and the Heat of the Hearth: Feeding, Personhood, and Relatedness among Malays in Pulau Langkawi', *American Ethnologist* 22(2): 223–41.

Case, David S., and David A. Voluck. 2012. *Alaska Natives and American Laws*. Fairbanks: University of Alaska Press.

Chatry-Komarek, Marie. 2003. *Literacy at Stake: Teaching Reading and Writing in African Schools*. Windhoek, Namibia: Gamsberg Macmillan.

Cohen, Ronald. 1967. *The Kanuri of Borneo*. New York: Holt, Rinehart and Winston.

————. 1971. 'Dominance and Defiance: A Study of Marital Instability in an Islamic African Society'. *Anthropological Studies*. Washington, DC: American Anthropological Association, pp. ix, 213.

Cole, Michael. 1985. 'The Zone of Proximal Development: Where Culture and Cognition Create Each Other', in James V. Wertsch (ed.), *Culture, Communication and Cognition*. Cambridge: Cambridge University Press, pp. 146–61.

Cummins, Jim. 1984. *Bilingualism and Special Education: Issues in Assessment and Pedagogy*. Clevedon, England: Multilingual Matters.

Drew, Paul. 1995. 'Interaction Sequences and Anticipatory Interactive Planning', in Esther N. Goody (ed.), *Social Intelligence and Interaction: Expressions and Implications of the Social Bias in Human Intelligence*. Cambridge: Cambridge University Press, pp. 111–38.

Ezzaki, Abdelkader, Jennifer E. Spratt and Daniel A. Wagner. 1987. 'Childhood Literacy Acquisition in Rural Morocco: Effects of Language Differences and Quranic Preschooling', in Daniel A. Wagner (ed.), *The Future of Literacy in a Changing World*. Oxford: Pergamon Press, pp. 159–73.

Famurewa, Jimi. 2022a. '"Farmed": Why Were So Many Black Children Fostered by White Families in the UK?', *The Guardian*, 15 September 2022.

————. 2022b. *Settlers: Journeys through the Food, Faith and Culture of Black African London*. London: Bloomsbury.

Fentiman, Alicia, Andrew Hall and Donald Bundy. 1999. 'School Enrolment Patterns in Rural Ghana: A Comparative Study of the Impact of Location, Gender, Age and Health on Children's Access to Basic Schooling', *Comparative Education* 35(3): 331–49.

_____. 2001. 'Health and Cultural Factors Associated with Enrolment in Basic Education: A Study in Rural Ghana', *Social Science and Medicine* 52(3): 429–39.

Fentiman, Alicia, Dominic Wyse and Lillian Vikiru. 2010. 'The Teaching of English in Sub-Saharan Africa', in *The Routledge International Handbook of English, Language and Literacy Training*. London: Routledge, pp. 484–95.

Foley, William A. 1997. *Anthropological Linguistics: An Introduction*. Oxford: Blackwell.

Fortes, Meyer. 1949. *The Web of Kinship among the Tallensi*. London: Oxford University Press.

_____. 1958. 'Introduction', in Jack Goody (ed.), *The Developmental Cycle in Domestic Groups*. Cambridge: Cambridge University Press, pp. 1–14.

_____. 1983. *Rules and the Emergence of Society*. London: Royal Anthropological Institute of Great Britain and Ireland.

Foster, Philip. 1965. *Education and Social Change in Ghana*. London: Routledge & Kegan Paul.

Gallagher, Shaun. 2020. *Action and Interaction*. Oxford: Oxford University Press.

Good, David. 2014. 'Intelligence, Interaction and Prayer'. Paper for Department of Social Anthropology Symposium organized by Alicia Fentiman, 1 November 2014, Cambridge University.

Goody, Esther N. 1961. 'Kinship, Marriage and the Developmental Cycle among the Gonja of Northern Ghana'. PhD thesis, University of Cambridge.

_____. 1966. 'Fostering of Children in Ghana: A Preliminary Report'. *Ghana Journal of Sociology* 2(1): 26–33.

_____. 1970a. 'The Kpembe Study: A Comparison of Fostered and Non-fostered Children in Eastern Gonja'. Unpublished report, Social Science Research Council Archives, London, and The Haddon Library, University of Cambridge. Excerpted in Esther N. Goody, *Parenthood and Social Reproduction*, Chapter 3. Cambridge: Cambridge University Press.

_____. 1970b. 'Legitimate and Illegitimate Aggression in a West African State', in Mary Douglas (ed.), *Witchcraft: Confessions and Accusations*. ASA Monographs 9. London: Tavistock Publications, pp. 207–44.

_____. 1971a. 'Forms of Pro-parenthood: The Sharing and Substitution of Parental Roles', in Jack Goody (ed.), *Kinship: Selected Readings*. Harmondsworth: Penguin Readings in Sociology, pp. 331–45.

_____. 1971b. 'Varieties of Fostering'. *New Society* 5: 237–39.

_____. 1972. '"Greeting", "Begging" and the Presentation of Respect', in Jean La Fontaine (ed.), *The Interpretation of Ritual: Essays in Honour of A.I. Richards*. London: Tavistock Press, pp. 39–72.

_____. 1973. *Contexts of Kinship: An Essay on the Family Sociology of the Gonja of Northern Ghana*. Cambridge Studies in Social Anthropology 7, Cambridge University Press.

_____. 1975a. 'Delegation of Parental Roles in West Africa and the West Indies', in Thomas R. Williams (ed.), *Socialization and Communication in Primary Groups*. The Hague: Mouton, pp. 447–84.

_____. 1975b. 'On Asking Questions'. Malinowski Memorial Lecture at the London School of Economics and Political Science, delivered 4 March 1975.

_____ (ed.). 1978a. *Questions and Politeness: Strategies in Social Interaction*. Cambridge Papers in Social Anthropology 8, Cambridge University Press.

_____. 1978b. 'Towards a Theory of Questions', in Esther N. Goody (ed.), *Questions and Politeness: Strategies in Social Interaction*. Cambridge: Cambridge University Press, pp. 17–43.

———. 1982a. *Parenthood and Social Reproduction: Fostering and Occupational Roles in West Africa*. Cambridge Studies in Anthropology 35, Cambridge University Press.

———. 1982b. 'Daboya Weavers: Relations of Production, Dependency and Reciprocity', in Esther N. Goody (ed.), *From Craft to Industry: The Ethnography of Proto-industrial Cloth Production*. Cambridge Papers in Social Anthropology 10, Cambridge University Press, pp. 50–84.

——— (ed.). 1982c. *From Craft to Industry: The Ethnography of Proto-industrial Cloth Production*. Cambridge Papers in Social Anthropology 10, Cambridge University Press.

———. 1982d. 'Introduction', in Esther N. Goody (ed.), *From Craft to Industry: The Ethnography of Proto-industrial Cloth Production*. Cambridge Papers in Social Anthropology 10, Cambridge University Press, pp. 1–37.

———. 1984a. 'Parental Strategies: Calculation or Sentiment?: Fostering Practices among West Africans', in Hans Medick and David W. Sabean (eds), *Interest and Emotion: Essays on the Study of Family and Kinship*. Cambridge: Cambridge University Press, pp. 266–77.

———. 1984b. 'Can Anthropology Contribute to Social Policy?' *RAIN* 63: 2–6.

———. 1986. 'Why Must Might Be Right? Observations on Sexual Herrschaft'. *Cambridge Journal of Anthropology* 11(3): 1–34.

———. 1987. 'Why Must Might Be Right? Observations on Sexual Herrschaft'. *Newsletter for the Laboratory of Comparative Human Cognition* 9(2): 55–75.

———. 1989. 'Learning, Apprenticeship and the Division of Labour', in Michael W. Coy (ed.), *Apprenticeship: From Theory to Method and Back Again*. Albany: State University of New York Press, pp. 233–56.

———. 1991a. 'Warum die Macht rechthaben muß: Bemerkungen zur Herrschaft eines Geschlechts über das andere', in Alf Lüdtke (ed.), *Herrschaft als Soziale Praxis: Historische und Sozial-anthropologische Studien*. Veröffentlichungen des Max-Planck-Instituts für Geschichte 91, Göttingen: Vandenhoeck & Ruprecht.

———. 1991b. 'The Learning of Prosocial Behaviour in Small-Scale Egalitarian Societies: An Anthropological View', in Robert A. Hinde and Jo Groebbel (eds), *Cooperation and Prosocial Behaviour*. Cambridge: Cambridge University Press, pp. 106–28.

———. 1993. 'Informal Learning of Adult Roles in Baale', in Michèle Fiéloux and Jacques Lombard (eds), with Jeanne-Marie Kambou-Ferrand, *Images d'Afrique et Sciences Sociales: Les Pays Lobi, Birifor et Dagara (Burkina Faso, Côte d'Ivoire et Ghana)*. Paris: Karthala-Orstom, pp. 482–91.

———. 1994. 'Authority and Learning in Northern Ghana. Phase II: Authority and Learning in Primary Schools. Report on First Year (July 1993–June 1994)'. Unpublished report for Economic and Social Research Council, UK. See Esther Newcomb Goody Archive, Centre of African Studies, Cambridge University.

——— (ed.). 1995a. *Social Intelligence and Interaction: Expressions and Implications of the Social Bias in Human Intelligence*. Cambridge: Cambridge University Press.

———. 1995b. Study team contributor in Richard Kraft et al. *A Tale of Two Ghanas: The View from the Classroom*. Accra, Ghana: Ministry of Education.

———. 1996a. 'Authority and Learning in Northern Ghana'. Unpublished End of Award Report for Economic and Social Research Council, UK. See Esther Newcomb Goody Archive, Centre of African Studies, Cambridge University.

———. 1996b. 'Modelling, Play and Responsible Practice: The Learning of Adult Role Skills in Baale'. Unpublished paper for Fyssen Foundation Conference *Culture et*

Usages du Corps, Paris, 1–4 March. See Esther Newcomb Goody Archive, Centre of African Studies, Cambridge University.

———. 1997a. 'Why Must Might Be Right? Observations on Sexual Herrschaft', in Michael Cole, Yrjo Engeström and Olga Vasquez (eds), *Mind, Culture, and Activity: Seminal Papers from the Laboratory of Comparative Human Cognition*. Cambridge: Cambridge University Press, pp. 432–72.

———. 1997b. 'Social Intelligence and Language: Another Rubicon?', in Andrew Whiten and Richard W. Byrne (eds), *Machiavellian Intelligence II: Extensions and Evaluations*. Cambridge: Cambridge University Press, pp. 364–96.

———. 1997c. 'Spencer Foundation First Annual Report: October 1996–September 1997'. Unpublished interim report. See Esther Newcomb Goody Archive, Centre of African Studies, Cambridge University.

———. 1998. 'Social Intelligence and the Emergence of Roles and Rules'. Radcliffe-Brown Lecture in Social Anthropology. *Proceedings of the British Academy* 97: 119–47. Retrieved 17 October 2024 from https://www.thebritishacademy.ac.uk/documents/2460/97p119.pdf.

———. 1999. 'Sharing and Transferring Components of Parenthood: The West African Case', in Mireille Corbier (ed.), *Adoption et Fosterage*. Collection De L'Archéologie à L'Histoire. Paris: De Boccard, pp. 370–88.

———. 2002. 'The Roles of Knowledge and Policy in Contributions of Research on Education to Development: Observations on Social Anthropological Research for the 21st Century'. Keynote address to 1997 Pan-African Association of Anthropologists. *Cambridge Journal of Anthropology* 23(1): 1–19.

———. 2003. 'Foreword' to Marie Chatry-Komarek, *Literacy at Stake: Teaching Reading and Writing in African Schools*. Windhoek, Namibia: Gamsberg Macmillan.

———. Ca. 2005. Draft unpublished report, Grant Number R000239984 (Penultimate Year of Award) to the Economic and Social Research Council, UK. See Esther Newcomb Goody Archive, Centre of African Studies, Cambridge University.

———. 2006a. 'Dynamics of the Emergence of Sociocultural Institutional Practices', in David R. Olson and Michael Cole (eds), *Technology, Literacy and the Evolution of Society: Implications of the Work of Jack Goody*. Mahwah, NJ: Laurence Erlbaum, pp. 241–64.

———. 2006b. 'Effects of Hierarchical and Egalitarian Modes of Teaching and Learning in Northern Ghana'. Grant number R000239984. Unpublished End of Award Report to the Economic and Social Research Council, UK. See Esther Newcomb Goody Archive, Centre of African Studies, Cambridge University.

———. 2009. 'The Role of Dialogue in Building Understanding in the Classroom'. Grant number 200700080. Unpublished End of Award Report for the Spencer Foundation, Chicago, IL. See Esther Newcomb Goody Archive, Centre of African Studies, Cambridge University.

———. 2011. 'Where Might GES Literacy Training Go after NALAP?' Unpublished report. Esther Newcomb Goody Archive, Centre of African Studies, Cambridge University.

———. 2012. 'Co-operation and the Origins of Spoken Language'. Review article. *Journal of the Royal Anthropological Institute* 18(2): 461–65.

———. 2019. 'About the Curious Power of Dialogue', in David Shankland (ed.), *Dunbar's Number*. Occasional Paper no. 45 of the Royal Anthropological Institute. London: Sean Kingston, pp. 125–35.

Goody, Esther N., and JoAnne Bennett. 2001. 'Literacy for Gonja and Birifor Children in Northern Ghana', in David R. Olson and Nancy Torrance (eds), *The Making of Literate Societies*. Oxford: Blackwell, pp. 178–200.

Goody, Esther N., and Jack Goody. 1992. 'Creating a Text: Alternative Interpretations of Gonja Drum History', *Africa* 62(2): 266–70.

Goody, Esther N., and Christine Muir Groothues. 1977. 'The West Africans: The Quest for Education', in James L. Watson (ed.), *Between Two Cultures: Migrants and Minorities in Britain*. Oxford: Basil Blackwell, pp. 151–80.

———. 1979. 'Stress in Marriage: West African Couples in London', in Verity Saifullah Khan (ed.), *Minority Families in Britain: Support and Stress*. Studies in Ethnicity No. 2. London: Macmillan, pp. 59–88.

———. 1982. 'The Quest for Education', in Esther N. Goody, *Parenthood and Social Reproduction: Fostering and Occupational Roles in West Africa*. Cambridge Studies in Anthropology 35, Cambridge University Press, pp. 217–33.

Goody, Jack, and Esther N. Goody. 1967. 'The Circulation of Women and Children in Northern Ghana', *MAN* 2(2): 226–48.

———. 1990. 'Marriage and the Family in Gujarat', in Jack Goody, *The Oriental, the Ancient and the Primitive: Systems of Marriage and the Family in the Pre-industrial Societies of Eurasia*. Cambridge: Cambridge University Press, pp. 160–78.

Gopal, Kusum. 2007. '"A Woman Exists Solely to Give Birth: An Ethnographic Study". Reduction of Maternal Mortality and Neonatal Deaths in the Dodoma Region, Tanzania'. Unpublished UNESCO Report.

Greenfield, Patricia, and Jean Lave. 1982. 'Cognitive Aspects of Informal Education', in Daniel A. Wagner and Harold W. Stevenson (eds), *Cultural Perspectives on Child Development*. San Francisco, CA: Freeman, pp. 181–207.

Hill, Polly. 1972. *Rural Hausa, a Village and a Setting*. Cambridge: Cambridge University Press.

Hipólito, Ines, and Thomas van Es. 2022. 'Enactive-Dynamic Social Cognition and Active Inference'. *Frontiers in Psychology* 13.

Hoelgaard, Suzanne. 1988a. 'Adoption Law, Policy and Practice in Colombia'. Report for Overseas Development Administration, Department of Social Anthropology, University of Cambridge.

———. 1988b. 'Child Protection Laws and Practice in Colombia'. Report for the World Health Organisation, Department of Social Anthropology, University of Cambridge.

———. 1998. 'Cultural Determinants of Adoption Policy: A Colombian Case Study', *International Journal of Law, Policy and the Family* 12: 202–24.

Humphreys, Nicholas. 1976. 'The Social Function of Intellect', in Patrick P.G. Bateson and Robert A. Hinde (eds), *Growing Points in Ethology*. Cambridge: Cambridge University Press, pp. 303–17.

Koll, Michael. 1969. *Crafts and Cooperation in Western Nigeria: A Sociological Contribution to Indigenous Economics*. Frieberg: Bertelsmann-Universitätsverlag.

Kraft, Richard, et al. 1995. *A Tale of Two Ghanas: The View from the Classroom*. Accra, Ghana: Ministry of Education.

Lallemand, Suzanne. 1976. 'Génetrices et Educatrices Mossi', *L'Homme* 16(1): 109–24.

Lave, Jean. 1977. 'Cognitive Consequences of Traditional Apprenticeship Training in West Africa', *Anthropology and Education Quarterly* 8(3): 177–80.

———. 2019. *Learning and Everyday Life: Access, Participation, and Changing Practice*. Cambridge: Cambridge University Press.

Lave, Jean, and Etienne Wenger. 1991. *Situated Learning: Legitimate Peripheral Participation*. Cambridge: Cambridge University Press.

Lloyd, Peter C. 1953. 'Craft Organization in Yoruba Towns', *Africa* 23(1): 30–44.

Ministry of Education. 1990. 'Enrolment Statistics for the Academic Year 1989–1990'. Accra, Ghana: Ministry of Education.

Mir-Hosseini, Ziba. 2010. 'Being From There: Dilemmas of a Native Anthropologist', in Shahnaz Nadjmabadi (ed.), *Conceptualizing Iranian Anthropology*. Oxford: Berghahn Books, pp. 180–91.

_____. 2012. 'The Politics of Divorce Laws in Iran: Ideology versus Practice', in Rubya Mehdi, Werner Menski and Jørgen Nielsen (eds), *Interpreting Divorce Laws in Islam*. Copenhagen: DJØF Publishing, pp. 65–83.

Muir, Christine L., and Esther N. Goody. c. 1971. Preliminary Report of a Survey of West African Families in London. Unpublished manuscript report. Social Science Research Council Archives. London: Mimeo.

_____. 1972. 'Student Parents: West African Families in London', *Race* 13: 329–36.

Newcomb, Theodore M. 1943. *Personality and Social Change: Attitude Formation in a Student Community*. New York: Dryden.

Oppong, Christine. 1973. *Growing up in Dagbon*. Accra: Ghana Publishing Corporation.

Peil, Margaret. 1970. 'The Apprenticeship System in Accra', *Africa* 40(2): 137–50.

_____. 1978. 'Self-employed Craftsmen'. Unpublished MS.

Rogoff, Barbara. 1990. *Apprenticeship in Thinking: Cognitive Development in Social Context*. Oxford: Oxford University Press.

Rosaldo, Michelle Z. 1980. 'The Use and Abuse of Anthropology: Reflections on Feminism and Cross-cultural Understanding', *Signs: Journal of Women in Culture and Society* 5(3): 389–417.

Rosekrans, Kristin, Arieh Sherris and Marie Chatry-Komarek. 2012. 'Education Reform for the Expansion of Mother-Tongue Education in Ghana', *International Review of Education* 58(5): 593–618.

Skinner, Elliot P. 1961. 'Intergenerational Conflict among the Mossi: Father and Son', *Journal of Conflict Resolution* 5(1): 55–60.

_____. 1964. *The Mossi of the Upper Volta*. Stanford, CA: Stanford University Press.

Smith, M.G. 1955. *The Economy of Hausa Communities of Zaria*. Colonial Research Studies 16. London: HMSO.

Strathern, Marilyn. 1972. 'Official and Unofficial Courts: Legal Assumptions and Expectations in a Highlands Community'. Canberra: New Guinea Research Bulletin No. 47.

_____. 1975a. 'Questionnaire Relating to Sexual Offences in the Criminal Code'. Report prepared for the Papua New Guinea Administration, Department of Law, Port Moresby.

_____. 1975b. 'Villagers' Attitudes Towards Corrective Institutions'. Report prepared for the Papua New Guinea Corrective Institutions Service, Port Moresby.

_____. 1993a. *Sex Selection: Social Issues*. British Medical Association, Conference on Sex Selection.

_____. 1993b. Contribution to *Virgin Birth*. Robert Silman (ed.), Proceedings of Symposium, London Hospital Medical College [1991]. London: WFT Press.

_____. 2000. Supplementary Notes, to accompany L. Kalinoe, 'Background Paper in Intellectual Rights and Related Social and Cultural Issues in Papua New Guinea'. Prepared for the PNG National Intellectual Property Rights Committee.

_____. 2011. 'Human Bodies: Donation for Medicine and Research'. London: Nuffield Council on Bioethics. Report prepared as Chair of NCOB Working Party.

_____. 2018. 'Persons and Partible Persons', in Matei Candea (ed.), *Schools and Styles of Anthropological Theory*. London: Routledge, pp. 236–46.

Streeck, Jürgen. 1995. 'On Projection', in Esther N. Goody (ed.), *Social Intelligence and Interaction: Expressions and Implications of the Social Bias in Human Intelligence*. Cambridge: Cambridge University Press, pp. 87–100.

Thomas, Roger G. 1974. 'Education in Northern Ghana, 1906–1940: A Study in Colonial Paradox', *The International Journal of African Historical Studies* 7(3): 427–67.

UNESCO (United Nations Educational, Scientific and Cultural Organization). 1953. 'The Use of the Vernacular Languages in Education'. Monographs on Fundamental Education. Paris.

———. 1990. 'World Declaration on Education for All and Framework for Action to Meet Basic Learning Needs'. Paris.

———. 2003. 'Education in a Multilingual World: UNESCO Education Position Paper'. Paris. Retrieved 17 October 2024 from http://unesdoc.unesco.org/ images/0012/001297/129728e.pdf.

UNICEF. 1991. *The State of the World's Children*. New York: Oxford University Press.

———. 2016. 'The Impact of Language Policy and Practice on Children's Learning: Evidence from Eastern and Southern Africa'. Retrieved 17 October 2024 from https://www.unicef.org/esa/sites/unicef.org.esa/files/2018-09/UNICEF-2016-Language-and-Learning-FullReport.pdf.

Vygotsky, Lev. 1978. *Mind in Society: The Development of Higher Psychological Processes*. Edited by Michael Cole et al. Cambridge, MA: Harvard University Press.

Weiner, Annette B. 1979. 'Trobriand Kinship from Another View: The Reproductive Power of Women and Men', *Man* 14(2): 328–48.

Weston, Kath. (1995) 2013. 'Forever Is a Long Time: Romancing the Real in Gay Kinship Ideologies', in Sylvia Yanagisako and Carol Delaney (eds), *Naturalizing Power: Essays in Feminist Cultural Analysis*. New York: Routledge, pp. 87–110.

Whiten, Andrew, and Richard W. Byrne (eds). 1997. *Machiavellian Intelligence II: Extensions and Evaluations*. Cambridge: Cambridge University Press.

Wood, David J., Jerome S. Bruner and Gail Ross. 1976. 'The Role of Tutoring in Problem Solving', *Journal of Child Psychology and Psychiatry* 17(2): 89–100.

1

Sisters into Wives, Wives into Sisters

Marilyn Strathern

At the time when Esther Goody was publishing her first fieldwork, in social
anthropology at large it was taken for granted that one described kinship
systems with a male reference point before considering a female one. The very
foundation of society through, as it was imagined, men's dependence on one
another for wives meant that separation of the sexual destinies of brothers and
sisters was understood as men giving up their sisters to other men. A concomi-
tant of this was that all kinds of institutions were presumed to exist in the ethnographic present to ensure the appropriate transformation of sisters into
(other men's) wives, sustained by residential rules and the like. Thus, anthropologists might interpret entry into conjugal status as the permanent mark of
female adulthood. Without making a song and dance about it, Goody's meticulous observations of Gonja life showed a social logic of another order. It was
common at a particular stage in the Gonja developmental cycle for wives to
become sisters again – not that they had not always been sisters, but in the
sense of now shedding their conjugal status in its all-important domestic
dimensions. Residence at a brother's place was one sign of this. Wives, we may
say, turned into sisters.

This is not the place to revisit debates of the time over residence and marriage, or over the primordial exchange of women, modes of production, and the
feminist critiques they engendered (notably in the present context Sacks 1979;
also Weiner 1992), although – as we will see – the idea of men giving up their
sisters would have resonated with certain sentiments that were current in the
nineteenth-century English-speaking world when the anthropological study of
kinship and marriage was beginning to take shape. The logic at issue in Goody's
Gonja study is indeed of a different order, and concerned the implications of
the enduring and often very practical interests that women and men had in one
another's affairs.

From a woman's point of view, marriage was not as it was in so many places a transformation that 'severed' relations with her own kin or put them on a more distanced basis. (The ruling group aside, Gonja commoners did not recognize localized kin groups of the kind that would give them interests in the matter.) Over time a woman was likely to move between different households; what was striking was that these were as often where their brothers farmed as where their husbands did. Moreover, men and women alike could call on the labour, that is, the co-residential support, of their siblings' children. Through the institution of fostering, children assumed the character of a joint resource between them [the siblings], men looking to their kinsfolk's sons, women to their daughters (e.g. Goody 1982: 47). In other words, women did not give up their brothers when they married, and they could always elicit brotherly support by the act of taking up residence with them. At the same time, while a woman's household jobs, such as cooking, could be undertaken for either a brother's or husband's children,[1] this was not a dimension along which these relations could be activated simultaneously. The nature of such enduring interests between siblings and spouses, and what is highlighted at particular moments during the course of a life, prompts address to an intriguing problematic that exists elsewhere.

A Problematic

Goody herself emphasized the permanency of sibling ties as against the contractual nature of marriage (1973: 131), especially under a regime where women might terminate more than one such contract over the course of a life, culminating in the woman's final withdrawal to her brother's place. Here we encounter an unexpected negativity. It was assumed that if a sister took up domestic roles in a brother's compound he would provide for her; yet, regardless of the regret that husbands might or might not express, such departure was often under a cloud of suspicion, even accusations of injury, against the woman. Moreover, if her husband had died, a widow knew she had no place with his kin. We might ask what kinds of relations these are. Or rather, how do we (English speakers) understand these modulations of expectations between diverse parties as 'relations'?

The question is prompted by one of the lessons I learnt from Goody and her colleagues in the Cambridge Department of Social Anthropology: that as far as anthropological analysis is concerned, negative relations are still relations. People may be in a state of war, but that does not imply an absence of relation; on the contrary, the relationship *is* that enmity. Rites of separation at funerals may seek to despatch the deceased so it will not bother the living, but we could as well regard these as rites of transformation; one kind of relation with the deceased becomes another. There is a concealed problem here: why it should have been necessary to be explicit in the first place. I suspect it was because the lesson goes against the grain of English vernacular usage. Hostile or distant relations can as easily be imagined as an absence of relation, as 'no relations' at all. This usage no doubt arises at least partly from the way the very concept of relation is loaded with positive connotations. The positive tenor that I see adhering to the English concept of 'relation' adheres to it in its abstract form.[2] When it comes to specific instances of relations, English usage allows it to encompass any affective modality. However, there is a specific domain of social relations where – again in the abstract but now applicable within this domain – a positive gloss is assumed before a negative one: kinship. Sahlins' (2013) reworking of Fortes' amity of kinship is a case in point.[3] What goes for kinship goes for relatives and relations in a kinship sense. It is a connotation of these particular terms (relatives/relations) that, before all the specific instances of not getting on are mentioned, kin are assumed to have positive feelings towards one another. Anything less may lead to a denial of relations. So relations can be 'broken off' or become attenuated or challenged to the point of English-speakers in effect claiming there is (now) 'no relation' between the parties concerned. It is possible to 'drop out' or 'lose touch', to the extent that there is 'no longer any connection with the family' (Edwards and Strathern 2000: 156).[4] The vernacular (English) formula is interesting for the bias it gives to the anthropologist's language of description. This is the problematic that I nibble at here.

Goody's Gonja material from 1956–57 is a provocative invitation to think about it. The affective gloss in English may well aid the anthropologist's analytic intentions (Fortes 1969), but it can also be a severe impediment to them when it comes to devising a language through which to address unfamiliar circumstances. Thus, it does not make sense in the Gonja context to assume that positive relations are the norm, and negatives ones aberrant. A further area of Goody's work is illuminating here, and I expand on it briefly. What follows is highly selective, and somewhat redundant for those who know her work well, but hopefully the point of both the selection and the detail will become apparent.

Positive and Negative Tenors

'Legitimate and illegitimate aggression in a West African state' was the title of a paper that Goody (1970) published before finalizing her two major works on kinship (1973, 1982). It is not irrelevant that the title neutralizes the tenor of 'aggression' that in English is otherwise negative. For what she conveyed was the dual aspects of a phenomenon that had in effect two sides – a male and a female one. Witchcraft in the hands of men had positive properties; it was used to secure protection for one's dependants or success in hunting or in competitive rivalry. While it might injure or kill it was not actionable, although it fuelled speculation and gossip. Witchcraft in the hands of women was interpreted negatively, as an enactment of malice. Female witches became objects of fear and terror, and as likely as not (about half the time) were punished, often with considerable cruelty. Covertly exercised, what enabled someone to practise witchcraft, and the forms it took, were the same in each case. Given the number of men's exploits that required witchcraft and the way that fears about women being witches dominated routine actions such as the distribution of food, the sexes could be defined by their witchcraft potential. Taken in its most general sense as a technique of mystical aggression, the positive and negative connotations of witchcraft were thus not simply a matter of specific circumstance – they were irrevocably attached to the difference between men and women.

In accounting for this asymmetry, Goody pointed to two salient social dimensions. On the one hand, it was chiefs par excellence who were known to wield such mystical influence, and who did so both to protect their dependants and to triumph over rivals. There was a parallel between village chiefs and compound heads (Goody 1970: 212), and indeed it would seem between chiefs and husbands in general. Thus suspected witches were sometimes sent as wives to a chief, because he would have the strength to control their activities (ibid.: 215). On the other hand, the primary arena in which women acted exposed men (and other women) to the possibilities of their disaffection; as Goody (ibid.: 240–41) observes, women were defined by domestic roles (spouse, co-wife, parent) whose mode was that of intimate dependence. As spouses, women were categorically subordinate to their husbands in a way they were not to their brothers, and wifely aggression could only take a covert form. Yet that archetype relationship of dependence, and of dominance and subordination, set up at marriage, did not wholly define the spheres in which women were feared. Husbands, co-wives and affines were prominent among women's victims, but so were consanguineal kin, including a woman's own child (also her husband's) or grandchild (also her husband's).

Not only did women frequently leave their husbands throughout their procreative years – in both separation and divorce – but women were also, to all intents and purposes, divested of the status of wife in the 'terminal separation' (from her husband) that came with old age (Goody 1973: 155). Indeed, throughout life a woman had the option of living 'as a sister, not only as a wife' (1982: 99), her brothers being obliged to support her as long as she wished. When death ended marriage, her deceased husband's kin did not expect her to stay, a mystically backed injunction forbidding her re-marriage to a deceased husband's brother. Rather than seeing periods of residence at the brother's home as interludes in a married life, as is the case in many societies,[5] Goody argued that sibling co-residence must be understood as an end in itself. It signified, tout court, the importance of the brother–sister tie. Fear of witchcraft accusation was a prime, though by no means the only, reason for women leaving their husband's compound in later life.

Witchcraft (positive or negative) was one of four modes that Goody singled out as 'idioms of relationship' (Goody 1973: 2–3), the others being greeting and begging behaviour, the sharing of cooked food, and the mystical influence of supernatural forces. These relational idioms were to do with the manner in which people were held to influence one another. Greeting and begging enacted the respect and subordination owed to seniors; sharing cooked food elicited the recipient's trust that it had not been doctored, while obligations to kin were upheld by the fear of mystical reprisal. In this context, witches' power to kill was an expression of the secret danger that they were to the health and life of others. This was so whether witchcraft was wielded by a strong man being 'protective' of those close to him or by a woman whose 'malice' against those she knew took effect. The (positive or negative) sentiments that were attributed to the perpetrator were elements of the influence he or she had. In the case of malevolent (female) witchcraft, might one understand this as an excess of influence between intimates? In any event, such a witch had to be killed or driven away. At the point when she could no longer exercise her influence, perhaps we could say relations were terminated.

Was there a parallel with divorce or separation? In sociological terms, these acts did not sever all relations. Goody (1973: 133) writes, 'once children have been born, the dissolution of a conjugal union can no longer terminate all relationship, for the couple is permanently united through parenthood'. Moreover, an enduring relationship of sexual rivalry existed between the successive spouses of one woman – she had brought them within the sphere of one another's influence – and former husbands might desperately hope for a wife's return. Supini Wuritche, the 'sister' of a divisional chief, had two ex-husbands, unmarried like herself; '[e]ach man complained that since she had left him, he had been wifeless, and each strongly resented the other as a possible obstacle to securing her return' (Goody 1962: 41). That she was of some status in her 'brother's' compound was another matter. It was the husband who might beg a woman to think again. Akuro's wife, Nyomba, had left him some fifteen years before, the four young children remaining with the father. When she once more refused his pleas that she return, he 'talked for days about her ingratitude in refusing, and her lack of maternal affection for her children, who, he said, had grown up as orphans' (ibid.: 33).

Nonetheless, there was perhaps a sense in which such relations were also terminated, namely, at the point when people sought to diminish the spheres of influence in which someone has an effect on another. In the model of chiefs using their (positive) witchcraft to seek out (negative) witchcraft, one may wonder if the female witch was seen by others as somehow presuming or assuming the kind of powers that men ('legitimately') exercised over dependants. Men's powers were backed by the state, by the authority of village and divisional chiefs. Women should not exercise such influence. This suggests an analogical relationship between male and female mystical influence and the positive and negative exercise of witchcraft.

It is not too far-fetched to see other arenas in which spheres of influence were deliberately kept in check. Kin networks should not be too dense. Was curbing an 'excess' of relational influence a component of the Gonja avoidance of repeated marriages? Marriage with a cross-cousin (bilaterally) was the only close form that was encouraged. Replicating unions, such as multiple marriages between siblings – two sisters or two first cousins marrying the same man (in vivo) or marrying two brothers – incurred sanctions. People might speak in the same breath of inappropriate marriage and inappropriate sexual relations. Indeed the concept of inappropriate sexual union, whether with kin or adulterously with the spouses of kin, could, so to speak, settle on any such dereliction, much in the way that witchcraft could be located in a variety of mystical effects (inhabiting medicines, expressing a will of its own, appearing as a skill that is learnt or as poison put into food). But Gonja could also draw specific parallels that reinforced the danger of too much influence. If the idea of a man sleeping with his brother's wife was met with the same repugnance as the idea of brother–sister incest, so was the idea of two sisters with one man.[6] 'If a man were to sleep with the wife of a full brother,' Supini Wuritche explained, 'it would be the same thing as sleeping with his own sister, because if your brother were a woman and both were to sleep with the same person, it is as though they had slept with each other' (Goody 1973: 219–20).

The ethnographic record at large speaks to diverse modes of relations between siblings, and especially cross-sex siblings, as they are worked out though domestic arrangements. Goody's material is a particularly good place through which to think about the positive and negative tenors that are given to ideas of relating. I have asserted there is a bias here in anthropological discourse, and turn to something of the vernacular context of that discourse.

Closeness and Distance

It is a peculiarity of the way interpersonal relations are often depicted by English speakers that distance is generally taken as a matter of degree before it is taken as a matter of alterity (cf. Strathern 2017). While there are innumerable situations where people encounter social barriers or glass ceilings, or talk of distance or closeness as constructs of class or race, the concepts lend themselves to apprehending a world in which there is a sliding scale in the degree to which one admits others as close or distant to oneself. The scale that calibrates closeness and distance can be coordinated with almost any dimension of life, among them assumptions about increasing and decreasing knowledge in the form of personal recognition, and the appropriateness of the feelings that accompany the knowledge. The map people may well have in their heads is of a kind of socio-geographic field of ever-widening concentric rings, in which one can place diverse intimates and acquaintances till one reaches the point where relations are no longer 'interpersonal' but become subsumed under interactions with such categories as 'stranger' or 'alien'.

On this map, family, friends and lovers may be typified as the closest intimates (e.g. Morgan 2009).[7] Indeed kinship relations in general may be regarded as 'close' before 'distant' connections are also remembered. Here is another example of a positive gloss: in vernacular usage, closeness is a matter of affect as well of relational degree. Close relatives are ideally close to one another. The negative things that 'close' relatives may do to one another is cause for comment.

To remain close, however, relations usually have to be activated, and the ethnographic record on English kinship contains numerous examples of relatives who break off their relations with one another, as well as those who seemingly slip out of the family from neglect or a desire to get away.

My interest in the issue comes from the way that, in the English-speaking world, the positive gloss given to the concept of relation informs all kinds of knowledge practices, including those of social science. Here is another double entendre, as the term 'positive' itself can refer either to the discernible presence or recognition of an entity (as in 'positivism') or to a benign value put on its appearance. And while they can always be separated by context, these connotations also run side by side. We might call it relational positivism. Time and again in social anthropology the mapping out of discernible relations has been articulated as the point of the exercise. This is true whether between people (including kin) or between elements of social life, and I think we must take the analytical or epistemic connotations alongside the value the term also carries. The combination almost gives a sense of agency to the analytical construct: relations can be 'activated', and to take action is to be positive.

An instructive example of relational positivism is found in the study Raymond Firth and his colleagues carried out in the early 1960s with a middle-class sector of North London, a stance that seemingly kept faith with their informants. Ideas about closeness and distance between kin were translated from the vernacular into an analytical distinction – that is, through a doubling of terms. The distinction was between kin who were recognized and kin who were effective kin, or as we might say these days who 'performed' kinship. Effective kin, those with whom contacts were maintained, with whom relations were activated, could also be thought of as carved out of a wider sphere of all those who were recognized as kin. ('Recognition' allows the same doubling, in that those whom you actively recognize may be part of the domain of those whom you simply 'know'.) The category of effective kin was in turn divisible into the 'intimate' with whom contact was close and frequent, and the 'peripheral' where contact was distant and sporadic (Firth, Hubert and Forge 1969: 156). And how was this model devised? Among other things it emerged from the research process. The researchers asked people to lay out who their kin were, starting out from the immediate family and then tracing everyone connected through birth or marriage. This produced a (positive) map of relations on which could be plotted the effectiveness of the relating that was at issue. Among the results was a host of equivocations about who were or were not considered to be relations or relatives – 'she is not a relation, only by marriage' (ibid.: 91).[8] Often people did this by reference as to who would count as family, and as the authors remark, 'family' does not just demarcate a category of kin but is 'a term of affective significance' (ibid.: 92).

Goody's analysis prompts a different vantage point, one that tries to step back from such a modelling of closeness and distance, and its presuppositions about the positive nature of relations. With her presentation of the Gonja in mind, we might consider both the positive and negative tenors of dealings between siblings and spouses. While they are embedded in the practicalities of enduring interests, this is not just a question of the variations in affect – from affection to aversion ('relations are a perishing nuisance', ibid.: 108) – to be found among close relatives, as Firth and his colleagues would be the first to admit. Rather the question is what we might learn from the distribution of values that Goody identified in Gonja witchcraft. Now this is not a step into the very considerable literatures on siblings and spouses that exist in other disciplines, nor even an attempt to summarize what could have been taken from countless ethnographic contexts. On the contrary, I narrow the exposition down to a quite specific moment in English history, although perhaps one of some interest to anthropologists given its proximity to the origins of anthropology in debates about the sexual destinies of siblings.

Incest and Intimacy

When in 1834 one John Melville married Sophia, sister of Henry Thornton, he was marrying someone who was at once his deceased wife's first cousin and his own first cousin. The Melvilles and Thorntons were banking partners, and no one who has delved into European kinship would be surprised to find marriages between business associates. However, this was a time when 'marriages between cousins or brothers- and sisters-in-law were just as common in families of doctors, lawyers and clergymen, or in the Anglo-Indian dynasties of high civil servants, as they were in business, not to speak of the intellectual and scientific bourgeois or evangelical sects'. I refer to Kuper's (2009: 135)[9] account of the (upper) middle class England of the nineteenth century. Marriage repeated between families merged into a sense of marriage 'within the family' (ibid.: 27).

This was a period in which modes of intimacy were subjects of public discourse; an ideal marital arrangement of the Victorian novel, for example, was adoption 'into the family [of] someone who is almost a member of the family already' (quoted, Kuper 2009: 17). 'These webs of relationships' shaped vocations, generated patronage and gave a special cast to the idea of alliance,[10] insofar as 'marriages between relations' generated interpersonal ties that overtly brought close people closer in connectedness and sentiment (ibid.: 24, 18). The sentiment was a matter of expressed feeling, and how first cousins, or brothers and sisters, *felt* about one another was part of the pattern. Here, then, marriage could be a device for reinforcing positive relations, bringing the close ever closer.

The family circles of bourgeois nineteenth-century England were sustained through different combinations of the resources of siblings and spouses.[11] A transfer of wealth was likely to accompany a woman's separation from her natal family. The union of husband and wife thereby freed capital assets ideally embodied within both their natal families for the new family's deployment. The latter's financial support was anticipated in a property settlement, one that may well have acknowledged the wife's distinct identity while also anticipating what the husband would do in supporting her. Husbands and wives themselves ideally combined their sentiment and feeling for each other. As we have seen, such sensibility was already shared within the family circle, and close marital alliances theoretically overcame the switch in the flow of emotion from relative to spouse. It is almost too obvious to say that marriage not just created new connections but rearranged old ones. However, even when it was between close kin, this expansive connotation of connection could fall short of the emotions generated by the expectation of familial intimacy. People also gave vent to feelings of extreme negativity, and wrote about them. There are descriptions of the extraordinary wrench it was for brothers and sisters to separate.

Kuper (2009: 167–69) tells how Henry Thornton, who had already suffered the defection of another sister, opposed Sophia's marriage to his cousin – not on grounds of its closeness but because he was so fond of her. If he alienated his sister by this 'preposterous' behaviour, his friend Tom Macaulay repeated the pattern. Tom could not bear the thought that his own two sisters might marry, in this case the women returning the anxiety (ibid.: 175–76). (Marriage could also be regarded as a betrayal of sisterhood.) He was broken-hearted on each occasion. Of the first, 'My loss is all pure loss'; of the second, 'The work of more than twenty years has vanished in a single month ... She was everything to me: and I am henceforth to be nothing to her' (ibid.: 176–77). When the first sister, Margaret, married, he wrote to the one then remaining (Hannah) that Margaret was dead to him (ibid.: 176; Davidoff 2012: 139). It is as though marriage severed relations, and relations severed were no relations at all. One of the prerequisites for the making of relations, then, could itself be the cause of breaking them: namely, the institution of marriage.

What was true between siblings was also true between families. If there was widespread value put on the effective recognition of relatives, there was equal possibility of its withering away. Several years earlier, so to speak, the heroine of Jane Austen's unfinished novel (*The Watsons*, begun about 1803), who has been brought up by a wealthy aunt in the mistaken expectation of a fortune, finds her brother reproaching the aunt for sending her back as 'a weight upon your family, without a sixpence'; he elaborates, 'keeping you at a distance from your family for such a length of time ... must [have done] away with all natural affection among us' (Austen (1871) 1923: 134–35).[12] Similarly, it would seem, *Persuasion*'s Mr Elliot, who had earlier 'throw[n] himself off' as far as his family was concerned, comes to the point of wishing 'to be received as a relation again', 'to be restored to the footing of a relation' ((1818) 1930: 150–51). But here marriage plays a crucial role. For the estrangement was in no small part due to the fact that Mr Elliot had earlier 'purchased independence [from his family] by uniting himself to a rich woman of inferior birth' (ibid.: 7). Extenuating circumstances for that union now had to be found.

Marriage could provide a source of independence (from their 'families') for both men and women, and novels of the time dwelt on what wealth and fortune, and its deprivation, meant for familial relations. From diaries, letters, biographies and other writings, the historical sociologist Leonore Davidoff documents just how marriage in and of itself was regarded as severing relations between siblings, whether between sisters, between brothers or between brothers and sisters: '[F]or those who had been exceptionally close, separation through long distances, but particularly through marriage[,] could evoke … feelings of grief and abandonment, the "desertion" of the loved companion's loyalty now transferred to another' (Davidoff 2012: 323).[13] The positive relation of marriage showed altogether another side. From the point of view of the sibling left behind it had the potential of being an act of profound negative consequence. There were certainly, in some instances, dire social repercussions for the bereft sibling, not only when it was a woman facing another taking over her home, but when it was a man losing a housekeeper and companion.

The latter should be put into the context of men's dependence on women, and if they had no wife then on their sister(s). The dependency was of a special kind, namely for 'domestic services' such as running the household. While either sex might suffer the consequences of a sibling's marriage, women's confinement to the sphere of household management and companionship gave their situation a particular cast. Unmarried daughters would be sent off by their parents to be 'housekeepers and companions in the homes of unmarried sisters or brothers' (Davidoff 2012: 137). As far as their natal home was concerned, there are many societies in which a bride's natal kin would mourn her departure in marriage. However, in these English cases, the departure was not restricted to the departure of a youthful bride on the verge of adulthood. An unmarried sister might have settled into an adult domestic routine (and in the large families of the time, older sisters would have an important role taking care of younger siblings).

Davidoff (2012: 129–30, 218) enlarges on Thornton's circumstances, and his dependence on his unmarried elder sister, Marianne, with whom he discussed financial matters, and whom he supported both before and after his own marriage. There was no question of her earning her own living. When he was widowed, he left the care of his children in her hands (he was still living in the original family home). She was the only one of his siblings who became reconciled to his subsequently marrying his wife's younger sister. Siblings were often closely involved in one another's marriages. On sibling intimacy of the time, 'feelings … often hovered on the edges of erotic desire. Literary scholars have noted that the legitimate desire for a cousin sometimes appears as a stand-in for forbidden attraction to a brother or sister' (ibid.: 239).[14] This is where, of all the different kinds of sibling intimacies that marriage might threaten, there was a special dimension to the cross-sex relation.

In terms of the personal feelings brother and sister might have for one another, the sister's defection in particular was, one might say, almost tantamount to a mystical attack. The metaphor grasps the tenor of expressions of intimacy among relations within the family, and between husband and wife. For the sister who assumed domestic support for a brother had become a kind of wife to him.[15] Sometimes it seems to have been more the withdrawal of this helpmeet, this wifely sister, than the interests of the other man that counted.

In the decades that followed, open discussion on the proper limits of intimacy turned all this into a public issue.[16] The challenge became uncertainty about incest. Kuper (2009: 57) is blunt: '[T]he English were uncertain as to what did, and what should, constitute incest. Incest was defined as an act of sexual intercourse between related persons whom the church prohibited from marrying ... [a] doctrine mired in centuries of theological argument'. Despite church rulings and parliamentary interventions, limits and their consequences were constantly put to the test of knowledge, and involved anthropologists of the day. If parliament was to become preoccupied with debating the propriety of marriage with the deceased wife's sister, the wider question concerned the consequences of relations born of intimacy. One suggestion from a literary historian is that interest in the prohibition on marriage with a dead wife's sister emphasized the primacy of the marital tie, and freedom of choice in the matter, in that in choosing a spouse a person also chose connections with the spouse's relatives. The possibility of cousin marriage, on the other hand, indicated that 'the sibling tie is dissolved by adulthood *and marriage* ... [for] marriage in some senses neutralizes siblinghood so that sibling incest taboos are not transmitted to the next generation' (Perry 2004: 121, my italics). Springing as they do from a close acquaintance with literature of the time, I would be surprised if Perry's comments had not caught something of the spirit of vernacular sentiments.

Analogies

So, what kinds of relations were being imagined for English siblings at these various junctures? Here Perry's (2004: 51) formula comes from extensive reading in history and anthropology, among other disciplines. Over the course of the eighteenth century, women of propertied families found their relations as daughter and sisters eclipsed by their positions as wives and mothers. With changing structures of inheritance, 'an emphasis on capital accumulation and the competition for resources for exchange rather than use undermines the reliance on kindred and opposes, rather than consolidates, the interests of siblings to one another' (ibid.: 129).[17] The relative power of sisters and wives in relation to their menfolk is explored in numerous eighteenth-century texts. Adopting Sack's focus on sisters and wives along with her argument about class and state formation, Perry draws attention to plots that play on the 'disinheritance' of women, their lack of independent means; specific legal and economic developments were leading to conflicts 'between one woman's sister-right and another's conjugal right' (ibid.: 131). The sexualization of the conjugal tie was an element here. 'As marriage became an increasingly important mechanism for the accumulation of wealth, the place of marriage in social life and the place of sex in marriage had to be reconceived' (ibid.: 237). If these trends are discernible, it may in part be to the extent that they had become consolidated by the nineteenth century.

We might remark, then, that some of the circumstances in which women of the following century were to find themselves included a heightened sentimentality in brother–sister relations as well as ideas about the desirability of close unions. A sister's departure 'attacked' the brother's feelings of affection and attachment; the person who was now 'nothing' had been even more acutely 'everything'. Henry's predicament might have been extreme in its expression, but perhaps what we are witnessing is an extreme development of ideas of closeness and distance, and the positive and negative resonances they carried. It was in emotional terms that a severed relation appeared to be no relation. Marriage displaced one set of 'close' feelings with another, the emotions involved becoming assimilated to the absolute union of conjugal love. At the same time, regarding sentiment and affection as being severed was to deny the possibility of continuing sentiment and affection bridging the gap brought about by marriage.

Let us recall the Gonja concerns with violation involving a sibling's wife ('You would surely die, it is the same as sleeping with your own sister' [Goody 1973: 75]) and, in at least one woman's mind, the substitutability of male and female: imagine a male sibling as though he were a female sibling. As though siblingship had male and female aspects? Possibly that substitutability reappears in what seems to be a Gonja analogy between the mystical powers of men and women. For all the contrast between them, were they also versions of each other, positive and negative aspects of the same phenomenon? For what Goody so clearly saw in Gonja was that there were not two kinds of witchcraft, but two values attached to the exercise of mystical power. They were values that had enduring consequence for men's and women's daily lives, precisely because aggression was something that either sex could express. The predicament of English wifely sisters was differently located.

Rather than the sexes being regarded as (analogical) versions of each other, English ideas of gender were developing towards a (positivist) emphasis on gender-appropriate attributions of identity. And here was a positive reduplication of both identity and affect: a close sister offered domestic support like a close wife.[18] It would seem that people were not so much playing on the positive and negative consequences of being close, as showing a preoccupation with 'closeness' imagined along some kind of scale. It could be felt as greater or lesser (when it became 'distance'); it could also be regarded as present or absent. The same was true of relationships. When Tom Macaulay's sister Hannah in due course married, as her bachelor brother he became heavily involved in her new family.[19] That did not heal the breach. Years later he told Hannah that her marriage was for ever a 'living death' for him. What had died at the moment of her defection was their intimate relation. A relationship was gone. We might surmise that what made such kinship-thinking possible was contributing to formulations about the nature of an intimacy that was also fashioning how, in the vernacular on which English-speaking anthropologists came to rely, 'relations' between persons were inflected with the desirability of closeness.

Acknowledgements

Esther Goody was my second-year undergraduate supervisor, and she then took me for my doctorate; I could not have had a more stimulating or kinder teacher. The excitement with which I went off to the university library to meet the challenge of the first essay she set me is still vivid. The debt endures. I pay my respects – even if I cannot repay the debt – by folding some of her early ethnographic and theoretical concerns into some recent concerns of my own. Her comments on an earlier draft of this attempt have been listened to!

Marilyn Strathern is a former William Wyse Professor of Social Anthropology, and currently life fellow of Girton College, Cambridge. Her ethnographic forays are divided between Papua New Guinea and Britain. Apart from gender and kinship, she has written on reproductive technologies, intellectual and cultural property, and audit culture.

Notes

1. Men cooked for themselves, but a woman cooked for men's children.
2. This develops an argument presented elsewhere (Strathern 2014). It is foreshadowed in Edwards and Strathern (2000: 152, footnotes omitted): "'Belonging', like "association", "relationship", and a host of similar connective terms, carries positive overtones. It is almost as though there were something productive and generative in making connections as such'.
3. 'Mutuality' in the 'mutuality of being' that Sahlins takes as the primary characteristic of kin relations has the same kind of positive gloss *in the abstract*. He goes on to find particular positive and negative correlates of each, apropos the argument below.
4. Mr Butterworth was part of the family when he was younger, but (a relative remarked) 'he sort of took himself out of the family sphere by not, you know, communicating sort of thing' (Edwards and Strathern 2000: 155).
5. Including the Lowiili, further to the north in Ghana, who are contrasted here. Necessarily this short account must be highly selective, and I do not rehearse here many pertinent factors, such as the presence of ranked estates, the absence of descent groups, expectations concerning the dispersed residence of children, or the significant factors that make fostering an end in itself, not to speak of the sociological understanding that Goody brings to the intricacy of motives and circumstances that lead women to shift residence.
6. Moreover, not only would an affair with a brother's wife be 'equivalent to sibling incest but marriage to a woman who has ever been in the relationship of spouse to a sibling, parent, or parent's sibling is not allowed' (Goody 1973: 136–37).
7. An image of 'overlapping circles', with 'the individual and close intimates at the centre and acquaintances further out', is drawn vividly by the sociologist Morgan for present-day Britain (Morgan 2009: 4). Running through many forms of acquaintance, he says (ibid.: 108), is a balance between closeness and distance. Strangers, on the other hand,

'tend to be defined in negative terms, as people who[m] we do not know or recognise' (ibid.: 3).

8. To take one example (1969: 95): 'Yes, I think of them as relatives ... if ever they wanted anything we would be pleased to help them ... but I don't think of the others as relatives ... they are older and it is not likely for us to ask them for any help as friends ... and not the distant ones ... my husband has hundreds of them'.

9. Often the unions were explicitly 'between families', as among elite Quaker families prominent in banking, or the Thorntons and Wilberforces of the evangelical Clapham Sect. Cousin marriages seem to have been a largely middle/upper class phenomenon (Kuper 2009: 18, 97).

10. 'I protest against the opinions of those sentimental people who think that marriage concerns only the two principals', wrote Charles Darwin's cousin Francis Galton; 'it has in reality the wider effect of an alliance between each of them and a new family' (Kuper 2009: 17–18).

11. Both sets of parents would be expected to settle capital on the newly-weds to secure their financial future. However, in this social stratum, a woman's family often circumvented the common law presumption that a wife's person and property came under the husband's jurisdiction, through trust laws that secured the daughter's capital and allowed her an independent income (after Kuper 2009: 16–17).

12. Firth's North Londoners have their own version of recognition. For example: [of consanguines of affines] 'I would hardly call them relatives. I would have called them relatives if I'd known them longer'; [of a wife's brother] 'He was so close to her that, yes, he was a relative' (Firth, Hubert and Forge 1969: 97).

13. Note the two senses of the epithet 'close' here. Of William and Henry James (born in 1842 and 1843), she writes: '[t]heirs had always been an intense relationship of love and mutual care ... [and when] William eventually married, ... his bachelor brother Henry felt "divorced"'. And the separation could be re-lived. When William died, Henry 'felt that "my beloved brother's death has cut into me, deep down, even as an absolute mutilation"' (Davidoff 2012: 328).

14. Indeed, an anthropologist might regard 'some forms of preferential cross-cousin marriage as ... an attempt to perpetuate the brother–sister tie in the following generation – the compensation for the incest taboo at one remove' (Goody 1982: 92).

15. In an era when lover-like language was used without inhibition between kin, it is perhaps not surprising to find unmarried intimates in domestic roles (same-sex or cross-sex) referring to one another in conjugal terms. Davidoff (2012: 137–38) describes an unmarried country curate, whose sister lived with him and helped him in his parish duties, speaking of their relationship as 'amateur man and wife'. One sister, inviting another to help run her household, said that with the housekeeping taken care of she herself would 'take the husband's part' (ibid.: 149).

16. Davidoff (2012: 239) comments on the gap between the anxieties of the scientific and intellectual establishment and 'the absence of adverse comment by members of the families involved'. Rates of close marriage continued to increase throughout the nineteenth century.

17. In particular, she notes the 'diverging destinies of brothers and sisters in the property-owning classes. ... As sisters came to be more dependent within their families, brothers were increasingly expected to take on the parental functions of protection, advice, regulation ... Tension between these responsibilities and the demands of the brothers' own [conjugal] lives came to be more and more a staple of eighteenth-century fiction' (Perry 2004: 111). 'Many a fictional heroine must apply to her brother for a place to stay, money to live, or permission to marry' (ibid.: 116).

18. Conversely with husbands and brothers, but for men – who had access to occupations beyond domestic ones – perhaps less intensely.

19. Davidoff 2012: 139–40; 185. He made living with them (initially) a condition of his approval to the marriage; on her part, Hannah is said to have remained besotted with Tom (Kuper 2009: 177).

References

Austen, Jane. (1871) 1923. *'Lady Susan' and 'The Watsons'*. London: Martin Secker.
_____. (1818) 1930. *Persuasion*. London: Martin Secker.
Davidoff, Leonore. 2012. *Thicker than Water: Siblings and their Relations, 1780–1920*. Oxford: Oxford University Press.
Edwards, Jeanette, and Marilyn Strathern. 2000. 'Including Our Own', in Janet Carsten (ed.), *Cultures of Relatedness: New Approaches to the Study of Kinship*. Cambridge: Cambridge University Press, pp. 149–65.
Firth, Raymond, Jane Hubert and Anthony Forge. 1969. *Families and Their Relatives: Kinship in a Middle-Class Sector of London. An Anthropological Study*. London: Routledge & Kegan Paul.
Fortes, Meyer. 1969. *Kinship and the Social Order: The Legacy of Lewis Henry Morgan*. Chicago: Aldine Publishing Co.
Goody, Esther N. 1962. 'Conjugal Separation and Divorce among the Gonja of Northern Ghana', in Meyer Fortes (ed.), *Marriage in Tribal Societies*. Cambridge: Cambridge University Press, pp. 14–54.
_____. 1970. 'Legitimate and Illegitimate Aggression in a West African State', in Mary Douglas (ed.), *Witchcraft: Confessions and Accusations*. London: Tavistock Publications, pp. 207–44.
_____. 1973. *Contexts of Kinship: An Essay in the Family Sociology of the Gonja of Northern Ghana*. Cambridge: Cambridge University Press.
_____. 1982. *Parenthood and Social Reproduction: Fostering and Occupational Roles in West Africa*. Cambridge: Cambridge University Press.
Kuper, Adam. 2009. *Incest and Influence: The Private Life of Bourgeois England*. Cambridge, MA: Harvard University Press.
Morgan, David. 2009. *Acquaintances: The Space between Intimates and Strangers*. Maidenhead: Open University Press.
Perry, Ruth. 2004. *Novel Relations: The Transformation of Kinship in English Literature and Culture, 1748–1818*. Cambridge: Cambridge University Press.
Sacks, Karen. 1979. *Sisters and Wives: The Past and Future of Sexual Equality*. Westport, CN: Greenwood Press.
Sahlins, Marshall. 2013. *What Kinship Is – And Is Not*. Chicago: University of Chicago Press.
Strathern, Marilyn. 2014. 'Reading Relations Backwards', *JRAI* (NS) 20(1): 3–19.
_____. 2017. 'Connections, Friends, and Their Relations: An Issue in Knowledge-Making', in Pierre Charbonnier, Gildas Salmon and Peter Skafish (eds), *Comparative Metaphysics: Ontology after Anthropology*. London: Rowman & Littlefield, pp. 61–83.
Weiner, Annette. 1992. *Inalienable Possessions: The Paradox of Keeping-While-Giving*. Berkeley: University of California Press.

2

Fragments of Intimacy and the Reassembling of Relations

Barbara Bodenhorn

Many of the works in this volume take a particular work of Goody's and revisit it. Although the present chapter does not do that, it reflects the alacrity with which I absorbed her article on 'forms of pro-parenthood' as a graduate student, and our intense conversations about whether I was discussing adoption or fosterage in my thesis chapter on Iñupiaq parents and children (1971). A close engagement with language and communication was never far behind (see in particular Goody 1978; 1982). But the chapter reflects, I think, a more general intellectual debt. I never left a supervision without a list of books that I could not wait to get my hands on. She encouraged me to think about the words people use as well as the complex relations they get up to. She never reduced 'kinship' to models of sexual reproduction, for which I thank her. Esther was my MPhil supervisor; Carrie Humphrey supervised my PhD. I have always counted myself extraordinarily fortunate to have had the opportunity to keep company with such formidable scholars, first as a student and subsequently as a colleague. That Marilyn Strathern then also came to Cambridge was one of the things that kept me here. What is reflected in this chapter, then, is an intellectual genealogy (and not a pedigree); it is a story of connection, travel, exploration and reconnection.

Introduction

A few years ago I watched a video documentary called *Paper Clips*, which explored a school project in Tennessee designed to increase students' comprehension of the enormity of the Holocaust by collecting 6 million paperclips.[1] Putting aside the passionate support of and the outraged opposition to this project for the moment, what struck me both in viewing the documentary and in reading about the complex reactions to the project – and what I want to explore here – was how active these paperclips seemed to be in their capacity to facilitate not only the memory of lost relations, but also the forging of new ones. I will explain what I mean later in the chapter. At about the same time, Kath Weston, then visiting William Wyse Professor at the Department of Social Anthropology at Cambridge, gave a series of thought-provoking public lectures that explored the concept of 'intimacy' – already the subject of wide-ranging discussion.[2] Two of Weston's lectures stood out with relation to the subject at hand. Her first, on 'lost intimacies', considers the vagaries of chip technologies that track information about the origins of fragmented and commodified substances such as beef or pork. She questions what we actually know through the production of intimate facts generated by the deployment of such technologies. Her second, on the 'unwanted intimacies' that came to mark many Japanese lives after the Fukushima Daiichi nuclear plant meltdown, makes an incontrovertible case for understanding intimacy as an analytic that reaches far beyond notions of intimacies established through sexuality and/or desire. At virtually the same time, Linda Layne – also a visiting scholar at the Centre for Family Research in Cambridge that year – gave a seminar on 'ghostly sperm', which developed her understanding of the persistence of kinned feeling and the notion of the 'uncanny'.[3] Here again was an account in which 'the intimate' seemed to be manifested in fragments of knowledge made visible through a series of materializing strategies. Although I had vowed that with my contribution to McKinnon and Cannell's volume on kinship in the twenty-first century (Bodenhorn 2013), I had 'finished' with kinship as a subject of inquiry, I suddenly found myself thinking about connectivities in new ways. The present chapter is the result.

Our core question, then, is to ask how the categories of intimacy and kinship intersect, interact and illuminate. My weak argument is that the terms we use to denote our moral universe (wherever the boundaries to that universe may be held to lie) – kinship, belonging, relatedness, intimacy – are 'and' rather than 'either/or' terms. Although they often emerge from robust critiques of the usage of already-established terms, they expand our understanding rather than provide analogues to some basic category that anthropologists are continually trying to uncover. In addition, what this material offers us, I think, is an awareness of the ambiguous power of knowledge made visible in the process of relation making and breaking. As such, then, we are firmly in Esther Goody territory, where she has so fruitfully joined the examination of knowing and practice.

My stronger argument has to do with the ambiguous capacity of things/ persons continuously to create each other through processes of fragmentation and reassembly. The recognition that kinship is more process than anything else – and that the process involves breaking relations off and building them up again, is in itself not new;[4] Marilyn Strathern, amongst others, has for some time been showing us, with particular attention to the partibility of persons and the connectivity of things, how that is the case.[5] What is striking about the material at hand is the extent to which we are not talking about a thing/person boundary crossing, but rather of boundary 'ambiguating' (for it is not always clear what these things are thought to 'be'), Following on from that, we see how although these technologies of intimacy all produce knowledge of a personal nature, it is inevitably only partial, and furthermore, the connections between these forms of knowledge and the relations that come into being through their deployment are neither direct nor predictable. In *Still Life*, Moore (2013: 2) challenges her readers to engage with 'the dilemmas posed by trying to think about the connections between the people we are and wish to become ... not only to give form to the self but the world'. It seems to me that the material to come offers an important middle ground to this provocative challenge, for the processes we are examining are not, I suggest, about self-fashioning, but rela-tion-fashioning. Individual selves and collective worlds are part of the story, but they do not occupy centre stage.

A Few Words about Intimacy

A significant amount of work using 'intimacy'[6] as an analytic has been done in recent decades that recognizes the link between sexual intimacy and politics – not only at the level of 'the personal is the political' but also in terms of the conduct of state and the spread of empire.[7] The figure of Malintzin (la Malinche) invites us to expand this material a bit; traded by her natal family to a Mayan community, she was then presented to Cortés as a sign of goodwill. She became both his concubine (producing a son who, in popular accounts, could represent the emergent Mexican nation, carrying the lineages of old and new worlds) and a key political player in her capacity to act as translator in both Nahua and Mayan. Relations between Cortés and Malintzin were inti-mate enough that he took (for Spaniards) the virtually unheard of decision to assign her a prominent role in face-to-face interactions with Moctezuma; by the same token, the Nahua emperor took the equally unusual decision to accept her as an interlocutor. Sixteenth-century accounts unfailingly refer to her as 'Doña Maria', a term of honour and respect; it is only during the mod-ernizing project of nineteenth-century Mexico that she is assigned the role of a traitor for not having resisted Cortés's sexual advances to the death.[8] Here, I suggest that what this example illustrates is precisely *not* that the intimacy in question was sexual in nature, but that the nature of these relations allowed the dissolution of barriers that ordinarily would have prevented the sorts of communication that evidently took place. This is very clearly a politics of inti-macy, but one where desire is directed towards an imagined outcome, rather than focused on a present relationship. Indeed this resonates with the Latin roots of the word *intimus*, translated as 'innermost': what is ordinarily most deeply hidden is made evident through particular sorts of contact.[9] The exami-nation of conditions under which personal barriers may dissolve, allowing what is innermost to be brought to the surface – or indeed the reverse –

becomes the first element of my own exploration of what 'intimacy' may be held to be.

Anne Hyde's (2011) alternative account of the American West in the late eighteenth and early nineteenth centuries provides a different entryway into our understanding of the intimate as profoundly central to political and economic processes. Her account of the development of the fur trade, and the growth of cosmopolitan hubs such as St. Louis, places on centre stage the complex and intertwined bonds of kinship, marriage, adoption and extended family relations between Sioux, Osages and (largely) French actors.

> Imagine the fur trade as a set of wheels, connected by cogs, linking very separate parts of the trade. Spatially the most significant cogs were forts, but operationally the most crucial links in the system were families. We need to understand the global spread of the system, the intimate patterns of gift giving, choosing spouses, and building families, as well as the rhythms of daily work in these forts and the communities that surrounded them. Fort Vancouver served as a microcosm of the social, familial and economic systems that characterized the fur trade in the first half of the nineteenth century. ... [O]perating underneath all of these was a set of new cultural arrangements centered on relationships with native women. ... [W]e think of the fur trade as primarily male ... However, from the start, to get furs these men needed women – specifically native women – to process furs and feed themselves [as well as to establish political alliances]. (Hyde 2011: 91)

> [T]he big men in the trade, their employees, and the people dependent on the communities they created often married into Indian families who had essential local knowledge and trade networks. Anglo-American and British observers, travellers and merchants found these cultural choices shocking, and commented on the presence of people of mixed race at the highest levels of leadership at nearly every fort, demonstrating the ubiquity of this métis world. (ibid.: 97)[10]

The importance of this example, for me, is the compelling recognition of 'the intimate' as a multifaceted world of networks made possible by many sorts of acts. This, then, becomes the second element of my understanding: that to focus too narrowly on intimacy as a function of relations between a small number of individual actors unproductively reduces our field of vision.

In her extended essay, 'Toward a Theory of Intimacy', Liza Povinelli (2006) brings these elements together with a focus that contributes a further 'flavour' to my definitional scaffolding.[11] Moving across her personal experiences in the worlds of les–bi–gay sexual politics in middle-class United States and the racialized politics of aboriginal Australia, Povinelli explores both the analytical potential of and the limits to discourses of individual sovereignty and social constraint as they are applied to an understanding of intimate worlds. Rejecting a stance that suggests a determined relationship between these two, Povinelli offers an account of what she calls 'immanent dependencies' amongst indigenous and queer people (ibid.: 8) and, drawing on Freud (via Wilson), looks to ways 'in which ... soma and psyche are ... the literal material of each other, different from each other but mutually obliged rather than caused or affected,

vulnerable to rather than subject of' (ibid.: 9). This attention to mutual obligation that creates vulnerabilities rather than subjects is, for me, a most fruitful
idea. Obligation and vulnerabilities, as ideas, point us in the direction of continuous process. This position resonates strongly with Weston's starting point
in *Animate Planet* (2017) where she suggests that intimacy 'must be animated',
through environmental conditions or social relations. This, in turn, strikes a
chord with Layne's earlier (2012) work on grieving processes of parents who
have lost children at their earliest stages. Here Layne explores the ways in
which 'animation' is a process of rendering visible what is otherwise invisible,
of creating an uncanny presence out of absence. As we shall see, however, it is
important to recognize that while 'animation' is by definition processual, it is
not necessarily intentional; and that even when intention is an important
player, the consequences may be unexpected.[12]

Finally, by way of Kath Weston's same work, I bring in Geeta Patel's (2006)
notion of 'techno-intimacies' as a final aspect of what I call my quadrahedric
scaffolding. By this she refers to (and Weston elaborates on) the capacity of
twenty-first-century technologies to produce and track intimate information
with or without the knowledge or consent of the trackee, who may or may not
be human. Unknowing tracking has of course gone on since spying was
invented, but techno-intimacies bring this possibility into high relief.

In sum, then, for 'the intimate' I include the conditions that permit an inver-
sion of internalities/externalities; these require animation, which may in turn
create vulnerabilities; they may extend well beyond the world of dyadic relations, and as well may point to an agentive human/non-human universe. In
three of the four examples below, I am taking parenthood as the focus of my
inquiry into the fragmentary nature of intimacy; with my fourth, paperclips,
example however, I intentionally broaden the frame to bring connectivity into
a more inclusive view.

Intimate Conceptions: Is Seeing Believing?

At first glance, my initial example resembles the conventional notion of intimacy: those intimacies related to conception and parenting. But they are conventional with a twist. We begin with Aizley's (2003) riotous account of
conception and consumption brought together in the process of 'Buying Dad' –
an adventure in finding, purchasing and using the sperm of an unknown person
to create a child of 'one's own'.[13] The author visits a series of clinics that can offer
a choice of sperm. The choice is based on compilations of photographs and bio-
snippets: ears, noses, hair, education, and personal achievements. 'Dad' in this
case is never a whole person, but is present only in the fragmented form of
reproductive substance and virtual representations. Based on these intimate
bits of personal information – which of course carry little predictive weight
about the person who might emerge if the genetic substance of the person
imagined on the basis of these fragments was to be combined with that of the

hopeful parents – the clients carry the book to the check-out desk (so to speak) and ask for a job lot of page 375. As often as not, they are told that number has been sold out, but in a manner reminiscent of Next, they are informed that page 468 is really very popular as well. The point I want to make here is that this is precisely *not* about techno-intimacy. Assisted Reproductive Technologies (ARTs) in this case have made it possible to extract sperm and reinsert it, but the intimate information of who is 'in there', so to speak, remains hidden in these new techno-forms. In Aizley's account, the potential relation embodied in the purchased sperm is held in a canister until the conditions for implantation are met. The canister itself may become further personalised, installed in the sitting room, draped with a scarf and included in meals. Thus, by the time the longed-for baby is born and a new relation has come into being, information-made-visible has taken many forms – even though the 'reassembly' has ultimately taken place in the entirely conventional way of combining male and female reproductive substances. It is commonplace to assert that making-visible is part of knowledge-fixing – the underpinnings of the Enlightenment project, positivism and its subsequent critiques. But in this case the actors understand that the visible intimate fragments they have access to cannot really predict the whole outcome – that the most intimate of genetic information may produce unexpected results, and that a life course is relational. Seeing, in this case, is not really believing but is, rather, I suggest, an instance of 'it's all we have to go on'.[14]

But that is not the end of the story, as Layne discusses in her exploration of 'ghostly fathers' and the uncanny (2012a/b). Once a third party is no longer necessary for conception, they may become 'a problem'. In Aizley's (2003) account, the physical representations of the sperm donor return to intrude, uncannily, on the couple's sense of themselves as the parents. Aizley's partner from the beginning had not wanted to see pictures of any fragmented bits, saying she wished to be able to imagine her partner as the other parent. Aizley herself comes to wish she had never seen any physical representations at all, because they remained to (re)animate a relation that the couple did not want to be reminded of.[15]

At the risk of restating the obvious, this is not about natural desire, but 'natural' desire – illustrating once again Strathern's observation that new forms of technology do not necessarily produce new forms of kinship.[16] This might seem counterintuitive in the present case – we are talking about same sex parents after all. But we are looking at the norm of two parents, linked to 'their' children through something called 'biology'. Iñupiaq adoption practices, for instance, can mirror gestational surrogacy almost exactly. One woman carries a child who, by an explicit agreement, is destined for another family as soon as s/he is born. There the resemblance ends, however. Relations between birth and adoptive parents are strengthened through the process as a rule; and it is generally left up to the child to decide the degree to which connections to both families are maintained.[17] 'Ilyagiit' – or relatives (in a two-way relationship, living) – translates literally as 'additions';[18] adoption whether decided before or after birth, is one way of generating such an addition. It implies neither subtraction nor substitution of those in recognized parental roles. What sorts of fragments of intimacy are thought to count, what they are held to mean, and whether or not they entail anything at all is a matter of cultural understanding.

The Intimacy of Vulnerabilities

Just as Layne examines parental uneasiness caused by ghostly fathers, Weston (2017) also examines what she calls 'unwanted intimacies', in this case, those emerging as a result of a nuclear plant meltdown in Japan. Parents, who cannot move to a place they know is reliably 'safe', also cannot know with certainty what sorts of toxic presences may be penetrating their children's bodies – intimacy without intention. In this case, on the one hand, Weston is talking about a sort of intimacy visited on children by virtue of an externality becoming innermost, rather than the reverse; and on the other, she is addressing the particular sorts of intimacies called forth in a parental relation. With this I would like to bring Weston and Povinelli together – thinking about what it might mean in this instance to 'animate' (Weston's term) vulnerability (Povinelli's concept). Although the vulnerabilities associated with personal intimacy are often linked to trust – leaving oneself open to another to hurt as well as to pleasure – this seems a different matter altogether. In this instance, I suggest, the intimacy is not that between child and radioactive invasion, but rather the vulnerability to anxiety that this invasive presence awakens in parents who feel at a loss to know how best to fulfil their parental obligation. It is a vulnerability to anxiety that is animated by non-human substances, and intensified by an already existing relationality. What this material further points towards, I suggest, is a recognition that, despite an ideology that defines intimacy as getting to the 'real', interior (imagined) whole of a person, what we see once again is its fragmentary nature.

Mourning, Materialities, Memory

In many ways, my final example is the exact opposite of the uncanny, constantly reinserting its unwanted presence that characterizes Aizley's and Weston's accounts and is instead the search for relations that might have been – or indeed, might be. Layne (2012a) talks about this in terms of 'angel babies' (infants who died at or before birth) who are not only commemorated, but in some ways are created through multiple materialities that allow the parents to keep them present in a non-trivial way. Clothing, photos, tattoos, cards commemorating life signposts that would have been, and balloons set free carrying messages for the lost child are all part of parental strategies for keeping the relationship vital.[19] I want to think about this with relation to David Magilow's

(2007) discussion of acts of memorialization, specifically the paperclips project of Whitwell, Tennessee, which I mentioned in my introduction.

The Project

In 1998, teachers at the Whitwell Tennessee Middle School (at the behest of some parents) began to explore ways in which their students, who were quite homogenous, might better comprehend their position in a world filled with diversity and political strife. The school began a voluntary after-school class about intolerance and its roots, focusing on the Holocaust as an exemplar of political violence that may be encountered in many forms and in many contexts. Students undertook to collect 6 million paper clips, choosing the symbol (as they understood it) of Norwegian resistance during the Second World War.[20] They set up a website, wrote to political figures and media celebrities asking for contributions of paperclips, were publicized by journalists Peter and Dagmar Schroeder – who facilitated the procurement and transportation of one of the few extant Nazi boxcars to Whitwell – and, on 9 November 2001, they opened the Children's Holocaust Memorial. Ultimately the children received more than thirty thousand letters and collected more than 25 million paperclips, 11 million of which were included in the final memorial exhibit. With this example, then, we move from the moral universe of 'parents' to a more Maussian vision of what he imagined as late modern human connectability (1985).[21]

The Reaction and Subsequent Analyses

This and similar projects have come in for considerable criticism. People are not paperclips, buttons, pennies, or grains of sand, the sceptics protest; we run the danger of thingifying people – people who were already treated as less than human, and we do so by giving into the childish pleasures in collecting.[22] But Magilow (2007) invites less dismissive consideration. In 'Counting to Six Million', he glosses Russell Belk (1995 [2013]: 67) to suggest that 'collecting ... is a process of actively, selectively and passionately acquiring and possessing things removed from ordinary use ..., [which] concurrently gain exchange value as symbols. ... [it involves] the collector's intense affective investment in them'. Belk links this explicitly with commodity fetishism. 'We must remember', Magilow exhorts us, 'that any relationship exists not between the coins, buttons, or paperclips themselves but in the minds of collectors'. Here I think we should be more Strathernian – this is about the generation and extension of relations, not between students and the things they are so assiduously collecting, but in the connection between the students and the people who are sending them paperclips for whatever reason. These objects are, in Weston's terms, animating. To explore this, I want to turn to some of the letters Magilow includes in his analysis – letters, mostly from Germany, that are filled with connective, vibrant tissue. The writers (who of course, by responding, have already entered into reciprocal relations with the students) have taken the time to be thoughtful in a way that will bring the students in: they recount their own histories, explain the reasoning behind the particular paperclips that have been sent, connect the events of the Holocaust to the present. They are personal; intimate. One writer explained that he was sending paperclips he had found on official files in an abandoned Nazi building: 'They simply did their duty. They held together pieces of writing that were stamped with swastikas...' Another explained she was sending a box of paperclips for each family member she had lost during the Nazi era; still another made connections between the role of paperclips not only in Nazi administrative procedures but in Germany's present political asylum process. Another explained that he could not send all of the paperclips he would like and so was sending only two: 'Both of the enclosed clips should symbolize the thousands of paperclips that I would have liked to have sent'. In his analysis, Magilow draws on Fritsche (2005) who speaks of 'the archive' as fragments of information, carefully selected, set apart, and then deployed to imagine a whole. Again, I think we can recognize the force of this, but with a caveat. They are indeed selected and contextualized but, I would suggest, they are not metanymic. No whole is being posited, represented or imagined.

Each of these paperclips embodies a relationship with the writers' pasts, but just as importantly acts as a medium through which new relations are not just imagined, but brought into possibility. To deploy a Strathernian term once again (although not, I suspect, in the way her Papua New Guinea interlocutors would), we can think of these paperclips as transplants – moving to new territory, enacting a moral relationship that simultaneously enables a continuity and fosters new growth. In both Layne's material, and that from Whitwell, we see the power of inanimate objects to move beyond the realm of the signifier – to be as well as to represent – and to act as animators themselves.

Discussion and Conclusion

I suddenly had the thought, as I was preparing to give a version of this chapter at University College London, that I was really reading these examples through my own understanding of Iñupiaq understandings of the power of names and naming (Bodenhorn 2006). As I have argued elsewhere, Iñupiat persons are simultaneously partible, multiple, and singular. Names carry with them essences of personhood which must be recognized in order for the names to be connected up to a new proper person. You ask *who* is your name (kiña atiñ), not what is it – and it is the 'who' of the name that must fit. Just as kinship is framed through the logic of additions, so names too may accumulate during a person's life. Each name has the capacity to create an Atiq/namesake relationship – an identity that is nevertheless also a relation created through a third person, in a manner Strathern has recently been discussing.[23] So each name 'sticks' you to others and is called forth through speech, but the sum total of your names forms a unique combination. Thus we have names as thing/intimate personal bits (because, to my knowledge, they are never held to be the totality of a person), which detach and stick, which must be animated through recognition and speech, and through these animating actions both reflect and constitute socialities. There are clear resonances between the fragmentary, animating capacity of Iñupiaq names with the material that I have been discussing, but not (in an Iñupiaq sense) an identity.

Iñupiaq names are held to *be* essential aspects of persons – personal essences that travel across time in a kind of reincarnation (so that people will say of a newborn, 'it is so nice to see so-and-so again') and that must be recognized by someone living so that the name in the person matches the name of the person. If you get it wrong, your child may get sick. What we have been discussing here, however, I shall call for the moment 'intimacy at a distance'. The intimate knowledge materialized on the pages of sperm donor descriptions does not determine the character of a child born with that donor's genetic substance; the photos, however, have the capacity to insert a ghostly father into the imaginations of the ART couple. They animate, not the child, but parental disquiet. In a similar way, Weston's material notes the capacity of inanimate radioactivity to penetrate a child's body – a most intimate act; its animating power, however, again lies in the realm of parental concern. The things that the grieving parents in Layne's account deploy to create a reality for their parent–child relationship are not, for the most part, things their infant had during its brief life – things that became meaningful through that brief lived life as lived, but are, rather, things put in place after the child's death: clothing made after the fact; photos in which the body is put in 'natural' poses; photos that image what a child might have looked like at five years of age. But they too, in a non-trivial way, are felt to have the power to animate a living relationship. Finally, pace the critics, no one in the Whitwell project thought that paperclips could be the people killed in the Holocaust. But to trivialize the intensity of reactions of the letter writers' engagement with this project – animated by those very paperclips – is to misread profoundly what was going on.

So what are we left with? Neither the notion of partible persons, nor the realization that persons/things can be extensions of each other is new. In some ways the philosophers of modern capitalism got it right: global techno-worlds have the capacity to fragment and unify in ways that cannot be divorced from political economy. We have been considering briefly ways in which recent anthropology offers tools for thinking about these processes in two regions dominated by logics of late modern capitalism, Japan and the United States – intimacies that produce assemblages; eclipsing as they reveal, requiring attention to an agentive person/thing universe. Two points emerge from this that bear a final mention: it is precisely the fragmentary nature of intimate knowledge that allows for recombinant socialities to emerge. And the extent to which the animating capacities of the things we have been examining are at the core of such socialities suggests that what we are looking at is the very opposite of commodity fetishism. The things may be infused with magical animating power, but at stake are the social relations made possible (or put under threat), not the value of the things themselves. It is the very sociality of those relations that are rendered visible – at a distance – rather than being eclipsed.

Barbara Bodenhorn is an Emeritus Fellow of Pembroke College, Cambridge. She has worked in Arctic Alaska since 1980 and in the Sierra Norte of Oaxaca since 2004, with a current focus on young people's environmental knowledge. Recent books include *Risky Futures*, edited with Olga Ulturgasheva (Berghahn Books 2022).

Notes

1. The documentary was shown on HBO in 2005.
2. The published version of these lectures can be found in Weston 2017. The assumed connections between intimacy, kinship and gender within anthropology has been explicit, at least since the 1990s. See, e.g., Leonard 1992.
3. This has since been published (Layne 2012b).
4. I am thinking of marriages, divorces, funerals, initiations – staples of anthropological analysis that rest on the recognition that rupture is as important as alliance in contributing to the resilience of social relations.
5. Starting with her work on Papua New Guinea, continuing with her attention to New Reproductive Technologies (Strathern 1988, 1996, 2004, 2005) as well as on 'the relation' more generally (2014). She is not alone in this, but she was most definitely a pioneer, and continues to push the boundaries of our understanding.
6. Although I am drawing on a number of concepts that inform recent theoretical argument – assemblages, partible persons, the agentive capacities of things as well as of persons – the ambiguous ways that 'intimacy' takes part in these discussions has made me feel I need to spend extra time thinking about the idea itself. My analysis draws on a large comparative base; the material itself, however, is almost entirely taken from colleagues who are working in the United States.
7. Fenella Cannell (1999) on the Philippines, Ann Stoler (e.g. 2002, 2006) on the spread of empire more generally, Veena Das (1995, 2007) on the sexual politics of Partition, and Perveez Mody (2008) on love marriages and the state in India, all explore ways in which sexual relations may be sought, coerced, created and eluded at the individual level while at the same time generating complex forms of attention from those wielding formal political power. Much, although not all, of this work draws on Foucaultian notions of power as existing at what he calls the 'capillary' level, with the body as its particular site (1973). No surprise, then, that feminist and queer theorists have been at the forefront of this thinking (for overviews, see, e.g., Povinelli 2006; Pratt and Rosner 2012). Giddens seems to provide a counter narrative in his 2013 exploration of intimacy and the sexual egalitarianism that he considers to be characteristic of late modern society.
8. See Townsend 2006 for a recent consideration of Malintzin's life; Bernal Diaz's (1963) memoires provide a respectful portrait of her; Paz (1961 [2005]) provides a side-splitting account of the nineteenth-century demonizing view. The irony of this is worth a separate paper.

9. See Pratt and Rosner 2012: 4. Also cited in Layne 2014. Thus the relationship between torturer and torturee may be as intimate as that between mother and newborn.
10. I provide this extended quote because it is so clear. For readers interested in the centrality of such relations for early US history, I refer them to James Axtell 1985 and James Brooks 2002. For colonial Spain, see, for instance, Lockhart 1994, Restall 2003, and Townsend, already mentioned.
11. I am echoing Julie Cruikshank's (1998) use of 'scaffolding' as a kind of skeletal structure, which, once erected, may hold the understanding of a story together, but may never be alluded to in its entirety again.
12. When I gave this paper at University College London, Jerome Lewis noted that we must recognize that the participants in such moments can by no means be assumed to be acting with the same sort, or degree, of intentionality. It is an important point.
13. For a wider engagement with the literature exploring this see, Layne 2012 a/b.
14. Paraphrased from Aizley 2003: 20–35. In 'How's the Baby Doing?', Layne (1999) provides a compelling example of this through her analysis of her own infant son's stay in a neonatal intensive care unit. Numbers were constantly produced as a result of many kinds of bodily monitorings. Neither hospital staff nor anxious parents knew what those numbers might mean in terms of the child's chances of survival.
15. Surrogate mothers often experience this kind of postpartum erasure as well (see Bonaccorso 2009), often made all the more painful because of the intimacy of the relationship between commissioning parents and surrogate during the pregnancy itself. In a different way, Layne has found that single mothers by choice often feel the need to build a positive father picture for their children.
16. This is an observation she has made in several contexts (e.g. Strathern 1996, 2005).
17. 'I like it myself', said my adoptive Iñupiaq grandmother, Mattie Bodfish, who was herself adopted. She was talking about the frequency with which she had to decide whether to go out camping with one family or the other (see, e.g., Bodenhorn 2000, 2006). Esther Goody (1982) was one of the first to note that 'parenting' as a cluster of responsibilities could be aggregated or separated as a matter of cultural convention.
18. Ernest S. Burch discusses Inupiaq kinship in historical perspective in many publications, but see in particular Burch 1975 for careful linguistic attention to kinship terms.
19. That these relations are shot through with the sorts of anxious vulnerabilities present in Weston's account I can only surmise. Layne does not talk about this; any conversation I have had with friends who have lost children has been dominated by such concerns.
20. See, e.g., Magilow 2007, Schroeder and Schroder-Hildebrand 2004, or the video documentary *Paper Clips* shown on HBO in 2005 for a fuller account of the project itself.
21. In his essay on 'the category of the person', Mauss argues that as 'persons' become more individuated, they simultaneously expand their awareness of themselves as part of a moral universe.
22. I am glossing Marc Gellman (2005), A.O. Scott (2004) and others as reported in Magilow 2007: 26ff.
23. Cambridge Friday seminar, October 2014.

References

Aizley, Harlyn. 2003. *Buying Dad: One Woman's Search for the Perfect Sperm Donor*. Alyson Publishing.

Axtell, James. 1985. *The Invasion Within: The Contest of Cultures in Colonial North America*. Oxford University Press.

Belk, Russell W. (1995) 2013. *Collecting in a Consumer Society*. London: Routledge.

Bodenhorn, Barbara. 2000. '"He Used to be My Relative": Exploring the Bases of Relatedness among Inupiat of Northern Alaska', in Janet Carsten (ed.), *Cultures of Relatedness: New Approaches to the Study of Kinship*. Cambridge University Press, pp. 128–48.

——. 2006. 'Calling into Being: Names and Speaking Names on Alaska's North Slope', in Gaby Vom Bruck and Barbara Bodenhorn (eds), *The Anthropology of Names and Naming*. Cambridge: Cambridge University Press, pp. 140–56.

——. 2013. 'On the Road Again: Movement, Marriage, Mestizaje and the Race of Kinship', in Susan McKinnon and Fenella Cannell (eds), *Vital Relations: Modernity and the Persistent Life of Kinship*. Santa Fe, NM: SAR Press, pp. 131–54.

Bonacnocorso, Monica. 2008. *Conceiving Kinship*. Oxford: Berghahn Books.

Burch, Ernest S., Jr. 1975. *Eskimo Kinsmen: Changing Family Relationships in Northwest Alaska*. St. Paul, MN: West Publishing Company.

Cannell, Fenella. 1999. *Power and Intimacy in the Christian Philippines*. Cambridge: Cambridge University Press.

Cruikshank, Julie. 1998. *The Social Life of Stories: Narratives and Knowledge in the Yukon Territory*. Lincoln: University of Nebraska Press.

Das, Veena. 1995. *Critical Events: An Anthropological Perspective on Contemporary India*. Delhi: Oxford University Press.

——. 2007. *Life and Words: Violence and the Descent into the Ordinary*. Berkeley: University of California Press.

Diaz, Bernal. (1632) 1963. *The True History of the Conquest of New Spain*. London: Penguin.

Foucault, Michel. 1973. 'Governmentality', in Graham Burchell, Colin Gordon and Peter Miller (eds), *The Foucault Effect: Essays in Governmentality*. Chicago: Chicago University Press.

Fritzsche, Peter. 2005. 'The Archive', *History & Memory* 17(1) (Spring/ Summer): 16.

Gellman, Marc. 2005. 'Paper Boats', *Newsweek* (online edition), 10 August 2005. Retrieved 30 October 2014 from http://www.msnbc.msn.com/id/8900133/site/newsweek.

Giddens, Anthony. 2013. *The Transformation of Intimacy, Sexuality, Love and Eroticism in Modern Society*. Cambridge: Polity Press.

Goody, Esther N. 1978. 'Towards a Theory of Questions', in Esther N. Goody (ed.), *Questions and Politeness: Strategies in Social Interaction*.

——. 1971. 'Forms of Pro-parenthood: The Sharing and Substitution of Parental Roles', in Jack Goody (ed.), *Kinship: Selected Readings*. Harmondsworth: Penguin Readings in Sociology, pp. 331–45. Cambridge: Cambridge University Press, pp. 17–43.

——. 1982. *Parenthood and Social Reproduction: Fostering and Occupational Roles in West Africa*. Cambridge: Cambridge University Press.

Hyde, Anne F. 2011. *Empires, Nations, and Families: A New History of the North American West: 1800–1860*. Lincoln: University of Nebraska Press.

Layne, Linda. 1999. 'How's the Baby Doing?', *Journal of Medical Anthropology* 10(4): 624–56.

——. 2012a. 'Troubling the Normal: Angel and the Canny/Uncanny Nexus', in Sarah Earle, Carol Komoromy and Linda Layne (eds), *Understanding Reproductive Loss: Perspextives on Life, Death and Fertility*. London: Ashgate, pp. 129–42.

——. 2012b. 'Creepy, Freaky and Strange: How the Uncanny Can Illuminate the Experience of Single Mothers by Choice and Lesbian Couples Who Buy "Dad"'. CUSAS seminar paper, Cambridge University, March 2013.

——. 2014. 'A Changing Landscape of Intimacy: The Case of Single Mothers by Choice'. Presentation at the 'Gender, Equality and Intimacy: (Un)comfortable Bedfellows?' workshop held at the Institute of Education, London, on 7 April 2014.

Leonard, Karen. 1992. 'Love, Intimacy and Passion: Shapers of Family and Kinship', *Reviews in Anthropology* 21(2): 85–93.

Lockhart, James. 1994. 'Sightings: Initial Nahua Reactions to Spanish Culture', in Stuart B. Schwartz (ed.), *Implicit Understandings: Observing, Reporting, and Reflecting on the Encounters between Europeans and Other Peoples in the Early Modern Era*. Cambridge: Cambridge University Press, pp. 218–48.

Magilow, Daniel. 2007. 'Counting to Six Million: Collecting Projects and Holocaust Memorialization', *Jewish Social Studies* 14(1): 23–39.

Mauss, Marcell. 1985. 'The Category of the Person', in Michael Carrithers, Steven Collins and Steven Lukes (eds), *The Category of the Person: Anthropology, Philosophy, and History*. Cambridge: Cambridge University Press, pp. 26–45.

Mody, Perveeze. 2008. *The Intimate State: Love-Marriage and the Law in Delhi*. London: Routledge.

Moore, Henrietta L. 2013. *Still Life: Hopes, Desires and Satisfactions*. Cambridge: Polity.

Patel, Geeta. 2006. *Risky Subjects: Insurance, Sexuality and Capital*. Duke University Press.

Paz, Octavio. (1961) 2005. 'Hijos de la chingada', in *The Labyrinth of Solitude*. London: Penguin Classics.

Povinelli, Elizabeth. 2006. *The Empire of Love: Toward a Theory of Intimacy*. Duke University Press.

Pratt, Geraldine, and Victoria Rosner. 2012. *The Global and the Intimate: Feminism in our Time*. New York: Columbia University Press.

Restall, Matthew. 2003. *Seven Myths of the Spanish Conquest*. Oxford: University Press.

Schroeder, Peter W., and Dagmar Schroder-Hildebrand. 2004. *Six Million Paper Clips: The Making of a Children's Holocaust Memorial*. Minneapolis, MN: Kar-Ben Publishing.

Scott, A.O. 2004. 'Grasping Extraordinary Evil Through the Very Ordinary', *New York Times*, 24 November 2004.

Stoler, Ann. 2002. *Carnal Knowledge and Imperial Power: Race and the Intimate in Colonial Rule*. London: University of California Press.

———. 2006. *Haunted by Empire: Geographies of Intimacy*. Durham, NC: Duke University Press.

Strathern, Marilyn. 1988. *The Gender of the Gift: Problems with Women and Problems with Society in Melanesia*. Berkeley: University of California Press.

———. 1996. 'Cutting the Network', in Henrietta Moore and Todd Sanders (eds), *Anthropology in Theory: Issues in Epistemology*. Wiley & Sons, pp. 400–410.

———. 2004. 'Losing (out on) Intellectual Resources', in Alain Pottage and Martha Mundy (eds), *Law, Anthropology, and the Constitution of the Social*. Cambridge: Cambridge University Press, pp. 204–9.

———. 2005. *Kinship, Law and the Unexpected: Relatives Are Always a Surprise*. Cambridge: Cambridge University Press.

———. 2014. 'The Relation'. Department of Social Anthropology Friday Seminar, Cambridge University, 17 October 2014.

Townsend, Camilla. 2006. *Malintzin's Choices: An Indian Woman in the Conquest of Mexico*. Albuquerque: University of New Mexico Press.

Weston, Kath. 2017. *Animate Planet: Making Visceral Sense of Living in a High-tech Ecologically Damaged World*. Durham, NC: Duke University Press.

3

The Visible Invisibilities of the Circulation of Women in the Ottoman Mediterranean and Their Implications

Paul Sant Cassia

Introduction

Two of Esther Goody's early interests, like many of her generation in Cambridge, were kinship and marriage. In two papers ('Forms of Pro-Parenthood', 1971, here called FPP), and another with Jack Goody ('The Circulation of Women and Children in Northern Ghana', 1967, here called CWCNG), she posed two questions. First, what are the *sociopolitical* reasons and consequences of fosterage as a particular elaboration of filiation? Second, what are the *identity-shaping* consequences of different matrimonial transfers in reproductive rights, and hence on filiation? Who do 'offspring' refer to in different types of unions? Substituting the above terms by others (e.g. 'surrogacy' for 'fosterage', 'biological contributions' for 'matrimonial transfers' or 'unions') renders Esther's concerns presciently contemporary.

In the West African societies examined by Esther and Jack Goody, descent and matrimonial transfers determine filiation. Additionally, various pro-parenthood arrangements circulate children between different domestic groups. This contribution approaches Esther Goody's interests by reference to the circulation in the eastern Mediterranean of preadolescent males through the Ottoman 'child-levy', and of women between religious groups through intermarriage and religious conversion that determined religious filiation. In Ottoman countries, Muslim men could take Christian wives, but the opposite was not permitted. Children born to a Muslim male and Christian woman had to be brought up as Muslims, and a Christian widow of a Muslim man would lose custody of her children to her Muslim affines unless she converted. This contribution explores the causes, dynamics and implications of (admittedly rare) cases of 'mixed marriages' between Muslim men and Christian women in the eastern Mediterranean, and the filiation of their offspring. Both intermarriage and religious conversion have often been treated inter alia as individual strategies of social mobility and unidirectional, converging on a single common result: the incorporation of (Christian) women and their offspring in the politically dominant religion (Islam). The overall societal structure and its constituent cultures are presumed to remain intact, albeit with group 'losses' and 'gains'. But in concentrating on the results, we risk missing the varied reasons and contexts for conversion and/or interfaith marriages, and the ways men and women adjusted to their novel situations. These adjustments, including mixed religious practices, are either disregarded as 'exceptional' or singled out as 'intentional' evidence of 'crypto religion'. But the 'exceptional' nevertheless has social effects that are not necessarily the latter, whilst the latter confuses the imputed results with intentionality.[1] We need to examine why men and women converted, who they married and why, and what were the consequences on filiation, both jural and religious. In the Ottoman Balkans, Crete and Cyprus (Jennings 1993b) (and earlier in late Muslim Iberia) not insignificant numbers of male first-generation Christian converts to Islam either remained in their (subsequently post-conversion) 'mixed marriages' or, if unmarried, drew spouses from their original community, sometimes followed by their male offspring. Women also converted as divorce strategies, and sometimes married other converts. Our classic picture of fixed distinct religiously endogamous groups in the Mediterranean traversed solely by the unidirectional integrationist converging pathways of conversion and intermarriage needs modification. Group boundaries were fuzzy, mediated by interfaith marriages, concubinage, and other conjugal arrangements, resulting in a social phenomenon that operated between the visible and the invisible. The circulation of women across formal religious boundaries through divorce, remarriage, and conversion at widowhood as a child retention strategy raised considerable difficulties in subsequent ethnic-religious classification. I begin by examining the circulation of children, and then explore the dynamics of the 'circulation' of women from Christian groups to Muslim ones.

Mediterranean Patterns in the Circulation of Children

In FPP, Goody identified four forms of parental role devolution: fosterage, ritual sponsorship, adoption, and (Roman) adrogation. Relationships between parents and children entail two types of reciprocities: *status reciprocity* and *reciprocities of rearing*. Status reciprocity 'carries with it rights and obligations: a share in, or management of property, worship of shrines, often burial of the status holder' (Goody 1971: 332), as distinct from reciprocities of rearing, which continue into old age with the change in direction from the younger to the older. These latter are moral in nature in contrast to the more jural status reciprocities, although many social systems (including in the West) imposed legal obligations on heirs for the care of the elderly.

Apart from 'crises fosterage' (Goody 1970), children circulate as infants through wet nursing (nurturant fostering) (Goody 1971: 336) as orphans through adoption, as apprentices through fosterage, and as young adults in domestic service. Wet nursing can have political functions. Parkes (2003) draws a parallel between the political links forged through milk-kinship or lactation pacts in Muslim North Africa and the Middle East, with Christian spiritual kinship (*compadrazgo*), that is, ritual sponsorship. Both establish alliances between the pro-parent/parent, and matrimonial prohibitions between their offspring.

Goody's attention to domestic horizontal arrangements by the unstratified Gonja led her to argue that 'co-parenthood seems designed for working in the gaps between the formal elements of the system' (1971: 339). In complex agro-literate polities, the disposition of children and women can become subject to much larger social forces, such as religious group membership. In the early modern Mediterranean, the Ottomans faced three political, military and repro-ductive dilemmas: how to administer contiguous ethnically and religiously diverse social groups without dependence on one group; how to ensure a pro-fessional military force loyal to the sultan; and how to ensure dynastic repro-ductive self-sufficiency escaping European-type dynastic marriage alliance compromises. A partial solution was the expansion of the sultan's household through the revolving incorporation of outsiders: ex-Christian youths and con-cubines, 'the only Muslim dynasty to confine reproduction to concubine con-sorts rather than legal wives' (Peirce 2007: 43).

The Ottoman system of *xeno*-fosterage apprenticeship, known as the *devs-hirme* or child-levy, operated between the late fourteenth century (1383–87) and the 1630s, and drew its administrative elite and military muscle from a selection of Christian preadolescent youths. Some one to three thousand youths were drafted annually. Single sons and sons of widows (Ménage 1966: 78), and native-born Muslim children and Turks, were initially excluded. The *piasmon paidion*, as it was called in Greek, was imposed on cities that had resisted Ottoman subjugation (Vryonis 1956: 443), excepting the Muslim Bosnians who voluntarily provided recruits (Imber 2002: 137). In contrast to its contemporary, Habsburg Spain, the Ottoman regime administered and repro-duced itself through naturalized uprooted outsiders, youths and concubines, prompting the Venetian patrician Morosini to characterize it as 'a republic governed by slaves'.

Fosterage, what Signe Howell (2006) called 'kinning', has been viewed as contrary to the 'natural' bonds of affection stemming from biological kinship (Bowie 2004). Goody's comparison between fostered and parentally raised children (1971, 1982) suggested that the former were not disadvantaged, and were sometimes benefited in their political careers. But the Gonja fostered children of kin (daughters to fathers' sisters, sons to mothers' brothers) in order to reinforce links between them. The *devshirme*, by contrast, was not voluntary and nor did it reinforce kin ties, but emphasized rupture, erasure, and displacement by a distant 'pro-parent'. Balkan historiography and folklore identified the levy as a hallmark of 'Ottoman oppression' or a 'blood levy' (Vryonis 1956: 443).[2] It provided the empire with Simmel's 'professional strangers': reliable scribes and warriors with no residual loyalties to community, religion or kin. The *devshirme* was accompanied by conversion, hence ritual sponsorship.[3] It possessed an element of fosterage in that youths were raised by selected Muslim foster families until reaching military training age. They then joined the elite salaried corps of Janissaries initially based in Istanbul, the big towns, or the sultan's household, the empire's nerve centre, becoming members of the *askeri* (military) class. Among Janissaries, horizontal solidarity was sustained through barrack residence, property reinherited within the group, and agamy. The most promising youths were trained as *icoglans* (pages) for the sultan's household, their symbolic pro-parent, as his '*kül/küller*' (pl.) ('slaves' or personal subject) (Ménage 1966: 66), and could rise to important positions of power and influence.

The child-levy substituted traditional temporary foster-child sponsorship by permanent dependency on the pro-parent. Sponsorship, Goody tells us, 'consists in the provision of a youth with the position and resources necessary for assumption of adult status ... (and) just what is required varies widely from society to society' (1971: 333). Ironically, the *devshirme* initially denied adult status to recruits by their exclusion from marriage, and sponsorship was determined not by their natal family needs but by the receiving one (the sultan's). If fosterage extends the 'filial relationship into the adult world, into the external system' (ibid.), here this relationship was subrogated by submission to a prodigious image: that of the sultan as symbolically 'castrating' 'father-master'. Recruits were forbidden to grow beards (symbols of manhood and Muslim identity)[4] and were de-vocalized – obliged to use a special sign language in his presence (Peirce 2007: 45). Their imposed situation, as well as what Peirce calls the Ottoman 'parthogenetic form of royal authority' (ibid.) due to dynastic reproductive reliance on concubines, could merit further psychoanalytic exploration.

Following Janissary discontentment, under Sultan Selim II (1566–74) recruits were allowed to marry prior to retirement, leading to further concessions in 1579 when they were permitted to enlist their sons in the corps (Radushev 2008: 458). By 1648, the child-levy was abandoned (ibid.: 452), replaced by volunteers, many of whom were apostatized Christians eager for a secure career, including children of retired Janissaries (such as converted Bosnian Slavs).[5] Some historians link the emergence of small-scale 'peasant Janissaries' with a corresponding growth of voluntary conversion as a means of social mobility. According to Radushev, 'the material benefits and social privileges provided by Janissary service became the major motive for many Balkan Christians to adopt Islam' (ibid.: 461). In 1834, a visitor to Crete noted that the *Yerli Yeniçeris* 'consisted solely of Cretan Mohammedans', i.e. Cretan converts (Dedes 2011: 331). Thus re-embedded in kin and community, Janissaries infiltrated and diversified into economic activities in the countryside (trade, land ownership, and tax farming), and in the towns where they had equal muscle, both literal and economic (comestible importation, shop ownership, guild membership, and money lending) (Yilmaz Diko 2015). Military connections and threats of violence strengthened their economic leverage. From 'political eunuchs' (Coser 1972), the Janissaries had become an economically privileged and self-reproducing (often destabilizing) 'interest group', what Inalcik called a 'semi-autonomous traditional status group with consolidated privileges' (1992: 58). The 'stranger', or more precisely the 'othered' ex-Christian, settled down as the farmer next door. Conversely, the neighbouring farmer could become the 'Other' through conversion – a member of the *askeri* military class collecting the *cizye* (head tax) from his neighbours. The 'Profession-as-Stranger' (Coser 1965) had evolved into the 'Stranger-as-Profession'.

Goody's focus on pro-parenthood arrangements can thus be expanded to show that they can be harnessed for political functions.[6] Another Esther Goody publication that is inspirational for my purposes is the paper she wrote jointly with Jack Goody on 'The Circulation of Women and Children in Northern Ghana' (1967). Its main purpose was to show the link between the two and their embeddedness in several variables (marriage prestations, divorce, widow inheritance, kinship fostering, concepts of paternity, and kinds of kin groups) – in short, how filiation is created. In the eastern Mediterranean, women's marriages and hence the filiation of children was governed by religious denomination. But interfaith marriages and conversions, although unusual, did occur with implications for filiation, intergroup relations, and the transmission of religious practices. Conversion was a means of social mobility that in turn inter-articulated with the matrimonial 'circulation' of women, and hence affected group filiation.

The Political Economy of Religious Conversion

Islam, as Lucette Valensi (1997) reminds us, is the easiest world religion to enter. It merely requires the recounting of the witness.[7] In its ease of access lie two distinct consequences. First, it is probable that not all converts to Islam in the early modern Mediterranean fully knew what they were doing. Like North African captive apostates returning to Europe, eastern neo-Muslims could probably declare 'I believe in God and in Mahomet seated at his right hand' (Bennassar 1988: 1352) without entertaining cognitive dissonance. Second, apostasy back to one's original religion was a (rarely implemented) capital offence. Bulliet suggested that 'a convert first became a member of the Muslim community, and later discovered, or tried to discover, what it meant to be a Muslim' (Bulliet 1979: 131). In contrast to the Christian 'Pauline' epiphanic model, Islamic conversion was a 'narrative non-event' (Krstić 2009: 44). Although there were periods of mass conversions in the Balkans (Krstić 2009), conversion was generally an individual tactical choice through social networks and sponsorship (Krstić 2011).

Deringil notes that 'mass conversion of non-Muslims was never an official policy in the Ottoman Empire as it was in the Spanish and Russian empires' (Deringil 2000: 567), although he acknowledges the conversive effects of coercion (including the un-Islamic *devshirme*) or apprehension. In a mirror reflection of previous Venetian practice, the Ottomans strategically settled Muslim populations in frontier or depopulated zones (e.g. Bosnia and Cyprus). In addition, substantial parts of the Mediterranean between the fifteenth and seventeenth centuries were alternating borderlands, resulting in movements of individuals for trade and economic or social advancement ('renegades'). The seas and mountainous regions also conjured new categories and identities: slaves, captives, fugitives from blood feuds, rootless adventurers, and so on, resulting in complex flows of fluid subjectivities forced into, or in search of, new social identities.[8]

Male conversions to Islam occurred at the extremes of Christian society: at the bottom involving the vulnerable, especially in border areas, and at the top (equally vulnerable) echelons of conquered societies. In Crete, Bulgaria, mainland Greece and Cyprus, it was initially often the landed aristocracy who converted, eventually inserting themselves in the Ottoman ruling group (Imber 2002: 28). Conversion had the ineluctable traction of success, further encouraged by the inevitable Christian apprehension following Ottoman military defeats and/or during campaigns against Christian powers (Vryonis 1981: 299).[9] Insurrections and suppression were often followed by apostasy or conversion. In Cyprus (as later in Crete [Kolovos 2008]), following the island's violent capture from Venice in 1571, the major period of conversion to Islam was between 1580 and 1637 (Jennings 1993a: 164). Subsequently, religious conversion was individual, suggesting an accommodation between Orthodox Christians and in-coming Ottoman Muslims, often settled on appropriated Latin estates (Beckingham 1957: 172).

There were differences between town and country, the former being important Islamic centres in contrast to the countryside (Lopasic 1994: 170). If urbanization and Islamization went together, in the countryside there was a complex intermingling and camouflaging of faiths and practices, partly because of peripherality and demographic mix, partly because of less stringent clerical and political pressures on religious conformity, and partly because of the interarticulation of 'social conversion' (Bulliet 1979) and mixed marriages. Missionary Dervish Orders such as the Bektashis (closely associated with the Janissaries) and Sufi sects made inroads in the Balkan countryside through the integration of old Christian pilgrimage sites,[10] and were an important vector for religious absorption through 'gradual and peaceful intrusion' (Hasluck 1929: 59), attracting intermixed religious clienteles. Their flourishing was as much due to their local flexibility as to (an admittedly oscillating) Ottoman encouragement (Doja 2008), which turned them into an 'enormous sponge' integrating local variability into Islamic culture (Gradeva and Ivanova 2001: 328). Scholars have drawn attention to the important role of social networks in conversion (Krstić 2011; Preiser-Kapeller 2012).

Male and female conversions to Islam had different motivations and trajectories. The former had a strong pragmatic element. The latter were responsive to critical hiatuses in the developmental cycle: to escape from arranged marriages, as divorce strategies in unpromising marriages, or to retain custody over offspring as widows. Conversion was the 'nuclear option' for women: they broke the bonds of patriarchal domination in their own community to move to another, obtaining new legal rights that they may have lacked but losing other less calculable benefits (support of kin, community, etc.) (Baer 2004), unless they themselves married similarly converted men, which was not uncommon. Baer notes that when (Jewish) women converted 'Muslim men gained the most, new Muslim women gained less than Muslim men, and non-Muslim men were the biggest losers' (ibid.: 440) – unless the latter themselves converted, which they sometimes did. If female conversion necessarily resulted in religious endogamous incorporation, male conversion did not for they could draw spouses from their natal community.

Gender Differences in Conversions to Islam

Male conversions to Islam were consequences of, and adaptations to, two types of porous boundaries: shifting external politico-religious frontiers between power blocks, and more fixed internal legal-juridical ones between the different religious groups. For the former, male conversions were either consequences of historical contingency (warfare, piracy, etc.), or adaptations through voluntary migration from one politico-religious domain to another for trade or social advancement. The two could shade into each other, and historical contingency (e.g. piratical capture) could provide a vocabulary of justification for opportunism.[11] Pragmatic conversion was often a function of adventurist relocation across geo-politico-religious divides in both directions in search of military or commercial advancement. These 'trans-imperial subjects' (Rothman 2012) included returnees from Ottoman captivity and Jewish, Armenian and Greek commercial brokers. But there were also undoubtedly 'inter-imperial irregulars' (such as escaped slaves) who rarely appeared in records, nor wished to.

In Cyprus, most conversions were individual and voluntary, even if strategic, facilitated by the proximity of different religious groups because of Ottoman settlement, and these lasted well into the late eighteenth century. Economic conversion (to escape from paying the *kharaj*, or capitation/military exemption tax, or debt release) was likely to have been resorted to by the very poor, and by men.[12] Social mobility was also an important motivation. Women, not subject to the capitation tax, tended to convert either at marriage (rare) or to exit unhappy ones (more common).[13] This confirms that female conversion was not the culmination of a spiritual journey but a drastic response to a new or difficult personal situation through a change in juridical status (Krstić 2011).[14]

Because of the prohibition on *zimmi* (Christian or Jewish) men having Muslim wives, it follows that married *zimmi* women who converted, but whose husbands did not, could not remain in that marriage. In effect, free female *zimmi* conversions were a means to achieve divorce/annulment and remarriage. Enslaved *zimmi* women, by contrast, often converted as a step towards emancipation (Baer 2004). Most women's conversions were geographically circumscribed.[15] If Minkov's (2004) Balkan data for 1670–1730 are applicable elsewhere, where there were mixed communities (as in Cyprus) conversion preceded marriage: some 85 per cent of conversion petitions were made by single men and women,[16] suggesting individualized strategies, and posing the question 'whom did they marry?' Some male converts undoubtedly took (paleo) Muslim wives, others Christian if they wished to mitigate their apostasy by retaining links; the converted women, by contrast, were theoretically lost to their natal communities, unless they married similar ex-converts.

Christian or Jewish women in the Ottoman Mediterranean were more resistant to conversion than men, as this would result in their exclusion from kin and community.[17] In early modern Istanbul, Jewish men had to return their wives' dowries if the latter converted to Islam. Their humiliation was further compounded when they 'witnessed their former wives marrying Muslim men, who were sometimes converts' (Baer 2004: 440), an indication that conversions could be a means both to divorce within one's community and to remarriage within the same ethnic pool but outside its religious boundaries. In Cyprus, 'conversion of women to Islam might have been a means to escape from unhappy marriages – the converted women, whether previously married or not, easily found husbands' (Jennings 1993a: 140), a practice that alarmed the Orthodox Church.

Church discomfiture at conversions to resolve matrimonial difficulties was a function of the tension between its desire to promote 'Christian marriage' and grass-roots communities' diverse customary laws. The church subscribed to exogamy up to seven degrees of consanguinity, including spiritual kin, life-long sacramental monogamous marriage with rarely granted divorce or annulment, a lifetime three-marriages ceiling, condemnation of concubinage, and equal partible inheritance. As in Western Europe (J. Goody 1983), this brought it into conflict with individual strategies and highly variable community customs (*adet* [Tu.]; *topikoi nomoi, synitheies* [Gr.]) (Pantazopoulos 1967). Its legal sovereignty over Christians (disputed by historians) was further constrained by the institutional dominance of Islamic law and practice (Çiçek 1992), accessible to all Ottoman subjects, on which it differed fundamentally regarding marriage. The overlapping and nesting of three domains of regulation, conflict resolution and decision-making (community customs through local elders, church law, and Ottoman sharia) (Kermeli 2017), and consequent uncertain outcomes, thus provided ample opportunity for strategic manipulation, 'appeal-shopping', and what Baldwin called 'intimidation through documentation' (Baldwin 2012: 516). If circumstances dictated, Christians were prepared to appeal to Kadi courts (Joseph 2009: 346; Doxiadis 2011).[18] A

Christian woman's desire to divorce and remarry could be resolved through: (a) ecclesiastical courts (lengthy, costly, awkward due to fault-based criteria, and disinclined to property settlements); or (b) cheaper, routine divorce-issuing, and financial-provisioning Ottoman courts, but which penalized female divorce applications (*hul'*) in suspending their dower rights; or (c) through conversion, suggesting that the divorce-seeking woman had a 'clean break' and a specific new spouse in mind. Her subsequent 'Muslim marriage' provided her with an indirect dowry (*mahr*) from the groom in two tranches, at marriage and at widowhood or divorce, thus loosening dotal dependence on natal kin.

Sharia courts thus offered divorce and remarriage strategies for Christian and Jewish men, and particularly women, who could facilitate, or even seal, such marriage dissolutions through religious conversion, though not always. The majority of Nicosia kadi-presided *zimmi* divorce (*hul'*) cases between 1698 and 1726 were initiated by women (Çiçek 1992: 114). *Zimmi* men may have perceived Islam as domestically subversive for it gave their women unfamiliar, potentially unwelcome, rights to divorce, remarriage, and child custody not contemplated by their religious law and culture. Laiou (2007: 252) gives examples of Christian widows of Muslim men in Macedonia 'converting' to retain custody of underage daughters who would otherwise have been raised by the deceased's (Muslim) kin. This also applied to single-faith marriages. *Zimmi* women in unpromising single-faith marriages could pre-empt the transference of their children to their husbands' care in cases of anticipated separation or divorce through conversion (Baer 2004). Underage children would then be placed under a Muslim guardian (*vasil*), normally the mother. Such instrumental extrications may have contributed to male *zimmi* bitterness at Muslim facilitated 'depredation' of not merely their womenfolk but also their offspring. Christian widows of Muslim men also strategically converted to retain custody of underage children who would otherwise have had to be under the care of Muslim affines. Whether such children were raised as 'Muslim' or 'Christian' is debateable. As in contemporary times, inter-legal shopping to resolve unpleasant personal issues such as divorce, maintenance and child custody could result in drastic, culturally unanticipated resolutions by one party, and abiding resentments by the other (Doxiadis 2011). Child circulation was thus dialectically related to the circulation of women via divorce or conversion, not just between religious communities but between domestic groups.

The Inherent Ambiguities of Mixed Marriages

In contrast to the western Mediterranean, which became homogenously Christian from the *Reconquista* onwards, the Ottoman Empire remained multiethnic and multi-religious. As Valensi (1997, 1986) observed, proximity brought promiscuity – inevitably of the flesh, more subtly of the spirit. *Ceteris paribus*, in any population of two geographically intermingled or even contiguous faiths (Islam, Christianity),[19] and if there were no impediments to intermarriage, there are three possible matrimonial outcomes: solely Muslim, solely Christian/Jewish, and mixed faith marriages. In the Ottoman system, Muslim men could take Christian or Jewish wives, but the inverse was not possible, though there were exceptions. The movement therefore was of Christian or Jewish women marrying into the Muslim groups/families, but not vice versa.[20] Such marriages were of the following types:

(1) As the result of Muslim 'abductions' of Christian women,[21] or as first marriages for Christian women with paleo-Muslims, often due to historical contingency: in 1660s Crete, towards the end of the lengthy invasion campaign, 'some 27.56% of all recorded marriages were between paleo-Muslims and Christian brides' in Nova Candia (Kolovos 2008: 114).

(2) As 'reclassified' Christian marriages where the husband (but not the wife) converted to Islam during the marriage; the marriages therefore become 'mixed' between neo-Muslim men and their Christian wives.

(3) As *ab initio* marriages between paleo-Muslim grooms and neo-convert females or daughters of converts to Islam: some (37.8% of Muslim-born grooms in Nova Candia, Crete) 'married either converts to Islam or daughters of converts to Islam (6.8%)' (Kolovos 2008: 114). The latter were probably daughters of male neo-converts and Christian mothers.

(4) As second marriages for Christian or Jewish women with (neo- or paleo-)Muslim men, either as widows (excepting the Jewish levirate) or as a divorce tactic for apostatized Christian/Jewish women (and men) sometimes escaping from arranged childhood marriages.

(5) As (mono or polygynous) marriages or concubinage for Christian or Jewish captive slave women of *zimmi* masters (and *a fortiori* of Muslim masters) manumitted through conversion to Islam, as *zimmis* could not own Muslim slaves.[22] Conversion to Islam obliged the woman to marry a Muslim man, necessitating the substitution of a *zimmi* master with a Muslim one. Captive slavery introduced large numbers of Christian and Jewish women into Ottoman society. By converting to Islam, women could be ransomed by pious Muslims, some of whom were ex-Christians and potential spouses. If their masters recognized any subsequent offspring, mothers and children obtained manumission and inheritance rights to his estate (Baer 2004).

(6) As part of a general pattern whereby descendants of converts to Islam (neo-Muslims) practised a sort of group endogamy[23] and/or complemented this by also drawing wives from their Christian co-villagers across time. This may be an intentional or contingent effect of extraneous factors such as reluctance by the receiving group to intermarry with new converts – as occurred in newly captured Crete in the 1660s, and earlier in *Al Andalus* for Christian converts (Sant Cassia 2018), and post-*Reconquista* Iberia for some Jewish communities (cf. Nirenberg 2003).

In Cyprus, marriages of Muslim men and Greek Orthodox women were 'certainly not uncommon. That was the verdict of several Western visitors to Cyprus, and it is evident from the judicial records as well' (Jennings 1993a: 29).

In Crete, the Muslim population mainly consisted of local Christian converts, not incoming Turkish-speaking settlers as in Cyprus, and many Cretan Muslims remained Greek-speaking. More Christian men converted than women (Greene 2002), who did so to end a marriage (with a Christian) and enter a new one (often with an ex-co-religionist/neo-Muslim (Kermeli 2013)). For 1660s Crete, in Candia Nova or Inadiye, 52.56 per cent of male converts married a Christian bride, 34.62 per cent married female concerts to Islam, or daughters of converts (8.97 per cent) (Kolovos 2008: 114). These figures must be contextualized as this was an Ottoman new town. Nevertheless, by the second half of the seventeenth century, the intertwined practices of conversions, intermarriages, and Christian appeals to Cretan Islamic courts had become so common that Hanafi jurists produced *Fatva* 'Case Law Manuals' to guide deliberations (Kermeli 2013). Female conversions to Islam and consequent divorce and remarriages to Muslims (neo or paleo) would not necessarily result in an Islamic education for the progeny (particularly daughters) of the new union, especially if the mother's knowledge of Islam was limited. Similar leniency could be extended towards underage sons of Christian male converts to Islam in mixed marriages who theoretically had to adopt Islam on reaching the age of reason (Kermeli 2013). Although Islamic jurists were aware that conversion was an attractive route to divorce, and tried to restrict this, they had limited success. As patriarchal complaints were initially ineffective (Baer 2004), including in Cyprus (Çiçek 1992), the church was obliged to adopt a more divorce-tolerant approach (Laiou 2007: 250). But by the late eighteenth and early nineteenth centuries, the church's sovereignty over its flock was enhanced (Ivanova 1999: 172) through being delegated to collect Christian community taxes (Kermeli 2017: 176), leading to a decline in interreligious matrimonial 'legal shopping'.

In the Balkans, Crete and Cyprus, conversion of Christian men to Islam, partly to escape the head tax (rare), but more likely as a means of social mobility, such as recruitment to the Janissaries, appears to have created a new matrimonial situation that resulted paradoxically not in full Islamization but in a type of religious synthesis or hybridity that nationalist historiography questionably interpreted as 'crypto-Christianity'. Initial Islamic conversion of men, especially if pragmatically motivated,[24] could be tempered by drawing wives from their ex-co-religionists. They could be called 'restorative' or 'compensatory' mixed marriages, compatible with (Muslim) wife-takers being then socially superior to (Christian) wife-givers (from a Muslim perspective).

Apart from reasons of social mobility, other factors contributed to marriages between Christian women and neo-Muslims in rural areas, including, firstly, to reamalgamate divided properties, as neo-Muslim men (being subject to Islamic marriage laws) could marry their female kin within the (church) prohibited degrees, as did occur (Kermeli 2017: 205; Ivanova 2007:163). They could include single (including orphaned) daughters, vulnerable through material poverty or lack of protective male kin (similar to the ancient Greek *epiklerete*).[25] Secondly, the economics of mixed marriages, as Islamic marriage required an indirect dowry or dower (*mahr*) from the groom at marriage and at divorce/widowhood, whereas it was customary for Christians in some (certainly not all) parts of the Greek world to provide a parental dowry for the bride as a premortem inheritance,[26] or even a cash 'groom-price' (*trachoma*), irretrievable in the case of divorce. Dowry inflation was acute in eighteenth-century urban Greece, rendering Kadi-officiated *kepin* marriages to dower (*mahr*) bearing grooms particularly attractive to impoverished Christian women.[27] These 'temporary' *kepin* (or *kiambin*) marriages specifying a sum to be paid by the groom on the termination of the marriage contract were particularly disturbing to the church, which viewed them as adulterous, potentially bigamous, and a travesty of marriage's sacramental character. They were popular not just among paleo- and neo-Muslims but also Christian women, as the 'Christian' *trachoma* 'groom-price' was replaced by a Sharia-required groom-bearing indirect dowry (that could of course be symbolic). Islamic law recognized children of such unions as legitimate, much to patriarchal chagrin. If no termination had been contractually specified, the marriage remained in force.[28] By the seventeenth and eighteenth centuries, *kepin* marriages were found in 'virtually every part of Ottoman South East Europe' (Zelepos 2013: 47). Thirdly, and finally, Islam made greater explicit financial (and less judgemental) provision for divorce. Christianity was hostile to divorce, and only granted it after intrusive investigations into culpability, which then determined child custody.

So attractive was the Sharia's contractual approach to marriage and its dissolution that significant numbers of 'Christian marriages' were ratified before a (state-appointed) Kadi, often at the bride's insistence, particularly but not exclusively in contexts of increasing male in and out migration, as was the case in eighteenth-century Rumelia (Ivanova 1999, 2007). The Muslims, by contrast, merely engaged the local imam. In a Kadi-ratified marriage, the groom was obliged to follow Sharia requirements by offering an indirect dowry (*mahr*), including provision for divorce or widowhood, preferable to Balkan Christian and northern Greek women who often offered an irretrievable prenuptial cash gift (*trachoma*) to the groom (Joseph 2009: 347). To bypass their customary law, pursue their interests, and neutralize lengthy ecclesiastical forensics in marital breakdown, some Christian women were adopting Islamic legal instruments (including in Damascus; Al-Qattan 1999). Some Kadis, as educated state officials, may have viewed their role as fostering social harmony; others to line their pockets.

Mixed-faith marriages are regularly recorded for most Ottoman regions with contiguous or intermixed religious groups.[29] In 1738, Pococke noted for Cyprus: 'the Mahometan men very often marry with the Christian women and keep the fasts with their wives. Many of them are thought to be not averse to Christianity' (Cobham 1908: 269). 'Not averse to Christianity', for some may have been first-generation married Christian men who had converted to Islam, or their descendants. The neo-convert husband with a Christian wife was the simplest and socially least disruptive conjugal molecule, straddling both communities. Links with the original maternal Christian community could be generationally sustained by marriages, including close-kin ones prohibited under canon law, as occurred in Crete (Kolovos 2008). Daughters' marriages, by contrast, although perforce with Muslim men, if preferentially oriented towards a new incoming first generation of converts or second generation neo-Muslim grooms, could reinforce pre-existing links to the original Christian community. In 1660s Nova Candia, nearly 47 per cent of daughters of neo-converts married similar neo-convert grooms (ibid.: 114).

If marriage could unite, property devolution could foster conflict, often exacerbated by conversions that resulted in Muslim-*Zimmi* joint ownerships. Muslims and *zimmis* could not inherit from each other, although converts retained their pre-conversion devolved property. With one-way conversions and intermarriages this could logically result in a haemorrhaging of property. Further research is necessary on the ultimate destination of mixed religious joint property ownership.[30]

Some confirmation that religious conversions together with mixed marriages did not necessarily result in ruptures from kith and kin comes from Turner's observations in Cyprus in 1815: 'Many professed Moslem are in secret Greeks and observe all the numerous fasts of that church. All drink wine freely, and many of them eat pork without scruple in secret, a thing unheard of in Turkey. They frequently marry the Greek women of the island, as their religion permits a Turkish man to marry an infidel woman' (Cobham 1908: 449). For seventeenth-century Albania, Doja notes that 'when the Catholic population began to diminish rapidly because of mass conversions to Islam, crypto-Christianity correspondingly expanded among the Albanians. Missionary reports frequently describe cases of whole Catholic communities engaging in men-only conversion … In some cases, the new converts are reported to have taken Christian rather than Muslim women as their wives, on the grounds that they did not want Christianity to vanish from their homes' (Doja 2008: 60).[31]

Mixed-faith marriages could be self-sustaining in religious socialization by default rather than legislative intention. Sons were necessarily oriented to the men's world (the mosque and public Islam), whilst their sisters would also be exposed through their mothers and female networks to more intimate religious practices congruent with Christianity's pervasive interactive tactile iconicity versus Islam's scripturalism. If the wives were Christian, or had Christian kin, priests could visit homes without incurring suspicion.

Mixed-faith marriages in rural contexts thus tend to an aggregation in religious practices, with formal (male) public participation in the mosque and more eclectic popular religious forms of devotion, including visits to Christian shrines by women and the preparation of ritual foods (Jacobs 1999). Such eclecticism shades into, and is camouflaged by, popular religion as a by-product of contiguous or intermixed populations.[32] Ritual foods were 'family custom', often domestically unquestioned and externally invisible, but could also in certain situations become reinterpreted as diacritical markers of 'crypto-religious' difference.[33] Clearly, conversion to Islam was irreversible, and descendants would be locked in the Muslim fold with no possibility of a formal return to Christianity, even had they so desired.[34] And participation in mixed devotional practices depended on a church's position towards conversion, ranging from hardline Catholic condemnation to the more flexible Orthodox (but not Athonite) policy of *economia* – that is, accommodation to the powers that be, including 'that they do not go to the Kadi' (Ivanova 2007: 165). In regions where Catholicism and Orthodoxy coexisted, such as the Balkans and Cyprus, a rejection of accommodation by the (Catholic) priest could result in a migration of 'crypto-Catholics' to the Maronite Church as occurred in Cyprus (Jennings 1993a: 150), or to Orthodoxy. As Orthodox priests were selected by their co-villagers (in contrast to Catholicism), they may have been more disposed to privately dispense blessings, prayers, offerings and Extreme Unction/ *Euchelaion* (equally sought by paleo-Muslims). Neither Catholicism nor Orthodoxy, however, recognized or registered mixed marriages, or conducted religious burials compromising the deceased's offspring.[35] Such individuals became invisible from the records, and any sacramental administration remained informal. Individuals entered and exited life as members of specific religious communities, but their life journeys were punctuated by participation in the numerous crossflows of mixed devotional practices.

Evidence for synthetic forms of religion through the matrilateral transmission of religious practices come from India and, more relevantly, from the Ottoman Balkans.[36] There, Hasluck noted that Muslim participation in Christian rituals was encouraged by mixed marriages (1929: 136). In 1909, Durham observed that border Albanian 'crypto-Catholics' (*laramane*: dappled) attended both church and mosque, adopted both private Christian and public Muslim names, followed both Christian and Ramadan fasts, and received last rites but were buried in Muslim graveyards. The Cypriot '*linovamvakoi*' (linencottons), until the late nineteenth century (Dietzel and Makrides 2009), held Muslim marriage rites on Fridays that were open to all, and a more restricted Sunday Christian wedding with a *koumbaros* (Michel 1908). Such practices were hard to bracket off from more prosaic forms of cultural diffusion and borrowing, especially of religious practices, including shared places of worship, a phenomenon that received attention from both Hasluck (1929) and Albera and Couroucli (2012).[37]

Between 'Discernible Invisibilities' and 'Indiscernible Visibilities'

I conclude by revisiting the implications of Jack and Esther Goody's concern with the circulation of women and children with respect to the historic eastern Mediterranean.

Esther's Gonja voluntarily circulated children through fosterage for the modest sociopolitical purpose of reinforcing kin ties (Goody 1970: 63). In the Ottoman world, children likewise circulated between kin, from child-wealthy families to child-poor ones, to learn trades, and such like. But additionally, through the child-levy, young males were abducted from the periphery to become the privileged, protected intimates of the sultan's extended household. Two processes occurred simultaneously: that of 'othering' (turning them into *xenoi*/strangers from their own kin and communities), followed by their fictive 'patri-filiation' (incorporating them as 'sons' of the sultan). Within the empire, Janissaries were 'professional strangers'; within the sultan's extended household, they were his slaves (*kül*), lacking genealogy, kin, and natal community. Correspondingly, these very slave-outsiders became his metaphorical 'guest-sons' through 'patri-filiation', and by extension, linked through 'sibling' rivalry. Although the sultan might phenomenologically appear as their 'foster parent', it was the biological parents who risked being reconjured as 'surrogate' parents, bearing children for a prodigious sultan, and generating simmering historical resentments. The Ottoman system of fictive patri-filiation thus bears comparison with contemporary surrogacy. In contrast to contemporary surrogacy, the 'appropriation' of biological reproduction is not by the commissioning conjugal unit to 'assist nature', but by a distant prodigious figure to overcome governing vulnerabilities by forging a radically new, but phenomenologically 'traditional', substantiation of power through fictive neo-filiation. What is of interest are the various political elaborations of filiation. Rather than harnessing kinship *qua* filiation (*qaraba*) as an organizing horizontal political principle of group solidarity (*assabiya*) as with dissident North African pastoral tribes, the 'New Rome' based Ottomans constructed a superimposed system of vertical fictive neo-filiation, recognized as such by the protagonists in palace choreographies of virility, linking each recruited generation to the sultan as his 'foster children'. Differentiating filial submission rather than egalitarian fused *assabiya* was the ordering value.

Group filiation in the Ottoman world was a function of religious group membership, whose main gateways were descent, conversion and intermarriage. From a conventional perspective, group identities were dependent on the ultimate matrimonial destination of women, and filiation (including child custody and religious affiliation) depended upon whether they were married to Christians or Muslims. Women could be 'lost' to their natal religious group through intermarriage and conversion. Conversions and intermarriages thus threatened group identities and integrities, particularly if such migrations involved women. However, such perspectives, common in nationalist accounts, bypass men's conversions and give a one-sided gynaeco-centric picture, where one group 'loses' and the other 'gains'.

This is partly what seems to have happened in the eastern Mediterranean: Christian women 'circulated' through interfaith marriages, including with neo-Muslims. But where married Christian men converted, it was not the women who were 'circulating' between groups but *their husbands' conversions* that performed the classificatory sleight of hand, re-bracketing women in subsequent popular historiography as married to/'abducted by Turks', and were thus 'lost' to their group. A man's canny (perhaps mercenary) conversion to Islam and a subsequent marriage to a Christian girl is substituted in subsequent popular recounting as a Christian girl's 'abduction' by an (anonymised) 'Turk', for the underlying causes of such humiliating 'losses' to dominant groups are often buried through shamed silence. The same sleight of the collective tongue would apply to a woman's conversion to Islam to escape from an arranged marriage, and her subsequent marriage to an (often neo) Muslim. We thus get a much more nuanced picture when we move from formal prescriptive legal systems that regulated marriages, divorces and remarriages within groups to encompass religious conversions to facilitate or bypass them. The intimate aetiologies of such 'ethnically embarrassing' individual strategies are subsequently erased in favour of more emotionally satisfying group ideal histories. 'Abductions' or 'elopements', often two sides of the same popular historical coin, although attested to and occurrent, are not sufficient transparent explanations.

The matrimonial 'circulation' of women may thus have been both their group membership *reclassification* by male conversive strategies and subsequent patriarchal vocabularies of counter-justification, and their active legal self-reclassification to pursue their emotional interests as divorcees through conversion, or their material ones as widow converts. The 'discernible invisibility' of interfaith marriages that contemporary travellers cynically recognized (especially as regards men), risks transmuting into an 'indiscernible visibility' to scholars grappling with the phenomenon (especially as regards women).

Within such a representational schema, groups may well appear as distinct and separate, subject to 'gains' and 'losses', and there is a sense in which groups have an investment in this, though for very different reasons. Group boundaries are generally fuzzier than the dominant one is prepared to admit, and the dominated wish to recognize, particularly with regards to the 'circulation' of their prized 'assets', women; because quite often it is the men as husbands or potential grooms who migrate from one group to another. Both groups had an investment in not acknowledging the emergence of an intermediate social group because the latter, squeezed between the two, had an interest in erasing any distinctive social markers by adopting exaggerated cultural responses, which Bateson (1972) identified as schismogenic. These included emphasizing their external visibility *qua* Muslims to Muslims, especially by the men, and adopting pious Muslim practices like emancipating slaves (Spyropoulos 2015: 197), partly because the receiving group is reluctant to fully accept them, *and* compensating through an intimate 'complementary religious filiation' to the Christian community via mother–daughter links.[38] Female participation in popular mixed religious rituals was dismissed by Muslim clerics as 'marginal', and thus invisible and inconsequential – including by subsequent generations of their menfolk who undoubtedly became fully Islamicized. Such cumulative challenges to the erosion of Freud's 'narcissism of minor differences' in Crete and the Balkans later provoked violent recrudescence, fed by Herderian nationalism.

This is not to suggest that mixed marriages were the rule; they were statistically rare and significant in specific political ecologies. Viswanathan (1998) characterized conversion – of which intermarriage is an important vector – as an 'unsettling (political) event' in the colonial and postcolonial nation state. This is only partly correct for the early modern Mediterranean. For the receiving group, conversion was a ratification of the superiority of their faith, 'honouring (the convert) with the glory of Islam' (Baer 2004). Within the sending group, reactions ranged from public shunning, and collective erasure through silence for women's conversions, to more personal barely concealed envy. In Crete, *burmades* (renegades) were particularly despised (Dedes 2011: 327), as probably elsewhere, but cross-cutting ties of kinship, affinity, residence, and shared religious places moderated divisions. Muslims regularly testified on behalf of Christians against other Muslims in Nicosia's courts (Çiçek 1992), so a converted Muslim kinsman/co-villager was not to be shunned. Exceptionalism, a psychic defence mechanism, pre-empted conversion from becoming 'an unsettling political event', rendering the visible invisible. In the ethnically turbulent 1960s, Loizos (1975) noted that in response to persistent questioning his Greek Cypriot village 'informants' had grudgingly admitted that interfaith marriages or 'elopements' were probably less unusual in the past than they then felt comfortable acknowledging (Asmussen 1996). Historical nationalist ideologies cling like Nessus's poisoned tunic to the body politic, compromising a fuller appreciation of the circulation of women and children that Esther and Jack Goody explored.

Interfaith marriages are dismissively marginal if approached from a nationalist a priori expectation of endogamous self-reproducing groups with distinct, consistent articulations of religions, languages, and cultural practices. But if we have little difficulty in lending credence to *zimmi* female slave conversions and their subsequent concubinage to ameliorate their fate (itself an important example of the 'circulation of women'), why should we be surprised if individual men or women in difficult unanticipated circumstances, or with motivations of social mobility, also converted or intermarried but tried to mitigate the implications, particularly with their natal communities? Conversion and intermarriage provided resolutions for the unanticipated, but the unexpected has sociological significance, including when it is evoked as a legitimizing tactic by the actors themselves. This is not to deny the structuring forces of power inequality, but to explore its pushes and pulls in the conjugal arrangements linking individuals to groups. The desire to partake in Ottoman high culture was an equally potent pull, evidenced by the high-status careers of some elite converts (Imber 2002: 163).

Conversions and compensatory intermarriages with one's ex-co-religionists are often individual tactics of the weak 'determined by the *absence of power* just as a strategy is organized by the postulation of power' (de Certeau 1984: 38, original emphasis). On the *individual* level, they may be the ultimate ruse of becoming *an*-Other to remain oneself. But *cumulatively* the unintended result is the risk that one becomes *the* Other, precisely because one must adopt that role. As a result of substantial conversions and consequent intermarriages, the Ottomans left Crete to be largely administered by indigenous Cretans *qua* Muslims. In this 'Janissaries island' (Greene 2002: 33) rebellions were common

(Sariyannis 2008), ironically demonstrating the pre-eminence of local ties over the trans-local fiction of imperial filiation. By the mid nineteenth century, in a virulent nationalist age, a dimly intuited fratricide masquerading as national liberation enabled Cretans to recapture their past through their ruses of resistance to their 'Turkish masters' (Herzfeld 1985). The historical multi-vectored trans-communitarian circulations of women and children can have unanticipated cumulative sociopolitical effects.

Paul Sant Cassia is a professor at the University of Malta in the Department of Anthropological Sciences, Faculty of Arts. He was a PhD student at the University of Cambridge under the supervision of Professor Jack Goody. He has conducted research in Cyprus. His research interests include Anthropology of Mediterranean Societies, Anthropology and Art, Kinship Studies, and the Political Economy of Memory.

Notes

1. Logically, a faith becomes 'crypto' retroactively only when one declares that one wants to leave it.
2. Vakalopoulos claims that Christian parents betrothed sons as children to prevent their drafting (1976: 36).
3. On the complex issue of retained Christian attachments, see Lybyer (1913: 68–69), Vryonis (1981: 272), Imber (2002: 136), and Hasluck (1929: 36).
4. See Bromberger (2006) on religion and trichoculture.
5. The *sunnetluler*, that is, circumcised youths, sons of recent Bosnian converts to Islam.
6. See Maksudyan (2008) for the more conventional nineteenth-century rural–urban movement of 'foster daughters'/maids (*beslemes*).
7. See Rothman (2012) for more bureaucratized contemporary Catholic responses.
8. Such as Montenegrin Christians fleeing from blood feuds to Muslim Albania, converting to Islam and taking local (Muslim) wives (Tošić 2017: 88).
9. For Albania, see Skendi (1967) for Albania.
10. See Duijzings (1993: 85, 89) and Reinkowski (2007: 421).
11. Particularly employed by Ottoman (re)converts to Catholicism (see Rothman 2012). See Tošić (201107) on the link between blood feuds and conversions.
12. Minkov (2004) notes that many Balkan conversion petitions between 1670 and –1730 were from the marginal (widows, orphans, etc.).
13. According to Minkov (2004), 20 per cent of Balkans petitioners were women.
14. Except for rare high-profile 'intellectual' conversions (Krstić 2009). By contrast, Venetians subscribed to a model of forced Islamic conversions thereby enabling Ottoman petitioners to dissimulate their personal motivations (Rothman 2012).
15. For exceptional female abductions/conversions, see Dursteler (2011: 80).
16. Including the vulnerable single, widows and orphans.
17. As in medieval Cairo (Goitein 1971), or Muslim Spain where a conversion resulted in an annulment not a divorce, and in exclusion from inheritance from blood relatives (Shatzmiller 1996: 237).
18. Some 40 per cent of all Kadi hearings in Nicosia between 1698 and 1726 involved at least one *zimmi*, mainly over buildings (Çiçek 1992).
19. I refer to Jewish conversions sporadically for limited comparative purposes.
20. And Jewish–Christian intermarriage (not discussed here).

21. Well attested by travellers – (e.g. Savary on Crete (1798: 340) on Crete.
22. Baer (2004: 438) notes that for Jewish women this was akin to a 'second birth'.
23. As with the Mallorcan (*converso*) *Xuetas* (Porqueres i Gene 1995).
24. Rather than merely as an individual route to an easy divorce (also common).
25. Dotal or female inherited property (if any) would become 'Muslim' through devolution to the Muslim offspring. See note below, however.
26. That disinherited sons and resulted in de facto inequalities (Papataxiarchis 1993).
27. Dowry inflation in certain parts of eighteenth-century18th Greece disadvantaged poor women who may have resorted to *kepin* marriages (cf. Sant Cassia and Bada 1992; Tsoukala 2010). See Loizos (1975) for the pre-1930's Greek Cypriot custom of grooms providing the dowry house and lands, rendering them like Turkish Cypriots. On exclusively dotal regimes found in homogeneous Christian regions such as the Aegean islands, see Doxiadis (2011).
28. For *kepin* marriages in Cyprus, see (Sant Cassia 1986: 22); for Greece, see (Tsoukala 2010: 886. Also, Hasluck 1929: 36, note 2.
29. Including both Catholic and Orthodox denominations.
30. In many mixed religious contexts (Balkans, northern and central Greece, Crete, and Cyprus), both Christians and Muslims practiced virilocality and an agnatic property devolution bias, with Muslim sons receiving double their sisters' shares. An accentuated Christian dotal regime and uxorilocality was strong in homogeneous Christian areas (e.g. the Aegean) and may have been adopted later in other contexts when, from the late eighteenth century onwards, mixed marriage challenges to property devolution subsided (from the late eighteenth century onwards).
31. Cf. also Skendi (1967).
32. For Bosnian Catholic monks performing exorcisms for Muslims and Ottoman authorities, see Lopasic (1994: 177).
33. See Jacobs (1996: 104) on the Jewish female transmission of unexplained prepared 'ritual foods'.
34. On a reluctance to admit ancestral conversion, see Lopsasic (1994), who noted deeper Bosnian Christian genealogies than Muslim ones.
35. For Cyprus, Jennings (1993a) notes that women suspected by priests of being Muslims (possibly in *kepin* mixed marriages) and refused church entry, had to resort to sSharia courts to gain church admittance.
36. See Kent (2010) on the so-called secret Christians of Tamil Nadu, where clusters of Christian women married Hindu husbands.
37. See Dursteler (2011) on veneration of the Virgin by Christian and Muslim women.
38. I am expanding Fortes' 1953 notion of 'complementary filiation' (1953) to include religion.

References

Albera, Diongi, and Maria Couroucli. 2012. *Sharing Sacred Spaces in the Mediterranean: Christians, Muslims, and Jews at Shrines and Sanctuaries*. Bloomington: Indiana University Press.

Al-Qattan, Najwa. 1999. 'Dhimmis in the Muslim Court: Legal Autonomy and Religious Discrimination', *International Journal of Middle East Studies* 31(3): 429–44.

Asmussen, Jan. 1996. 'Life and Strife in Mixed Villages: Some Aspects of Inter-ethnic Relations in Cyprus under British Rule', *Cyprus Review* 8(1): 101–10.

Baer, Mark David. 2004. 'Islamic Conversion Narratives of Women: Social Change and Gendered Religious Hierarchy in Early Modern Ottoman Istanbul', *Gender & History* 16(2): 425–58.

Baldwin, James E. 2012. 'Petitioning the Sultan in Ottoman Egypt', *Bulletin of the School of Oriental and African Studies* 75(3): 499–524.

Bateson, Gregory. 1972. *Steps to an Ecology of Mind: Collected Essays in Anthropology, Psychiatry, Evolution, and Epistemology*. Chicago: University of Chicago Press.

Beckingham, C.F. 1957. 'The Turks of Cyprus', *Journal of the Royal Anthropological Institute of Great Britain and Ireland* 87(2): 165–74.

Bennassar, B. 1988. 'Conversion ou Reniement? Modalités d'une Adhésion Ambiguë des Chrétiens à l'Islam (XVIe–XVIIe siècles)', *Annales. Histoire, Sciences Sociales* 43(6): 1349–66.

Bowie, Fiona. 2004. 'Adoption and the Circulation of Children: A Comparative Perspective', in Fiona Bowie (ed.), *Cross-cultural Approaches to Adoption*. London: Routledge, pp. 3–20.

Bromberger, Christian. 2006. 'Towards an Anthropology of the Mediterranean', *History and Anthropology* 17(2): 91–107.

Bulliet, Richard W. 1979. *Conversion to Islam in the Medieval Period: An Essay in Quantitative History*. Cambridge, MA: Harvard University Press.

Çiçek, Kemal. 1992. 'Zimmis (Non-Muslims) of Cyprus in the Sharia Court: 1110/39AH/1698–1726 AD'. PhD thesis submitted to the Centre for Byzantine, Ottoman and Modern Greek Studies. University of Birmingham, UK.

Cobham, Claude Delaval. 1908. *Excerpta Cypria* [Cypriot Excerpts]. Cambridge: Cambridge University Press.

Coser, Lewis A. 1965. 'The Political Functions of Eunuchism', *American Sociological Review* 29(6): 880–85.

———. 1972. 'The Alien as a Servant of Power: Court Jews and Christian Renegades', *American Sociological Review* 37(5): 574–81.

de Certeau, Michael. 1984. *The Practice of Everyday Life*. Berkeley: University of California Press.

Dedes, Yorgo. 2011. 'Blame It on the Turko-Romnioi (Turkish Rums): A Muslim Cretan Song on the Abolition of the Janissaries', in Evangelia Balta and M. Ölmez (eds), *Between Religion and Language: Turkish-Speaking Christians, Jews and Greek-Speaking Muslims and Catholics in the Ottoman Empire*. Istanbul: Eren, pp. 321–76.

Deringil, Selim. 2000. '"There Is No Compulsion in Religion": On Conversion and Apostasy in the Late Ottoman Empire, 1839–1856', *Comparative Studies in Society and History* 42(3): 547–75.

Dietzel, Irene, and Vasilios N. Makrides. 2009. 'Ethno-Religious Coexistence and Plurality in Cyprus under British Rule (1878–1960)', *Social Compass* 56(1): 69–83.

Doja, Albert. 2008. 'Instrumental Borders of Gender and Religious Conversion in the Balkans', *Religion, State and Society* 36(1): 55–63.

Doxiadis, Evdoxios. 2011. 'Legal Trickery: Men, Women, and Justice in Late Ottoman Greece', *Past & Present* (210): 129–53.

Duijzings, Ger. 1993. 'Pilgrimage, Politics and Ethnicity: Joint Pilgrimages of Muslims and Christians, and Conflicts over Ambiguous Sanctuaries in Yugoslavia and Albania', in Mart Bax and Adrianus Koster (eds), *Power and Prayer: Religious and Political Processes in Past and Present*. Amsterdam: VU University Press, pp. 79–90.

Durham, M. Edith. 1909. *High Albania*. London: Edward Arnold.

Dursteler, Eric. 2011. *Renegade Women: Gender, Identity and Boundaries in the Early Modern Mediterranean*. Baltimore, MD: Johns Hopkins University Press.

Fortes, Meyer. 1953. 'The Structure of Unilineal Descent Groups', *American Anthropologist* 55(1): 17–41.

Goitein, Shelomo Dov. 1971. *A Mediterranean Society: The Jewish Communities of the Arab World as Portrayed in the Documents of the Cairo Geniza, Vol. 2: The Community*. Berkeley: University of California Press.

Goody, Esther N. 1970. 'Kinship Fostering in Gonja: Deprivation or Advantage?', in Philip Mayer (ed.), *Socialization: The Approach from Social Anthropology*, ASA Monograph 8. London: Tavistock Publications, pp. 37–54.

———. 1971. 'Forms of Pro-Parenthood: The Sharing and Substitution of Parental Roles', in Jack Goody (ed.), *Kinship: Selected Readings*. Harmondsworth: Penguin Readings in Sociology, pp. 331–45.

———. 1982. *Parenthood and Social Reproduction: Fostering and Occupational Roles in West Africa*. Cambridge Studies in Anthropology 35. Cambridge: Cambridge University Press.

Goody, Jack. 1983. *The Development of Family and Marriage in Europe*. Cambridge: Cambridge University Press.

Goody, Jack, and Esther Goody. 1967. 'The Circulation of Women and Children in Northern Ghana', *Man* 2(2): 226–48.

Gradeva, Rosita, and Svetlana Ivanova. 2001. 'Researching the Past and Present of Muslim Culture in Bulgaria: The "Popular" and "High" Layers', *Islam and Christian–Muslim Relations* 12(3): 317–37.

Greene, Molly. 2002. *A Shared World: Christians and Muslims in the Early Modern Mediterranean*. Princeton, NJ: Princeton University Press.

Hasluck, Frederick W. 1929. *Christianity and Islam under the Sultans: Vols. 1 & 2*. Oxford: Clarendon Press.

Herzfeld, Michael. 1985. *The Poetics of Manhood: Contest and Identity in a Cretan Mountain Village*. Princeton, NJ: Princeton University Press.

Howell, Signe. 2006. *The Kinning of Foreigners: Transnational Adoption in a Global Perspective*. Oxford: Berghahn Books.

Imber, Colin. 2002. *The Ottoman Empire, 1300–1650*. Hampshire, UK: Palgrave Macmillan.

Inalcik, Halil. 1992. 'Comments on "Sultanism": Max Weber's Typification of the Ottoman Polity', in Charles Issawi and Bernard Lewis (eds), *Princeton Papers in Near Eastern Studies* 1: 49–72.

Ivanova, Svetlana. 1999. 'Muslim and Christian Women before the Kadi Court in Eighteenth-Century Rumeli: Marriage Problems', *Oriente Moderno* 18 (79), NR 1: 161–76.

———. 2007. 'Judicial Treatment of the Matrimonial Problems of Christian Women in Rumeli during the Seventeenth and Eighteenth Centuries', in Amila Buturović and İrvin C. Schick (eds), *Women in the Ottoman Balkans: Gender, Culture and History*. London: I.B. Tauris, pp. 153–200.

Jacobs, Janet L. 1996. 'Women, Ritual, and Secrecy: The Creation of Crypto-Jewish Culture', *Journal for the Scientific Study of Religion* 35(2): 97–108.

———. 1999. 'Conversa Heritage, Crypto-Jewish Practice and Women's Rituals', *Shofar: An Interdisciplinary Journal of Jewish Studies* 18(1): 101–8.

Jennings, Ronald C. 1993a. *Christians and Muslims in Ottoman Cyprus and the Mediterranean World, 1571–1640*. New York: New York University Press.

———. 1993b. 'Divorce in the Ottoman Sharia Court of Cyprus, 1580–1640', *Studia Islamica* (78): 155–67.

Joseph, Sabrina. 2009. 'Communicating Justice: Shari'a Courts and the Christian Community in Seventeenth- and Eighteenth-Century Ottoman Greece', *Islam and Christian–Muslim Relations* 20(3): 333–50.

Kent, Eliza F. 2011. 'Secret Christians of Sivakasi: Gender, Syncretism, and Crypto Religion in Early Twentieth-Century South India', *Social Compass* 79(3): 676–705.

Kermeli, Eugenia. 2013. 'Marriage and Divorce of Christians and New Muslims in Early Modern Ottoman Empire: Crete 1645–1670', *Oriente Moderno* 93(2): 495–514.

———. 2017. 'The Right to Choice: Ottoman Justice vis-à-vis Ecclesiastical and Communal Justice in the Balkans, Seventeenth–Nineteenth Centuries', in Andreas Christmann and Robert Gleave (eds), *Studies in Islamic Law: A Festschrift for Colin Imber*. Oxford: Oxford University Press, pp. 165–210.

Kolovos, Elias. 2008. 'A Town for the Besiegers: Social Life and Marriage in Ottoman Candia outside Candia (1650–1669)', in Antonis Anastopoulos (ed.), *The Eastern Mediterranean under Ottoman Rule, Crete: 1645–1840*. Rethymno: Crete University Press, pp. 103–75.

Krstić, Tijana. 2009. 'Illuminated by the Light of Islam and the Glory of the Ottoman Sultanate: Self-Narratives of Conversion to Islam in the Age of Confessionalization', *Comparative Studies in Society and History* 51(1): 35–63.

———. 2011. *Contested Conversions to Islam: Narratives of Religious Change in the Early Modern Ottoman Empire*. Stanford, CA: Stanford University Press.

Laiou, Sophia. 2007. 'Christian Women in an Ottoman world: Interpersonal and Family Cases Brought before the Shari'a Courts during the Seventeenth and Eighteenth Centuries (Cases Involving the Greek Community)', in Amila Buturović and İrvin C. Schick (eds), *Women in the Ottoman Balkans: Gender, Culture and History*. London: I.B. Tauris, pp. 243–71.

Loizos, Peter. 1975. 'Changes in Property Transfer among Greek Cypriot Villagers', *Man* 10(4): 503–23.

Lopasic, Alexander. 1994. 'Islamization of the Balkans with Special Reference to Bosnia', *Journal of Islamic Studies* 5(2): 163–86.

Lybyer, Albert H. 1913. *The Government of the Ottoman Empire in the Time of Suleiman the Magnificent*. Cambridge, MA: Harvard University Press.

Maksudyan, Nazan. 2008. 'Foster-Daughter or Servant, Charity or Abuse: *Beslemes* in the Late Ottoman Empire', *Journal of Historical Sociology* 21(1): 488–512.

Ménage, Victor Louis. 1966. 'Some Notes on the Devshirme', *Bulletin of the School of Oriental and African Studies* 29(1): 64–78.

Michel, Roland L.N. 1908. 'Muslim–Christian Sect in Cyprus', *The Nineteenth Century Journal* (63): 751–62.

Minkov, Anton. 2004. *Conversion to Islam in the Balkans: Kisve Bahası Petitions and Ottoman Social Life, 1670–1730*. Leiden: Brill.

Nirenberg, David. 2003. 'Enmity and Assimilation: Jews, Christians, and Converts in Medieval Spain', *Common Knowledge* 9(1): 137–55.

Pantazopoulos, Nikolaos J. 1967. *Church and Law in the Balkan Peninsula During the Ottoman Rule*. Thessaloniki: Institute for Balkan Studies 92.

Papataxiarchis, Evthymios. 1993. 'La Valeur du Ménage: Classes Sociales, Stratégies Matrimoniales et Lois Ecclésiastiques à Lesbos au XIXe siècle', in Stuart J. Woolf (ed.), *Espaces et Familles dans l'Europe du Sud à l'âge moderne*. Paris : Editions de la Maison des Sciences de l'Homme, pp. 109–42.

Parkes, Peter. 2003. 'Fostering Fealty: A Comparative Analysis of Tributary Allegiances of Adoptive Kinship', *Comparative Studies in Society and History* 45(4): 741–82.

Peirce, Leslie. 2007. 'An Imperial Caste: Inverted Racialization in the Architecture of Ottoman Sovereignty', in Margaret Greer, Walter D. Mignolo and Maureen Quilligan (eds), *Rereading the Black Legend: The Discourses of Religious and Racial Difference in the Renaissance Empires*. Chicago: University of Chicago Press, pp. 27–47.

Porqueres i Gené, Enric. 1995. *Lourde Alliance: Mariage et Identité Chez les Descendants de Juifs Convertis à Majorque, 1435–1750*. Paris: Kimé.

Preiser-Kapeller, Johannes. 2012. 'Webs of Conversion: An Analysis of Social Networks of Converts across Islamic–Christian Borders in Anatolia, South-Eastern Europe and the Black Sea from the 13th to the 15th Century'. Workshop *Cross-Cultural Life-Worlds in Pre-Modern Islamic Societies: Actors, Evidences and Strategies*, 22–24 June, University of Bamburg, Germany.

Radushev, Eugeni. 2008. '"Peasant" Janissaries?', *Journal of Social History* 42(2): 447–67.

Reinkowski, Maurus. 2007. 'Hidden Believers, Hidden Apostates: The Phenomenon of Crypto-Jews and Crypto-Christians in the Middle East', in Denis C. Washburn and A. Kevin Reinhart (eds), *Converting Cultures: Religion, Ideology, and Transformations of Modernity*. Leiden: Brill, pp. 409–33.

Rothman, E. Natalie. 2012. *Brokering Empire: Trans-Imperial Subjects between Venice and Istanbul*. Cornell, NY: Cornell University Press.

Sant Cassia, Paul. 1986. 'Religion, Politics and Ethnicity in Cyprus during the *Turkocratia* (1571–1878)', *European Journal of Sociology* 27(1): 3–28.

⸻ . 2018. 'Marriages at the Margins: Interfaith Marriages in the Mediterranean', *Journal of Mediterranean Studies*. 27(2): 111–32.

Sant Cassia, Paul, and Constantina Bada. 1992. *The Making of the Modern Greek Family: Marriage and Exchange in Nineteenth-Century Athens*. Cambridge: Cambridge University Press.

Sariyannis, Marinos. 2008. 'Rebellious Janissaries: Two Military Mutinies in Candia (1688, 1762) and their Aftermaths', in Antonis Anastasopoulos (ed.), *The Eastern Mediterranean Under Ottoman Rule: Crete, 1645–1840*. Athens: University of Crete Press., pp. 255–74.

Savary, Claude Etienne. 1798. *Letters on Greece Being a Sequel to Letters on Egypt*. London: Robinson.

Shatzmiller, Maya. 1996. 'Marriage, Family, and the Faith: Women's Conversion to Islam', *Journal of Family History* 21(3): 235–66.

Skendi, Stavro. 1967. 'Crypto-Christianity in the Balkan Area under the Ottomans', *Slavic Review* 26(2): 227–46.

Spyropoulos, Yannis. 2015. 'Slaves and Freedmen in 17th and early 18th Century Crete', *Turcica* 46: 177–204.

Tošić, Jelena. 2017. 'Travelling Genealogies: Tracing Relatedness and Diversity in the Albanian–Montenegrin Borderland', in Hastings Donnan, Madeleine Hurd and Carolin Leutloff-Grandits (eds), *Migrating Borders and Moving Times: Temporality and the Crossing of Borders in Europe*. Manchester: Manchester University Press, pp. 80–101.

Tsoukala, Philomila. 2010. 'Marrying Family Law to the Nation', *The American Journal of Comparative Law* 58(4): 873–910.

Vakalopoulos, Apostolus Evangelou. 1976. *Origins of the Greek Nation: The Byzantine Period, 1204–1461*. New Brunswick, NJ: Rutgers University Press.

Valensi, Lucette. 1986. 'La Tour de Babel: Groupes et Relations Ethniques au Moyen-Orient et en Afrique du Nord', *Annales Histoire, Sciences Sociales* 41(4): 817–38.

⸻ . 1997. 'Inter-Communal Relations and Changes in Religious Affiliation in the Middle East (Seventeenth to Nineteenth Centuries)', *Comparative Studies in Society and History* 39(2): 251–69.

Viswanathan, Gavri. 1998. *Outside the Fold: Conversion, Modernity, and Belief.* Princeton, NJ: Princeton University Press.

Vryonis, Speros. 1956. 'Isidore Glabas and the Turkish Devshirme', *Speculum* 31(3): 433–43.

———. 1981. *Studies on Byzantium, Seljuks, and Ottomans, Vol: 13.* Malibu: Undena Publications.

Yilmaz Diko, Gulay. 2015. 'Blurred Boundaries between Soldiers and Civilians: Artisan Janissaries in Seventeenth-Century Istanbul', in Suraiya Faroqhi (ed.), *Bread from the Lion's Mouth: Artisans Struggling for a Livelihood in Ottoman Cities.* International Studies in Social History, Vol. 25. New York: Berghahn Books, pp. 175–93.

Zelepos, Ioannis. 2013. 'Multi-denominational Interactions in the Ottoman Balkans from a Legal Point of View: The Institution of *Kiambin*-Marriage', in E. Papo and N. Makuljevic (eds), *Common Culture and Particular Identities: Christians, Jews and Muslims in the Ottoman Balkans.* Moshe David Gaon Center For Ladino Culture & Ben-Gurion University of the Negev, pp. 43–53.

4

The Circulation of Women and Children – and Everybody Else – Half a Century Later

Lynne Brydon

I originally intended in this piece to write about recent work on international migration and fostering from and to Ghana with the ultimate aim of trying to show how the presentation and conclusions from recent work in this field seemed, in many instances, to lack context. It taps into interesting stuff on transnationalism in many ways, but the local-level work and overall contextualization I think is a little thin, not at all 'thick'. The general point of this – to paraphrase Meyer Fortes – was to urge that conclusions should be based in sound ethnography, not simply the natty presentation of results of focus groups and surveys, with a nod to some theoretical perspective, whether relevant or not, and without reference to contexts and their changes, the ethnography on the ground.[1] I came to the conclusion, however, that this was merely a tool for me to vent my post-retirement crabbiness about the ways in which things had changed. Having spent much time and spleen-venting in this direction, I decided that it all just seemed rather shrill and, perhaps more appropriately left to a calmer framework, and I thought I might better write in a book for Esther Goody about how her early ideas, and those developed through the 1980s, on fostering and the fluidity of family and childcare arrangements, beginning with 'The Circulation of Women and Children in Northern Ghana' (1967, with Jack Goody), seem to have influenced my work through the past almost forty years to illustrate, if indirectly, the centrality of Esther's own work in these areas.

I say, 'seem to have influenced' because I have no recollection and had no realization that I had been so influenced. When I first worked in the Avatime village of Amedzofe in 1973, my initial priority was language learning. I did not have a 'theoretical perspective' or a well-worked-out research proposal.[2] I was interested in looking at the dynamics of family organization in a relatively remote village in Ghana's Volta Region, particularly in the light of then current ideas about the incorporation of small groups into nation states and the influences of modernity, then conceived. So I spent the first four or so months of fieldwork, having been granted permission by the paramount and the village chiefs to do research, with someone to help me with language learning (Avatime is not a written language)[3], usually using the mornings to work on language and the afternoons/ early evenings to walk around the village practising. Of course, if there was anything happening in the village *qua* village – communal work by women to clear weeds from around the post office prior to its 'upgrading'; town meetings early in the morning; a range of non-Christian rituals; funerals; trying to learn the etiquette of palm-wine drinking – I went, practised my language skills, was thoroughly laughed at, and encouraged both to watch and to take part.

I learned the organization of Amedzofe its division into five localized clans, each further subdivided into lineage groups. In addition, this included the Christian area that contained families from all the clans in the village, descendants of the earliest converts whom the German missionaries had encouraged to move away from their family areas (with their temptations to backsliding) and resettle around the Mission House. I embarked on writing down genealogies in each clan and its lineages, all the while speaking more and more in Avatime, and learning new things about local Christianity, local culture, local history, local gossip. Back then, the only fieldwork advice, apart from that of supervisors and Elenore Smith Bowen (Laura Bohannan)'s *Return to Laughter* (1954), was Epstein's *The Craft of Social Anthropology* (1967), where genealogical information was presented as key in helping students to understand local organization and how the society worked, structurally and functionally. But, in listening to the genealogical information, apart from wonderful conjecture about past connections (Did A really have four wives in succession to each other? Was woman B the same woman who appeared in this bit of the pattern as a sister, but in that bit as a wife? Shades of Evans-Pritchard and debates about African models in the New Guinea Highlands, only vaguely remembered), what really stood out was the geographical spread of people's lives. Not only had those who were working with me on the genealogies and their siblings been born in a range of places, but their fathers and mothers and their siblings had been born in a range of places, and their children were currently away from the village living in villages and towns throughout Ghana, although mostly in the south. Despite the village's relative remoteness and inaccessibility (and from the 1890s, because of the presence of the mission station and school there), its inhabitants' lives showed a multitude of connections to and networks with other parts of the area.

Keeping the 'ethnographic' focus in mind, establishing my ethnographic credibility, a couple of months later I, with the chiefs' permission, undertook a village-wide census: who was living in each house at the moment, where were they born, how were they all related to one another, and more importantly, what were the effective subunits in the family houses? While people might sleep in one particular building, a 'residence', their interconnections were not uniform:

there were multiple consumption groups – those eating from one pot – and often different and rather fluid production groups, depending on the task in hand. In addition, I asked about those who were away at the time: who would stay at this house if they came back to visit (for a funeral, for their annual leave), where they were, and how they were related to those at home? What this revealed, in addition to confirming the network of Amedzofe people throughout, mainly southern, Ghana, was the number of family groups in which the children of absent daughters and sons were living with grandparents or uncles and aunts, either paternal or maternal. So, this revealed a pattern of kin fostering in an area of Ghana that had not, according to Goody's earlier work, had a tradition of fostering.

And these kinds of families were common[4] in a village where, ostensibly, kinship was patrilineal (so why are all of the daughters' children living in the houses?) and according to what I was learning was traditional practice, in addition to my collected genealogies and gossip, extended three generation families were not the norm and where, on marriage and the birth of children, a new residential group was set up. So I began to look further into the variety in family patterns. A range of family patterns was, apparently, not new in the 1970s. Barbara Ward's work (1950, 1955) in the late 1940s, and undertaken as an extension of the Ashanti Social Survey, showed that, at that time, there was a range of family patterns in Vane, the Avatime paramount's village, about three miles from Amedzofe. Of course, this discovery had to wait until I was back in Cambridge and had access to a library, there being no internet then, effectively no telephone connections, and a postal system that was decidedly tardy.

As the twentieth century progressed, more and more the peoples of what became Ghana began to participate in the economic and social changes brought by colonialism, capitalism and Christianity. The increasing impact of money as currency, from the late nineteenth century onwards, and the novel idea that labour could be sold as 'work', something that had locally perceived benefits in terms of cash incomes, took root and flourished. Well before 1900, Amedzofe people knew about 'work' and what they saw as the benefits of having money.[5] One source of indigenous cash generation was cocoa cultivation. The cocoa boom in southern Ghana through the first two-thirds of the twentieth century, primarily focused on the areas just north of the Accra plains and into Asante, brought more income and more ideas about investment, both in tangible things like houses for rent and businesses, and less tangible things like education for children.[6] A secondary focus for cocoa growing centred on the middle part of the Volta Region (around Ahamansu and Buem); Amedzofe (and Vane) men, having worked away in the south, some as labourers, domestic servants, teachers or Church officials, used their cash savings to buy cocoa land in the Volta Region.[7] In addition, some did acquire land in the Afram Plains, on the other side of the River Volta (before the dam was built and the lake created).[8] Some simply moved to the cocoa areas to work on a share-cropping basis, and then gradually accrued enough cash and/or service to negotiate for land in their own right.

When Barbara Ward (1950) wrote about Vane in the late 1940s she found that a significant number of men were working away, mainly in cocoa cultivation, but also that some women were away independently of men, working on their own accounts. Her data do not indicate any preponderance of three-generation 'fostering' families in Vane, although she did write about the existence of quite complex households and what she termed 'dwelling groups'.⁹ With respect to Amedzofe migrants, about twenty-five years later I also found that both men and women were away working. In the 1970s, however, being away because of cocoa cultivation was relatively rare for those from Amedzofe. Amedzofe migrants over twenty years old, both men and women, were largely still in education or were teachers, with a range of other saleable occupations – from labourers or informally trained artisans and traders to businessmen and professionals.

Amedzofe migrants in the 1970s chose to work away to earn money; and results from further surveys between 1976 and 1979 from current and returned migrants from all the Avatime villages supported my initial findings. A key difference between the 1940s and the 1970s, however, seems to be that many more of the later migrants moved to urban areas, and that they stayed away for longer. In addition, they had children; some, in fact, married and stayed away throughout their children's childhoods. Another trend through the 1950s and 1960s was that a growing number of Amedzofe/Avatime women had children without being formally married. Many of them did subsequently marry the fathers of their children, but there were a number who did not; and also those who, having been married at one time, divorced their husbands. The vast majority of marriages and consensual unions took place between people from the same village, or certainly from the Avatime villages. Not only were destinations and occupations different between the Vane and Amedzofe migrants in the late 1940s and early 1970s respectively, but so were the consequences of their absences.

For those who were away, whether couples or single women, it was, and perhaps still is, perceived to be much easier, and cheaper (and healthier), to look after children in a village such as Amedzofe and the other villages. Parents did not have to pay a baby nurse or nursery fees, and the children themselves could eat fresh foods from farms; they could play outside without fear of traffic; they were in no danger from the pollution found in crowded low-income areas in the towns; and children, at least of primary school age, suffered no disadvantage as Amedzofe had two good and well-staffed primary schools.¹⁰ Parents working away sent money, soap, sugar and tinned goods for their children and their carers, and villagers sent fresh produce to those in towns: fresh and processed yams, cassava and maize, and fruits such as avocados, oranges and bananas. Thus many children were sent back to the villages to live with grandparents, or aunts, or sisters (women were the primary carers). This relatively new arrangement had another advantage, too: it meant that children would learn the Avatime language and about village life and customs. In the 1970s, before the vast majority of anthropological work on identity, local people put a premium on learning to be 'Avatime', as they saw it, and a premium in returning home eventually.

So from being a village where 'traditionally', as I was told, children lived with their parents in nuclear family households, even before the coming of Christianity, by the 1970s Amedzofe was full of complex multigenerational arrangements where children's parents were absent and children were cared for by a range of older women in fostering arrangements. In addition, in this formally patrilineal society, the older women tended to be the mothers, mothers' mothers, or sisters of those working away such that the majority of 'third generation children' in Amedzofe households were 'daughters' children'. At that same time as more and more young Amedzofe people were leaving to work, norms with respect to adulthood and marriage shifted hugely, and women's children, the children of as yet unmarried women, formed a significant part of this population of fostered children. This does not mean that these children were illegitimate, but simply that their mothers and fathers, in many instances, had not managed to organize the appropriate adulthood and marriage ceremonies; where women were not married, they preferred to send the children to their own rather than to their possible/probable future husbands' family members to be cared for.

Crisis fostering (if a child's parents had died, for example) was known and practised in Amedzofe at least from the late nineteenth century. There were also cases through the twentieth century where girl children in particular were sent to live with a female relative, perhaps if she had no children of her own, to help with daily household tasks and be supported by her. Such women had obligations to provide for their foster children's adulthood and marriage ceremonies, to provide their dowries, at the appropriate time, and in return, the foster-carer should be helped in old age. But the mid to late twentieth-century pattern of migration-prompted fostering in Amedzofe was new.

From Avatime-wide surveys I undertook in the later 1970s, I realized that there was also a pattern, seemingly in existence throughout the twentieth century with the growing significance of education, training and work, of a kind of instrumental fostering. Children could be sent to relatives who were working away, on one hand to help in the household, but on the other to receive training about life away, life skills if you like, about modernity, and to attend school. In one of the first papers I wrote (1979), I discussed the development and existence of these kinds of fostering strategies in Amedzofe in relation to women working away: 'grandmother' and 'helper' kinds of fostering in effect, specifically in the light of Esther's work in Gonja, but also in the aftermath of her published work on the West Indies, where women, often single, who were working away sent their children home to be looked after by their mothers. It was only later from the early 2000s that I managed to embed these findings in a historical context.

Work with the archives of the Bremen Mission, whose missionaries built a mission station and school in Amedzofe from 1889, showed that the early missionaries, despairing of converts, spent their frugal funds on redeeming slaves (from the domestic arena), particularly children.[11] From about the 1860s onwards, these redeemed children were effectively fostered by the missionaries: fed, clothed, taught literacy and numeracy, and trained in more practical areas such as craft production, housework, sewing, and cultivation of introduced crops. Local people saw that there were advantages to training children in this way, and even if parents themselves were not inclined to join the new religion, they seem to have realized the benefits both for the children, and them too: if the children lived with the missionaries and worked for and with them, it did not cost the parents anything. The missionaries referred to these children, slave and freeborn, as '*Hauskinder*', and there were often perhaps twenty to thirty children attached to mission stations in this way. As time went on, the children grew up and many became Christians; they married and they in their turn became the 'trainers', the fosterers for new generations of children who appeared as Christianity became more pervasive, and the need to work outside of the subsistence sector became more pressing. So, an instrumental/helper version of fostering developed and flourished through the twentieth century.

The historical contexts for these arrangements for child 'care' had a further precedent (see Brydon 2007, 2009). These were relationships/domestic arrangements of pawnage that had existed – on the coast at least since the seventeenth century, and probably inland both east of the Volta (where Avatime is) and west, in states like Asante, Akwamu and Akyem – from the eighteenth century onwards. As economic, if not social, differentiation became widespread with the entrenchment of trade through the import of European goods and export of locally produced goods changing through time (cotton, palm oil, rubber, coffee and, later, cocoa), so indebtedness became a commonplace. While there were obviously seriously exploitative connotations to pawnship, pawns could also establish longer term more familial kinds of relationships (including marriage) with their creditors (ibid.). Whatever the origins and/or evolution of these kinds of relationships – of pawnage, of helper relationships including the *Hauskinder*, of crisis fostering – by the mid-twentieth century the fact of the circulation, not only of women and children, but also of boys, was unremarkable, even commonplace, throughout what became Ghana and West Africa. The perceived advantages to the children, their natal families, and the fosterers were virtually universal in the region.[12]

In 1982, Esther published the results of further work on fostering in Ghana, taking into account the areas where she had already worked and, in addition, areas in the south where, as in Avatime, new patterns of training were developing. Her report included comparative material from Creole society, from the West Indies, and from West Africans in Britain. She also specifically looked at informal apprenticeships, and the local patterns of training in a range of craft skills that had developed in what became Ghana through the twentieth century. Here a child's parents sought a master or mistress with a good local reputation with whom to apprentice their children in order for them to learn a trade. The parents paid a set amount at the beginning of the apprenticeship, the child lived with, worked for and learned from the master/mistress for the duration of the apprenticeship, and at the end of the term the parents paid another amount. I know from my own survey work that the sums involved up to the middle years of the twentieth century involved payments in kind and relatively little cash (that is, they were affordable to many rural families); more recently, and particularly in Accra, these informal apprenticeships have become more monetized and the costs have increased.[13]

The kinds of craft skills for which informal apprenticeships existed throughout the twentieth century ranged from blacksmithing (in the early part of the century) through the skills associated with building (carpentry/joinery, masonry and brick making and laying), to those associated with motor transport (driving and repairing, referred to in Ghana as 'fitting'), cobbling (shoe repairing), tailoring (boys) and seamstress–ing (girls), and cooking/stewarding for both boys and girls. In addition, girls might learn baking (bread and cakes) for sale. With time, the relevance of some skills dwindled, but others gained importance (painting and decorating; sign-writing; hairdressing/barbering), and the last forty years or so has seen informal training in occupations such as electricians, plumbers, refrigeration, air-conditioning engineers, mobile phone and computer repairers, and even cake decorators.[14] Amedzofe, and Avatime, people have taken advantage of this array of informally accessible occupations, in addition to the white-collar work based on their church derived literacy (mainly teaching). Many trained in these skills through the twentieth century, spending time away from the villages when they were younger or in their middle years, but tending to return to the villages when they were older, to retire and take their places in family and village hierarchies and daily life. The 1970s to 1990s in particular saw a huge growth in housebuilding on the outskirts of the existing village and in the Christian section as returning migrants built houses for their retirement.

Through the twentieth century, Amedzofe and Avatime people's training opportunities tended to be organized by families and depended on the references and recommendations about the skills, competences and good character of the 'masters' from either relatives or the families of people they knew well. Parents approached a master or mistress directly and saw where their children would live and work. Conditions of service were set and agreed by both parents and master together, and, in any case, distances were not great. This, perhaps rose-tinted and rather cosy image of child training and child labour in twentieth-century Ghana is not grossly overstated, at least for the first three-quarters of the century. But the economic crisis in the 1980s, the effects of the World Bank and IMF economic stringency measures, in conjunction with the huge upsurge in international migration as other parts of the world were perceived to offer so many more opportunities than 'home', shifted parameters. Now the world was smaller: local towns, even Accra and Kumase, which had been the focus for Avatime people's work and training over the century were all just local, and subject to the same constraints and economic stringencies as 'home', where opportunities were perceived to be few and far between. Ghana, and

Avatime, had had a taste of what might be on offer in the wider world in the rush to Nigeria after the discovery of oil there in the late 1970s. Avatime joined thousands of other Ghanaians who went to find money by practising their skills, both as artisans and as teachers, in Nigeria through the latter part of the 1970s and into the 1980s. But they also experienced the problems of stranger-hood, of being 'aliens', in feeling the effects of Nigeria's draconian expulsion order in the early part of 1983. But at least Avatime were not subject to the worst horrors of the journey back from Nigeria as Togo closed its borders. As Ewe (the *lingua franca* of southern Togo) speakers, at least bilingually, they could pretend they were Togolese, cross Togo and filter across the Togo/Ghana borders along bush paths (Brydon 1985). As the effects of structural adjustment began to bite through the 1980s, many moved away again, some back to Nigeria, but others further afield. A significant African destination for Avatime was Sierra Leone (before the civil wars), and the South African Bantustans also drew in Ghanaian migrants.

The search for work and money took Ghanaians out of Africa, to Europe (Holland, Germany and Britain, primarily), to the USA and Canada, but also to the Middle East and Libya where there was demand for labourers in the con-struction and oil industries, and for skilled workers such as nurses. Esther's work in the late 1970s and early 1980s (see Goody 1982) showed how young Ghanaians, mainly students studying and working to support themselves in Britain, had their children fostered by British families, mostly around London. There were occasional newspaper headlines through the 1970s commenting on the shock and distress of the British foster-parents as Ghanaian (and other West African) parents reclaimed their children to go back to Ghana with them once they had obtained their qualifications and gained some work experience. Understandably, the British press (and British fosterers) did not understand what were effectively Ghanaian norms of fostering: the idea that 'their' foster children were following a long-established pattern, albeit a geographically extended one, whereby at the appropriate time the West African families wanted to go 'home' with their children, with all their newfound skills and knowledge and capacities for earning, in order to make good in Ghana.

These kinds of patterns where children are fostered in a host country while parents are working and studying, attending classes and working night shifts, may still exist. More recently, however, the extended search by many more Ghanaians for work overseas has seen young Ghanaians leaving small children behind in Ghana, and perhaps sending any children born to Ghanaian parents in host countries back to Ghana to be fostered; First World childcare costs and no access to family care from grandmothers and aunts, makes fostering in Ghana a cost-effective option. This is the kind of fostering/childcare arrange-ment that Esther wrote about as the 'West Indian model' in her own work, through the 1970s and 1980s.[15]

While those left behind or sent back might desperately want to join their parents, and communication revolutions in phones and internet mean that they can talk to (and see) their parents, their lives are embedded in Ghana, and in Ghanaian cultures. Their aspirations and their views about life 'abroad' are probably not different from those with local parents whose lives are entirely focused in Ghana and who dream of going abroad at some point in the future. I suspect that what happens now is that poorer, first-generation Ghanaian migrants, or perhaps students, leave their children at home or send them back, as outlined above, while the wealthier migrants keep their children with them and raise them wherever they are. The overseas children grow up with some Ghanaian language skills, depending on the assiduity and embeddedness of parents in overseas communities, and with some knowledge of cultures and histories. But the overseas children straddle cultures and classes, and a new and vast range of cultural hybridities is emerging. Within Ghana the 'old' practices and ideas about fostering to help a single relative, or to learn/train as an apprentice to help themselves and their families, still do have relevance, but transnational migration on a large scale has expanded and begun to create a whole new bubble of possibilities and dreams.

Meanwhile, in Ghana and in West Africa through the last, say, quarter of the twentieth century, new and what might be called attenuated patterns and practices of fostering were emerging, and it is these that have given rise to what we see in the West as the vicious practices of child labour/slavery in the cocoa industry and more broadly. Whether we can call these practices 'fostering' in the sense intended by Esther when she wrote so extensively about the care elements and positive advantages of fostering is a moot point. Knowledge of these practices first came to non-specialist Western notice towards the end of the 1990s in relation to cocoa cultivation, where boys from Sahel countries like Mali and Niger were brought through 'agents'/traffickers to work on cocoa farms, mainly in the south of the Ivory Coast, largely without pay and in poor conditions. However, initial concerns in this field seem to have been confined largely to activist NGOs, although there have subsequently been much more widespread efforts to mitigate, if not eradicate, the malpractices. But it was the case of Victoria Climbié that made horrific headline news in February 2000 in Britain that indicated a new twist to fostering kinds of relationships. Victoria, using the name and passport of another child from the same Ivorian village, Anna Kouao, was brought to Britain via France, probably early in 1999, to live with an 'aunt', a cousin of her father, to go to school, to help the aunt and eventually to get a job to help her parents and siblings at home – a version of the 'helper' kind of fostering, perhaps. But the aunt and her partner inflicted horrific abuse on the child and she died, emaciated and beaten, in February 2000.

Even this notorious case of fostering gone badly wrong, with the relationships, rights and obligations skewed out of all recognition, is recognizable as a fostering relationship in the 'common' West African sense.[16] Cases such as the cocoa 'slaves' and that of the *Etireno*, the ship ostensibly full of children bound for Gabon from Cotonou in early 2001 (Brydon, 2001), demonstrate even less recognizable versions of the circulation of children in West Africa. Key differences in the case of the cocoa slaves and of the *Etireno*'s children are distance (whether geographical or in terms of social barriers) and the development of a class of 'middle' people, brokering deals with parents about their children's life chances, safety and development. Parents no longer know, even by repute, the 'masters' to whom their children are sent, and there can be no easy familial redress where distances are great.

So, in the second decade of the twenty-first century, the practice that was core to Esther's early fieldwork, 'the circulation of women and children' drawn from her Gonja experience, has continued, albeit changed, developed, adapted; it has also been twisted and turned out of all recognition, been wrenched inside out to become, in some cases, a travesty of itself. We can trace the trajectory of fostering's developments within Ghana through the latter part of the twentieth century, in the continuation of the old kin and 'helper' versions of fostering; in the existence of the massively increasing array of informal apprenticeships now becoming more monetized and 'formal' as different economic factors pound Ghana's societies; in the 'West Indian' pattern of fostering I saw in Amedzofe in the 1970s, where migrant parents send children to their home villages and small towns as the best option for both them and their children's future, a pattern that still continues; in the new transnational versions of this West Indian pattern of fostering, mediated by new communications systems; and finally trafficking, whether for domestic or agricultural work in Africa, or for domestic or sex work overseas. All of these have different implications for family patterns and relationships on the ground, both there and here, depending on vantage point.

It was only when I came to think about this chapter that I realized how much I had piggybacked on Esther Goody's original ideas in my own work over the years, in terms of the insights, detail and clarity with which she elucidated a particular set of practices and its spin-offs in the latter half of the twentieth century. In my own work I have looked at gendered impacts of work in relation to fostering and at new patterns of family organization, at least in the 1970s. Gender and migration, and their relationship to novel family patterns in particular in relation to childcare, have long been key interests. But I have also tried to contextualize fostering and childcare patterns in relation to the history of Amedzofe and Avatime as I have come to know it, in terms of institutions such as pawnship, and looked at the impact of Christianity and introduced ways of working on gaining livelihoods. More generally, I have suggested that contemporary child trafficking in and from West Africa can be interpreted as a kind of cancerous offshoot of fostering/training relationships.

But there are still many more questions radiating from the nexus of family relationships and the differential impacts of wildly changing social and economic factors that can be asked and investigated, and these issues have a firm place in future research. What are the relationships between fundamental Christianity and child trafficking, particularly with respect to the fear shown by (mainly) young African sex workers in Europe of mystical threats both to themselves and their families back home? And there are questions in relation to

transnational movement and the care of children in relation to cultural identities and hybridities that need to be asked. Closer to home, and relating to my
own ethnographic perspective, it is noticeable that Amedzofe/Avatime
migrants now often keep their children with them when they work away in
Ghana (the dwindling of the 'West Indian' pattern, at least within a Ghanaian
context?), so such children have much less chance of learning about the place.
The connections afforded by fostering young children in the village in the 1970s
are being severed, the creation of a next generation of Avatime who know the
place and its peculiarities as home, as well as the worlds outside of the village,
is just not happening. In spite of a common language and the pull of relationships and family celebrations 'at home', many come very irregularly and stay for
a very short time; retiring at home, a prominent ambition in the 1970s, seems
to have fallen down the agenda of the elderly. They prefer to stay in the urban
areas where they have worked, and where, now, their children are also probably
working. The meaning of 'home' has also shifted.

Lynne Brydon studied with Esther Goody at Cambridge between 1969 and
1976. She moved to the Centre of West African Studies in Birmingham in 1996,
which she headed in 2006–8. Between 1991 and 2001 she worked with col-
leagues at the Institute of African Studies, University of Ghana, Legon and
Fourah Bay University (Sierra Leone) under the British Council Links Scheme.
Her publications include *Women in the Third World*, with Sylvia Chant (Talyor
& Francis [1989] 1993), and *Adjusting Society: The World Bank, the IMF and
Ghana*, with Karen Legge (Bloomsbury 1996).

Notes

1. My first PhD supervisor, before Esther, was Meyer Fortes, and he could not stress enough
   the importance of ethnography. I paraphrase from a pre-fieldwork letter he wrote to me,
   'Always focus on the ethnographic perspective'.
2. From the same letter from Meyer, this time I remember the exact words (how could I
   forget them?): 'Dear Lynne, I have received and read with interest your research proposal
   and I am bound to express the hope that once you get into the field it will dissipate into
   a forgotten exercise...' And this about a week before I boarded a ship for Ghana.
3. Russian missionaries affiliated to the Wycliffe Bible Translators, and who speak neither
   English nor Avatime, are now working on the Avatime language: further fuel to my post-
   retirement ire.
4. If anyone is interested enough to want more information here, please contact me.
5. My perspective here is obviously bottom up: I am aware of the Marxist material on the
   exploitative nature of colonial rule, but the view from Amedzofe people, almost uniformly, was that they wanted 'to work to get money'.
6. The classic work here is Polly Hill (1963), but see also Gareth Austin (2005) for an introduction to this literature.
7. It was mainly men who moved at this time; if women went away it tended to be as wives
   or as teachers.
8. Until 1957, the vast majority of the area that became the Volta Region was administra-
   tively separate from what was the Gold Coast. Until the outbreak of the First World War

it was the German Colony of Togoland, and thereafter Trans-Volta Togoland, initially Mandated Territory of the League of Nations, and after the Second World War, Trust Territory of the United Nations.

9. Please see my thesis (1976) Chapter VI for a full and rather laboured discussion of differences between Ward's work and my findings.

10. Esther came to visit me once in the field; she was amazed, she said, that for so many children in the village going to school was the norm.

11. I first worked in Bremen in 1982 and have been working on the material from there since then: I read/translate German very slowly.

12. For a description of an exploitative patron/client, or, possibly, pawnship relationship, see also Coe 2010.

13. See, for example, Edwards 1997.

14. I am not going to comment here on the gendering of these skills, except to say that there were always more opportunities for boys than girls. For an early perspective on this, see Alison MacEwan Scott 1986.

15. See Goody, E. N., 1970, 1971, 1973 and 1975.

16. See also the interview given by Victoria Climbié's mother to the *Daily Mail* in 2008, explaining the prevalence of the practice and the ordinariness of it, in the face of accusations of blame from some quarters of the press and public during the inquiry that followed the case (Harding 2008).

References

Austin, Gareth. 2005. *Labour, Land and Capital in Ghana: From Slavery to Free Labour in Asante, 1807–1956*. Rochester, NY: Rochester University Press.

Bowen, Elenore Smith. 1954. *Return to Laughter*. London: Victor Gollancz.

Brydon, Lynne. 1976. 'Status Ambiguity in Amedzofe–Avatime: Men and Women in a Changing Patrilineal Society'. Unpublished PhD thesis, University of Cambridge.

_____ . 1979. 'Women at Work: Some Changes in Family Structure in Amedzofe–Avatime'. *Africa* 49(2): 97–111.

_____ . 1985. 'Ghanaian Responses to the Nigerian Expulsions of 1983'. *African Affairs* 84(337): 561–85.

_____ . 2001. 'Slavery and Labour in West Africa'. *Review of African Political Economy* 28(87): 137–40.

_____ . 2007. 'Extensions of Extended Families: A Case Study from Avatime, Ghana'. Working Paper no 1, *MEBAO*.wp01.pdf.

_____ . 2009. 'After Slavery What Next? Productive Relations in Early Twentieth Century Krepe and Beyond', in Toyin Falola and Matt Childs (eds), *The Changing Worlds of Atlantic Africa: Essays in Honor of Robin Law*. Durham, NC: Carolina Academic Press, pp. 479–96.

Coe, Cati. 2010. 'Domestic Violence and Child Circulation in the Southeastern Gold Coast, 1905–1928', in Emily Burrill, Richard Roberts and Elizabeth Thornberry (eds), *Domestic Violence and the Law in Colonial and Postcolonial Africa*. Athens, OH: Ohio University Press, pp. 54–73.

Edwards, Susan Teresa. 1997. 'Yeepam Fatawo: We Sew and It Fits You: The Social and Cultural Context of Small-Scale Enterprise in the Tailoring and Dressmaking Sector of Southern Ghana'. Unpublished PhD thesis, University of Hull (Department of Sociology).

Epstein, Arnold L. (ed.). 1967. *The Craft of Social Anthropology*. London: Tavistock.

Goody, Esther N. 1970. 'Kinship Fostering in Gonja: Deprivation or Advantage?' in Philip Mayer (ed.), *Socialization: The Approach from Social Anthropology*. ASA Monograph 9. London: Tavistock, pp. 51–74.

———. 1971. 'Forms of Pro–Parenthood: The Sharing and Substitution of Parental Roles', in Jack Goody (ed.), *Kinship: Selected Readings*. Harmondsworth: Penguin Readings in Sociology, pp. 331–45.

———. 1973. *Contexts of Kinship: An Essay on the Family Sociology of the Gonja of Northern Ghana*. Cambridge Studies in Social Anthropology 7. Cambridge: Cambridge University Press.

———. 1975. 'Delegation of Parental Roles in West Africa and the West Indies', in Jack Goody (ed.), *Changing Social Structures in Ghana*. London: International African Institute, pp. 137–66.

———. 1982. *Parenthood and Social Reproduction: Fostering and Occupational Roles in West Africa*. Cambridge Studies in Anthropology 35. Cambridge: Cambridge University Press.

Goody, Esther, and Jack Rankin. 1967. 'The Circulation of Women and Children in Northern Ghana'. *Man* 2(2): 226–48.

Harding, Louette. 2008. 'Victoria Climbié's Mother Speaks Out: "I am shocked that I have been attacked for what I did"'. London, *Mail Online*. Retrieved 18 October 2024 from http://www.dailymail.co.uk/home/you/article–1034908/Victoria–Climbi––8217–s–mother–speaks––8216–I–shocked–I–attacked–I–did–8217.html.

Hill, Polly. 1963. *The Migrant Cocoa Farmers of Southern Ghana: A Study in Rural Capitalism*. Cambridge: Cambridge University Press.

Scott, Alison MacEwan. 1986. 'Industrialisation, Gender Segregation and Stratification Theory', in Rosemary Crompton and Michael Mann (eds), *Gender and Stratification*. Cambridge: Polity Press, pp. 154–89.

Ward, Barbara. 1950. 'Some Notes on Migration from Togoland', *African Affairs* 49: 129–35.

———. 1955. 'An Analysis of the Distribution of Population in a Town in British Togo', *Man* 55(43): 35–39.

Antioch College yearbook portrait of Esther Newcomb, ca. 1952.
© Goody Family Archive.

Esther Goody during her first fieldwork in northern Ghana in 1956.
© Esther Newcomb Goody Archive (photograph Jack Goody).

Esther Goody with her daughters, Ghana, 1965. © Esther Newcomb Goody
Archive (photograph Jack Goody).

Esther and Jack Goody in California, late 1970s. © Goody Family Archive.

Esther Goody on a walk with friends in south-west France, 1980s.
© Goody Family Archive (photograph Jack Goody).

Esther and Jack Goody in Japan, 1980s. © Goody Family Archive.

Esther Goody working at the Goody's house in Lacapelle, Lot, southwest France, 1980s. © Esther Newcomb Goody Archive (photograph Jack Goody).

Esther Goody visiting local LLIL project teachers in Baale, northern Ghana, 2000s. © Esther Newcomb Goody Archive.

Esther Goody with her daughter-in-law Ranjana Goody, Hatfield Broad Oak, Hertfordshire, June 2016. © Goody Family Archive.

5

Video, Voice and Vygotsky
Narratives of Learning among the Konkomba of Northern Ghana

Alicia Fentiman

Introduction

This chapter is based on ethnographic field research carried out among the Konkomba of Northern Ghana. The research discussed here was a component of a larger comparative research project developed by Esther Goody on 'Roles of Authority and Learning in Northern Ghana',[1] during which I was her research officer for two years. The first phase of the project design documented and compared informal learning in two egalitarian and two hierarchical societies.[2] The key research questions of the project were: Are hierarchy and authority at the level of polity and community related to modes of informal learning? What are the informal modes of learning related to the effective learning of adult role skills?

The two hierarchical studies in the research were the Gonja (Goody) and the Wala (Bennett). The two egalitarian studies were the Birifor (Goody) and the Konkomba (Fentiman). Detailed ethnographic work was carried out in all four societies, and ethnographic accounts and extensive video recordings were made. The marked difference in status between egalitarian and hierarchical societies provided a framework for comparing the influence of status and its expression of institutionalized patterns of authority amongst the four ethnic groups (see e.g. J. and E. Goody 1967; E. Goody 1990 and 1991).

The second phase of the project was to examine the patterns of learning and authority in the classroom. However, the original research design was altered to look specifically at effective learning in primary schools in northern Ghana through a controlled comparison of the effects of initial literacy in the child's own language and initial literacy in English for effective learning in primary school. An article based on Phase Two of the research was published in *The Making of Literate Societies* (Goody and Bennett 2001: 178–200). This chapter, however, is based exclusively on the research carried out in Phase One of the project, and examines the comparative data between the two acephalous societies: the Birifor and the Konkomba. The aim is to shed light on the informal modes of learning of adult roles among children in these two societies.

Theoretical Background of the Research Study

The theoretical basis of the research study derived from Goody's earlier work on the role of status in determining the ways in which questions were asked and understood (Goody 1978). In 1974, Goody undertook field research in Daboya, the capital of one of the subregions of the Kingdom of Gonja. She experienced and observed firsthand how apprentice weavers mastered the skills of weaving that had been transmitted over generations. During this period, she noted two themes that were central to the learning of weaving. First, the work of apprentices was a major factor in the production of cloth. Each master adapts the ways tasks within the weaving process are assigned so as to make effective use of the level of skill and experience of particular apprentices. She observed that as an apprentice became more and more skilled they would take on more responsibility until they became master weavers themselves (Goody 1982). As an apprentice, Goody recollected, 'I tried to model my behaviour on that of the boys and youths working around me. So I had to inhibit my own constant urge to ask why, how, where?'

It was this experience that led her to the fundamental observation that none of the apprentices asked questions of the master weaver. She observed that the apprentices questioned each other but did not address questions to their master. The analysis of this data enabled her to see that the meaning of questions was embedded in the relative status of questioner and respondent. In her seminal work *Towards a Theory of Questions*, she noted that an apprentice could never ask the master a question merely to obtain information because it would be perceived as challenging his master's authority (Goody 1978). Her ethnographic observations of how apprentices learned in Daboya provided the foundation for her academic interest in the differences between hierarchical and egalitarian political systems (Goody 1972). This also provided the link between kinds of questioning and their relationship to status and power. She observed that there was a bar on apprentices asking questions of their seniors. This sparked her theoretical interest in asking whether there was a link between authority and learning. Her extensive ethnographic fieldwork among the Gonja (hierarchical) and the Birfor (egalitarian) provided the initial framework to examine the striking differences in status between hierarchical and egalitarian societies, and to research the influence of status and institutionalized patterns of authority. This was then expanded to include other ethnographic examples.

During the course of the research project, the activity and practice view of learning was primarily based on the work of Vygotsky and his colleagues (Vygotsky 1962, 1978; Luria 1979; Cole 1971, 1985, 1998; Wertsch 1985; Moll 1990). Vygotsky argued that performance (with the support of experts) precedes competence, and refers to the 'space' between what a child can do with support (performance) and what a child can do unassisted (competence); this is defined as the zone of proximal development. Cole interpreted Vygotsky's definition of the 'zone of proximal development' as the difference between a child's 'actual development as determined by independent problem solving' and the higher level of 'potential development as determined through problem solving under adult guidance or in collaboration with more capable peers' (Cole 1985).

The interpretation of this view is that skills are first encountered as a child participates with others in her sociocultural world, and this was grounded in Goody's thinking. She wrote: 'This approach views learning as the product of an activity carried out in a social context, … jointly with an "expert"'. She explained that this does not necessarily need to be a teacher, but it may be a peer or a parent. This creates the basis for internalizing its component skills and meanings. The expert initially carries out the task before the child joins in, taking over more and more difficult aspects. Eventually the child can take on responsibility for the whole task. The 'zone of proximal development' refers to the area in which the child understands to a varying degree through participating with an expert, but in which the child is not yet ready to carry out the process independently. Cole supports this view by explaining that Vygotsky and his students observed the actual processes by which children came to adopt the role of adults in culturally organized activities. Lave and Wenger (1991) also discuss the importance of 'situated learning' in which, she argues, learning occurs in the *function* of the activity, context and culture in which it occurs. The next section provides a brief overview of Konkomba society which helps to explain the culturally specific context of the narratives discussed below.

The Konkomba of Northern Ghana

I spent over two years conducting ethnographic research amongst the Konkomba in northern Ghana. I lived in one of the traditional compounds in a remote rural village, and immersed myself into the everyday life of the people. I stayed in a mud hut within the confines of a large compound comprising over twenty people. It consisted of the elder of the village and his four wives and ten children, and his senior son, his wife and four children. This multigenerational household was an ideal place to observe interaction between household members and to participate in daily activities. Fortunately, there were excellent ethnographic studies already carried out amongst the Konkomba (Tait 1953, 1958, 1961; and Froehlich 1954) that supplied a good background and understanding of the politico-jural relationships, kinship structures, religious beliefs, and economic activities. These provided an ethnographic foundation on which to build while undertaking my own detailed research. As a female anthropologist I was able to record and observe gender specific rites and rituals that neither Tait nor Froehlich had experienced or recorded. This was especially important when it came to observing childbirth, marriage rites and death rituals. However, I was fortunate to be allowed access to all rituals in the community, and I was given permission to document, photograph and videorecord all activities. This provided the basis for understanding the local and domestic authority roles, which were central to our study.

The Konkomba are a patrilineal, acephalous ethnic group, and they lack any form of centralized or hierarchical government. Roles of authority are based on age. Elders are treated with respect and deference by their junior counterparts. The oldest male in the village is the *unikpel*, and he is regarded as the 'head' of the community. He and his council of elders (the male heads of the compounds) meet and collectively discuss and decide on matters concerning the village. Two of the most important rituals among the Konkomba are the *obua* (known as second burials, when the cause of death of a member of the community is revealed by soothsaying) and the *libawol* (indigenous beliefs, which involve sacrifices to the shrines and ancestors). These rituals are also in the hands of the male elders. These rituals are important for social cohesion among clan members, many of whom are dispersed. The only sacred position that does not necessarily go to an elder is the position of the *untindaa* (owner of the Earth shrine). This ritual position is exclusive to the Konkombas living in the Saboba area, which is regarded as their traditional homeland. Konkombas who have migrated outside the area do not have the position of *untindaa* in their villages because they are not the 'owners' of the land. They do, however, have village shrines to protect them. They have a unique marriage system in which they practise infant betrothal. Female infants are betrothed at birth to a clan member. In return, the prospective 'husband' and his clan have to perform a series of rituals and services, including economic activities over fifteen years or more. It is a long and binding courtship between clans rather than individuals.

The Konkomba reside predominantly in north-eastern Ghana, straddling the border with Togo. Their homeland is Saboba, but they have migrated extensively throughout the northern region, into the Volta and Brong Ahafo regions, mainly in search of arable farmland. They are predominantly rural, subsistence farmers, and they are known to be hardworking, industrious and devoted to their farming activities. Their lives revolve around the rural environment. The main cash crops are yams, guinea corn, maize and groundnuts. Yams are the most economically fruitful crop. Other crops are grown for 'soup' ingredients such as chilies, beans, vegetables and herbs. In addition, the Konkomba are known as 'fearless warriors'. The men employ a variety of violent methods in fighting, and women often support them during fights by praising them and reciting stories of courageous ancestors; they also supply water and encouragement. Within this context, it can help us to understand the social norms, attitudes and social roles of what it means to be an adult in Konkomba society.

Methodology

The main methods of data collection in the comparative study were qualitative in nature, and included participant observation, in depth interviews, and the use of videorecordings.[3] In the first phase of the study (1990–92), Goody and I systematically observed and made videorecords of the settings (i.e. places for situations) where activities took place among five designated domains in the villages: work activities, domestic activities, dispute settlement, rituals and play. Video was used as a major tool to ensure later comparability of material, and to check observer reliability. A major focus of the research was to look at the 'learning' settings – the contexts in which informal learning[4] took place.

A key reason for designing the study around the use of videorecords was to facilitate an objective comparison between the societies. It was intended that the video data from each society would provide systematic records of situated behaviour. A format was devised by Goody and me for observations, video-recordings and basic ethnographies. Most of the observation was directed at what seemed important in the daily life going on around us. These opportunistic observations led to an insight into what was perhaps the underlying problem in understanding the informal learning of adult roles. The key question we wanted to answer was: How does the child select from her/his environment those elements out of which adult role skills are constructed? An important empirical question was to ask whether the activities we recorded were goal orientated and what levels of awareness the children had of this process.

An additional component of the original research proposal was to return to the communities, show them the videos, and gather their views and perspectives of the tasks being performed. Unfortunately, due to escalating ethnopolitical conflict in the region during my field research it was not possible for me to return to the communities until several years later.[5] However, during recent research visits (2017, 2019), I returned to the field and revisited the village I had worked in, and I showed the videos to some of the participants/actors who took part in the original films. Their voices are also included in the analysis, as discussed further in the chapter.

Narratives of Learning

This section provides examples of narratives of everyday activities that depict how Konkomba children learn adult roles through participating in everyday activities. I have selected two activities that we deemed important for our understanding of the roles for comparability. These activities captured in the videos[6] provide an insight in how children 'learn' adult roles by taking part in both work and play activities. Goody documented some of her findings from her work among the Birifor, and these are discussed and compared with the Konkomba data further on in the chapter.

Figure 5.1. Children and young adults carrying sand for building construction, Kachilinde Village, Kpandai, Ghana, April 1992. © Alicia Fentiman.

Women and Children at the Farm Peeling Cassava as a Work Activity

The first video[7] shows a group of women and a wide age range of children at Tabwor's farm, approximately five kilometres from the village. The women and children are all from the same compound, and comprise Chanwein and her 4 daughters Jilima (12 years), Kumah (9 years), Yajabrum (7 years) and Mbigmabo (2 years), as well as Chanwein's co-wife Unana, her infant son Ntibi (1 year), Tali (mother-in-law to Chanwein, Tingbani and Uanana), Tingbani, and co-wife Nakool and her two daughters Nankamba (6 years) and Mbmawha (8 years). The video shows the women at the farm carrying cassava from the granary and then sitting down under a tree to peel the cassava with machetes. There is very little instruction going on, and one observes that the children know what to do. Without any prompting or instruction, the girls go to the granary to collect more cassava and then sit and help to peel it. Significantly, in the observation between mother Chanwein and her young daughter Mbigmabo, one can see a gradual learning process in motion. For example, Chanwein is sitting on the ground peeling cassava. Her daughter Jilima comes to where she is sitting and empties a bowl full of cassava, which she harvested from the farm. Significantly, Mbgimabo also tries to contribute to the pile by following her elder sister to the granary. She carries a very small piece of cassava on her head because she is very young has not yet acquired the skill, strength or coordination to carry a heavy load. Nevertheless, her 'small' contribution is included with the larger pieces of cassava. The significant point in this clip is that Mbigmabo wants to help and take part, and she is combining this 'work activity' with playful gestures. More importantly, she is not asked to do this, but merely wants to participate with the others.

Further on in the video, Mbigmabo joins her mother and picks up a knife. She tries to peel a small piece of cassava without success. She then says, 'Mother, help me peel it'. Her mother takes the knife from her young daughter and helps her to peel off some of the skin of the cassava, and then hands the knife and piece of cassava back to her daughter to continue with peeling. Mbigmabo does not really have the strength, and she struggles with the knife and the peeling. After a while, she hands it back to her mother so her mother can finish peeling it. What is significant to note is that the mother takes the time and has the patience to aid her young daughter in this work activity. She does not get angry or cross with her for interrupting her during this busy time of food preparation. The mother knows that she cannot peel it properly, but instead of discouraging her she encourages her to attempt to peel it. Afterwards, Mbigmabo gets up and places a pan on her head, she starts shouting 'kaya'. Interestingly, she is imitating women hawkers who carry baskets on their heads with items for sale throughout the markets and street shouting 'kaya, kaya'. Mbigmabo is playing at imitating the hawkers. Later in the video Chanwein's older daughters (Jilima-, Yajabrum and Kumah) continue peeling the mound of cassava with ease. Then other participants enter the farm.

Figure 5.2. Konkomba women and children at the farm peeling cassava, Kachilinde Village, Kpandai, Ghana, March 1992.
© Alicia Fentiman.

Nakool's two daughters appear at the farm, and Nankamba joins the group, picks up a knife and begins peeling the cassava. No one instructed her to do it, she just did it on her own initiative. This is important because there is no leader in this activity. It is not hierarchical in terms of one person in charge. The women and children participate in this group activity according to their skills and abilities collectively. Another important observation is to see how quickly children acquire skills. Two sisters, Nankamba and Mbamawah, are about two years apart in age, however their work skills and abilities vary considerably. As Nankamba peels the cassava her younger sister holds a knife and tries to peel the cassava. She gives up and then starts to play with the knife. For quite a while the knife is in her mouth. Although she is surrounded by older children and women, no one takes the knife from the young girl.

Participants Voices

The video described above was shown to two of the participants in the video. Jilima (who was a teenager in the video) and is now a mother of three children living in Accra. She remarked:

> You see, there is very little teaching/instruction going on in the video. As you can see in the video, the children learn by observing and participating, no one tells them to do anything. Look at me! I am a young girl of 11 years and I am carrying cassava from the farm and then I sit and start peeling it. If you watch and listen carefully, no one is telling my sisters [or] me what to do. We just do it and we take the initiative. We do what we can based on our strength; we want to be like our mothers. The activities in our daily life become such a routine that you just know what to do, whether it be at the farm with our mothers and kin members or other domestic chores in the compound. For example, as you have seen in our village when you lived with us, we wake up, we sweep, we light the fire and then we go to fetch water. This is what every girl does every day – no one will instruct her to do it; she just does it. If you go to the bore hole, you will see children of all ages going to fetch water, even a very small girl will go with her own small pot to carry the water. She just follows the others and, as she grows, she will be able to carry more and more water based on her physical strength. In Konkomba society, we learn by doing not by being told what to do. We just know what to do. It is instinctive. If my father says he is going to cut guinea corn at the farm, we know that we should carry our pans to collect the guinea corn; he does not tell us to get the pan, we just know what to do. I look at what I was capable of doing when I was a young girl in the video. My daughter is a similar age that I was in the video, but she is in the city [Accra] going to school. She is exposed to a different type of learning – being told what to do and when to do it – in the classroom. If you look [at] how hard we worked in the village it is based on our physical strength and acquiring the necessary skills to survive. The food we are preparing is for our own subsistence, and any surplus will be sold in the market. From a very young age, we are learning very important skills that will help us in our

society. We had very little, and we worked hard. Children in the city do not suffer like we did back in the village. My daughter cannot do what I did at her age. I knew all the skills that were necessary to be a hard-working adolescent and to be a Konkomba woman. The skills I learnt then as a child are the skills that help me now in my business as a yam trader at the Konkomba market in Accra. These skills are not taught through a book or a teacher; they [were aquired] by watching and learning from my mother, my grandmother, my peers and the other women in my village. These are the skills that are so important in being a Konkomba woman.

Mbigmabo, who is the two-year-old girl in the video, also commented on the video. She lives in Accra and is currently at university. When I asked her what she thought of the video, she replied:

Childhood is a time when you are not mature or sophisticated enough to realize that the way you are acting, disturbing, moving up and down [is] all unguided. It is exciting watching these videos at the moment; it gives me an idea of where I came from and how far I have come. It makes me wonder what life would have been like if I had not been brought to Accra by my [eldest] sister. Seeing myself with no clothes on at my father's farm, without a care in the world, makes me imagine the kind of lifestyle I would be having if I had stayed in the village! The recollection of my childhood days through the video reminds me of some of the family members who are still in the village, and it also gives me the opportunity to see some of the kin members that have died. By watching the video, it shows me how united our extended family was. The extended family (all those who lived in my father's compound) used to come together to work collectively; they would all contribute until the tasks were completed, as shown at the farm. I am really touched at seeing my mother, my older sister Jilima and sisters; they are all working so hard at the farm without shirts [or] sandals, with their children there. Imagine, I was only 2 years old and I am holding a machete trying to peel cassava! I really wanted to help and participate in the activity with the other women, but I did not have the strength to do it. I can imagine that it was not easy for them but they endured it, and that shows how determined they were. Growing up there as a child made me learn a lot, such as being a hard-working and truthful person. In my village, both young and old are working hard to survive and trying to make a living. This is instilled in me and is really helping me now.

Video 2: Play Activities

Another activity that I observed frequently during my fieldwork was child's play (Piaget, 1951). I often spent several hours watching and videorecording children playing. Many of the activities in play were based on real-life activities. It was fascinating to see how children, male and female, performed activities according to their gender. The division of labour according to sex was inherent in many of the play activities. The following two examples highlight these roles. The first shows girls play cooking, and the second shows children at play performing traditional dancing and drumming.

Girls Play Cooking

This video[8] shows a group of children – Bakamfu (6 years) and Maadi (7 years), Kumah (9 years) holding her sister Mbigmabo (2 years), and Nankamba (4 years) – sitting outside the compound near a tree and the girls are play cooking. The girls are imitating the various activities associated with cooking: collecting firewood, preparing a fire, blowing the embers, pounding ingredients, stirring, tasting the soup for salt, adding water, and sweeping up after food preparation. The parents have gone to the market and these young children have been left behind at the homestead, and they are being looked after by an older sibling. In the video, one of the children decides to go and fetch firewood – she says, 'You need to add firewood to your fire so I will go to the bush and collect some for you'. She goes to the side of the tree and gathers some small branches. A more senior child, Kumah, says to Nalison, 'Stop what you are doing, let me show you, this is the fish that I will put into your soup'. The firewood is put onto the make-believe fire and Kuma instructs the young girl how to place it well. Then, she says, 'Now move away from that place because Bakamfu is going to pound fufu. This is my pestle and mortar and I will now pound the fufu'. Nalison is summoned, and Kumah says you are strong so you must come and pound the fufu. Then another of the children decides to sweep and keep the area of the 'compound' clean and neat. The interesting point about this 'play' activity and dialogue is that the children who are playing are not yet capable of performing these adult tasks in the household. However, they do imitate what they have observed what their mothers, older sisters, and other women perform in the real-life kitchen.

The video clips show Konkomba girls' learning of occupational roles through play, imitation and modelling. They are constructing a pretend world in which they are women performing important adult skills. In a second example of girls play cooking outside a compound, the young girls have built a proper *ifaku* (a cooking area) by arranging three stones on the ground and then placing the firewood they collected on top. In this instance, the 'pretend fire' becomes a real fire when an older girl goes into her mother's cooking area and comes back with lit charcoal, which is then placed on top of the branches. The girls then spend time blowing at the charcoal to make it flame; this is exactly what their mothers would do. It is also interesting to note that each of the girls has her own cooking area, like their mothers have within the compound. In the polygamous compounds, each wife has her own hearth and kitchen area. The girls then prepare the soup ingredients, put the soup on the fire, and pound fufu with a pestle and mortar. Once they have finished the food preparation, the food is distributed as it would be in the compound. One bowl is given to the boys and the other to the girls. They never share a bowl – the food is served separately according to gender. Mothers scaffold the learning of cooking tasks for girls. In the play kitchens that are located outside the compound, the girls practise tasks they have never performed in the household. In scaffolding in role play there is no expert, and both authority and risk are minimized while children are practising real-life skills and skill development.

Play at Rituals: Young Boys Drumming; Girls and Boys Singing and Dancing

Eleven children from two compounds are sitting under a large mango tree.[9] The boys and girls are singing and dancing the *kenatschun*, a dance that is a Konkomba tradition at funerals and celebrations. The oldest boy in the group is drumming using a broken metal bucket with sticks, while the boys are dancing and the girls are singing, clapping and dancing. They are imitating the dance movements and singing the traditional Konkomba songs that they perform at funerals. The dance movements are also prescribed by gender. Boys dance in a particular way and then compete with each other to show who has the most stamina and endurance.

The spatial aspect of play was also significant. Most of the girls would play very close to the compound, whereas boys tended to venture further afield because they normally go out hunting for rodents and birds and looking after livestock.

Comparison with Goody's Work on the Birifor

The Birifor, like the Konkomba, are acephalous and predominantly farmers. In one of Goody's earlier papers on the Birifor she starts with a question – What is the nature of learning adult roles skills in a small-scale preliterate society? (Goody 1991) Goody collected extensive ethnographic data and videorecordings of a number of similar activities of work and play in the village of Baale. A paper was published on her initial findings (Goody 1993). Unfortunately, a significant amount of the data from this archive of Phase One has never been published. However, a few unpublished papers provide an insight into her research. During a workshop in 1992, Goody presented a paper and a selection of video clips from her research in Baale on informal learning.[10]

I have extracted two of the examples she describes, which make interesting comparisons with the Konkomba data cited above. The first is a work activity and the second is a play activity.

Work Activity: Young Boy with His Father Hoeing

Goody shows a video of Sei, a four-year-old boy who has followed his father to a farm where he is hoeing. She describes the situation:

[#3.] Sei is intent on managing the
large hoe so he can dig earth
with his father.

[#7.] These tiny kitchens behind Bisen
Yir are used each evening by three
girls (8, 9 and 10 years old) to
cook minute portions of porridge
and soup which they share with
their 'husbands'.

Figure 5.3. Sei Hoeing/Tiny kitchens: Esther Goody's Baale fieldwork video stills, ca. 1990. © Esther Newcomb Goody Archive.

Four-year-old Sei follows his father everywhere, often to his annoyance. One morning when his father was hoeing earth for building, I noticed Sei had found himself a hoe and was also silently scraping up earth. Although his father apparently ignores Sei, he works around him, and doesn't disturb his intense concentration. Sei's earth is included, without comment, in the final pile. Even at this early age, being allowed to use a hoe and being able to use it, are emblems of being 'like father', and thus of masculinity. What is very clear from this role is that Sei is concentrating intently on managing the hoe, planning the direction of his work in relation to his father's path, and not particularly interested in his father's approval or attention. It is the task itself that fascinates him – though obviously the task is inseparable from his father's role.

If we compare this work activity with the first video clip of the Konkomba material described above, it is very similar in the way Mbigmabo (2 years) was at the farm with her mother. She was holding a machete and trying desperately to help; although her contribution to the pile of cassava was very small, nevertheless it was included. The young girl was trying to be 'like her mother' and the other girls and women performing the task.

Girls Play Cooking

Goody provides an example of 'play cooking', when a group of young girls 'cook' soup against the outer wall of the compound.[11] She shows six girls from the same compound, but each one is cooking separately with her own fire and her own 'soup' ingredients, but then when the cooking is finished they go to an area to share it. Goody also presents a video on girls playing at grinding grain into flour. She shows three sisters (aged 2, 3 and 7) sharing a grinding slab, each girl with her own grinding stone, grinding according to her skill – the 2-year-old only manages to hold and push the stone intermittently, the 4-year-old understands the grinding process, and the 7-year-old has mastered the process.

The work activities described above depict situations where a child/novice participates jointly with an expert, and gradually develops the understanding and skills to carry out the tasks independently. This is defined as situational scaffolding (see Lave 1995). Whereas the play activities are not intentional or planned, they are important in providing an insight into children's own active construction of their knowledge. In play certain adult skills are focused upon and practised.

In Goody's paper, it was shown that both boys and girls were given more responsibility for progressively more complex tasks to build adult roles. For girls it was shown through the various domestic and agricultural tasks, and for the boys through tasks relating to farming and herding. Significantly, both boys and girls engaged in elaborate role play in which they performed elements of adult tasks that they had not yet performed in real situations, such as in kitchens or on farms. As Goody observed while videorecording Baale children, the process of modelling was central to girls' development of cooking skills. This was similarly true amongst the Konkomba society, as shown in the videos above. At a very young age, girls are constantly with their mothers and sisters who are engaged in daily activities of food preparation, fetching water, farming, trading, and selling things in the market. The important thing is that they are constantly watching and participating in everyday activities.

The Konkomba data of children play cooking reveal striking similarities to the data collected by Goody during her fieldwork among the Baale. The informal modes of learning that proved most effective were those in which children were highly motivated to learn adult role skills, modelled these skills in peer role play and had rich opportunities for practising them through responsible participation in adult activities. The effectiveness of this mode lies in the way these three elements reinforce each other in scaffolding learning. Scaffolding is the process in which a child participates jointly with an 'expert' in an activity that is gradually mastered through practical action. Scaffolding can often occur as a result of the way a setting is structured without being intentional, which is the most significant feature underlying the differences between societies. As the data showed, play activities provided the basis for understanding situational scaffolding, which is built upon by children making sense of their world. In the Konkomba and the Birifor societies, children are active agents in constructing their own worldview.

Our research findings are also pertinent in Fortes's research when he studied the acephalous Tallensi in northern Ghana. In the extract below he shows how 'education' in the informal sense is taught but never forced upon a child. He remarked:

> As between adults and children in Tale society, the social sphere is differentiated only in terms of relative capacity. All participate in the same culture, the same round of life, but in varying degrees, corresponding to the stage of physical and mental development. Nothing in the universe of adult behaviour is hidden from children, or barred to them. They are actively and responsibly part of the social structure, of the economic structure, the ritual and ideological system. Education, it is clear, is regarded as a joint enterprise in which parents are as eager to lead as children to follow ... A child is never forced beyond its capacity. (Fortes [1936] 1970: 19, 23)

This is consistent with Goody's view that in small-scale, undifferentiated societies, learning occurs within the domestic group – sons learning from fathers and girls learning from mothers (1992).

Conclusion: Video, Voice and Vygotsky

The in-depth studies of informal learning of adult role skills described in the narratives above collected by Goody (1978, 1982) and myself (Fentiman, 1990–1992) illustrate the importance of the situations linking a child's contribution in daily activities to valued skills in carefully graduated stages. Informal learning of adult role skills was characterized by the replication of meaningful, closely aligned sub-routines of work, play, and responsible practice. As shown above, the use of video was a key research tool for our project, and enabled us to compare various activities within prescribed ethnographic settings. We collected a large volume of data that documented everyday activities in a variety of settings almost thirty years ago. It provides a historical and audio-visual record of events. In a recent visit to Ghana, I deposited copies of all my data to the village I had worked in.

The research discussed here was not merely an academic exercise but had much wider implications for how children acquire and learn adult roles in the context of the community, and how they learn in the formal education (classroom) sector. The data was applicable to our understanding of how children learn in the informal setting and how children could learn in the formal setting. The research poses important questions, such as: Can the ways children learn at home be applied to how children learn at school? By comparing the various ways children ask questions in different settings (i.e. acephalous and hierarchical) it may be possible to provide an important insight for educational research (see e.g. Goody and Bennett's work on LLIL in the classroom).

Acknowledgements

I am grateful to Esther Goody for her guidance and assistance as my PhD supervisor and as my postdoctoral colleague. I was fortunate to work and to learn from her during my research in Northern Ghana. Her inspiration, passion and commitment to work with rural communities in Ghana had a significant impact on my life.

Alicia Fentiman is a social anthropologist who conducted her PhD under the supervision of Esther Goody at the Department of Social Anthropology, University of Cambridge. She has worked extensively in the field of international development in sub-Saharan Africa. She has also worked as a consultant and as a senior researcher at the Faculty of Education, University of Cambridge.

Notes

1. This research was funded by the ESRC Grant R000 223 1852. (Fentiman, 1991–1992) I was appointed as Goody's postdoctoral research officer on the project, and worked exclusively with the Konkomba during the first phase of the research. Unfortunately, due to political conflict in the Northern Region, I was unable to continue in the second phase of the project due to insecurity in the region.
2. See, for example, an earlier work by Goody which discusses a comparative study between hierarchical and egalitarian societies of kinship structure and movement among the Gonja and Lowilli in Northern Ghana. Also, see Fentiman 1991, Middleton and Tait (1958) for a discussion of segmentary lineage systems in African societies.
3. In Erickson's article on the Use of Video in Social Research, he illustrates how ethnographic narrative reports in the form of video case studies emerged from educational

research (mainly in the classroom) as an important tool for documentation, and how they became known as 'videography' (Erickson 2011: 184). For further information of the diverse uses of video in social sciences and through micro-ethnography, see Goldman et al. 2007.

4   The definition of 'informal learning' is complex and debated. It is often used to contrast the difference with 'formal' learning, which tends to be an organized and structured learning activity that leads to a qualification or certificate, e.g. in classroom, whereas informal or non-formal does not lead to a certificate. There is a significant literature on this. See Lave 2019 for a discussion on formal versus informal learning.

5. The army occupied the area where I was working, which made fieldwork extremely difficult, so it was not possible to continue the second phase of the research in schools.

6. Video data examples of play and work activities from Alicia Fentiman and Esther Goody will be included for the electronic copy of the book.

7. Video available to watch on https://iplayerhd.com/player/video/e0529534-ae05-4cc7-b235-9acb80a5acdc/share.

8. Video available to watch on https://iplayerhd.com/player/video/07b2e383-6ca0-437c-8ff8-0145cd222109/share.

9. Video available to watch on https://iplayerhd.com/player/video/07b2e383-6ca0-437c-8ff8-0145cd222109/share.

10. Video available to watch on https://iplayerhd.com/player/video/91ff15f0-37e8-48ff-bbd5-ff419afb0213/share.

11. Video available to watch on https://youtu.be/96al5M_Xu-s.

References

Cole, Michael. 1985. 'The Zone of Proximal Development: Where Culture and Cognition Create Each Other', in James Wertsh (ed.), *Culture, Communication and Cognition: Vygotskian Perspectives*. Cambridge: Cambridge University Press.

Cole, Michael, et al. 1971. *The Cultural Context of Learning and Thinking*. New York: Basic Books.

Erickson, Frederick. 2011. 'Use of Video in Social Research: A Brief History'. *International Journal of Social Research Methodology* 14(3): 179–89.

Fentiman, Alicia. 1990–1992. *Field Notes from Ethnographic Research in Northern Ghana*.

———. 1991. 'Tribes without Rulers or Rulers without Tribes? Political Conflict in Northern Ghana', in Jon Kirby (ed.), *Tamale Institute of Cross-Cultural Studies*, pp. 4–6.

Fortes, Meyer. (1936) 1970. 'Social and Psychological Aspects of Education in Taleland', in Meyer Fortes (ed.), *Time in Social Structure and other Essays*. London: Athlone.

Froelich, Jean Claude. 1954. *La Tribu Konkomba du Nord Togo*. Memoires de l'Institute Francais d'Afrique Noire, No. 37, Dakar.

Goldman, Ricki, et al. 2007. *Video Research in the Learning Sciences*. Mahwaw, NJ: Lawrence Erlbaum.

Goody, Esther N. 1972. '"Greeting", "Begging" and the Representation of Respect', in Jean S. La Fontaine (ed.), *The Interpretation of Ritual: Essays in Honour of A.I. Richards*. London: Tavistock Press, pp. 39–72.

———. 1978. 'Towards a Theory of Questions', in Esther N. Goody (ed.), *Questions and Politeness: Strategies in Social Interaction*. Cambridge: Cambridge University Press, pp. 17–43.

_____ . 1982. 'Daboya Weavers: Relations of Production, Dependency and Reciprocity', in Esther N. Goody (ed.), *From Craft to Industry: The Ethnography of Proto-Industrial Cloth Production*. Cambridge Papers in Social Anthropology 10. Cambridge: Cambridge University Press, pp. 50–84.

_____ . 1990. ESRC Grant Application on Authority and Learning in Northern Ghana.

_____ . 1991. 'The Learning of Pro-social Behavior in Small-Scale Egalitarian Societies: An Anthropological View', in Robert A. Hinde and Jo Groebbel (eds), *Cooperation and Prosocial Behaviour*. Cambridge: Cambridge University Press, pp. 106–28.

_____ . 1992. 'Modelling, Work and the Situational Scaffolding of Adult Roles in Northern Ghana', *Apprenticeship* symposium. American Anthropological Association, San Francisco. Esther N. Goody archive, Centre for African Studies, Cambridge University.

_____ . 1993. 'Informal Learning of Adult Roles in Baale', in Michele Fieloux and Jaques Lombard (eds), *Images D'Afrique et Sciences Sociales: Les Pays Lobi, Birifor et Dagara (Burkina Faso, Cote d' Ivoire et Ghana)*. Paris: Karthala-Orstom, pp. 482–91.

_____ . 1996. 'Authority and Learning in Northern Ghana'. End of Award Report, Economic and Social Research Council, UK. Esther N. Goody archive, Centre for African Studies, Cambridge University.

Goody, Jack, and Esther Goody. 1967. 'The Circulation of Women and Children in Northern Ghana'. *Man* 2(2): 226–48.

Goody, Esther N., and JoAnne Bennett. 2001. 'Literacy for Gonja and Birifor Children in Northern Ghana', in David R. Olson and Nancy Torrance (eds), *The Making of Literate Societies*. Oxford: Blackwell Publishers Ltd, pp. 178–200.

Lave, Jean. 1991. 'Situated Learning in Communities of Practice', in Lauren Resnick, John Levine and StephanieTeasly (eds), *Perspective on Socially Shared Cognition*. Washington, DC: American Psychological Association, pp. 63–82.

_____ . 2019. *Learning and Everyday Life: Access, Participation, and Changing Practice*. Cambridge: Cambridge University Press.

Lave, Jean, and Etienne Wenger. 1991. *Situated Learning: Legitimate Peripheral Participation*. Cambridge: Cambridge University Press.

Luria, Aleksandr R. 1979. *The Making of the Mind: A Personal Account of Soviet Psychology*. Cambridge, MA: Harvard University Press.

Middleton, John, and David Tait (eds). 1958. *Tribes Without Rulers: Studies in African Segmentary Systems*. London: Routledge & Kegan Paul.

Moll, Luis C. 1990. *Vygotsky and Education: Instructional Implications of Sociohistorical Psychology*. Cambridge: Cambridge University Press.

Piaget, Jean. 1951. *Play, Dreams and Imitation in Childhood*. London: Routledge & Kegan Paul.

Tait, David. 1953. 'The Political System of the Konkomba'. *Africa* 23: 213–23.

_____ . 1958. 'The Territorial Pattern and Lineage System of the Konkomba', in John Middleton and David Tait (eds), *Tribes Without Rulers: Studies in African Segmentary Systems*. London: Routledge & Kegan Paul, pp. 167–202.

_____ . 1961. *The Konkomba of Northern Ghana*. Oxford: Oxford University Press.

Vygotsky, Lev. 1962. *Thought and Language*. Cambridge: MIT Press.

_____ . 1978. *Mind in Society: The Development of Higher Psychological Processes*. Cambridge, MA: Harvard University Press.

Wertsch, James B. 1985. *Vygotsky and the Social Formation of Mind*. Cambridge, MA: Harvard University Press.

6

Lessons in Milking and Lessons in Maths
A Case Study of Andean Children in Colombia

Catalina Laserna

Introduction

I begin with a puzzle: children from rural areas of Colombia become competent in a wide variety of tasks around the household, solving problems and dealing with complex situations that arise. Yet in the government school, these same children seem to learn with great difficulty. The differences in learning became particularly evident to me as I carried out fieldwork in San Juan – a community of indigenous peasants in the south of Colombia. There, conditions of acute land shortage, increased deforestation and erosion of the soil, and scarce resources make labour-intensive methods of land utilization imperative for survival. Characterized by a strong work ethic, time is not to be wasted. From very early on it is normal and expected that children partake of the workload of their domestic unit.

By contrast, while daily attendance at school is customary, students seem to have difficulty understanding what is taught. Only a small fraction of the students who begin primary school complete the five years offered by the local school. As one dropout student put it: 'I have a hard head... books are just not for me. In school I was wasting time. I better earn my living with the shovel'. This marked contrast between the effectiveness of one type of educational form over the other provided the key stimulus to undertake an investigation into how the organization of knowledge and skills and the learning process varies between the domestically based chore curriculum and the school-based academic curriculum (Laserna 1988).

I viewed learning to do chores as a kind of apprenticeship where, over time, children gradually assume the productive roles of their parents (Goody 1982). Hence, in the milking lesson described below, I show how the mother scaffolds her daughter as an emergent milker. I also build on Goody's work on questions

(Goody 1978) to illuminate the way language is used by the mother and her daughter. Similar to Esther Goody's research in Ghana, I explored apprenticeship, family sociology, parent–child relations and teacher–student interactions in San Juan, a remote peasant village in the Andes mountains of Colombia.

At the time of fieldwork, I was struck by the fact that while doing chores with or for their parents, children very rarely asked questions. Close observation revealed that, as a speech act, asking questions was associated with power (i.e. the way someone in authority 'questions' someone with less authority). Working along with their parents, apprentices were expected to observe attentively and quietly. The only questions allowed were those intended to elicit information to coordinate joint action with their parent. For example, a child might ask, 'Should I hold the calf now?' This linguistic ideology around avoiding questions explains why, when these same children attend school, they very rarely ask questions of the teacher.

This chapter will compare the teaching of two types of procedures involving a sequence of steps, one in the chore curriculum and the other in the academic curriculum: the concrete procedure of learning to milk a cow, and symbolically mediated arithmetical procedures.

Why Compare Milking and Maths?

The choice may appear odd at first. After all, they *are* such disparate activities. My claim is that precisely because these two procedures are so different (and yet both are 'procedures'), they provide a unique opportunity to contrast

Figure 6.1. The village of San Juan and surrounding landscape, Department of El Cauca, Colombia, 1978. © Catalina Laserna.

'embedded' versus 'formal' teaching of procedures. Their sharp differences yet fundamental similarities make milking and maths ideal points of departure for understanding how embedded and formal education operate. There are two reasons for this.

First, as procedures or algorithms, milking and maths are both made up of a series of steps that the novice/student needs to master. Mastering any procedure necessarily involves acquiring control over one or more operations: one needs to learn how to *do something*. From this need to transfer control, at least on the level of operation, scaffolding arises as a spontaneous teaching method. Scaffolding a procedure is easier than scaffolding the acquisition of a conceptual network, because by having some mutual understanding of where the procedure is leading, the actions of the novice provide a solid ground for specific feedback. In this regard, procedures are ideal activities for Vygotskian-type learning in that external monitoring can gradually be replaced by self-monitoring (Cole 1985; also see Fentiman's chapter in this volume).

Second, milking and maths are close to 'ideal types' of academic and practical lessons: milking is not taught at school, nor is maths taught at home. Other subjects, like religion, are taught in both contexts. In sum, the fact that both milking and maths entail procedures and at the same time represent typical examples of academic and embedded content provides an excellent opportunity to elucidate some of the factors determining the educational process within two distinct forms of social organization: the domestic unit and the school. Esther Goody explored this in her work on informal and formal learning (Goody 1996).

This chapter emphasizes the power of context or 'set-ups' in promoting learning. The consequences of learning and teaching within activities that are set up in different ways are explored. The polarity presented here is between two types of set-up: holistic or 'same-script', and fragmented or 'assembly-line'. The same-script formats are characteristic of embedded learning/teaching. By contrast, assembly-line formats are typical of formal, academic teaching/learning. The maths curriculum is used to illustrate the assembly-line format, whereas milking is used to exemplify the same-script format.

The three questions and claims addressed in this chapter are as follows:

1. How is milking organized? The pattern described is that of the same-script. The claim is that this same-script format, coupled with the activity being 'the real task', makes milking a good set-up to promote the integrated development of skills and knowledge around milking.
2. How is the maths programme organized? The pattern described is that of an assembly-line. The claim is that this assembly-line format promotes the fragmentation of knowledge into often dry, drill-type exercises, at the expense of true conceptual development, and results in mostly rote memorization. I support this claim by analysing five classroom episodes taken from first and second grade. The episodes presented in the text are selected from random recordings of typical maths lessons. Although three different teachers are involved, the same patterns are observable in all the lessons.

3. How can these two activities be contrasted? The claim here is that although milking and maths differ in many important aspects, much can be gained from analysing a setting like milking, where connected knowledge and skills are promoted. Four dimensions of coherence are proposed and analysed for the maths and milking material. It is noted that fragmentation within the maths curriculum is not derived from the nature of mathematical knowledge as such, but from the way the teaching of this content is being 'set up' by the formal curriculum.

The nature of the scaffolding provided by the expert or teacher is a crucial mechanism for making the embedded learning/teaching of milking connected, while the formal teaching of maths is fragmented. In an embedded, concrete situation it is common to provide instructional 'scaffolding' to the novice. Scaffolding here refers to a range of instructional techniques that support the learner's performance. In the case of a practical activity like milking, this support is provided verbally, non-verbally, or some combination of the two. Non-verbal support is provided by having the novice participate in the activity and allowing a meshing of actions between expert and novice. The expert offers verbal support in the form of commands that have a causal explanation embedded in them, for example: 'Tie the cow's legs! Don't you see that she is going to kick!' By contrast, causal explanations are either delayed or never provided in the school's assembly-line format.

In sum, my argument is that a fundamental constraint on the effectiveness of learning processes originates in the organization of the activity. The question arises as to whether this organization is or is not made surveyable to the learner. In same-script, repetitive lessons in practical everyday situations such as milking (where the overall routine remains the same) it is the degree of participation of the learner that gradually evolves. I contrast this with the school-based assembly-line lessons in which, following the state-mandated curriculum, learners are led from one curricular unit to the next.

I argue that the embedded set-up 'naturally' (a better word?) induces connectiveness as verbal explanations are embedded in the task, thereby contributing towards connecting the various aspects of the task: semantic, syntactic and pragmatic.

A Field Lesson in Milking

As a cultural practice, milking is routinely done by women. They are in charge of cheese production and sale. They also administer the money that is generated from selling cheese. It is customary for women to take a child (of eight or older) to help to manage the animals and to transport things to and from the field. Depending on the number of cows and their productivity, it may be impossible in some cases for one person to carry back all the milk. Analysed at a higher level of teaching, learning to milk needs to be also understood as a part of a larger socialization process, where the girl is learning to 'become a woman', 'to be a useful daughter', and so forth. This larger motive is recognized by both the mother and the daughter, who are aware of the rhythm and orientation of the domestic cycle as the daughter acquires knowledge. At this stage, parents do not need the children's help. In fact, they may be more of a burden than a help. However, when possible, children are taken along explicitly to 'get them used to working'. While later on the child's help may be necessary, teaching remains an important secondary goal of the participants: parents are interested in their children acquiring such skills, and the children are generally eager to assume the duties (and associated rights) of becoming a full working member of the domestic unit.

The identification of the daughter with the mother provides strong motivation for the child to learn. Mothers often reinforce such identification by telling their daughters 'Now you are learning to be a good woman' and by offering young girls deals such as 'If you help me raise this calf, I will buy you a pair of shoes at the market when I sell it'. By offering the child this kind of reward, the mother is allowing the child to participate in the 'social space' of an adult woman, who may also buy some new shoes for herself after she has successfully raised an animal for sale.

As an educational form, one can characterize milking as an 'immediate' form of cultural reproduction, wherein social replacement and the transmission of knowledge occur in a short, immediate cycle of mother/daughter communication. Hence, in Fortes' terms, the social space of the mother and

Figure 6.2. A four-year-old son observes and assists his mother making cheese in the village of San Juan, El Cauca, Colombia, May 1978. © Catalina Laserna.

daughter are 'undivided' (Fortes 1938). As an everyday work routine, milking is 'opportunistic'. An expert milker does not miss the chance of combining the outing for milking with some other chore like fetching firewood, or grass for the hamsters. These materials need to be transported back to the village, and children are often in charge of the lighter but sometimes bulkier loads.

Once in the field, the structure of the milking routine can be described in terms of three phases, each one with a series of steps or actions.

Phase A: Selling Up
Step 1. Driving the cow
Step 2. Driving the calf
Step 3. Tying the cow's hind legs
Step 4. Letting the calf suckle until milk is 'let down'
Step 5. Tying the calf to the fence near its mother

Phase B: Getting the Product
Step 1. Milking the cow

Phase C: Clearing the Stage
Step 1. Releasing the cow
Step 2. Releasing the calf
Step 3. Pouring the milk into a larger container to transport it back to the village

Phases A, B and C are repeated until all the cows are milked. At a finer level of analysis, that of operations, one needs to consider how, as the actor executes various steps, specific constraints arise that call for variations in the basic pattern. These will be discussed in the context of presenting the specific details of a milking lesson.

The series of events described below start as the mother, Flor (34 years old, unschooled), her daughter Zora (10 years old, in second grade) and the observer arrive at the pasture where the cows are grazing. The calves are in one pasture and the cows in another. Zora's main role is to watch the gate controlling the entrance of the cows into the milking area, and handling the calves as they approach their mother.

The first cow comes in and Flor ties its legs. Zora ropes the calf as it approaches its mother. She then lets the calf loose so that Flor may guide the calf to suckle a few times on each of the teats. The mother explains to the observer (me, also an apprentice in this setting) that one needs to let the calf suckle the cow's teats to 'release' the milk. After a short time, one can see the calf's mouth full of milk. Zora observes this, pulls the calf back, and ties it to the fence near the cow.

Flor prepares for milking by sitting on a small stool. She places the container on the ground. 'Should I hold it?', asks Zora. Her mother nods and Zora holds the container while her mother milks. Flor remarks that this is the cow's first calf and therefore it is hard to milk. When the teats are small, as on this cow, it is difficult to grab them, and the hands get tired easily. Also, the cow has a black udder, and those cows are known to be difficult to milk. Once Flor has finished, she pours the milk into the bigger container.

Zora drives the second cow. They repeat the same procedure as for the first cow: Flor ties up the cow's legs, the calf is allowed to suckle and is then pulled back and tied to the fence by Zora.

As Flor milks the cow, she observes that the udder is still full in its upper part. She says that the cow is 'hiding' the milk and asks Zora to release the calf a second time. The calf suckles for a few seconds and then Flor continues to milk. The milk flows abundantly. The mother explains: 'Some cows are difficult because they hide the milk, for example this one. You can tell she is hiding the milk because she is still *ubrona* (an enlarged udder)'. In such a case, to stimulate milk production, Zora releases the calf periodically and lets it suckle a little at each of the teats. Flor resumes milking, and as she finishes she remarks: 'See how much she was hiding! A whole pound!'

The mother suggests that Zora should try milking this cow. As Zora prepares to milk, Flor warns her to place the container correctly: 'See that you place it steady on the ground'. Zora extracts some milk, however she lacks strength in her hands to get a good flow. After three or four minutes Flor takes over, finishes the milking and releases the cow.

As the next cow comes up to be milked, another constraint of the milking task becomes evident: some cows have blisters and need to be milked in a particular way to avoid having them kick and spill the milk. Milking a cow with blisters is risky, as the milker can get hurt and the milk may be spilt by the cow's jumps or kicks. When I enquire about the cause of these blisters, Flor explains the belief that if a cow's milk boils over while cooking and is left unwiped on the stove, the cow gets these blisters.

Zora is afraid of being kicked by the cow and does not hold the container for her mother as she milks. Flor, who is a real *practica* (skilled girl), stays there by herself and milks the cow without any problem. Mother and daughter chat and anticipate that at home the oldest daughter (14 years old) is preparing a sweet dish for when they return from the countryside. Zora tells me, 'I love those *mejicanas*, (if I could) I would eat them every day!' The mother pours the milk into the big container, and when she releases the cow, Zora releases the calf.

'Which one should I bring now?' asks Zora. Her mother tells her one of the names. The next cow also has blisters. This time, Flor offers a different explanation for the appearance of blisters: 'They also say that it (these blisters) may be due to some *peste* (disease)'.

Flor makes a comment on low milk production, and explains to me that on some plots of land, cows produce more milk because they have running water: 'Here where we are, they do not let down as much milk as over there. There (where there is running water), they produce one gallon and you still have one cow left! Here there are only small wells and the animals give less milk'.

As the fourth cow enters the area, Flor leads the calf to suckle alternately on each of the teats two or three times – for such a short time, the calf gets a surprising amount of milk. 'Zora can milk this cow, although she is pretty hard', so

Flor tells Zora to try. Mother and daughter sit on either side of the cow. Zora starts to milk for two or three minutes and then her mother takes over, then again Zora, then mother, alternating four times. The mother explains to the observer that switching off gives the girl a chance to rest her hands while at the same time ensuring that the milk flow does not stop. The one-gallon container is not filled. The calf is released a second time to stimulate the cow to release a second batch of milk. After the calf has suckled for a brief time, Flor tells Zora: 'Pull it away!', and she wraps up the milking. After all the cows have been milked, they need to be moved to a new pasture and the milk needs to be carried home.

As 'lessons', chore lessons are highly repetitive, or 'same-script': every day cows and calves need to be separated and then brought together to milk the cows. Milk needs to be extracted and so on, regardless of whether or not a novice is present to learn. Embedded in a practical chore, the milking 'curriculum' is not defined by the overall activity but by the role participants play. In other words, it is the cooperative process and its evolution that provide insight into the organization of the embedded curriculum. As novices increase their competence in various aspects of the activity, their roles evolve, leading to the partial and eventual total delegation of control over the activity to the novice. This same script format of the chore curriculum has significant implications at the level of learning and teaching.

From the point of view of learning, three important consequences derive:

1. The novice has a good amount of pre-knowledge about the actions and operations she is about to master. Having participated in milking outings from early on, Zora has a conceptual model of what the performance entails and what the critical variables are. For example, while she does not know how to handle a cow with blisters, she has the correct expectation that such animals will be difficult to milk.

2. The novice's conceptual model becomes enriched by a series of details that she 'picks up' over time – for example, she may learn why cows get blisters and how to cure them (including the fact that two alternative diagnoses coexist), or how to recognize when a cow is 'hiding her milk'. In other words, as Zora gains experience, her depth of understanding of the craft of milking increases.

3. The repetitive nature of the activity, coupled with the fact that it is a concrete activity, leads the learner to develop a holistic understanding of the activity; in other words, the procedure becomes 'surveyable' to the learner. This happens in a dual sense. On a general level it helps to develop an increasing understanding of what the activity is about and how it fits within other social routines, its value, and so on. On a local level, or within the routine itself, sub-routines are gradually identified and understood in terms of the larger routine. In sum, the same-script format fosters 'mental surveyability'. A practical routine like milking is also 'visually surveyable' because

the actions are overt and organized in a sequence, and therefore can be scrutinized, whereas oral verbal discourse cannot.

Surveyability[1] provides the learner with an opportunity to watch what she does not yet know, to review what she does know, and to elicit appropriate scaffolding (guidance for the sake of practice) in steps that are still emergent – in other words, 'knowing why' and 'knowing how' to carry out a procedure become integrated into a coherent functional system, which enables the learner to associate new information with its relative dimensions, and tie it into practice.

The Multiple Identities of the Learner

To characterize Zora as a 'novice' is somewhat misleading because when it comes to dealing with the calves, Zora is a 'local expert'. In this particular subtask, she is truly helpful to her mother. At other points however, she will be treated like an apprentice. The expert has overall control over the activity and, when appropriate, provides the novice with an opportunity to try out emergent skills. This is typical of other chore lessons: a mixture of true cooperation interspersed with short pedagogical episodes.

Becoming a *practica* entails the articulation of three aspects of Zora's behaviour: her knowledge about facts and rules that relate to the craft of milking; her actual skill in carrying out the procedure; and not least, her willingness to do so. 'Place the bucket firmly on the ground' may well be followed by, 'because if not, the cow can easily move and tip it over'. However, at Zora's level of mastery, such explanations are left out because the mother assumes that the reason for placing the container firmly on the ground is obvious to Zora, albeit that at this stage of her mastery she might forget to actually *do* so.

Fragmentation at the level of the domain has three features associated with it: fragmentation at the level of scaffolding; separation between learning how to carry out a procedure and why it 'works'; and separation between the preknowledge that students have derived from their everyday experiences, and classroom maths.

In the 'milking lesson', animals, the environment and the actors are engaged in a dynamic system that stimulates the mother to teach and the daughter to learn as she increasingly participates in different ways. The concrete activity has a compulsiveness of its own, which the child learns to understand. For example, the novice learns to identify cues such as a loose calf, which can 'signal' trouble for the milker. Hence, the signals of trouble or need for action are not necessarily provided by the teacher (as in the case of, say, blackboard problems) but the novice milker gradually learns to 'read' the signals from the physical environment itself. In the same way, as mentioned above, the expert also uses cues from the environment to support her guidance and instruction. In sum, the context provides 'free contextual scaffolding' both to the learner trying to master the activity and to the teacher trying to transmit knowledge and skills.

Figure 6.3. *Minga* (community labour): weeding the school garden in the village of San Juan, El Cauca, Colombia, April 1978. © Catalina Laserna.

Teaching Maths: Sample Lessons

On a descriptive level, the aim is to demonstrate that the maths content is fragmented. Phrased metaphorically, maths is presented according to the 'assembly-line' format; that is, the whole content is broken down into subcomponents, which are introduced sequentially to the students. The expectation seems to be that at the end of this assembly line, the learner will be able to put together a coherent 'product' out of the fragments of knowledge and the skills that he/she has acquired throughout the school years.

The developmental stages of the maths curriculum implemented by one of the first-grade teachers observed are: (1) 'getting ready' to learn maths; (2) learning the components (the numbers); and (3) learning to do basic arithmetic operations. The three stages are briefly described below. Stages 2 and 3 are each followed by sample lessons (one sample lesson for Stage 2, and four sample lessons for Stage 3). Where relevant, the lesson dialogue is presented under 'Observation Protocol', followed by an analysis of the teaching and learning process.

Stage 1. Getting ready.

During the first four months of the year, students are trained in using pencil and paper. The emphasis is on fine manual coordination, which many of the new students lack. The teacher writes samples, which the students copy.

Stage 2. Learning the components – the numbers.

Next the numbers from 1 to 10 are introduced. Following the same format as in the preceding stage, the teacher provides the students with samples and then the students have to write a page of the sample numbers. An example of Stage 2 is summarized below.

The Number Example

The teacher calls students to the blackboard and dictates the numbers between 1 and 20. At the level of student performance, the emphasis is on being able to read and write the numbers correctly. Later in that same lesson, the teacher introduces the numbers between 20 and 30. The teacher promises he will provide 'a key' (the formula) for writing all the numbers up to one hundred. The teacher, however, gets sidetracked by other issues and forgets about the general construction rule.

To make the class more fun, the teacher proposes a 'game': he dictates numbers and the students write them down. The goal of the game is to write the numbers down correctly.

Analysis

Four aspects of the teaching/learning process will be analysed: content, pedagogical technique, evaluation, and the social consequences of having acquired certain knowledge.

The Content

The lesson described above is a representative example of a traditional maths class, in which the numbers are introduced without any actual application. In other words, rather than dealing with 'the number system', the students only learn its individual components. The teacher assumes that written numbers are somehow separate from the child's ability to count or use money. As students do not engage in any operations involving numbers, at this stage learning numbers and learning the letters of the alphabet are very much the same: the students' goal is to be able to read and write the appropriate symbol when the teacher tells them to. In both cases, the task for the students is to fill page after page with numbers and letters – following a sample provided by the teacher (*la muestra*). Sometimes students accidentally mix up their maths and language workbooks.

Fragmentation appears even at the content level: drill exercises often have little relation to each other. In the example given above, the students attempted to master the numbers between 20 and 30. There is no general motivation for this lesson except that 'we need to learn the numbers'.

Pedagogical Techniques

Scaffolding: Because the students are involved in learning to do something, there are repeated instances in which the teacher intervenes to help the students achieve their goal. Fragmentation also appears in the teacher's scaffolding, which is often highly contextual. For example, when a student writes a 14 instead of a 24, the teacher may suggest: 'Not that number [meaning the 1], but the one we are dealing with today [meaning the 2]'. No effort is made to teach general principles such as, 'All numbers that are read as twenty-something start with a two'. An example of non-verbal scaffolding occurs when the teacher points to space on the blackboard, anticipating where students will be writing.

Errors and scaffolding: When errors have to do with the mechanics of writing, the teacher quickly provides goal-effective support by helping the student to write the correct answer. So, for example, when a student is asked to write the number 27 and she does not know how to write the 7, the teacher takes over and writes the 7 on the blackboard. After this he asks the student to rehearse the number by writing it a few times on the blackboard. However – and this supports our characterization of an assembly-line format – when the errors relate to some part of the content that is not within the immediate objectives of the lesson, the teacher is reluctant to deal with them. For example, when a student is asked to write the numbers from 10 to 20, and forgets to draw the hyphen that separates the numbers 13 and 14, writing instead 1314, the teacher simply says 'That is not 13 and 14 ... that is another number ... what's happening? What's happening?' [meaning 'hurry up']. The student cannot find the mistake and continues writing the other numbers. After the student returns to his bench, another student is asked to read what the first student had written down. The mistake is not discussed, but simply corrected by the teacher without any explanation.

Emphasis on Routine Verbalization: It is common for the teacher to ask questions such as: 'What did you do to write?' or 'How do you read that number?' In addition, the students are constantly reminded to recite aloud when they write a number – whether on the blackboard or in their workbooks. Making what they are doing explicit is typical of maths instruction throughout primary education, and it serves a pragmatic purpose: to help the teacher hear what the student is doing. Verbalization allows the teacher to track the student's mental activities. However, what the students are encouraged to verbalize is restricted to highly routinized 'maths talk', and they are allowed only to name the numbers. As we will see in later stages, this discourse evolves into verbal routines such as: 'Two minus eight, I cannot do it; I borrow one'.

Reason Giving: There was not a single instance in the lesson where the teacher, while talking about maths, provided an explanation to the students. They are told what to do and how to do it, but the teacher does not give any reasons for doing so – as indicated by the absence of 'because' elaborations or 'why' questions. Nor do the students provide any explanations or ask any questions.

The only 'because' in the entire lesson occurs in the teacher's sentence, 'We are going to applaud her [a student] because last week she had difficulty and now she has studied and now she is not confused'. It is interesting that as in the chore curriculum, the reason is provided as part of a command. Such a 'because' elaboration increases the depth of the understanding, an issue that will be dealt with more systematically later on.

Evaluation

Throughout the lesson the teacher quizzes the students about numbers that are written on the blackboard. Once again, the only criterion for evaluation is that the students be able to read and write the numbers. The teacher continually tells the students to 'Remember', and 'Do not forget', encouraging them to memorize the numbers.

Social Consequences of Having Acquired the Knowledge

The students are aware that the teacher will be pleased if they know the numbers well. Some children tell their parents what they have learnt that day and show them how many pages they have filled with numbers. In some households, older siblings who have attended school may amuse themselves by 'quizzing' their younger siblings and having them read or write numbers. However, at this stage knowledge of numbers does not seem to affect their assignment of chores, such as buying groceries.

The most important consequence of having acquired knowledge is within the maths programme itself: the students are now ready to move on to the next stage in the curriculum. They will not have a chance to go over a given topic again, and thus students who fail to master the numbers initially may find themselves left behind by the end of the year.

In conclusion, analysis of the number example confirms that at the levels of content, pedagogical technique, and evaluation, the teaching/learning of the components (the numbers) is done in isolation from any other type of knowledge or problem-solving. The transmission and evaluation interactions are equally decontextualized. Students are not encouraged to either use any prior knowledge they may have about what is being taught (i.e. relate it to everyday experiences of numbering, counting or sequencing), or to form a mental schema of what the whole activity is about, such as developing a sense of the 'number system' and a grasp of some of its properties.

This deep fragmentation encourages a separation of rules from the underlying schemata which justify and explain them. For example, the problem of writing the numbers between 20 and 30 is not related to the problem of writing any other number sequence; the local form is provided without any explanation as to how this fits into the holistic schema of 'writing numbers' or 'numbering'. This trend towards fragmentation becomes even more obvious in the case of more elaborate maths instruction at the next stage of the school programme.

Stage 3. Basic Arithmetic Operations.

Once the students have learnt the components (i.e. the numbers between 1 and 100), they learn the basic operations of adding and subtracting. These basic arithmetic operations are taught with the aid of sets of objects. This representation of problems stated in terms of spoken words (or written symbolism in terms of sticks) is crucial to the development of addition and subtraction skills.

Later on, control is transferred to the student, who now possesses his own set of sticks and learns to manipulate them. With experience, the student internalizes and automates the concrete model – and learns basic addition by rote, as in the case of 2+2=4, so that he does not need to count to get the answer. Four examples of basic arithmetic lessons are presented below:

Lesson 1. Addition Using Sticks

This example demonstrates how the scaffolding process occurs at the stage of using sticks to represent and solve a problem in addition.

Observation Protocol (Excerpt), Lesson 1

[The student is given the problem 6+5. The teacher scaffolds him verbally.]

T: You have five and how many are you going to add?
S: *Six.*
T: How much is it? It is equal to...? What are you going to do first...?

[The teacher hints.] The sticks to figure out the result ... Which ones are you going to do first?

S: *The five.* [He draws them.]
T: And next?
S: *Six.*
T: Draw them...
S: *Seven, couldn't there be seven?*
T: Count them all!
S: [The student counts them all and asks:] *Eleven?*

[The teacher nods.]

Analysis, Lesson 1

This episode illustrates how scaffolding helps the student to achieve his end, in this instance doing addition. At this stage control is firmly in the hands of the teacher: the teacher's interventions are direct and leave little room for mistakes. The student is not even allowed to explore what to do next. (Later, the teacher gradually shifts the control over to the students, leaving them increasingly on their own.)

In the above example the expert's interest does not seem to be in having the child understand why or how something is done (e.g. why use sticks to add), but simply in helping the novice to 'get through the procedure'. Again, the teacher's scaffolding is goal-effective, not simply supportive of the student's attempts. There is, however, one fundamental difference between the mother and the teacher: unlike the kitchen sequence, in maths instruction 'why' explanations are not even part of the command.

Such goal-effective instruction leads to mechanical execution of procedures. This becomes evident when the students learn the procedure for checking addition by means of subtraction, and vice versa – or, as it is called, 'the proof' of the addition. To understand how this checking procedure is taught, it is instructive to examine an excerpt of a second-grade lesson, which vividly represents what will later be referred to as 'the minuend syndrome'.

Lesson 2. The Minuend

Summary of the Activity: The second-grade teacher wants to teach the students how to prove (check) whether subtraction has been performed properly. The teacher therefore gives the students the following rule for checking a subtraction problem: 'If the addition of the subtrahend and the difference is equal to the minuend, then the subtraction has been done right'. In essence, the rules says that the reverse operation should be used for checking. So, for example, to verify that 6 (the minuend) – 4 (the subtrahend) = 2 (the difference), all one needs to do is add what one has taken away – that is, to perform the operation 2+4=6. Throughout the lesson the teacher insists upon appropriate use of the various technical terms and uses them as the basis for establishing whether the proof has been done properly or not. At no point is there a straightforward explanation of how or why reversing the operation is the way to check for accuracy. There is no attempt to evaluate whether or not the students have understood why this rule works. All the teacher seeks from the students is the correct use of the terms.

Observation Protocol, Lesson 2
T: So what is it that she's going to add? Let's see, Fabio.
S: The difference.
T: The difference with the subtrahend. If the subtraction is done properly, what will the result be? Janet, stand up. Stand up.
S: The same result.
T: The same result? As what?
S: [Other students volunteer:] Me, teacher, me!
T: [To Janet:] Pay attention. If we are going to add the minuend to the difference, what comes out if it is done right?
S: [No answer.]
T: The minuend. What results? The minuend. This one over here [The teacher points on the blackboard] … this one should come out. Whenever you do a subtraction, what is it you have to take into account to check if it has been done properly?
S: Me teacher, the minuend …the minuend.
T: We get the min-u-end. This one over here [The teacher points to the blackboard] – the larger one – should be the result. That is what you always have to consider when you do subtraction, and you get as a result the minuend – and what does that mean?
S: That it's right.
T: That it is right. And if not, you have to erase it and do it again. OK, now, my child, do it. [Finally, the girl at the blackboard gets a chance to do the proof.]
S: Seven plus one is eight; five plus two… seven. Three plus five… eight.
T: Good, eight. What does Dora say? Is it right or wrong? Has this subtraction been done right? Stand up and answer in a loud voice.
S: Yes, teacher.

[Notice that in the following passage the only time the teacher uses a 'why' question is when it refers to the terminology:]

T: Why?
S: Because you got the result from above.
T: 'You got the result from up there'. No! You have to give it a name. The one up there is called? We got the same…?
S: Minuend.
T: Minuend, good. Who wants to come up and do another subtraction?

Analysis, Lesson 2

The student's answer, 'We got the same result as above', is correct and in fact expresses what the operation is about. Instead, the teacher insists on the formal category name, 'minuend', which is presented only as a label and obscures the logic of the procedure. This 'minuend syndrome' appears repeatedly, not only in maths but in most other subjects: the emphasis is on 'correct' vocabulary at the expense of conceptual development and understanding. In other words, the symbolic level is emphasized without a corresponding conceptual and pragmatic connection.

The syndrome represents 'formal teaching' in a dual sense: on the one hand, formal in that a 'form' or general 'formula' is taught; on the other, it is formal in the sense of introducing a 'formal' label for the parts of a subtraction problem. The combination of recipe-like performance and obscure labels coupled with the lack of any explanation through which the student could connect this formula to his 'sense of reality' and intuitive understanding makes the 'minuend syndrome' the epitome of decontextualized teaching.

Lesson 3. Subtraction – Rice Example

The next example is not an excerpt from an ordinary lesson. It is drawn from a lesson taught by the anthropologist during fieldwork – hence the use of the personal pronoun. My aim was to get some sense of how well students understood mathematical concepts and related problems; in particular, I wanted to probe into students' understanding of the rule that in addition the order of the factors does not alter the result, although it does alter the result in subtraction – for example, 5+6=6+5 but 7-2≠ 2-7.

Observation Protocol, Lesson 3

[Jesus, eight years old, is at the blackboard. The regular teacher, Socorro, is also present. T = anthropologist's dialogue, S = Jesus's dialogue, and Socorro = the teacher's dialogue.]

By chance I start with a 'wrong' subtraction problem, which reveals the student's understanding of the number system, despite formal teaching. I begin by giving Jesus a problem:

T: Write: 3-8.
S: [Jesus writes an X under it.]
Socorro: Why did you write an X under this operation?
S: *[No answer]*
Socorro: You cannot do it.

[I recognized the opportunity to test the student's understanding of quantitative reasoning as applied to practical money exchanges. What happened next did not surprise me. I proposed the following problem:]

T: Let's think about this. When do we apply subtraction? When you go shopping, do you subtract?
S: *[No answer]*

T: Suppose I send you to the store to buy some rice [something Jesus had often done for his mother]. I give you three pesos and the rice costs eight pesos. What happens?

S: *Five pesos are missing.*

T: What do you do?

S: *[No answer]*

T: Do you ask for credit?

S: *No.*

T: What do you do then?

S: *I go back and ask for the five pesos that I am short.*

Analysis, Lesson 3

Jesus's quick and confident answer indicates that he has had plenty of 'informal' experience with not having enough money to buy something. The practical problem of lacking enough money was not solved by simply saying: 'I cannot do it'. There are other forms to deal with not having enough money: borrowing, or going to ask for more money as he did. For any of these solutions it was vital to know how much money was missing. He played two games, back to back, relating to two versions of 'the same' problem: at school you 'cannot' do those subtractions because there is a rule; in reality, however, the problem is one of finding a way to get the missing money.

How is the inconsistency between school maths and practical maths to be explained in this case? The key to this problem lies in the fact that these are arbitrary rules (as are the ones taught to Jesus), which may apply to some types of everyday problems, but not to others. One cannot produce money one does not have; the same applies to taking six oranges from three oranges. However, the number system is a very broad conceptual system, applicable to different 'target systems', whether oranges in a bag or the circulation of money in the village. However, as experienced by Jesus, you *can* get the missing three pesos. Confusion arises because the implemented curriculum largely ignores the pre-knowledge that students have about quantitative operations in everyday life.

Lesson 4. Subtraction Drill

Another episode from second-grade maths instruction illustrates a related point. Again, the teacher asks the student to perform a subtraction problem which 'is not possible' according to what has been covered in the maths programme so far. However, the student makes the 'mistake' of ignoring the formal rule and proceeds with the subtraction. As a last resort, the teacher asks the student to 'think'.

Observation Protocol, Lesson 4

Summary of the activity: The class is an intensive drill session of subtraction problems. One student makes up a problem and then another student has to solve it. The problem at hand is: 330-567. The girl starts to apply the subtraction algorithm: 'Zero minus seven I cannot do, so I borrow one'. The teacher interrupts: 'Before doing the problem, think about it!' (According to the implemented curriculum this operation is not possible.) The girl freezes. The teacher probes but cannot get the student to 'see' that the operation is impossible. In despair, the teacher finally seeks contextualization: ' Think! If you have 330 pesos and someone asks you to lend him 567: can you do it?' The girl replies 'No'. Imagining a concrete situation (you cannot lend what you do not have) where the operation is impossible helps the student to regain control over the rule as used in the classroom.

Analysis, Lesson 4
Although the teacher's approach works in that particular problem, it contains serious inconsistencies. In this case, the problem with more digits reveals an internal inconsistency: the student discovers that she can borrow within the subtraction itself, but later, as a whole, the answer cannot be 'borrowed'. This, then is another type of fragmentation – rules that work in the parts do not work in the whole.

Maths Lessons: Summary and Conclusions

Fragmentation

To support the claim of 'assembly-line' fragmentation of the maths curriculum and of the lessons themselves, evidence was explored both at the level of the curriculum structure and at the level of the lessons themselves. Fragmentation due to the assembly-line format occurs at various levels. At the level of the overall curriculum, topics often do not relate to each other. If rote memorization is common in conceptual routines, drill is the norm in maths lessons. Both drill and memorization occur detached from real-life problems where mathematical reasoning could be relevant, and isolated from other topics within the curriculum itself. At the level of individual lessons, objectives are narrowly defined and segregated from other segments of the curriculum. Sometimes such fragmentation leads to internal inconsistencies, as was the case in the long subtraction that 'could not be done', where, in fact, the girl was doing it.

In addition, mathematical problems in school are solved with pencil and paper. The mediation of written notation introduces (and makes possible) different algorithms in the form of symbolic routines, which may be completely separated from the conceptual routine that they supposedly help to develop, 'run' or convey. The way children symbolically try to add fractions, for example, shows that they are using symbolic routines independently of any conceptual routine – they act like calculators symbolically executing algorithms. This difference between maths as mediated by pencil and paper and as performed in the mind (sometimes with the support of finger counting) is the primary reason for findings that street children in Recife, Brazil, can perform arithmetic operations in the marketplace but fail when they are asked to do the 'same' problem in the school.

Formal labels are woven into the maths programme in the form of definitions that are memorized but frequently not understood by the students. This heavy-handed labelling seems to contribute towards separating maths as taught in school from the practical mathematical applications students encounter in their daily lives.

What Is 'Logical' at Some Level May Not Be Pedagogical

The teaching/learning of maths is broken down according to logical criteria for the sake of the student and the teacher. The teacher leads the class one step at a time from simple to complex, partially because this makes it easier to manage such a large and relatively heterogeneous group of students. Simplification leads to fragmentation of knowledge, and diminishes drastically the possibilities for the student to experience and consequently internalize what a given activity is about. As the activity lacks broad significance, student curiosity and motivation are difficult to sustain. In an effort to motivate the students, teachers foster extrinsic reinforcement strategies, such as competition among students.

Virtually insulated from any connection with the students' everyday lives, school maths could be described as 'autotelic' (i.e. for its own sake). The maths programme continues as if one learns the numbers so as to learn to add, learns to add so as to learn to multiply, and so on. The usefulness of maths is, at best, once removed. Solving real-life problems that involve arithmetic reasoning is not part of the instruction. As in play, errors during the maths class have no real price tag beyond that of public shame for failing. But unlike play (another autotelic activity), maths as presented in San Juan is not fun.

Time on Task

One important consequence of the assembly-line format is that students lack motivation for working towards a meaningful goal. According to the lesson schedule, students do one or even two hours of maths a day. If, however, one were able to follow the students' real focus of attention, one would find that, as the teacher says, 'They are not [present] in class most of the time (*no están en clase*)'. Another consequence of this assembly-line format is that the class moved along to the next item in the programme as soon as most seemed to have mastered the previous step, but before some of the students had done so.

Consequences of Having Acquired the Knowledge

For students in school, mastery of knowledge increases their status with the teacher. In general, good students are treated better, given certain privileges (medals and other distinctions), and much positive reinforcement. Mastering a skill prepares the student for the next topic. Good students rarely drop out.

Students who have trouble mastering a stage are gradually left so far behind that they anticipate they will be 'left back'. Such students often feel uncomfortable and tend to drop out even before the end of the year.

There is an important sense in which 'out of context' in school translates to 'out of context' at home too: it is rare for first- and second-grade students to use any of the maths skills acquired in school when they are in the home environment. They do, however, occasionally reproduce a context similar to that of the school: older siblings 'quiz' younger ones, or they play at 'giving each other homework'.

Lessons in Milking Reconsidered

Earlier, I characterized the acquisition of knowledge and skills related to milking in terms of an 'apprenticeship'. This means that the learning/teaching processes are embedded within a routine not designed primarily to teach, but rather to 'get the job done'. As the routine is valuable in itself, it is repeated many times, regardless of the presence of a novice. From this constant repetition derives the characterization 'same-script'.

Same-Script Approach and Surveyability

What does 'same-script' imply in terms of the curriculum? As opposed to the maths curriculum, which has been 'set up' to teach, the milking 'curriculum' is not defined by the activity but by the role played by the participants. In other words, it is the transmission process and its evolution that provide insight into the organization of the embedded curriculum.

Consequently, the organization of the content by itself (i.e. without the roles of the participants) tells little about the teaching or learning process. However, from the point of view of the learner, there are important consequences to repeating the same procedure over and over. The most important result is that the procedure becomes 'surveyable' to the learner; in other words, the learner develops a holistic understanding of the activity. The same-script format of milking makes the activity surveyable by the learner in a dual sense. First, on a general level, it helps to develop an increasing understanding of its value, and what the activity is about and how it fits within other social routines. On a local level, or within the routine itself, sub-routines are gradually identified and understood in terms of the larger routine. In sum, same-script fosters 'mental surveyability'. Secondly, a practical routine like milking is also 'visually surveyable', because the actions are overt and organized in a sequence, and therefore they can be scrutinized in a way that 'conceptual routines' cannot.

Surveyability (both mental and visual) is used and promoted throughout the learning process at the chore curriculum stages identified elsewhere by me as 'dumb', 'getting-the idea', 'way-in', and 'practical'. Surveyability provides the learner with an opportunity to watch what he does not yet know, review what he does know, and elicit appropriate scaffolding in steps that are still emergent. In fact, the development from 'getting the idea' to 'way-in' only seems possible if the procedure is surveyable by the learner.

Types of Cohesiveness

In this investigation of what and how people learn/teach, one focus has been to account for the degree of connection between the corpus of knowledge and the skills as a whole. Based on the milking example, four types of cohesiveness (or complexity) can be distinguished.

1. *Multiple Purposes of the Activity*
The activity has one obvious purpose: to get the milk. Aside from this, the mother utilizes milking as an opportunity to: teach her daughter 'how to be a responsible young woman'; train her in a practical skill 'that she may use to earn her keep elsewhere' (with her husband or working for other people); teach her discipline and how to 'make herself useful'; and teach her not to waste time. All these are 'parallel lessons' that the child is getting and are based on the fact that learning is *polyphasic*, meaning that people can learn many things at the same time.

2. *Mastery Over the Craft of Milking*
In the case of milking, learning the craft means not just learning the physical movements, but grasping the functional logic of the activity. As learning/practice continues, such knowledge and skill become more elaborate within a pragmatic domain. Because small variations are part of the procedure, details regarding particular steps become overt, and the aspiring milker needs to incorporate them into her previous knowledge scheme.

Explanations – one way to make a domain more cohesive – are initially embedded within corresponding commands. The novice is expected to have gradually internalized the reasons. Conversely, the novice is expected to respond to intrinsic signals within the situation: for example, a piece of rope on the ground 'signals' that the milker may have forgotten to tie the cow's legs.

In terms of the levels of mastery fostered by the milking lessons, all sub-stages are developed at the same time. During the steps in which the child is still 'dumb', they have an opportunity to observe, such as watching an older sibling learning. The stages where they are on their 'way-in' are scaffolded and/or supervised. As mastery is achieved, autonomy increases. The level of performance expected and the corresponding depth of understanding are scaffolded via commands that contain the 'because' connection. In this way, responsibility training (the command part) and the acquisition of skill (the embedded explanation part) occur simultaneously. In the ideal case, what is expected from the novice depends on their state of development as the mother follows and generates her child's zone of proximal development. At the end of the process the novice is expected to take over and be accountable for the whole routine. This is an instance of self-contained or 'perfect' cultural and social reproduction, where one milker reproduces another milker, both at the level of transmitting the cultural knowledge and skills, and in terms of social replacement.

3. *Multiple Roles of the Activity*
As the novice learns to milk, she also acquires a sense of the different roles of the activity within the larger system of activities and values. In other words, the 'milking script' becomes associated with other social scripts, such as 'milking the cows for an in-law who is sick is a duty', or 'milking the cows of the Church is doing a good deed for the Virgin Mary'.

Learning to milk is also a form of group and family identity: this is 'how we survive', as opposed to people elsewhere who do other things. In this context, it seems clear that parents who prefer that their children learn to milk instead of going to school are making the choice of training them to stay around the house. The choice relates to the social consequences of having acquired the skill.

4. *Multiple Levels of Understanding*
How does 'craft'-level understanding relate to other forms of understanding? For example, how much does the novice learn about *why* the cow lets down the milk when the calf suckles? Multilevel understanding may be least developed in the case of learning to milk.

What levels of understanding are fostered by the 'same-script' practical format of milking? The effect of surveyability has been mentioned in terms of promoting pre-knowledge about steps the novice is not yet able to perform. Having pre-knowledge translates into developing a 'working model' or script of what the activity is about, even when the aspiring milker may not yet be able to do it by herself. Such a script includes knowledge about both the goal structure, and the relationship between algorithmic knowledge and the reasons for a particular procedural order (i.e. why you need to tie the cow's legs before you milk her). Same-script, practical milking also accounts for:

(a) No separation between the teaching/learning of various aspects of the activity; the novice experiences semantic, syntactic (algorithmic), and pragmatic aspects of the learning/teaching process at the same time.

(b) No separation between the script for acquiring a skill and real-life application; with a same-script format there are no discontinuities between the teaching of milking and 'real' milking, as there would be in the teaching of maths and the application of this knowledge in 'real' maths problems in a store. Milking, then, is not only 'same'-script but 'real'-script.

Reinforcement and Mastery

Earlier I described how as the child becomes more competent she assumes increasingly complicated and risky steps in the milking routine. Mastery provides intrinsic reinforcement for a child who, identifying with her mother, aspires to be a milker like her. Identification with the mother provides one source of reinforcement, and the products of the task are another. Both error and success have real price tags. It is the custom in many families that after milking, especially at the weekends, some special sweet dish is prepared upon returning to the house with the fresh milk.

Constraints on Exploration and Creativity

The toll for learning within the context of 'getting the job done' is that novices are allowed little room for free exploration. Errors are avoided via 'over-scaffolding'. Learning, therefore, is restricted to the level of 'craft', with little or no time for multilevel inquiry. The purpose of 'getting the job done' tends to reproduce traditional forms of problem-solving without encouraging innovation or creativity on the part of the novice. Economic constraints also determine what type of direct experience the learner can access.

Contrasting Milking and Maths

In contrasting the way these two procedures are taught and learnt, the following two aspects will be examined in detail: at the level of abstraction, maths is a formal language and milking is a practical procedure; and at the levels of student understanding that are promoted, maths and milking differ significantly.

Levels of Abstraction

A fundamental disparity between maths and milking is their level of abstraction. Milking is a practical procedure, and maths is a formal language. Of all the subject matter taught in school, maths is presumably the most abstract. Students need to learn a series of already abstract elements (the numbers), and then learn to perform operations with them. A further layer of remoteness is added when students are asked to establish relationships between operations – as when addition is the reverse of subtraction. Thus, in the teaching of maths, knowledge and skills quickly become disassociated from normal everyday problems that require practical reasoning.

While, in principle, mathematical reasoning demands a high level of abstract thought, as taught in San Juan it is not primarily the abstraction level but other 'distortions' of maths as a subject that account for its cumbersome treatment, in particular the emphasis on rules and formal labels at the expense of conceptual understanding (i.e. conceptual control over the routine). In other words, the key issue is not the level of abstraction but the levels of understanding fostered by the teaching of maths.

However, to frame the discussion on levels of understanding, it is important to establish maths as a language in order to clarify the dimensions that need to be taken into account when investigating levels of understanding. Unlike other subjects, like biology or history, which can be expressed in everyday language, mathematics is a language in itself – a highly formal language invented to talk about the quantitative aspects of sets of objects and their relationships. As with any other language, one may distinguish between semantic and syntactic aspects of instruction. What is unique about maths is the unambiguous, formal organization of mathematical systems. The power of purely syntactic algorithms is derived from this, and they can become automatizable tools that may be used either by machines or by people. People, like calculators, can simply memorize a formula, apply it, and get the correct answer.

This thought can be expanded by asking a simple question: Why is it that small calculators can perform long mathematical operations, while even the largest computers cannot do what all children can do: *understand* language? In the answer to this question lies an essential feature of the language of mathematics, namely, that mathematical operations can be performed automatically at a syntactic level, without understanding the semantic component. In other words, we do *not* need to understand connections between a given algorithm and the underlying rules and principles that explain why it works. Routines for 'doing' can be separated from routines for 'understanding'.

The situation of natural language is very different. Its interpretation is plagued with ambiguities. Native speakers use 'context' to resolve such ambiguities. As learning to deal with the context is essential for effective communication, it is easy to understand why the most effective way to teach natural language is in context.

In pure mathematics, context is not necessary because the rules are universal, formal, and not context dependent. Because maths is presumed to be a 'universal' language that is not affected by context, the aspects into which languages are broken down (syntax, semantics and pragmatics) can be taught in considerable isolation from each other. This new form of fragmentation allows one to talk about 'levels of understanding' fostered by instruction.

Levels of Understanding

The formal nature of maths lends itself to a separation between semantic and syntactic aspects of the domain. In part, this separation accounts for fragmentation and drill within the curriculum. By contrast, the applied nature of milking does not permit such separation.

On the separation of semantic and syntactic components of the procedure in maths but not in milking, people can and do perform mathematical operations 'like a calculator' by simply following a formula, without needing to understand anything else about the formula. This 'craft level' can be boosted with practice. The formula is syntactic in that it tells the person how to proceed.

Understanding, on the other hand, needs to be semantic and conceptual. Following formulas is akin to rote learning, while mastery over the semantic understanding associated with the syntactic procedure demands complex levels of conceptual understanding and abstraction.

How does this affect the curriculum? 'Getting the job done' in maths often means turning the students into 'calculators'. The trouble with this approach is that fragmented formulas have no semantic networks to keep them connected to other forms of knowledge. Without use, these formulas are easily forgotten, and because the learner lacks a robust semantic base, he/she has no way to reconstruct them. (Maths appears as the epitome of 'formal' or 'formula' teaching in the sense of teaching a recipe.) While applying the formulas mechanically may be a question of simple memory and does not involve a great level of abstraction, understanding the formulas (or reconstructing them when forgotten) requires abstraction and model building.

One should note that traditional second-language instruction has also disassociated the syntactic and semantic components, with people learning grammar on the one hand and vocabulary on the other. By contrast, modern methods of second-language instruction come closer to same-script or embedded teaching methods, where learners are exposed to syntactic and semantic aspects of a foreign language in the pragmatic context of trying to communicate. This organization of the pedagogical context comes closer to the 'embedded' teaching/learning of one's first language.

Could this separation between syntax and semantics occur in the practical milking context? Basically not, because there are no formal, universal rules; instead, variation is part and parcel of these practical contexts. In contrast to maths, in a practical same-script learning situation like milking, the novice needs to understand semantic/syntactic relationships, because there are no formal, rigid rules that always work. In some respects, the script is not strictly the same, but the adaptations are necessary.

Analogous reasons lie behind the difficulty in designing machines that do 'automatic' reading comprehension, like automated 'milkers'. (Machines can only deal with one step in the whole milking routine, the extraction of milk.) The reason is that the context determines which rule or variation of the rule to use. Animals behave differently on different days depending, for example, on their health; procedures to deal with them one day may be inappropriate the next. In sum, variation and the need for contextual judgement are intrinsic to the milking situation.

This implies that in the case of milking, understanding the connections between actions also needs to be scaffolded by the expert, because it is vital that the aspiring milker be able to solve unforeseen problems independently. Errors and 'accidents' that could result from applying strict rules when inappropriate need to be minimized because of the value of the product.

In sum, in a practical procedure like milking the value of the end product combined with the unpredictable nature of certain aspects of the activity constrain the syntactic routinization of the milking procedure. In classroom maths, routinization and the application of formal rules is not only possible, but desirable – despite the dissonance it may create in a student's mind.

The teaching strategy then reflects these different 'set-up' strategies. What characterizes the mother's instruction in milking is the combination of syntactic rules with semantic explanations. There are reasons for each step, reasons that may be transparent to an initiated observer, or that, in the case of young children, are provided by the expert embedded in the form of commands. It is at this level that the 'thickness' of the domain is constructed, according to the number of semantic layers that are woven together in the acquisition of a routine. By contrast, the maths teacher tends to delay the explanation by saying something like, 'Learn this now and later you will understand', or 'I will explain this to you in the next grade'.

How domains of expertise become more complex, coherent and elaborate can be organized according to four types of 'elaborateness' discussed previously for the milking example:

(1) Within the Domain (i.e. at the craft level):

While in milking all aspects of the activity are woven together, in school maths the calculator-like aspect of mathematical performances is emphasized, as are the appropriate labels and vocabulary. In sum, the symbolic level of the craft is emphasized at the expense of the practical and the conceptual.

(2) Multilevel Understanding:

In maths this would mean that symbolic routines are tied to conceptual models, which in turn relate to practical problems as experienced by students, and try to account for rules and the full range of concrete instances in which the formal rules do not seem to work. This type of multilevel understanding is not developed. In milking, the elaborateness or amount of connection to explanatory principles is occasional and ad hoc because often scaffolding is provided in the goal-effective spirit of 'getting the job done'. However, in other contexts novices may overhear or be provided with explanatory principles, such as when adults discuss with each other the causes of decreased milk production, and the possible solutions.

(3) Multiple Purposes

In maths lessons, the main objective is to get the students through the programme. Other secondary purposes are mentioned in isolated ways. In milking, the multiple purposes are constantly expressed in interactions surrounding tasks: 'You will never be able to get a job in milking', or 'How is anyone going to hire someone who milks as clumsily as you do!'

(4) Multiple Roles of the Activity

The multiple uses of mathematical skills are not part of maths lessons, except for word problems. However, these word problems are all of a similar type and selected by the teacher. In milking, the activity is embedded in a system of services/goods exchange that fosters identification with the teacher, the domestic work unit, and the community.

The Nature of the Physical Set-up

Finally, in contrasting milking and maths, the concrete setting of the activities needs to be discussed. The situation in the assembly-line format is 'set up' in advance for the student. There is a complex organization of material to be explained and problems to be solved – everything is prearranged for the student to work on. As in a factory where everything is 'set up', the student moves from stage to stage in an environment that is designed outside of their own experience. The way the routine is organized remains invisible to the learner. A professional educator knows what the teaching sequence should be like. The teacher prepares topics and materials, thereby providing a ready-made scenario for the students. By contrast, in milking, the novice has access to all the preparatory stages of the milking 'lesson'. After all, the learner will soon be expected to set up the activity himself, and eventually to teach it to the next generation.

The scenarios in maths change and there is no room to go back over previous 'set-ups', nor really enough time to assimilate them (as soon as some students have mastered the material it is time to move on to the next workstation). Such 'scaffolding' cannot be internalized by the novice.

Milking is 'overscaffolded', but in a different way. The context itself has many intrinsic signals that the novice learns and is told how to read: for example, a calf near the cow one is about to milk 'signals' trouble. Commands such as, 'Watch that calf, he is going to drink the milk and make the cow overturn the bucket' will be replaced by simple commands such as 'Look out, the calf'. The 'because ...' part can be left out now, as previous experience has demonstrated the consequences of such situations to the novice. This simplification of commands leads to the gradual internalization of a literal 'working model' of the situation, where sights like loose calves are intrinsic signals for specific action. The scaffold is internalized in that the novice develops a mental model of the activity. Not only that, but the activity itself provides external 'mnemonic support'.

In addition, the overtness of the activity provides the learner with the opportunity to observe aspects of the situation in which he may be interested. We could call this *'free contextual teaching/learning in milking'*. In the classroom, however, the situation presented is restricted to the particular problem at hand. Furthermore, in the milking context there are plenty of opportunities for 'ad hoc' or opportunistic teaching and learning, something that is not often done in the formal context because it is not part of the 'objectives of the class'. The criteria for deciding what should be dealt with and what should be ignored are much more rigid in the classroom situation.

The Tabula Rasa Fallacy vs. Integrated Schemata of Learning about Milking

When analysing the school curriculum in the context of conceptual routines in previous chapters, it was crucial to take into account how much students already knew about a particular subject matter (i.e. their everyday knowledge), so as to provide insight into how the teacher and/or student could 'make sense' of what was being taught in the classroom. The same holds true for maths, where sensitivity to the student's pre-knowledge would seem essential, but is largely ignored.

This 'tabula rasa fallacy', coupled with assembly-line fragmentation of the content described above, goes directly against the facts that (a) children have had plenty of experience with domains where quantitative reasoning comes into play, notably buying and selling in the store, and (b) those practical learning experiences have been of a same-script format. In other words, most children first go with their older siblings to shop, until gradually they go by themselves. They experience having a limited amount of money, prices going up, people owing money, giving back change, checking the change, and so on. The children may not understand all the elaborate details, but they do have a non-trivial amount of pre-knowledge of practical, monetary operations. While these practical calculations are carried out without the aid of pencil and paper (Nunes, Carraher and Schliemann 1985), they represent the 'target systems' by which the children have learned quantitative reasoning, and should be used to give meaning to formal school maths.

And yet school maths is based on the drilling of symbolic routines virtually separated from the real-life business of monetary calculations! As a woman owner of a store expressed it, 'I used to be terrible at maths in school. Only now that I own a store I do understand this business with numbers'. School emphasizes symbolic routines at the expense of conceptual (semantic), and practical (pragmatic) aspects of mastery, which are what a store owner needs to know, to apply maths effectively in solving real problems. In this context, it is significant that when parents were asked why they send their children to school, they mentioned to learn about religion but never to learn maths. Nor did not having been to school prevent any of the local women from getting involved in market transactions. Clearly, as Nunes, Carraher and Schliemann (1985) show, there are embedded forms of learning to deal with money.

Catalina Laserna is a social anthropologist who takes a sociocultural perspective on how people learn. She has conducted policy-oriented research on innovations for online education at Harvard's Division of Continuing Education. At the Harvard Extension School, she conceived and directed the Master of Liberal Arts in Technologies of Education. Dr Laserna has taught at the Harvard Graduate School of Education, the Department of Social Anthropology, and has advised the ministries of education in El Salvador, Paraguay and Colombia on advancing national e-educational reform.

Note

1. In using the term 'surveyable', I want to emphasize that learners have the opportunity of looking carefully and thoroughly at someone doing something. In this way, the novice gets a general impression of the routine as a whole and of particular details. Instead of providing the learner with careful instructions (as is the practice in school), learners are encouraged to observe carefully and ask few questions.

References

Cole, Michael. 1985. 'The Zone of Proximal Development: Where Culture and Cognition Create Each Other', in James V. Wertsch (ed.), Culture, Communication and Cognition: Vygotskian Perspectives. Cambridge: Cambridge University Press, pp. 146–61.

Fortes, Meyer. 1938. *Social and Psychological Aspects of Education in Taleland.* Oxford: Oxford University Press [Reprinted in John Middleton (ed.). 1970. *From Child to Adult.* Austin: University of Texas Press].

Goody, Esther N. 1978. 'Towards a Theory of Questions', in Esther N. Goody (ed.), *Questions and Politeness: Strategies in Social Interaction.* Cambridge: Cambridge University Press.

———. 1982. *Parenthood and Social Reproduction: Fostering and Occupational Roles in West Africa.* Cambridge Studies in Anthropology 35. Cambridge: Cambridge University Press.

———. 1996. 'Authority and Learning in Northern Ghana' . End of Award Report, Economic and Social Research Council, UK. Esther N. Goody archive, Centre for African Studies, Cambridge University.

Laserna, Catalina. 1988. 'Embedded and Formal Education in San Juan, an Indigenous Peasant Community in the Southern Andes of Colombia'. PhD dissertation, University of Cambridge.

Nunes, Terezinha, David W. Carraher and Analucia D. Schliemann. 1985. 'Mathematics in the Streets and in Schools'. *British Journal of Developmental Psychology* 3(1): 21–29.

Wertsch, James (ed.). 1981. *The Concept of Activity in Soviet Psychology.* New York: M.E. Sharp.

7

Singing the Names
Custom and Chronology in Mamprusi Drum Histories

Susan Drucker Brown

Editors' Note: With the passing of Susan Drucker Brown in May 2023, this chapter will most probably be her final publication. Although we have not altered her text, we did want to reflect briefly on how she saw her work in relation to Esther Goody's. As Fentiman recounted at Drucker Brown's commemoration in 2024, Susan (like Esther) met Meyer Fortes in the United States, who convinced her to come to the UK for advanced study. She (and Lynne Brydon already mentioned) became his doctoral student, and the beautifully thick description contained in this chapter is testimony to Fortes' insistence on the importance of ethnography before anything else. Drucker Brown was in fact working on the Meyer Fortes archive, held at the Cambridge University Library, during the final years of her life.

Although the abstract submitted for this chapter does not mention Esther Goody directly, an earlier unpublished abstract was explicit about ways in which Drucker Brown both extended and departed from Goody's material; we draw on some of that here: 'The paper here is an attempt to extend some of Goody's insights from Gonja questioning to the "speech" performed by Mamprusi drummers in the musical form that accompanies major ritual. ... [This] has critical political importance in the competitive system of succession. ... [However, this] drum language contrasts sharply with Goody ... [as] the performance of Mamprusi drums is limited to specialists'. Drucker Brown's discussion of the extent to which audience interpretation is context-dependent also invites comparison with a paper jointly written by Esther and Jack Goody (1992, see Introduction) on Gonja drum history. In this, Drucker Brown provides an extensive analysis of the ways in which the content of both drumming and song offers chronological as well as synchronic accounts of Mamprusi kingship.

Introduction

Esther Goody's work 'Towards a Theory of Questions' (1978) opens a fascinating window on the complex nature and interrelationship of the speech acts we would call 'questions' and the wider social world of hierarchy and social status. Because many of the phrases played by the Mamprusi drums are in the form of questions, I was inspired to analyse them using her frame of reference. The texts presented here demonstrate the nature of that ritual questioning. However, while studying these texts I was struck by the manner in which they represent the passage of time.

The core narrative of the musicians' performances consists of the names of kings and royal chiefs. These are known as *Naamyuya* – the names (sing. *yuri*, pl. *yuya*) of *'naam'*. *Naam* is the transcendental element embodied in *Nayiiri*, the king (literally, 'the house of *Naam*'). During his installation ritual, a *nabia* (a royal child of *naam*) becomes the incarnation of *naam*, able to allocate portions of *naam* to other royals who then become chiefs.

The singers and drummers address both the living royal chiefs and king as well as their ancestral predecessors. The king's musicians (*lungsi* – drummers and singers) are regarded as custodians of a narrative that is chronological in that it is believed to be a record of the kingship from its origins in the person of the founder, Na Gbewa, to its embodiment in the living king. However, the performance also links the living and the dead in ways that emphasize the circulation of royal office through generations in pairs of fathers and sons. The circulation of office is a process that underlies contemporary Mamprusi politics.

The name of the drum with which we are concerned is *lunga* (pl. *lungsi*). *Lunga* is also the drummer's title, though the solo-singer and leader of the drummers as a group is titled 'chief drummer' (*Lunaba*). The solo performer at the king's installation is titled 'Baamyo' (he who praises).

Drummers claimed that on the greatest ritual occasions they sing all the names of all the kings who have ever reigned; from the very first founding ancestor, Na Gbewa, to the living/reigning king and his contemporary royal chiefs. If, on many occasions, they do not sing the entire number, they claim it is because it would take too long. However, during most public occasions the *lungsi* performance is determined by the audience present to hear and, incidentally, to pay for the drumming.

Although writers in English often refer to the drummers' narrative as 'drum history', the *lungsi* do not narrate a single chronology of succession to any given office. Rather, they name the genealogically related holders of different royal offices, always emphasizing the connections between titled fathers and sons, citing the places in which those named held court. Similar though less elaborate performances occur in the courts of princes who hold important chiefly office.

The *lungsi* play an hourglass-shaped drum which is held under the drummer's right arm. He uses his left hand to wield the curved drumstick. The upper and lower skins of the drum are strung together across the frame with twisted grass rope. By the differing placements of drumstick and fingers on the upper skin, and by changing the pressure of his right arm on the strings, thus tightening or loosening the drum skins, the drummer can produce a nearly tonal scale (Chernoff 1979). In this way, *lungsi* drummers reproduce both the intonation and the rhythms of speech. Given that Mampruli is a tonal language, the reproduction of the rise and fall as well as the rhythm of speech makes recognition of phrases possible (Kawada 1982). Such drums are often referred to in English as 'talking drums'. However, the drumbeat can only be translated back into spoken words if the listener already knows the message. There are degrees of recognition which enable different listeners to retrieve more or less information from the same drumbeat, depending on how much information they already have.

For example, my own drum-name is '*Pwa'a kam sumla veilm*'. Those who know the drumbeat, having seen me enter the palace when it is played, may recognize the specific tonal pattern and rhythm as my name. Those who know me better will know the words the drummer is playing. Very few people will know why the name was given to me, or by whom, or what it means in a much more complete sense.

The *Baamsi*: 'Those Who Praise'

The musicians attached to the king's court, or to the court of a royal chief, are called *baamsi* ('those who praise'. See Drucker Brown 1975: 64–65). In addition to the *lungsi*, the category includes calabash drummers, the drummers who play the two large standing drums (timpani) located in front of the king's palace, whistle blowers, players of stringed instrument, and others. The timpani can also reproduce speech, but they are not mobile and are used to announce visitors to the palace. By contrast, *lungsi* accompany dancers, and most importantly they accompany the king as he moves. They announce when he is seated on the skins of office, and their drumbeat heralds dismissal of the court. Thrice weekly, before dawn, *lungsi* praise the past and the living king and royal chiefs who are descendants of ancestral kings. The spirits of these royal ancestors gather in the outer hall of the palace on these occasions. The thunderous drumming can be heard throughout the king's village. *Lungsi* may also patrol the village at night, beating drums which say: 'Quiet! Listen!' (*Shina ka iwum*), the drumbeat followed by a shouted announcement.

There were, in 1985, three drummers' families in Nalerigu, the capital village. One of these was a patrilineage headed by the *Lunaba* (chief/*naba* of the *lungsi*). The other two households were headed by drummers who had come from different parts of the neighbouring Dagomba region. It is not unusual for drummers to move from one court to another, and Dagomba kings, like those of Wa and Nanumba, claim descent from Mamprusi kings. Men of the three drummers' families perform together but only the Mamprusi *Lunaba* is permitted to sing the royal names on major ritual occasions, such as those described below. However, drummers are also present at the most routine of court occasions. They accompany the *Nayiiri* as he moves from inside the palace into public space. They are sent by the *Nayiiri* to outlying villages where they perform during the funerals of royal chiefs. They accompany the returning effigy of a royal chief to the palace (Drucker Brown 1988). At this point in the funerals of royal chiefs, there are two separate occasions when children of the deceased chief are named and individually present themselves, first to the court elders and then to the *Nayiiri*. These presentations are witnessed by the *lungsi*, who should, in future, recognize and name the children. *Lungsi* are in fact omnipresent witnesses to the public activities of kings and chiefs, and they move about the country performing with other musicians in ways that enable them to accumulate information they will use in their performances.

The *Nayiiri*'s Installation

Drummers perform the '*naamyuya*' throughout the entire night of the secret ceremony which transforms the king's body from that of a child of *naam* (*nabia*) to its most powerful incarnation as *Nayiiri*. At this time the palace is guarded by armed warriors, and the villagers remain in their houses. The ritual of installation, as described below, is clearly of major political and religious significance.

Nevertheless, when I asked the elders to name the different classes of titled persons who constitute the king's court, it was the king himself who added the praise-singers to the list. The *lungsi*, he said, 'are very important'. It is interesting that they had not been mentioned by any other member of the court. Like other elders, *lungsi* have a specific task. They perform names which summon and please the living and the dead. However, unlike other members of the court, they are paid with currency for their public performances; both royals and commoners together make gifts of currency. *Lungsi* also advise the king as well as praising him. Other elders also advise the king, but their comments are never made publicly. *Lungsi* advice has a particularly sharp edge, as it both praises the powers of kingship but also emphasizes its limitations (see below, and Appendix: Baamyo's Text).

King's Names

The name of a reigning king is chosen after his investiture, an event that will have been accompanied by the all-night performance of the names of his predecessors and their descendants. During the secret part of the ritual the new king will announce to the drummers the three names that he has chosen to be his kingship names. These may be chosen from a store of 'proverbial names' invented by past kings, or the new king may invent a new name to commemorate the circumstances of his accession and his hopes for the future. Of the three names the king announces, only one will be the name by which he is to be known. The drummers choose that name from the three he has announced, and set it to a beat of their drums. From then on, that drumbeat accompanies the king at all times, and still refers to him after his death.

Some names are aggressive, referring to victories over rivals, or vengeance to be taken in case of rebellion. Kings have, for example, been named razor, iron, crocodile, poisonous snake, and hawk. Na Sheriga's father was named for a snake which, it is said, 'does not bother you unless you rouse its anger'. Recent kings' names have been more concerned with the future well-being of the people. The *Nayiiri* reigning in the 1960s was named *Sheriga* (needle). He said the name meant that 'He would stitch his people together'. Other nonaggressive names that have been chosen are *Gamni* (door) 'to protect them against harm', *Saa* (rain) 'to be good to them like rain', and *Bongo*, 'a grove of shade trees'.

Some kings' names, like *Bongo*, are known but I did not hear them performed, nor are they spoken of as relevant to the present-day competition for office. They seem to be exemplary rather than a practical part of the publicly performed recitations. However, they are used as referents to what kings have done and may do. Among these are *Moa'are* (river), the name of a *Nayiiri* who did not take his elders' advice but built his house in a river. When he tried to enter the house, he sank in the water and turned to stone. The stone is now used to make each new *Nayiiri*, who, during the installation ritual, is seated on the stone seven times.

Another name, similarly unmentioned but known, is that of the usurping Na Sweep (*Na Kpism*), who swept up the kingship and sat on the stone that makes kings. He was killed immediately after that, but his children thus became princes and eligible for kingship. *Na Jeringa* (the poisonous snake), killed young men and women to embed their bodies in the wall he built around Nalerigu, the capital village, where remains of the wall can still be found.

When the king is brought out of seclusion after his secret installation, his name is performed by the *lungsi* to the crowds of people who will have gathered in the capital. This public phase of installation is called 'the outdooring', as is the ceremony performed for a Mamprusi infant. In an ordinary outdooring ceremony, the child is brought out of the mother's room into the public space at the front of the compound, where the infant's name will be announced to a gathering of kin, neighbours and friends. The 'rebirth' of a chosen prince as *Nayiiri* is thus explicitly presented as analogous to the birth of a child. The elder who is custodian of the new king during the period of seclusion refers to the installation and investiture as the birth of a female child (Drucker Brown

1992, 1999). At the king's outdooring, his name is announced in front of his predecessor's abandoned palace, where the secret installation was performed. The new *Nayiiri* will have a new palace built for him. Once announced, his name will be known throughout the kingdom during his reign and for some time after his death. The word chosen as his name will be avoided by the entire Mamprusi population. Euphemisms are substituted for the word that has become a king's name – for example, 'needle' became 'sharp pointed thing', 'snake' became 'rope'. Some words, taken as names by more than one king, seem to drop out of the common vocabulary entirely to be used only as king's names.

Mamprusi routinely avoid the use of personal names. A host of nicknames, and kin terms replace personal names. However, the prohibition on the use of a kingship name is unique in that the entire population, undifferentiated by kinship, place of origin or title, observes the prohibition against uttering the word. In addition to the name of the reigning king, which changes over time, Mamprusi are also forbidden to mention the name of the founder of the kingship or the name of the king-making stone. Both the founder's name and that of the living king are oaths. If mentioned in a dispute the case must be brought directly to the king's court.

Solima

The drummed names of kings and royal chiefs belong to a class of names called '*Solima*'. They are distinct from other *solima*, in that they are said to 'cover' the birth names and previous titles of their holders. Such names are said to be 'heavy'. They summon powerful ancestors who may be dangerous, and their living kin mention the names when offering sacrifice, but never in normal conversation. Most adult men and women have *solima*, which I have translated as 'proverbial names'. The word *solima* refers in other contexts to a particular kind of story, supposedly told only by women and children, though men are also easily persuaded to tell them. These *solima* begin with the phrase '*Nsolima bene*' (this is my *solima*), just as our fairy stories in English begin with 'Once upon a time'. *Solima* consist of a story told by a narrator, but they also contain a song or songs which the narrator sings together with his audience. This combination of solo narrative and chorus is also the pattern of a *lungsi* performance in which the *lungsi* chorus and lead-singer cooperate.

'*Solini*' (to perform a *solima*) thus means both to tell a story and to praise a name. An individual's praise name or praise names are stories about that person – proverbial phrases referring to real or imagined events, relationships and desires. A *solima*, in the sense of a proverbial or a praise name, may be of one's own invention, or the invention of others. Such names may be played by the drummers on festival occasions, and as noted above, the drummers must be paid.

Succession and Praise

To fully understand the performance of the praise singers and drummers it is essential to know something of the patterns of succession to Mamprusi kingship. Unlike some of the neighbouring kings historically related to them, the Mamprusi have no rule of automatic succession to kingship. The single most important rule is a negative one. The king may not be succeeded by his own son, nor by a close patrikinsman. The royal patrilineage segments that Mamprusi call 'gates' are ideally made up of three generations of patrikin, descended from the same kingly ancestor. Ideally the kingship rotates among these royal gates, moving from the deceased king's gate to the one that has been longest without a king. Mamprusi call this 'the gate farthest removed' from the kingship. Succession is recognized, however, to be the product of competition among rival princes; and the ideal, that circulation should favour the most distant gate, is rarely achieved (Drucker Brown 1989).

The commoner elders who choose the new king assert that only the true sons of kings are eligible to become *Nayiiri*. However, grandsons dispute this, and as grandsons may compete for lesser chiefly office and all royal chiefs may be praised as 'sons' of kings, confusion is possible. In any case, the results of a competition for the kingship are always regarded as unpredictable. Remember *Na Kpisim*, the usurper who swept up the kingship by sitting on the stone that makes kings. He had, in effect, founded a new gate and so his sons became eligible for kingship. His name would seem to indicate the powers of the initiation ritual to transform even a usurping candidate into a *Nayiiri*.

The *lungsi* performances are inextricably linked to the competitive succession because they publicize the names of living descendants of deceased kings and princes who hold office as royal village chiefs. These individuals may compete for the succession whether or not they are eligible. The names of the potential replacements of kings and chiefs are constantly repeated by drummers, along with the names of the royal ancestors who provide the genealogical basis for their claims to office. The demand, repeated explicitly by the drummers but well known to all Mamprusi, that *lungsi* must be paid for their performance, is equally publicized. This demand for payment is a pressure that some royals cannot endure. They may avoid public occasions and thus avoid paying the drummers, but this option endangers not only their individual claims but the continuing inclusion of the names of their ancestors in the drummers' repertoire. In effect, one can see the process of competitive succession leading inevitably to a loss of ancestral names as the names of fathers and living sons who are successful in the competition displace the names of kings whose descendants fail to gain office.

Damma (based on field notes from 1965)

Editors' Note: The following ethnographic description combines Drucker Brown's observations of a particular event (generally marked by the usage of past tense) and her knowledge of the ritual as established practice (generally described through the ethnographic present). Although the moves between past and present tense are at times unclear, she is not here to clarify and so we have left the tense changes as they appear in the text.

I describe this festival in some detail as it is the most important public performance by the *lungsi*. It occurs annually at the king's court, and simpler versions may also occur throughout the Mamprusi region at the courts of royal chiefs. The month named 'Damma' is preceded by a month called 'the slave of Damma', indicating the importance of Damma. In the course of the Damma ritual, *Nayiiri* moves first within his palace, and then outside, from one seating place (*ziziiya*) to another. He moves in an east to west direction, which I believe identifies him with the cyclical movement of the sun. Damma is a ritual whole; a single performance with a dramatic narrative within which each episode of *Nayiiri's* movement corresponds to a time of day or night. It also commemorates the transhumant nature of the Mamprusi kingship.

Typically, in ceremonies that celebrate the origins of polities, as Adler (2000) remarks of the Mondang in Chad, the emergence of the political and ritual apparatus is the result of an exchange; a pact between the Mamprusi in this case, and the generous indigenous earth-priest (*Tozugu*) who granted Na Gbewa permission to remain in his territory.

Although the drumming and singing of names is only one part of the ceremony, it is the thread that links the various sections, and it culminates in the king's private sacrifice of a cow to his ancestors; the meat to be shared among the praise-singers and members of the court. The description that follows is based on my fieldnotes of 1965. I recorded the performance, and a translation from the Mampruli words and drumming was made by a drummer's son.

The First Performance: Morning (*'asuba'*)
Drum Rhythm (*'gingaanga'*)

Before dawn the drummers gathered in the outer hall of the palace to praise royal ancestors. Dawn and dusk are the times of day when ancestral spirits are believed to gather, and the outer palace hall is their preferred gathering place. *'Gingaanga'* is the specific drumbeat used on this occasion.

After *gingaanga*, the hall was carefully swept. The king's skins and the pillows he normally uses were spread on the dais. A pair of curved metal swords (*takobi*) were placed beneath the skins. Outside the palace the timpani drummer and the *Nayiiri's lungsi* began to drum the names of Nalerigu village elders and their guests. Chiefs and their entourages had arrived from villages throughout the kingdom for the Damma ceremonies. These groups, first of elders, later of chiefs, princes and other visitors, converged in stately processions at the palace gate. As each elder entered the palace followed by the chiefs and notables lodging with him, the timpani announced their arrival using their individual drum names. The *Nayiiri*, sitting on the skins and accompanied by elders and servants, received the visitors' greetings. Elders and chiefly retinues

Figure 7.1. Mamprusi performer, musician and drummer during the installation of a chief, Nalerigu, northern Ghana, 1956.
© Estate of Susan Drucker Brown.

then dispersed, each individual to sit in the allotted position at court which corresponded to his title. Distinctive greetings were used by the guests: Muslims greeting with prayers, *Kambonsi* (warriors) greeting from a standing position, princes and untitled persons squatting forward on their haunches with downcast eyes, clapping slowly and repeating *'naa, naa'* in soft falling tones. An elder then transmitted words of greeting from the *Nayiiri* to the court. Calling officials and notables in turn, another priest-elder distributed kola from the kettle that always accompanies the *Nayiiri*. Chiefs were called by the names of their villages, other notables addressed as 'father'. Each senior person came forward to receive kola, and on returning to his place redistributed half of the kola nut, or even smaller portions, among his juniors. Once the kola had been consumed and the greetings exchanged, the court was dismissed.

Noon Gingaanga (*wintang gingaanga*)

At midday, the skins and pillows were again spread by the palace servants; this time on the outdoor dais adjacent to the west-facing wall and doors of the palace. Timpani drummers, again using the *gingaanga* beat, called the *Nayiiri* to emerge from the palace. Led by one specific elder, followed by another, and flanked to his right and to his left by two more elders, the *Nayiiri* proceeded from the outer hall through the north door, into the palace yard (*samani*) to sit on the waiting skins, which had been guarded by other servants and elders. It took the procession nearly one hour to make this progress of some fifty metres. The leading elder stopped every few paces to pick up a twig or a leaf, indicating that he was clearing the path. The king moved with a special rolling step. As the king walked, holding his gold-covered walking stick and tapping the ground before him, the *lungsi* drummers beat a replication of the following phrases in the high-pitched drums:

Mra Ka boa'ari; Mra ka I lu'
[Watch out for the holes. Watch out or you will fall!]

To which the bass drums replied:

Ti nin diai ti kobuga, Pa Nkwa!
[We will receive our hundred (cowries)! SOON!]

These drummed phrases are always played when the *Nayiiri* emerges from the palace on ritual occasions. They might refer to, and certainly recall, the founding king who disappeared into the earth upon hearing the news that the son he had chosen as his successor had been killed by a rival son. The rival had dug a large hole, covered it with skins, and invited his brother to be seated. Thus, the unfortunate favourite was trapped and killed. On the other hand, the reference to the drummers' payment could not be more explicit.

It was just before midday when the *Nayiiri* was again seated outside the palace facing the timpani drums and the shaded enclosure (*leenga*). The court regrouped, and the many visitors again greeted him. A commoner-elder, instructed by the *Nayiiri*, then 'opened the *damma*' – that is to say, he began the dance. Various of the commoner, warrior-elders danced to the special drumbeats of their own drummers. When the *Nayiiri* returned to the palace, a few princes also danced to their special rhythm. When the *lungsi*, who accompanied the king into the palace, announced with their special beat that the king was again seated on his skins, an elder emerged from the south door of the outer hall to disperse the court. This event lasted about an hour and a half. After the midday meal and rest at the palace, the *Nayiiri*'s horse was brought into the stable area of the palace and dressed in quilted cotton armour. The elaborately decorated leather saddle, the horse's headgear and other ornaments, some eight distinct pieces of gear in all, were separately named and fitted on the horse.

Twilight Damma (*wintang lu*)

Towards the end of the afternoon, roughly at 4.30 p.m., the timpani drummer began again to drum the names of visitors and the elders to convene the court. The visitors converged at the west corner of the palace, waiting for the *Nayiiri* to emerge. The *lungsi* again beat *gingaani*, which would accompany the *Nayiiri*'s slow progress from the palace to the shaded enclosure facing the palace gate. On this occasion, however, the procession of *Nayiiri* and his elders was preceded by the fully dressed, riderless horse who was led through the palace gate by one of the *Nayiiri*'s servants. Holding the bridle, the servant took up a position at the south-west corner of the palace wall, some five metres from the gate. Facing south, he held the horse in that position throughout the entire performance that followed.

Then the *Nayiiri*, wearing a hooded white robe of shimmering cotton and silk, shaded by a huge red umbrella, moved slowly to the *gingaani* beat, from the palace to the shaded enclosure (*leenga*). Among his elders, one whose title is 'custodian of the spears' (*kpanaraana*), carried three spears decorated with leopard skin. These had been taken from the palace shrine-room. Drummers and elders accompanied the *Nayiiri* to the skins where the warrior elders sat in a rank behind the dais. Once the *Nayiiri* was seated, the waiting princes moved towards the enclosure but remained squatting outside the entrance. Only when the *Nayiiri* was seated and the drumbeat had changed from the *gingaani* processional beat to the final '*Ti nin gmea ti kobuga*' ('we will receive our hundred cowries'), which heralds the singing of names, did the princes finally seat themselves outside the enclosure facing the dais.

Beating their drums, the mass of *lungsi* then moved in a phalanx from the shaded enclosure to the palace, led by the chief drummer. Then, turning to face the *Nayiiri* with their backs to the palace gate, the *lungsi* stood drumming, while the *Lunaba* knelt on the ground and began to sing. He praised first the founder of the Mamprusi Kingdom, Na Gbewa, naming him as father of the Mamprusi, the Dagomba and the Mossi peoples, and then as father of the kings of Pusiga, Bulugu and other ancient settlements of Mamprusi kings.

Lunaba's sung praises of specific kings and royal chiefs were interspersed with drumming. Each set of named chiefs and each king was first identified as Gbewa's child through repetition of the founder's name. Thus:

'*Pusigana Seidu ba, Na Gbewa*' – Chief of Pusiga's father, Na Gbewa
'*Gulugunaba ba, Na Gbewa*' – Chief of Gulugu's father, Na Gbewa …

Each successive *Nayiiri* was introduced, by naming the names of his titled sons. In this way *Lunaba*'s singing of the names grouped individuals as fathers and sons. The singing of royal names was interspersed with the drummers' solo performance. In the drummed intervals between each sung set of names, the singer, followed by the drummers, inched forward on the ground, ever closer to the king.

This grouping of fathers and sons is typical of the *lungsi* performances. The singer praises each individual as the child of his father, and occasionally also of his mother. In Mamprusi belief it is important to note that the identification of father and child established at birth is not ended by the father's death. The act of sacrifice is known as 'making, or making good, one's father's names' (*mali I bayuya*). These names, normally forbidden, are mentioned as one calls the ancestors to receive the sacrifice. Furthermore, death itself is linked to the utterance of names, for at death an individual is believed to be called by his ancestors.

It is clear that the slow crawl of the *Lunaba* from the palace gate to the seated king represents a movement in space which is meant to parallel a movement in time, from the foundation of the kingship to the present moment. The names are sung and drummed in a presumed chronology of kingly succession from the founder to the reigning king. However, chiefs' as well as kings' names are sung in sets corresponding to their membership of gates. The time of succession differs with each chiefly office. Royal chiefs are normally only installed after a father's death, and a royal chief may well outlive the successor of a king in the same gate, or of a king named in a succeeding gate. Thus, rather than the chronology of succession to a single office, the text asserts the chronology of succession of members of a particular patrilineage segment.

In this Damma performance, when the singer reached the name of the reigning king's father, a musket was fired. At this point the drummers and *Lunaba* had reached the entrance to the enclosure where *Nayiiri* was seated. One of the visiting priest-chiefs arose at this point, with a loud shout. The drummers had just named all the living children of the reigning king's own father. At the chief's shout, the drummers suddenly changed their drumbeat, moving from Damma rhythm to the beat characteristic of the commoner-warriors' dance. Three commoner priest-chiefs then came forward, each holding one of the ancestral spears. Walking towards the palace gate they turned and, following the new rhythm, they danced towards the *Nayiiri*, brandishing the spears. When they arrived at the entrance to the enclosure, they pointed the spears at the king's chest, and three times mimed an attack on him. I was told later that this is the most important part of Damma: the king must weep, 'a tear must come down from his eye'.

This dramatic climax of Damma is differently interpreted by commoners and royals. Commoners claim that the gestures that threaten the king mean the elders are saying, 'We own you!' Princes told me the *Nayiiri* wept for his followers who had died when they fled from their original homeland (to the northeast of the Mamprusi region) but that the presence of the horse was to show that, if he wished, the *Nayiiri* could ride off and leave his people behind. When their dance is completed, the elders return to the palace and the drums accompany the king as he too re-enters the palace. Once more the drums announce that he is seated on the skins, and an elder dismisses the court. This phase of Damma is followed by the sacrifice of a cow, performed inside the palace by the king to his ancestors. The meat is cooked, and later distributed to the musicians and other members of the court.

Night-Time Damm (*yungu*)

At night the people of the capital village, and their many guests, return to the palace. The king's drummers appear along with other groups of musicians. The different classes of elders, commoners and royals all dance with their distinct music. The royals, unlike many of the commoners, danced singly, competing with one another to show off their flowing robes and billowing pantaloons. They pay the drummers, and themselves receive contributions from onlookers who rush in to press coins to a dancer's forehead or into his hands. At midnight the king appears again with his senior wife. They sit for a time overlooking the dance. Damma produces a sense of unity among the public and even among the princes, despite their strong rivalries. Pride in their specific ancestors and in the kingship as a source of their common origins is elicited by the drummers.

The *Baamsi* Performance at the King's Installation

Unlike the Damma performance described above, which commands the attention of the entire Mamprusi population, the investiture of a *Nayiiri* is performed secretly in the abandoned palace of the deceased king, which in 1986, as is customary, was surrounded by armed warriors during the ceremony. I reproduce below a text recorded for me in 1965 by the leading singer (titled 'Baamyo') of the king's *lungsi*. He agreed to record the text if I gave him a sheep to sacrifice to his ancestors, which I did. The text is reproduced as an appendix to this chapter, and was translated for me by Thomas Musah Yakubu, son of one of the leading drummers.

In the recording, Baamyo begins by separating himself from the king, whom he is addressing: 'How did I become a praise singer? What did my fathers do to keep the title?', and he ends the recording in a similar fashion, referring to himself as 'tradition' (tradition sits all night), and to his performance at the investiture: 'He who makes Gbewa sits all night till dawn making Gbewa. His sitting is done and he chose his kingship name. He is *Kuliguba* (crocodile), Kuliguba's son. Step and let the earth cool'.

The phrase 'step, let the earth cool' is often sung. But most of Baamyo's text, performed during the *Nayiiri*'s installation, is very different from those commonly performed. Baamyo's narrative refers to specific elements of the ritual (the seating, bathing and feeding of the new king), and he emphasizes the differences between kings and the creator God (*Nawuni*). He refers to the kings as 'children of Belangu', thus naming the sacred stone which should never be mentioned.

After naming a long list of ancient chiefs, whom he calls children of the founding king, Na Gbewa, Baamyo refers again to himself and to the payment he requires: 'You aren't drumming. I can't sing. Mouth, speak for me. Mouth says, "Give me something!"' Returning to the distinction between *Nawuni* and the *Nayiiri*, Baamyo refers to events he attributes to the agency of 'God' (*Nawuni*) rather than *Nayiiri*: 'Big houses become small. Small houses become big. The barren woman waits to conceive and tires. She cries to God'. Baamyo addresses the new *Nayiiri* directly:

We say you are not God! And he says: Who is God?
Our grandfather is not God who made the leper.
Nas' wives are no one. They didn't create God.
He who made stones and made hills. We say God created them.
What is God? First king, Powerful one.
He created the farmer and created grass.
He created the kingship without an owner.
He created heads and made their covering.
Creation's God. My owner
Step! Let the earth cool. Kingship knows nothing!]/vs[

Here the reference to Na Gbewa, the founder, is also unique; he is praised as both father and mother of kings, 'mother of those who serve' and 'mother of the dead' (that is, everybody's ancestors). The ambivalent separation and identification of the first king with the creator god ends in this stanza with the phrases: 'Step! Let the earth cool. Kingship knows nothing!' Although the contrast of *Nayiiri* with *Nawuni* is clear in this secret performance, it is not routinely sung. By contrast, the phrase 'Kingship knows nothing!' is commonly drummed.

There are other sections that refer to the king's walk. Michel Cartry writes that among the Grumache, the drummers teach the king his special walk as part of his installation ceremony (Cartry 1987). The *Nayiiri* never moves quickly, but his walk on ceremonial occasions is theatrically slow, swaggering.

His senior wife pointed out to me that his walk was like the movement of a lion, and lions are indeed regarded as embodiments of dead kings. Na Sheriga asked me if I had not noticed that he moved like a chameleon, another special creature. The chameleon moves both slowly and tentatively, perhaps as though testing the ground as the *Nayiiri* is advised to do.

Baamyo refers to 'King of *gba gba*, king of *yo-yo*. Thighs support buttocks and buttocks go *gbari-gbari*. *Gba-gba naba, yo-yo naba!*' Here Baamyo is singing that the king's ceremonial walk depends on the buttocks, as the buttocks depend on the thighs.

The refrain: 'Step my lover, let the earth cool!' is commonly played by the *lungsi* to accompany the king as he walks. 'Cooling the earth' is a reference to peace-making, to ending conflicts with neighbouring peoples. Baamyo names the Nanumba and the Gonja (*Sibagsi*). In the past, conflicts with the peoples might well have preceded a king's installation as battles have been part of the preselection competition, and candidates are known to have enlisted mercenaries to support them. But also important is that the notion of 'cooling the earth' is a reference to the king's ability to make peace in his role as judge and arbitrator of disputes. The image of *Nayiiri* cooling the earth may also recall its opposite, for the *Nayiiri* is said to curse his people by stepping barefooted on the earth, which will cause them to suffer a skin rash.

'Kingship knows nothing' is a phrase often drummed, particularly when used as the introduction to the names of separate gates as these are sung at Damma and on other occasions. Here the drummers, in addition to recommending humility, are also reminding the *Nayiiri* of his dependence on others (including themselves) in order to perform his kingship.

Conclusions

Baamsi and royals both regard the *lungsi* performance as a chronicle that moves in time from the past founder and ancient kings to the living Mamprusi king and chiefs. However, the performance also illustrates the powerful temporal identification of fathers and sons. A friend once explained to me that 'you are your father's head'; the word for 'head' in the Mamprusi language (*zugu*) is also the word for 'luck'. He continued, 'that is because you are your father's destiny (*wuni*)'.

This conception of fathers and sons enacting a continuous, and even a simultaneous, destiny creates a kind of 'time-horizon' in which living princes or kings are presented as the embodiment of past generations as well as living agents. Because the genealogies of living princes vary in terms of how many generations removed they are from any particular living king, the names that are sung in praise of a living king or prince will encompass varying time spans. The singing of a king's name as the founder's child (*Gbewabia*) encompasses the entire time span from the origins of kingship to the present moment. On the other hand, the sons of kings who have no direct living descendants may be praised as though they were contemporaries of princes who are in fact sons of a reigning king.

What is essential is that royal ancestry be advertised for the rival princes who will compete for kingship and chiefship at a future time. To that end, the Mamprusi elders will try to keep the pool of princes eligible for chiefship and kingship as large as possible. As noted, the *baamsi* must be paid for the performance of the names, and elders too must receive gifts in the course of competition for royal office. Clearly, the wider the range of competitors, the greater the source of gifts. However, the names of rival gates will tend to be performed less often when the descendants of kings and chiefs either become too poor to provide payment and gifts, or generations pass without members of a gate becoming successful in the competition for office. Gifts are not necessarily decisive in the competition, but the ability to make a gift, like the ability to pay the *lungsi*, does more than simply strengthen a claim to office. It glorifies the office, and by extension, the kingship as a whole.

It is no exaggeration to say that the *lungsi* provide a collective memory for Mamprusi kingship and chiefship. The fact that the names are not written

Figure 7.2. 'The *Nayiiri*'s court in Nalerigu', aquatint etching by Susan Drucker Brown, ca. 2010. © Estate of Susan Drucker Brown.

enables the essential flexibility that constantly accommodates the drummers' repertoire to the fortunes of royal gates. The consensus that results from the repeated public performance of the names can be seen as one of the sources of stability in a potentially unstable system. The *lungsi* performances are subject to criticism as well as to approval, and they help to provide legitimacy and continuity for succession. The representation of time in their performance, whether it be cyclical or chronological, emphasizes above all the identification of father and son, and presents the kingship as the sum total of countless sequences of those connections.

Baamyo's Text
(As recorded in February 1965, translated by Thomas Musah Yakubu)

I cry to my lord god
They cannot leave god. People cry to the wise god.
A good skin makes bush-buck gather.
The well near an ebony tree sees many visitors.
How did I become a praise singer?
What did my grandfathers do to keep the title (*naam*)?
What did my fathers do to keep the title?
I call my lord god (*ndaana, nawuni*)
Let me call Belangu's children
Gbewa and who else is god?
We say you are not God.
God made the trees.
God created the crocodile with its head like three hearthstones
God created the crocodile with its teeth bared and twisting
God created the crocodile with its teeth like a dog.
Mother of the dead, Na Gbewa
Mother of those who serve, Na Gbewa
Zuurana Garidima's father, Na Gbewa
Binduri Gberi-Mori's father, Na Gbewa
Yunyoraana Da-zuku's father, Na Gbewa
Lumurana Yelintima's father, Na Gbewa
Misoraana Zorikum's father, Na Gbewa
Wungurana Daribioo's father Na Bewa
Yamdana Andani's father Na Gbewa

You aren't drumming. I can't sing.
Mouth: speak for me!
Mouth says 'give me something'
I cry to my lord God
King of streams, powerful god
Big houses become small

Small houses become big
The barren woman waits to conceive and tires
She cries to god.
The farmer cuts grass
And cries to a wise god.

Lover of good children; Na Gbewa
King of Gba-gba
King of yo-yo
God made trees.
What else did he make
Gbewa and who else is god?

We say you are not god.
And he said, Who is god?
Our grandfather is not god who made the leper.
Na's wives are no one.
They didn't create god. He who made stones and made hills.
We say god created them.

He who made stones and made hills
We say didn't god create them?
He who made farmers made grass.
We say didn't god create them?
Didn't god make stones?

What is god?
The day the granary is built, millet brings money.
Owner of he who cries for millet
First king, powerful one.
He created the farmer and created grass.
He created the kingship without an owner
He created heads and made their covering.
Creation's god. My owner.
Step!
Let the earth cool!
Kingship knows nothing...
I call my God. Let me call Belingu's children.
Belingu owner Dahmanoi finished.
We made his own child rise and he cut and finished.
He brought forth Belingu-owner Mahami.
Step! Let the earth cool.
He sat on the skins and stayed in kingship
The well near an ebony tree sees many visitors.

Bloody compounds child, Kuliguba.
Kuliguba opens ferocious teeth.
They want to bite.
Let them cool.
Nanumbas agree and cool.
Zibagsi agree. And cool.
Kingship knows nothing.

Susan Drucker Brown gained her first degree in ethnology from the Escuela Nacional de Antropología e Historia in Mexico City. She worked for the Indianist Institute among the Mixtec people of Oaxaca. As a graduate student at the Cambridge Department of Social Anthropology, she worked with the Mamprusi people of Northern Ghana. She was a senior lecturer at the University of Hull and a senior member of the Cambridge Department of Social Anthropology. Her publications include 'Cambio de Indumentaria en Santiago Jamiltepec', *Malinowski in Mexico*, and many articles on ritual aspects of Mamprusi kingship.

References

Adler, Alfred. 2000. *Le Pouvoir et l'interdit*. Paris: Albin Michel.

Cartry, Michel. 1987. 'Le Suaire du Chef', in *Sous le Masque de l'Animal*, Presses Universitaires de France, Paris, Bibliotheque de L'ecole des Hautes Etudes, Section des Sciences Religeuses, Vol. LXXXVIII, pp. 131–233.

Chernoff, John Miller. 1979. *African Rhythm and African Sensibility*. Chicago: University of Chicago Press.

Drucker Brown, Susan. 1975. *Ritual Aspects of the Mamprusi Kingship*. African Social Research Documents, Volume 8. Cambridge: African Studies Centre.

———. 1988. 'L'intronization du roi Mamprusi'. *Journal des Africanistes* 38(1): 88–97.

———. 1989. 'Mamprusi Installation Ritual and Centralization: A Convection Model'. *Man* 24(2): 485–501.

———. 1992. 'Horse, Dog and Donkey: The Making of a Mamprusi King'. *MAN* 27(1): 71–90.

———. 1999. 'The Grandchildren's Play at the Mamprusi King's Funeral: Ritual Rebellion Revisited in Northern Ghana'. *Journal of the Royal Anthropological Institute* 15(2): 181–92.

Goody, Esther. 1978. 'Towards a Theory of Questions', in Esther N. Goody (ed.), *Questions and Politeness: Strategies in Social Interaction*. Cambridge: Cambridge University Press, pp. 17–43.

Kawada, Junzo. 1982. 'Recordings of Drum Music for Japan Festival of African Music 2002'. Genese et dynamique de la royaute: les Mosi Meridionaux (Burkina Faso). Paris: L'Harmattan.

8

'One Snake is the Biggest in the Pond'
Linguistic Fragments from Mambila Funerals as Evidence for Religious Change

David Zeitlyn

Introduction

As has long been noted in anthropology, funerals are critical rites de passage in which social change is managed, orchestrated and marked, especially when a death is that of a senior, and so corresponds to the passing of the generations. Following Meyer Fortes, we might note that funerals are part of the developmental cycle of domestic groups. The following observations are taken from a larger work on religious change in Mambila. They provide, I hope, an example of how details of social interaction (how people talk to one another) can connect to wider themes of social anthropology as demonstrated in the work of Esther Goody. Her work exemplifies a great sensitivity to the intimate, contextually sensitive web of connections between language, social action and cultural history. For example, her discussion of questioning (1978) is a salutary warning about the misleading stereotype of 'just asking', which I regularly pass on to new research students. Indirectly this is an argument for participant observation and for following conversational flows that eventually can provide answers to unasked questions, albeit not always in predictable fashion. And Esther would have been the first to appreciate and to applaud the new directions that this would open up. She saw language as the main means by which culture (in all senses) reproduces and changes in response to challenges, both internal and external. Moreover, internal variation in patterns of usage can provide tools to help anthropologists, turning the linguistic analysis on its head, as it were. This is exemplified by politeness factors in pronoun use:[1] we can infer that these two people are, in some sense, equals because they use the familiar pronoun to each other. Such an observation would give us something concrete to discuss. In this chapter I am more descriptive and ethnographic: I use some fragments of speech from the planning discussions of a Mambila funeral as hooks on which to hang some ethnographic observations about religious change.

Mambila and Funerals

The Mambila people live on both sides of the Nigeria/Cameroon border, mostly on the Mambila Plateau in Nigeria. A smaller number (around twelve thousand) live in Cameroon, especially at the foot of the Mambila Plateau escarpment, on the Tikar Plain. My fieldwork has concentrated on these groups, and in particular on the village of Somié (see Zeitlyn 1994). According (contentiously) to the official 1986 tax census, Somié then had a population of approximately one thousand. It has now more than trebled, mainly as a result of immigration by Nigerian Mambila. Self-sufficient in food, the villagers have grown coffee as a cash crop since the early 1960s (maize is grown both as staple and as a cash crop). The local language is Mambila, a Mambiloid language which has a complex tone system but lacks Bantu noun classes. The group of Mambila languages has considerable dialectical variation: Nigerian Mambila immigrants use Fulfulde to speak to Cameroonian Mambila because the dialects are so different.

If asked, everyone in the village will describe themselves as Christian (Catholic or Protestant) or Muslim. In the late 1980s, the rough breakdown was two-thirds Christian and one-third Muslim, but as most Nigerian immigrants are Muslim the confessional breakdown is now approximately 50 per cent. Again it should be stressed that saying one is Christian or Muslim does not mean that one does not practise elements of traditional religion, although increasingly some people see a problem with this. Both the 'religions of the book' have been helped in their acceptance by a basic monotheism in Mambila religion in which the Semitic 'God' has been identified with the Mambila *Càŋ*, which leaves open the question of how to deal with and intercede with God. Granted considerable uncertainty about how to do this, the general attitude has been 'the more the better'. By the late 1990s this attitude has shown signs of changing as people have had more exposure to different forms of the world religions, and in response to those professing more radical or purer forms of them there are definite signs of the emergence of what I hesitate to call 'fundamentalism', but certainly can label 'religious purism' as manifested in the conversation discussed below.

On the one hand, it is easy to elicit information about funerals in Mambila. Many people will sit and give you accounts of how funerals are organized. If you ask, you may be told about how they used to be. This fluency, sadly, befits a society in which death is commonplace, one in which adults are seen to be dying more often in their prime as a consequence of AIDS, and one in which attendance at funerals is a widely followed social obligation: in the days following a death, large numbers of people gather to sit with those immediately bereaved. On the other hand, such accounts like so many 'official stories' gloss over uncertainty, division and dispute. These tend to occur backstage, off the record, and are resolved (more or less) before the performance takes place. As I will demonstrate, such disputes can be particularly informative for ethnographers.

The official accounts are incomplete, and in particular, they do not reveal the tensions between traditional funerary ritual and both Christian and Muslim rites, which are evident in local practice. That the tension is openly acknowledged is demonstrated by the discussion about arrangements following a death that I recorded on the evening of 26 July 1997, as I illustrate with some fragmentary quotations below.

More moves towards religious purity have been seen in the organization of funerals over the last thirty years. I have witnessed several arguments about this, either immediately following the death when the funeral is being planned or even, in some cases, during the funeral proceedings. One culminated in a series of arguments (which I did not witness) about how Chief Degah himself should have been buried (see below). These arguments are not as dramatic as the celebrated Kenyan case of 'Burying SM' (Cohen and Odhiambo 1992) in which the natal family and the wife clashed about where the body of the prominent Kenyan lawyer should be buried: according to Christian tradition in a consecrated graveyard in Nairobi or, following Luo tradition, in his natal compound, in the same place that his umbilical cord was buried. But, just as that case exemplified and brought into the open many tensions about the relationship of tradition and modernity in Kenya, so too do arguments about how senior Mambila should be buried, bringing into the open the tensions between Mambila traditional religion (and the *sùàgà* masquerades in particular) and the religions of the book – Christianity in the cases I have witnessed, and Islam in the case of the late Chief Degah.

Mambila funeral rites can be summarized as follows: burial takes place as soon as possible, although no preparations are made until after death. Shaft and chamber graves have been replaced by a grave style borrowed from the Fulbe by the middle of the twentieth century. A wide shaft has a small body size trench cut in the bottom. The body is placed in this wrapped in a cloth, or in a wooden coffin if the family can afford one. Both sexes are placed facing West, with the right hand held up. When there is no coffin, a raffia-pith mat is placed over the body and then the trench is roofed in with a screen of poles to prevent the earth directly touching the body. When filling the grave, the soil is replaced so that the darker soil from the surface is put in first. Red subsurface soil is thus left at the top. This serves to mark the location of the grave. Those who dig the grave and/ or touch the body must be treated afterwards to prevent arthritis: they hold their hands over a fire then shake all their limbs as if 'shaking off' something. Burial is performed by men, with women attending. It is now usually accompanied by Muslim or Christian prayers. In the past, women used not to accompany the body to the graveside, as they were not supposed to see the grave until it had been filled. I could not elicit any explanation for this.

Meanwhile people gather at the home of the deceased and sit there for some days. Food is brought so that no one in the compound needs to cook, and money is collected to pay for the beer and cola offered to the guests. Each guest on leaving pays their respects to the most senior member of the bereaved's family, and may discreetly hand them some money. A feast in which food is given to all comers is held on the third day after death. If death occurs in the evening there is often some debate as to when to start counting; practical considerations may sway the issue – for example, so that the feast day falls on a Sunday, allowing more people to attend.

Often included as part of the third-day feast is sweeping the house of the deceased with leaves of the *fuo yə* plant (one of the Labiatae sp., possibly plectranthus), the smell of which is said to drive the spirit (*Càŋ*) of the deceased out into the bush. Close relatives (and affines) are also treated 'to prevent them dreaming of the deceased'.

A second feast is held forty days afterwards, and this is a more elaborate affair as there has been more time to plan it. The second feast often does not occur after exactly forty days: it is very likely to be held on the Sunday after forty days have elapsed, and is sometimes postponed until sufficient funds are available. This is very likely to coincide with the 'summer holidays' when 'rich' city dwellers return to the village and may contribute towards the funeral feast of their siblings. However, these feasts do not compare in any way with the 'crydie' complex of the Grassfields (described, for example, by Brain and Pollock 1971 among many others, and somewhat more recently in Lancit's video *Funeral Season*, reviewed in Zeitlyn 2011). The feasts are notable for the absence of ritual other than the sweeping with the *fuo yə* plant and the commensality implicit in their existence, although either Christian or Muslim prayers are now included before the meal.

Quite separate from the feasts is the dancing of *sùàgà* for senior people. This occurs on the night following the death – or for a death in the evening, it happens the night after. Men's *sùàgà* is danced for a deceased male, women's *sùàgà* for a female.[2] The death of a very senior man occasions an appearance by the masquerade itself, but this is rare. The dancing occurs as a further elaboration of the visiting already described. No express mention of the deceased is made, and there is no difference (except in scale and hence dress of the dancers) between these funeral dances and the dances that accompany the masquerade.

When talking about dancing *sùàgà* at funerals no reasons were given for the practice, nor were criteria explicitly stated for the decision as to whether a certain person warranted the dancing of *sùàgà*, apart from generalizations such as 'if they are very old' or 'if a Notable'. It seems that an old and respected person with prominent children resident in the village will have *sùàgà* danced for them – unless, that is, either they or their children are devout Christians; this has been a cause of dispute.

In the past, funerary rites were certainly more complex. The anthropologist Farnham Rehfisch and the missionary Gilbert Schneider, who were both based in Warwar in the early 1950s, reported funerals of senior men at which the body was displayed, tied upright to a ladder or to stakes placed in the ground – indeed Schneider published photographs of this (1992). Death was announced by a special drum beat (*jùàr jùm*) on the *jùàr mbə* drum. No burial took place until close kin had seen the body, to verify that the person was, in fact, dead. Senior participants in *sùàgà* were treated by their peers before burial. Men did this beside the grave and women in the house before the corpse was carried out for burial. Some such rites are still performed. The ladder on which the corpse was carried was left to rot on top of the grave. Today, if the body was carried on a raffia bed, it will be dismantled and left on top of the grave. We should also note that Farnham Rehfisch photographed funeral dances in Warwar in 1953 where a collection of bells and other objects were dragged along the ground. Although there are currently none such in Somié village, they are known there and they do exist in neighbouring villages where they are produced at major oath-takings and during the male masquerade.

As already mentioned, abstract accounts of practice tend to be idealized, and this masks not so much uncertainty as conflicting pressures from different aspects of current religious practice. Consider some examples of how funeral arrangements are worked out in action. First, when Mbiyuo Bernard died in April 2000, men's *sùàgà* was danced at his funeral despite him, unusually, not having been a full initiate of the masquerade group. But he was senior, the husband of a *Gənmgbe* (the senior women of the village, in this case a sister to the chief and one of the leaders of the two moieties of women's *sùàgà*), and the father of twins, which gave him an extra honorific title. Second, and contrastingly, when a devout Christian, Huɔmbɔn Madeleine, died in autumn of 2000, they did not do any form of the *sùàgà* dance that would have been appropriate for a woman of her age and status in the village. She had asked for *just* Christian prayer, and as a devout Christian (senior in *Femmes Pour Christe*) her wishes were respected. I note that when her husband died in November 2001 *sùàgà* was danced for him before the funeral feast held three days after the death, but not at the later forty-day feast. But he had respected her wishes, and their funerals proceeded without argument. Other instances have not been so easy. In another case where I was present following the death of a senior woman, the funeral effectively split into two: the Christians saying their prayers, singing their songs (teetotal, as these were Lutherans), and next door the traditionalists, the women singing the songs of women's *sùàgà* and everyone drinking maize beer.

The Skull Cult of the Chief

These issues came to the fore in the disputes that surrounded the burial of the late chief Degah François in April 2002. I should stress that I was not present for these events, and even ten years afterwards it was still a sensitive subject which inhibited its discussion, so the following must be seen as a tentative and provisional first report.

First let me give the formal and abstract account I have received of how the death of a chief 'should' be managed. A chief is not an ordinary person. One of the ways this manifests itself is that there is a skull cult of the chief (almost certainly a borrowing from the Tikar, because there is no documentation of this occurring among Nigerian Mambila). Generally, however, there is no skull cult; and, it should be stressed, Mambila do not make connections between skulls, stones, pots and rain as has been reported in the north of Cameroon (see e.g. David, Sterner and Gavua 1988). The skulls of chiefs are removed and given a secondary 'burial' in the 'chiefs' skull house' behind the palace. Only sister's sons of the chief may enter this building.

Following the death of a chief, the dances associated with both *Ngwun* and men's *sùàgà* are performed. Chiefs are buried sitting upright in a circular shaft grave. Approximately a month after the burial, the head is removed and washed. The skull is placed in a small four-handled Mambila basket (*sɔgɔ bà*) in the skull house (*gùà fə*) to the west of the palace.

I have not been allowed access to the skull house, nor were the sister's sons forthcoming about the rites performed there. In particular, the relationship between the current chief and the skulls of his predecessors remains unclear. The rites described to me did not involve the chief himself. Annually, the heads are taken from their baskets and 'washed', being sprayed with palm wine by the sister's sons. The day on which this takes place is made '*súu*': it is forbidden to break the soil or to cut elephant grass, so no farmwork is undertaken.

In the past, non-Mambila immigrants to the village acted as guards and had permanent sleeping-quarters in the skull house, but this practice ceased in the 1950s. The heads are said to shake in their baskets when a Notable is going to die, and the guards were supposed to report this to the chief so that he could initiate divination in order to discover whose death was portended, and whether any action could be taken to avert it.

The late Chief Degah both performed *sùàgà* and was a practising Muslim. When he died this led to trouble. It seems that he had told some people that he wanted Islamic rites, and others, on different occasions, that he wanted a traditional burial. The most senior Muslim in the village at that time was not Mambila but a 'fonctionnaire' (an employee of the state, heading the village agricultural development post). As I understand it, he pressed for a swift burial following Islamic practice. The first clash concerned whether or not they would wait before the burial until Degah's adult sons (one of whom was a soldier working several hundred kilometres away) could view the corpse (see above). The second was whether he would be buried according to Islamic tradition or would follow the special 'royal tradition' (as detailed above) in such a way as to enable the removal of the skull. My understanding is that, having waited for the sons to return, he was buried according to Islamic custom. In the years following the death there were rumours in the village that he was later secretly reburied according to 'custom'. Whether or not this is the case, in 2003 the village seniors were cross with Muslims. I heard it being said that they should not be allowed into the palace, or even, according to some, to become chief at all. This is an extreme and very prominent case, and I must emphasize how uncertain my information is. As a Christian and traditionalist, Diko Madeleine (the first wife of Degah's father, so a respected and authoritative source; see Zeitlyn 2008)[3] was clear on this subject: he should be buried according to tradition and his skull should be removed.

Talking about Funerals, July 1997

That these tensions are appreciated and explicitly discussed is demonstrated by the discussion that I recorded almost by accident on the evening of 26 July 1997 when Mike Fischer and I had just returned to the village. Hearing that there had been a death we went to pay our respects. Although it was after dark I had a video camera with me, and once the discussion started I used it (effectively as a tape recorder) to record the conversation. It was only later that I realized that I had recorded a group of bereaved kin and church members passionately discussing whether Christian prayer was compatible with the singing of *sùàgà* songs. The active Christians were threatening not to allow the choir to attend if *sùàgà* songs were to be sung, let alone if the *sùàgà* dance were to take place. There is not space to include a full transcript here, so all I can do is point to the key idioms used and say something about who was saying what, or rather who was adopting which position. Broadly, the older speakers were more syncretic, the younger ones more monotheistic or purist. This patterning is particularly significant, as one of the older speakers was a prominent member of the local Catholic church and had been a catechist for many years. In one of his contributions to the discussion he explicitly invoked the memory of an early French missionary priest who had been based in Bankim before the nearer mission station at Atta was established in the late 1960s. The disagreement was pitched by the younger speakers using a suitable politeness strategy of indirect speech – the purist position was attributed to the non-present leader of the choir, of whom it was said that if he heard that *sùàgà* was being danced then he would instruct the choir not to perform. This form of speaking meant that the younger speakers were not themselves clearly contradicting their elders, 'merely' reporting a potential problem.

As was explained above, the recorded discussion was about whether both traditional and Christian ritual could be performed or whether they had to make an either/or choice. The key idioms being used were as follows:

For making a choice one or other

Time / Speaker	Mambila	English Translation
02.50 / XX	bí weh bí cén	You'll just take one
	fà dɔɔ̀ŋ bí wá ndé ŋgwèh	You'll not take two

| 26.15 / Youo | mì jeh bí a: sàb cén kwaá bèéh sôm kɔ | I say to you: one snake is the biggest in the pond |

For equivalence, and therefore that both are acceptable

| 03.45 / NJ | koral né mé feh seé seèn beè, sùàgà né mé njéh mona ndɔ | The choir has its own head, and so does *sùàgà* |

04.30 / NJ	de veen déì dua tam ŋgweéh	There's nothing evil there
	Sùàgà né dédé, korale né dédé	There is *sùàgà* and there is the choir
	bɔ njèh fà hen deeh bɔ né dédé	The two are there

Overall, nothing was decided and the actions that followed were inconclusive; the choir sang and *sùàgà* was clapped separately, so both sides took solace.

Conclusions

This was a small event, a micro-drama, in which, at one level, not much happened. However, it has larger social implications. The important anthropological conclusions are that, as analysts, we can see how the discussion is being played out and how actors orientate to such discussion. In the terms used by ethnomethodology (see Zeitlyn 2004), it is a question of *accountability*. It used to be taken for granted that *sùàgà* would be performed, and if Christians wanted to say prayers or sing hymns that was up to them. Now accounts are given to explain why a certain course of action is appropriate, where previously no explanation was felt necessary. Sometimes, of course, no questions are asked, but the action is accountable nonetheless in the sense that there is a socially recognized means of explaining why one rather than another option has been chosen. Against the conventional position that there are many 'heads',[4] the proverb is offered: 'Only one snake can be the biggest in the pond'. This implies that a choice must be made as to which one it should be (here, either Christian hymns or *sùàgà*). By using the proverb, Youo was insinuating that there was a new understanding of the world in which explicit affiliations must be made. The rhetoric treads a delicate path, maintaining a balance between the authority of age and position and the new sense of a religious purism. This balance is exemplified in Brown and Levinson's politeness theory (1978), which originally appeared in a volume edited by Esther Goody. In this theory the weightiness of an imposition is balanced by attention given to the (positive and negative) face of the people affected, so we can identify and understand linguistic components of social action. These can also be seen as analogues and accompaniments to those actions, but Esther would insist they are not secondary but rather are part and parcel of action itself.

In themselves the changes I have been discussing are relatively small but they point to larger currents of social change. As Esther Goody was so careful to alert us, the linguistic reflex, the nuance of utterance, is an important social indicator, and as such provides a means for an anthropologist to gain understanding without asking explicit questions (Goody 1978). Such conclusions take us back to Durkheim and the nineteenth-century foundations of anthropology, and argue, with Esther, for the centrality of sociolinguistics in social anthropology today.

David Zeitlyn is a professor of social anthropology at the University of Oxford, and a fellow of Wolfson College. His PhD studies in the 1980s were supervised by Esther Goody. His fieldwork with Mambila in the Cameroon started in 1985. Following his doctorate, he taught at the University of Kent for fifteen years and then moved to Oxford in 2010. His research focuses on traditional religion (especially spider divination), sociolinguistics and, more recently, Cameroonian photography.

Notes

1. The T/V choices, which were the starting point for the Brown and Levinson analysis of politeness (1978, republished 1987).
2. Both male and female masquerades exist in the Mambila traditional religion system. Normally the male masquerade takes place every year, the female once every two years.
3. More information about her is available online: http://www.mambila.info/Diko_Web/index.html. Accessed 25 September 2024.
4. Sometimes in similar discussions the metaphor used is, 'There are many roads but only one God (*Càŋ*)'.

References

Brain, Robert, and Adam Pollock. 1971. *Bangwa Funerary Sculpture*. London: Duckworth.

Brown, Penelope, and Stephen C. Levinson. 1978. 'Universals in Language Usage: Politeness Phenomena', in Esther N. Goody (ed.), *Questions and Politeness*. Cambridge: Cambridge University Press, pp. 56–290.

——. 1987. *Politeness: Some Universals in Language Usage*. Cambridge: Cambridge University Press.

Cohen, David W., and Atieno Odhiambo. 1992. *Burying SM: The Politics of Knowledge and the Sociology of Power in Africa* (Social History of Africa). Portsmouth, NH: Heinemann.

David, Nicholas, Judy Sterner and Kodzo Gavua. 1988. 'Why Pots Are Decorated'. *Current Anthropology* 29: 365–89.

Goody, Esther N. 1978. 'Towards a Theory of Questions', in *Questions and Politeness*. Cambridge: Cambridge University Press, pp. 17–43.

Lancit, Matthew. 2010. *Funeral Season (ou La Saison des funérailles): Marking Death in Cameroon*. Video.

Schneider, Gilbert D. 1992. *Norikam: Images and Field Notes*. Portland, OR: Intercultural Education Services.

Zeitlyn, David. 1994. *Sua in Somié: Mambila Traditional Religion*. Collectanea Instituti Anthropos 41. Sankt Augustin, Germany: Academia Verlag.

———. 2004. 'The Gift of the Gab: Anthropology and Conversation Analysis'. *Anthropos* 99: 452–68.

———. 2008. 'Life History Writing and the Anthropological Silhouette'. *Social Anthropology* 16: 154–71.

———. 2011. Review of 'Matthew Lancit. Funeral Season (la saison des funérailles): Marking Death in Cameroon. 2010'. *Journal of the Royal Anthropological Institute* (N.S.) (17): 645.

9

Childrearing through Social Interaction on Rossel Island, Papua New Guinea

Penelope Brown and Marisa Casillas

Introduction: Anthropology of Child Socialization and Language

The first detailed ethnographic studies of child upbringing in non-Western set-tings were focused on Papua New Guinea (PNG) and Oceania. Margaret Mead initiated the field with her (1928, 1930) studies of childhood and adolescence in Samoa and PNG. Malinowski expended some of his many pages on childhood in the Trobriands (summarized in Malinowski 2008). But the modern study of child socialization through language began with the collaboration of Bambi Schieffelin (1986a and b, 1990), working among the Kaluli of mainland PNG, and Elinor Ochs (1982, 1988), on Samoa. Together they developed the study of *language socialization*, examining the ways in which, through social interac-tion, children are initiated into their language and culture and into the associ-ated ways of talking, thinking, feeling, and understanding the world (Schieffelin and Ochs 1986a and b; Ochs and Schieffelin 1984, 2008; Kulick and Schieffelin 2004). Further PNG research in this paradigm was conducted by Kulick (1992), and there is ongoing research by San Roque (2018), San Roque and Schieffelin (2018) and Rumsey (2013, 2015), among others.

This research brought the extensive cross-cultural variation in child-rearing behaviours and attitudes to the attention of scholars interested in child development from various disciplinary perspectives – from those working in the traditions of Freud and Piaget to modern developmental psychologists and psycholinguists, and linguistic anthropologists. Questions raised include the effect of cultural practices on personality development, emotional development, and later, language development, socialization issues, interactional style and language acquisition. One theme in common across these diverse investigations is the claim that the social and cultural variability of interactional contexts for child-rearing has important implications for all aspects of child development. In no part of the world, perhaps, has the diversity of approaches been as great as in work in Africa, where contributions have been made from the viewpoint of developmental psychology (e.g. Whiting and Whiting 1975; LeVine et al. 1994), cognitive psychology (Cole et al. 1971), psychological anthropology (e.g. Weisner 1982; Weisner and Gallimore 1977), psycholinguistics (e.g. Demuth 1992 on language acquisition in Sesotho, and Demuth 2003 on Bantu languages), language socialization (e.g. Takada 2005 on the Central Kalahari San), and most importantly, for current purposes, Esther Goody's work in Ghana on children, social roles, and language (e.g. Goody 1972, 1973, 1974, 1975, 1978, 1982, 2006). What stands out from that is her emphasis on dialogue as a tool with which sociocultural worlds – such as roles and associated norms – are actually constructed.

Data of This Study

This chapter is based on two sets of research into caregiver–child interactions conducted in the Melanesian society of Rossel Island. The first is material collected during eight field trips by the first author over fourteen years. The data include parental interviews, videotaped interactions between caregivers and small children, observational time-sampling of child activities, and systematic focused elicitation to probe joint attention and pointing behaviour in infants, child interaction patterns, and early vocabulary acquisition. Interviews were conducted in English; videotaped naturally occurring interactions were in the Rossel language Yélî Dnye and transcribed and translated into English with the help of indigenous assistants. A second source of data was collected by the second author who, in a 2016 field trip, made extensive day-long recordings of fifty-five children, carried out psycholinguistic experiments, and assembled the demographic data for our samples. The field site of both was at the eastern end of the island in the region centred around the Catholic mission site at Jinjo.

Plan for the Chapter

This chapter describes the social and interactional context of children growing up on Rossel Island. It then sketches the ethnographic background and the social context of childhood and parental attitudes on Rossel. The next section presents some detailed examples of naturally occurring interactions with babies and small children, and considers their implications for socialization. Then we briefly compare Rossel child–caregiver interaction patterns with those of other well-documented situations of child-rearing in small-scale societies. Finally, we draw out some implications for socialization theory.

The Social Context of Childhood on Rossel Island: Setting

Rossel is the easternmost island of Papua New Guinea, at the end of the Louisiades chain, some 400 km from mainland PNG. It is a mountainous island about 25 km long, and surrounded by reefs. The island is remote and fairly isolated due to the difficulties of transport across the surrounding seas, although it has long been connected by trade to neighbouring islands. While not part of the Kula ring, Rossel supplied important shells for Kula exchange, and the island is still a major source of bagi. The language and culture of Rossel Island are distinct from those of neighbouring islands. The population of about six thousand people speak a linguistic isolate – a so-called Papuan[1] language called Yélî Dnye – which is entirely unrelated to the mostly Austronesian languages of the other islands, and with no known relation to any other language. English is the second language, learnt through church and school, and used for contact with virtually all outsiders, who consider the highly complex Rossel language to be unlearnable for adults.[2] Occasional work on the mainland, along with a certain amount of intermarriage with people from other islands, ensures a degree of multilingualism with some of the surrounding Austronesian languages.

Rossel Islanders have a dual descent kinship system (Levinson 2006a). Rossel social organization is partly based on matrilineal clans, which provide the core structures for the organization of marriage, the shell money system, and cooperative networks. The residence pattern is predominantly patrilocal, however, and most land is inherited through the patriline. Personal names also are the prerogative of the father's line. Subsistence agriculture is based on sago, taro, yams, sweet potatoes and manioc; these are supplemented with fish and (occasionally) pigs, providing protein. Coconuts are the main source of fat in the diet. Diving for beche de mer can be a seasonal source of PNG money (kina) for young men, as can copra production from the many coconut trees. With the exception of school fees and intermittent boat travel, however, kina are of little use on the island.

Without any infrastructure of roads, electricity, or piped water, and with no regular boat service connecting the island to the outside world, life on Rossel is an intriguing combination of ancient artifacts and customs – bush houses on stilts, outrigger canoes, shell money, grass skirts, sacred places and stories, witchcraft – and some modern accoutrements: for example, churches and schools, secondhand Australian clothes, pop music on battery-run radio, and occasional videos powered by generator. Rossel Islanders have a strong sense of identity, including pride in their famously difficult-to-learn language, and they span these two worlds with exceptional grace and dignity. Previous ethnographic work by Armstrong (1928) and Liep (1983, 2009) focuses on the famous shell currency of Rossel. Levinson has conducted anthropological linguistic work on Yélî Dnye since 1995 (e.g. Levinson 2006a and b). Levinson 2022 is a full reference grammar of the language.

Local Institutions

In the area of study (the Jinjo region at the eastern end of the island),[3] the infra-structure relevant to children is largely provided by the Catholic church, which arrived on the island in the 1950s. They developed a large mission site and built a church. They used to travel around the island to provide local church services, and initially provided boat services, schools, and health clinics for the commu-nity. The official Catholic presence has gradually been withdrawn, and funding for the schools and health clinic has now been partly taken over by the PNG government, but they are still only minimally integrated with the mainland system. A health clinic staffed with (mostly) local nurses provides vaccinations for children and monitors their health and growth monthly for the first five years. As rivals to the Catholic church, off and on there have been other denominations (Methodist, evangelical, and cargo cults). For the last fifteen years there have been preschools run by local teachers trained off the island, and literacy begins in the indigenous language. The primary school mainly uses English, however, running through to 8th grade. For pupils who do well in school, further education (increasingly being taken up) is available on other islands and on the mainland. Community activities centre around church, school, and the health clinic, as well as traditional ceremonies and feasts. Football (soccer) is a favourite community sport for boys and men – until recently with bare feet and a homemade ball, but now with team strips and an official soccer ball. Netball is the girls' and women's equivalent. Women run a small market selling their garden produce twice a week, a service especially relevant for the teachers and nurses whose work precludes their tending a garden. Local councillors provide the first level of official organization, and a connection to the PNG government through regional officials, elections and services. Occasional handouts are produced by the local government or by foreign governments and the WHO – for example, medicines, mosquito nets, and food aid after calamities like cyclones – but essentially Rossel Islanders are aware that they are on their own, at least potentially, for long periods. The lack of any regular form of boat transport to the island means that those who travel to other islands or to the mainland may have to wait many weeks to find a boat going back. Rapid changes are afoot, however; the recent addition of a cell tower at Jinjo has quickly resulted in many people having access to a mobile phone service, providing a dramatic change in the possibilities of communica-tion both within the island and with the outside world.

Roles

Subsistence activities centre on growing root crops in gardens, shellfish hunting, and fishing on the reef. All children learn these skills as well as those of canoeing, swimming, sago production, nut and coconut gathering, and acting as caregiver of younger ones. Many families raise chickens, virtually all have dogs, and some raise pigs. Some families engage in entrepreneurial activities (running small shops, or making and selling clothing) in which children may participate, though the lack of transport and hence access to fuel and goods severely limits this. Other roles are associated with particular expertise that only some obtain – for example, songwriter of indigenous vocal music genres, carpenter and house builder, outrigger canoe maker, local official (peacekeeper), store manager, church official, teacher, nurse, ritual specialist and caretaker of sacred sites, expert handler of shell money.

There are a handful of gender-differentiated roles. Men are the primary experts in managing shell money transactions, the sole singers of Rossel opera (*tpile wee*), the ones who go spear fishing or diving for beche de mer, slaughter pigs, build houses, and work on boats. Girls prepare themselves to be wife, mother, main cook, and to acquire the women's skills of collecting wild food and making baskets, grass skirts, and mats. Both men and women can be teachers, nurses, and church officials; teachers and nurses are often sent to work on other islands, or to a distant part of Rossel Island. All participate in fishing/ gleaning on the reef, and working in the gardens, and all take part in church services, traditional funerals, marriage ceremonies, and informal court hearings. (Speaking roles in these latter three are gender-differentiated: men dominate the proceedings, but women do speak up sometimes, especially as protagonists called upon in the dispute, and women can heckle the foregrounded male speakers.) Both parents are highly active in childcare and rearing.

Demographics of Households with Young Children in the Jinjo Area

The impression of Rossel Islanders as isolated from the rest of the world is mitigated by data that were collected by Casillas for an ongoing study of early communicative development from forty-three families on the island who had children aged under five in August 2016. The families in this sample primarily live at the eastern end of the island in hamlets around the villages of Jinjo, Nok:ia, Cheme, Pumba and Kimbikpâpu. The data reveal that in this mission-influenced region considerable intermarriage occurs with people from other islands: 21 per cent of the sampled families have mothers from elsewhere in PNG, and 23 per cent of the households are multilingual (70 per cent Yélî Dnye-English bilingual and 30 per cent Yélî Dnye-English-Other trilingual). Women who marry into life on Rossel Island typically find the language difficult to acquire as adults, and so generally use English to communicate with others.

On average, a child under five lives in a household with three adults and two siblings. The average time between births is two and a half years, and most mothers of young children are typically young themselves, so only 26 per cent of the households had more than one child who was aged under four. However, because Rossel hamlets are structured as tight clusters of houses, children – even those living in 'small' households – typically grow up with a very large number of other children around. Take, for example, the hamlets around the village of Cheme, where we have a complete catalogue of young children present in August 2016. Among the eighteen families with children under five, there are twenty-one children between the ages of two and five. These children spend much of their day in large independent playgroups, and it is not unusual to see groups of eight or more children playing together in the late afternoon.

Childrearing Practices, Beliefs

Interviews conducted by Brown with eighteen Rossel mothers of different ages provide a fairly consistent picture of customs, attitudes and beliefs concerning child-rearing and development. Pregnant women continue working in their gardens till late in the pregnancy, then they tend to stay near home and do only light housework. There are various food taboos, for example pregnant women and new mothers do not eat octopus or red fruit, both of which are believed to make a baby's skin spotty, nor do they eat 'big fish' like shark.

All the women in the villages where we worked go to the Jinjo health clinic to give birth, those living nearby waiting until labour begins before they go, while women from farther away may come early and stay in a maternity facility in Jinjo to await the birth. There is no doctor on the island but the nurses are skilled in delivering babies and looking after new mothers. Cases that require a doctor's intervention are referred to the mainland hospital in Alotau, though getting them there in time depends on transport, and stillbirths and maternal death in childbirth are relatively common.[4] If a mother dies in childbirth – or if she does not want to keep the baby – the baby is adopted, normally by a clan member of the mother, but otherwise, after consultation, by any woman who will undertake to care for it.[5]

The new baby receives its name while still in the hospital, which will come from the repertoire of the father's clan names. Women tend to stay for about a week and then walk home, carrying the new baby. For the first month or so they stay near home, but as soon as possible resume normal activities in the garden, and they routinely take babies if travelling on foot, or by boat, dinghy, or dugout canoe. Babies are cared for principally by their mother in the first months, but there is considerable handing around of babies, and childcare is regularly shared with the father, siblings, relatives and neighbours.

A baby from its first days is exposed to many people who stop to admire, greet, smile and talk to the infant as a matter of course while passing by. There is a minimal baby talk register, consisting of high pitch and affect-laden intonation, as well as certain words (e.g. *taataa*, to show something interesting; *apuu* 'don't do that!'), but generally people talk to babies as if they understand, and get them involved in interactional routines (peekaboo, greeting exchanges) from very early on.

Mothers do not have special terms for developmental stages, though they may well note that the baby is smiling, crawling, talking (i.e. babbling). They do recognize walking as a significant achievement, and often provide physical help in the form of sticks planted in a row for the child to hold as it takes its first steps, or patiently walk holding the child's hand saying 'walk, walk, walk'.

Children's development is monitored through regular health clinic visits. Every month the mothers return to Jinjo clinic to get the child weighed, and vaccinated or medicated as necessary; a record is kept and sent to the mainland authorities. This continues till the child is five years of age. The nurses use this opportunity to tell mothers about appropriate nutrition and safeguarding of their children.

The most remarkable thing about Rossel upbringing is how soon small children are encouraged to be independent. A large degree of freedom of movement is seen from the moment they are able to walk. They may wander all over the village area, following bigger children or playing by themselves with leaves, flowers, sticks, shells or rocks. By age two, many are in the river shallows on their own, with other children, and they learn to swim without any overt teaching. By two or three they can dress themselves, light a fire, look after their own breakfasts, crack nuts between rocks, and participate in peer-group games. By five or six, some will be out in the lagoon paddling a dugout canoe. Not until age six or seven do they start school, so they have many years of relative freedom to hang out, participate in chores, go places with peers or family members, and invent play activities. Once they are schooling, they may go and live with a relative to be near the school; the local primary school draws children from the entire east end of the island, which for some will be a couple of hours' walk away.

Parenthood is considered both a joy and a serious responsibility. Children are much loved; indeed they provide probably the main source of daily entertainment in Rossel lives. There is a communal sense of responsibility for bringing them up – anyone may discipline a child, though (as we will see) this is usually done indirectly and non-aggressively. Discipline centres on socializing children about the local dangers (the river, the fire), on decent behaviour (clothing, managing excretion, not swearing), and on treating others with consideration.

Interactional Style with Infants and Small Children

We present four examples of interactions with small children (one- to three-year-olds), recorded between 2003 and 2006 in the hamlet of our field site. This is a large settlement (of perhaps 500m²) with households of four families: three brothers with their wives and fifteen children and their unmarried brother, and their elder sister with her husband, children and grandchildren. The houses are set out along a river, a major resource for drinking and cooking water, washing clothes, bathing and swimming for all the villages around. Houses are built of local materials on stilts, with sitting areas underneath and porches for socializing; the inside of the house is private space. At any one time, some older children may be off the island schooling, others may be living here with uncles in order to go to the local school, grandchildren and married-away daughters may be visiting. There are usually about a dozen small children (of preschool age) around, playing in communal inter-house spaces or in the river.

These examples of daily life surrounding the activities of eating, play and caregiving are drawn from the first author's video corpus of about eighty hours of naturally occurring interactions, transcribed and annotated with the help of native speakers. They illustrate characteristic ways of interacting with small children in Rossel, and give us some insights into how this Rossel interactional style with children socializes particular ways of being in the world. In the excerpts, the focal child's turns are highlighted in boldface.

The first episode portrays efforts to engage in joint attention and interact with a one-year-old before he has any overt words, using various attention-getters, and then getting him to produce for their entertainment his imitation of a local old lady. They summon his attention by calling *hee ee* or *a pwiye* 'come', or *a pinda* 'my namesake', saying *yaa* and hiding their face (invitation to play peekaboo) or showing things (e.g. pencil, dog) and saying *taataa*. Several try to get him to engage in a favourite party game of imitating and thereby mocking an elderly relative. It is intriguing that in this society where old age commands respect and even reverence, it is considered funny for babies to mock elders.

Episode 1. 2005, v16

This episode of about two minutes is taken from an hour-long session on our house porch, featuring BK, a 15-year-old, caring for **Kak** (the 12-month-old son of his cousin). Other people are present some of the time or passing by: Mar/Kad and Top (off screen), (both are FaMoDa, aunts) Mgîm (Mo), Luc (FaMoBrWi), and cousins Ndu, Nii, Toon (age 9) and Kem (age 5) (all are FaMoBrCh).

> 02:12:000 Kak is standing on our porch about 6 feet from BK, who is sitting on the edge of it. Kad is also sitting on the porch seat near Kak. BK summons Kak:

> BK: sst. (0.8) a pénta. a pénta. a pwiye.
>   'sst. My namesake, my namesake. Come.'
> **Kak**:   ee [doesn't look to BK, and doesn't come]
> BK: a pénta. a pwiye.
>   'My namesake. Come.'
> BK: [holds hand half-way over face, playfully]
> **Kak**:   [looks, then looks away, doesn't come]
> BK: [gives up, looks away, while others off screen try to catch Kak's attention by calling his name]

2:40:
Kak: [whimpers a bit; all ignore this for half a minute]
Luc: Kakana Kakana Kakana Kakana Kakana.
?:   Kaawa [name of elderly man up the hill]

2:51:
Ndu: Chaadî. kââpyââ Chaadî ló nté?
       'Chaadî [name of elderly woman up the hill]. Granny Chaadî how (is she)?'
Kak: [raises eyes briefly, looks away, holds hand out towards Ndu] eee
BK: [throws marker pen to him]
Kak: [picks up marker, bangs on porch seat with it]

~3:30:
[Niinii comes to porch side, stands looking but doesn't interact]

3:49:
Ndu: kââpyââ Chaadî.
       'Granny Chaadî.'
BK: Chaadî ló nté ka. Chaadî ló nté wunté.
       'Chaadî how (is she)? Chaadî how (is she), how does she do?'
Kak: [lowers chin, raises eyes, his version of how she looks]
       [all laugh, Kak puts face down on his hands, looks away]

4:13: [another try]
Ndu: Kakana. kââpyââ Chaadî.
       'Kak [child's name], Granny Chaadî.'
Luc: ka Chaadî ka. kââpyââ ló nté ka.
       'OK Chaadî OK. Granny how is she, ok?'
       [Kak ignores them and continues banging marker on porch seat]

This episode illustrates the communal nature of childcare at this age, and anyone over the age of about five in the village can freely take over. It displays the small child as entertainment: getting him to imitate Chaadî's eyes, or funny walks, or asking joke questions like 'How did granny pass air?' Getting one-year-olds to mock respected elders is a favourite game, and this is handled by giving the child control over it – others can invite him to produce his party trick, but he alone decides whether and how much to play.

Our second episode of about ten minutes illustrates a process of prosociality training, with **Kââ** (2 years and 5 months) being encouraged to share a treat he is eating in front of the other children. Notably the person urging him to share is not his mother (though she is present) but his aunt (MoSi), and the process is one of persuasion rather than overt force, as well as overt praise of an older child's cooperative gesture, and implicit disapproval of Kââ initially for not sharing.

Episode 2. 2006 (4 Aug.), v4s1.

Participants: **Kââ** (2;5)[6] sharing food with K:ââm (3;1), Kap (3;2), Kak (1;11) interacting with each other and with Anna (aunt) and Too (K:ââm's sister, age 10). Three adult women, Anna (aunt), Luc (K:ââm's mother) and Marg (Kââ's mother) are also in the vicinity, but only Anna (briefly) participates. K:ââm is Kââ's 'uncle' (son of Kââ's MoFaBr), and Kak's cousin (son of his MoBr); Kap is Kââ's elder brother.

[video starts up at B's house, Kadam (prompted by P) summoning Kak to play with K:ââm (at 1:06:). Kââti comes up hill, holding a large scone (a treat). Kids ignore it (and him), he runs back down hill, and eats scone under Y's house. Kak and K:ââm come to him, summon him to play (a pwiye 'come'). The three boys are in the middle of the houses area (**Kââ** still eating, Kak kicking ball), K:ââm first mentions the scone – to his mother.

[-> marks turns with overt urging to share]

3:39:
K:ââm: (whining) Maami. angene scone w:uu?
            'Mama, where's a scone (for me)?'
Mo   [ignores, goes past carrying Marg's baby Pwee]

5:04:   [Anna urges Kââ to give some scone to boys]
Anna: ka K:ââmgaa pee ngmê naa y:eemî, apii, ka lîmî k:ii, teetee.
            'Ok give K:ââm a piece, ok? Hurry up, uncle'.
Kââ: eeee [holds his scone away from her, goes away]
-> Anna: Kââti pee u kwo ngmê yini, ka.
            'Kââ, give him a bit, ok.'
Kap: ... [offering his scone]
Anna: ii Kapini ka nyi mb:aamb:aa.
            'ii Kap, ok you are good.'   [praise for good behaviour modelled]
            oo ball nya y:ii, ball. ball k:ii. balli ka tóó.
            'Oh, get the ball. Ball over there. Ball is there.' [pointing]
            ka pee ngmê y:ee yi, K:ââmgaa, Kakan ye.
            'OK give a bit to K'aamgaa and Kakan.'
            ball n:aa nya, ball
            'I'll bring the ball'
            ee, Kapini, Kââti nyi mb:aamb:aa.
            'Eh, Kap, Kââ, you are good.'
            ball n:aa nya, nyi wuwu, nyi daa t:a.
            'I'll get the ball, you play, not you' [to Kââti, implicit sanction for not sharing food]
            chi lêpî.
            'Go away.' [to Kââti for not sharing his food]
            ball naa nya, nmo wuwu té mwi. [pointing]
            'I'll get the ball, we're all going to play there.'

-> 5:41:   ka pee ngmê y:ee yi Kakana, K:ââmgaa ye.

'Give half to Kakan and K:ââm.'

5:58:
Kââ: ka a pwiye [walks up to Kak] wule. wule.
          'OK come. Here you are' [presentative]

6:07:
Kââ: ala.
          'Here.' [hands Kak a bit of scone]
Toon: oo K:ââmgaa. Aamgaa ka chi lêpî u kwo. u kwo chi lêp. ka chi lêpî.
          K:ââmgaa chi lêpî.
          'Oh K:aam, K:aam, ok go to him. Go to him. OK go to him. OK K:ââm go.'

6:36:   [K:ââm goes to the two boys]
Kak: a tp:oo.
          'Little (ones)' [points to puppies nearby]
Kââ: [looks] ee
K:ââm: ee. ee. [holds out hand to Kââ, who gives him a bit of scone]
K:ââm: [eats it] (in yi tââ i)
Kââ: u ni tâ. u ni a ta [non-word sound play, while giving some scone]
Kak: u ni a ta te ... ni ta.

7:15:
Anna: [comes up with another scone] Kak ala.
          'Kak, here.' [holding out scone]
Kak: [takes it]
Anna: mb:aamb:aa. mbwodo ya dmyinê.
          'Good, you guys sit down.'
          K:ââmgaa k:ii nyi yeyi.
          'K:aam, come sit down here.'

[The children sit there on the ground for about four minutes eating/sharing scones, asking for 'a bit more' *ka pee tp:oo* (or sometimes English 'more').

These children are well on the way to automatic food sharing, a highly valued behaviour. It is considered very bad form to eat in front of others – especially in front of children – without sharing the food.

The third case illustrates one of the limits to freedom: small children cannot be allowed to play with sharp knives. (Other potential dangers guarded against include climbing steps or trees, falling off the veranda, or going into the river without supervision.) Yet in this case extracting a bush knife (a machete, a two-foot-long sharp knife) from a two-year-old takes five minutes and exposes those trying to remove it to serious risk. The mother is summoned to intervene but resorts to the usual tactics of long-distance advice, empty threats to the delinquent child, and getting other children to do what is needed to solve the problem.

Episode 3. 2003, v4, from 20:45: to ~ 25:51

Moop (2;9) is playing outside the house compound in Cheme, which has the houses of five families (four brothers and their elderly parents). Others present include Jud's mother Ann, sitting on ground with her Si-in-law's baby Eliz near house some thirty feet away, Jud's father Mbu (off screen), and her cousins Kep and Pwee (both age ~10).

20:45:
Moop: [walks over to below the other house, picks up machete, singing to herself. Walks over to banana trees and starts hacking at their dead leaves. Completely ignored by others around]

21:06:
Moop: hee! [brandishing machete and looking back towards the others]

21:10:
Kep: Moop! t:aa ngê ngê a chopwo. [he's off camera, about 20 feet away]
        'Moop! You'll cut your hand with the bush knife.'
Moop: [continues hacking at banana leaves with bush knife]

21:22:
Kep: kââkââ Mbulu
        'Uncle Mbulu' (Moop's father) [calling to get him to intervene]
Ann: [calls something unintelligible from house 30 or more feet away]
Moop: [stops hacking at banana tree, moves to log on ground and chops at it with bush knife]
Ann: Moop, a pwiyé
        'Moop, come.'

21:39:
wom: Pweepyu u kuwo mbwili.
        'Pwee, call out to her.'
Pwe: [standing 15 feet from Moop, he turns and looks towards woman who called to him, turns back away]
wom: Pweepyu u kuwo mbwili!
        'Pwee, call out to her.'
Pwe: [looks at Moop happily chopping at log, walks away, then calls:]
        Moop a pwiyé. (1.5) Moop a pwiyé.
        'Moop come. (1.5) Moop come.'
Moop: [ignores summons, continues to chop]

22:09:
Kep: [comes towards Moop, calls out]
        Moop! (1.8) Kakan u mutpili naa ngê ngê. Anna!
        'Moop! Don't touch Kak's something.' [then, summoning M's mother]
        'Anna!'

22:16:
Kep: o t:aa ngê kuu a chopwo
        'She's going to cut her hand with the bush knife.'
Ann: [calls something unintelligible]
        [Kep bends down and tries to take the knife from Moop]
Kep: a kii!
        'Give it to me!'
        [Moop holds it up and threatens him with it, and he backs off]

22:24:
Moop: ngââ!! [protest noise]
(1:0)
Ann: Kêpê u kwo naa ngê lee
        'Kep, don't go to her!' [she'll cut you]
Kep: [rolls her log with his foot, distracting her?]
Moop: [unintelligible, protest noises]

22:40: [Pwee goes over to Kep and Moop, rolls the log with his foot, and says gently, persuasively] hee!

22:46:
Moop: I'll hit you with this thing.
        [Kep walks away, comes back with an empty tinned-fish can]
22:53:
Kep: te dââ mu du ma, :aa te dââ mu du ma
        'I ate tinned fish, I ate tinned fish.' [ploy to get her to give up machete]
Moop: [swings machete at/towards Pwee, who runs off]

22:57:
Ann: taa ngê a ngmê numu chopwo
        'They will cut themselves with the bush knife.' [still calling from far away house]
Kep: see te dââ
        'See the tinned fish.' [holding container out towards Moop]
Kep: apuu ala tpile, a lama [complaining voice, to Pwee, who is playing with a small knife?]
        'No, this thing is mine, I know.'
Pwee: Moop! Mootpi kwi ala tpile
        'Moop, tell him this one is mine.' [thing that Pwee has]
Moop: a nani!
        'It's mine!' [machete]
Kep: ala tpile kwi
        'This is mine, tell her/him.'
Moop: [resumes hacking at log]
Pwee: Kêpê ngê nani mu da ngê ngee tpii
        'Kêpê has got yours, and he's holding it.'
(5.4)
Kep: apuu ala daa nani, ee!
        'No, this is not yours!'

Ann: Kêpê yi tpile na ma tpii k:ii ngi k:ii ngi. yi naa ngê k:ii chii u mênê nyi k:ii
       y:i. Moop u po wa ghê, dê da ngê, ai ai ...
       'Kêpê don't hold that thing [a tin lid]! Throw it away, throw it away. Don't
       throw it there, go and throw it in the bush. Otherwise Moop will stand on
       it.'
       [Kep throws tin lid into bush]
Ann: ??? na ngê a k:i ee! chii u mênê u kwo na ngmê mê kee.
       '?? don't give? it! Don't go into the bush!'
(3.0)
Ann: al:ii nu yu p:o nu yu p:o
       'Come home here, come home.'

24:03:
Kep: [puts hand on Moop's shoulder and tries to shove her towards home]
       a pwiyé. a pwiyé!
       'Come. Come!'
Ann: [calling] a pwiyé!
       'Come!'
Ann: Moop taa a nuwo yi taa a nuwo yi yâpwo têdê naa lêpî
       'Moop, bring the bush knife, I'll go to the garden.' [enticement]
(1.6) [the two boys walk away, go off camera]
Ann: taa nuwo yi taa nuwo yi Moopwé taa nêdê nyi kêlê kêlê hospital daa nê lee
       'Moop bring the bush knife, if you get hurt with the bush knife I'm not
       going to take you to the hospital.' [threat]
       alê ntênê nga té vyi. taa ngaa pee p:uu mênê dimi o!
       'I'm telling the truth!'
       taa ngaa pee p:uu mênê dimi o!
       'I'm gonna get the bush knife and hit you on the bottom!' [threat]
       [throughout this, Moop continues hitting at the log with the machete]
       Moop pêla ngê yimi mênê vy:ee yi, pêla ngê yimi mênê vy:ee yi.
       'Moop, I'm gonna hit you with a stick, I'm gonna hit you with a stick.'
       [threat]
       [Ann continues scolding about using the pêla, but Moop swings the
       machete a couple of times and scrapes the ground with it, then picks up a
       stick]
       nkéli pyââ nkéli pyââ
       'The foreign woman (will do something)'
       [Moop holds stick in left hand, hacks at it with machete in right hand.
       Then sits on ground and cuts at the stick with the machete.]
Ann: eee ee ee. daa ngê! ee ee. wu uu!
       'She got it!'
(1.5)
Kep: kuu dê kpaa (ka) tóó
       'Smack her hands, smack her hands.'
(1.3)
Ann: [sings singsong attractor nonsense song]

25:16:
Moop: [hacks two-handed at grass with machete]

Kep: ee Moop! Anna! u kuu a chapwo!
        'Hey Moop! Anna! She's going to cut her hand!'
Ann: [says something unintelligible, not directed at Moop]
        [Moop stands up, hacks at ground with machete. Ann from far away sings
        'My hands are clapping' song.]
Kep: [stands and turns to Moop, saying]
        'Moop!'
Moop: nyââ
        'Yes'
Kep: Moop a pwiyé ...
        'Moop, come!'
        [puts hand on her shoulder and leads her towards Mo]
Ann: [singing: 'My hands are clapping, clapping, clapping, my hands are clap-
        ping just like this.'

[25:46: As they are walking, Kep discretely takes the machete from Moop's hand,
saying: 'Got it'. Moop runs and sits down next to her mother on ground and singing
some 30 feet away.]

This event illustrates the respect for a small child's autonomy that is evident in
this society. Although safety considerations impose limits on her freedom of
action – in this case, the knife must be extracted – this is done in a very communal, and very non-heavy-handed way. No force or violence is used; rather
persuasion and distraction are the techniques used by her cousins, and fake
enticements ('I'm going to the garden') and threats ('If you cut yourself, I won't
take you to the hospital') by her mother sitting 30 feet away. Note that despite
the threats of physical punishment ('I'll hit you with the bush knife, or a stick'),
smacking small children is rarely resorted to.

Another limit to personal freedom is the necessity of complying with social
expectations about personal hygiene. Small children are mostly naked, so toilet
training is relatively simple – children are encouraged to go to the relevant area
of bush and are taken to the mangroves, where adults excrete, and shown what
to do. Occasional mishaps are handled in a very casual way: overt mention
(these events are 'mentionables') and sometimes a query ('Who did this?') or a
negative comment (*apuu* 'don't do that' or 'yucky') without any other sanctions.
This episode illustrates the communal 'noticing' of one such case, after K (age
1;2) calmly squatted and excreted on the path. The noticings (and clean-up
process) went on for about 7 minutes. Again, there is communal disciplining
but the child's autonomy is respected.

Episode 4. 2004, v9muumuu picnic, 39:14: to ~ 39:43

This extract comes from a one-and-a-half-hour session at a stone oven cooking
place about 100 yards upriver from the village. Adults are busy cooking food on
hot stones, all off camera, including Luc, **K:ââm's** mother, until she comes to

clean up his mess. **K:ââm** is wearing nothing but a G-string. Note: this family speaks English, Yélî, and sometimes a bit of pidgin; the mother is from Sudest (the next island westwards).

Participants: Luc's and Lore's families: 7 children age 1–10: **K:ââm** (1;2), Din (2;3), Ana (4;5), Nji (5;5), Wââ (6;0), Taa (almost 11), Kak (15). (Others there but not in this extract: Marg, Kap (3.3), Lore's Mo Ann, Pat and Agn, and Mar's Si Mir.)

39:14:
    [**K:ââm** squats, excretes on the path, says ee ee, runs off]

39:38:
    [K comes back, looks at his poop on the path, runs off again]
    [Nji comes by, sees poop, points at it, goes off silently]
    [Wââ comes running up path yelling yaa!]

40:03:
Wââ: [sees poop, points, comments on it and laughs at K]

40:15:
Taa: [calling to Luc] n:uu yi kn:aa. auntie kê vyi yi.
    'Who pooped? Tell auntie' [Luc]
(3.3)
    auntie o. auntie! (6.0) ee! auntie kê vyi yi!
    'Eh, tell auntie!'
Wââ: eeee! K kêdê kn:aa
    'Auntie Lucy! K is pooping.'
    auntie ka vy:i
    'Tell auntie'

40:49:   auntie o!

40:59:   auntie o! auntie! aunti ee! aunti ee!

41:04:
Nji: iiee K:ââm! ee K:ââm!
    'Oh K! eh K!'
Nji: u pwo chi ghêê
    'You stood on it!' [to 2 small children there: K, Din]

41:16:
Kak: auntie kê vyi yoo. kn:ii lukwe diy:o nmye wuwu té
    'Tell auntie. Good one. Why are you children playing?'
Taa: áuntie. auntie u! [calling her] auntie ka vy:i yoo
    'Go tell auntie'

41:18:
Taa: áuntie. auntie. K:ââmgaa's pekpek
    'Auntie! Kââm's pekpek' [pekpek is the Pidgin word for excrement]

Ana: K:ââm i pekpek [on the road]
'K's pekpek'
auntie! Kêm ka kp:ee
'Auntie! Kêm is swearing'

Nji: [pointing] k:ii mu dê kn:aa mu ngee kwo
'He pekpeked there, and there's another one here.'

Nji: o k:ii kn:ââ mboo ngee kwo
'There, pekpek is there.'

42:38:
Wââ: [pretending to vomit] oo K:ââm [first overt sanction to K, + negative affect]

42:43:
Nji: [pointing] o mu ngee tóó
'There's some more there.'

Taa: km:ii dênê mu nya nyoo
'Go and get another coconut husk.'

42:56:
Taa: [lifts K off the path onto side bushes, saying] oo chi (po). [points at poop]
chup chup apuu, apuu, apuu! knîknî [stinky]! [second overt sanction to K]

Taa: [grabbing/teasing K's penis] oo oo oo!

43:29:
Taa: k:ââ puu mu dê pii, auntie.
'I cleaned the bottom (of K), auntie.'

Luc: ee?

Taa: k:ââ puu mu dê pi
'I cleaned his bottom.'

Luc: mw:ââkó
'Thank you.'

K:ââm: aa

?:   al:ii. auntie al:ii [pointing]
'Here. It's here auntie.'

Nji: Wââ. ...

Wââ: kê nyi myénte [you too]
Taa to K:ââmgaa!
[babytalk version of his name. She cleans his bottom with coconut husk.]

44:25:   [Luc now appears, bends over and cleans up mess on path]

44:33:
Taa to Din: kn:î kn:î kn:î   [third overt sanction, this time to D]
[disgust sound]
[Taa walks past K:ââm and pats him on the head. Reassurance, it's ok]
[D bounces ball on K's head, playing]

45:01:   [L is cleaning up, and talking to K:ââm about his delict, softly]
K:ââm: [walks up and hands me a keemî nut]
         ee ma 'eat'. ee ee. [offering game, back to normality]
Kêm: Din a dé
         'Din, you throw it' [ball]
         later, 45:56:
Kêm: Penny, Kââm pekpek there.
         'Penny (i.e. researcher), K pooped there.'

Although there are multiple mentions of the delict, and jokey comments on its unpleasantness, and the children make sure that K's mother (their 'auntie') intervenes, K is not scolded. It is noteworthy that Rossel adults do not quarrel openly or upbraid each other over small delicts. For large offenses (e.g. stealing, adultery, rape, witchcraft) there will be a public hearing, an informal court case where anyone (usually men) can speak out and harangue the offender; these are usually resolved with the payment of shell money by the offender to the victim. Overt adult aggression is restricted to this kind of verbal haranguing in a court case, except for a few special contexts – for example, at funerals it is customary for certain relatives of the deceased to hit the bereaved wife/husband with a hard smack on the back, and to throw coconut stem chunks at young male relatives, who are presumed to have neglected the one who died. Violence in this society is very much behind the scenes, in the form of witchcraft.[7]

Discussion

In sum, in this Rossel community small children are socialized through interaction in a secure, supportive, free and creative environment, manifesting the 'secure' mode of training for prosociality (behaviour carried out for the benefit of others) identified by Esther Goody (1991). This, she suggests, tends to co-occur with a high level of mother–child intersubjectivity and with independent interdependence with peers, as evidenced, for example, by Mbuti pygmies, and the Fore of PNG, as also in our Rossel case. The processes Goody mentions for influencing prosociality – shaping, scaffolding, modelling, training – are all abundantly present in the interactions we have observed, and generally in an atmosphere of good-humoured affectionate patience. There is a change in a child's status when a new sibling is born which can produce a temporary shock – the mother's attention turns to the newborn, and the child is shifted to an elder sibling or other relative as a primary caregiver, and to peers for interaction – but this does not seem to produce long-lasting emotional effects (in contrast to what Carstairs (1958) observed in India). The early training in independence takes hold, and by age three or four the Rossel child can pretty much stand on her own feet, immersed in her peer group activities.

The result, for most Rossel children, is very happy childhoods and confident adults. The data are compatible with Goody's suggestion (1991) that there may well be general cross-cultural patterns in prosocial actions: nurturance and care of infants, sharing of scarce resources, and protection of others from harm, are all emphasized by caregivers, of all ages, in this community as well. Another thing that is emphasized is ethnic pride – children are incorporated in cultural activities; for example, attending rituals, boys singing the all-night male opera form *tpile wee*, and school Fridays which focus on local cultural activities.

We can make an explicit contrast with a community on the other side of the world, that of the Tzeltal Maya of Tenejapa in Chiapas, Mexico, where we have also studied child interactions.[8] Interactional styles in these two cultural contexts are radically different, with the Tzeltal non-child-centred; babies are carried tied onto the mother's back and very little interaction with babies occurs until they are about 9–10 months of age and beginning to make initiatory moves to interact. In addition, Tzeltal infants have extreme constraints on their physical mobility – many Tenejapan babies are not put down on the ground and do not learn to crawl. Brown (2011) found radically different rates of interaction in the two settings: children initiate interactions with others twice as frequently in the Rossel data. Nonetheless, there are commonalities in their interactional development – pointing behaviour, for example, appears to emerge at about the same time as among the Rossel babies (ibid.), suggesting a biological predisposition – what Levinson (2006b) has called the 'interactional engine' – to the development of communicative interaction. There are sociocultural factors in common as well: there is a comparable emphasis on actions, rather than on objects, in the content of interactions in these two settings; in both societies, other children do a major part of the child-caring, and most interactions are multi-participant rather than the two party (mother–child) ones familiar in Western contexts. Yet Tzeltal children are not encouraged to be independent actors from a young age, and they do not develop into the markedly competent and self-confident small children that we observe on Rossel Island.

The similarities and differences in these two contexts suggest that the contrast between 'child-centred' and 'situation-centred' styles of child-rearing (Ochs and Schieffelin 1984) is too blunt an instrument. We need a finer-grained typology of interactional styles of caregivers and children to capture the multiplicity of variations across societies and across contexts. To this end, the study of this process of socialization into language and culture is critical to understanding the biological bases, learning, and cross-cultural variability of social interaction, as well as the role of social constructs and of culture more broadly in the social, cognitive and linguistic development of children around the world.

Acknowledgements

I (PB) am indebted to Esther in a number of ways. She played an important role at the start of my career, by suggesting that the mammoth paper on politeness that Stephen Levinson and I had written as graduate students was worthy of publication, and following this through to include it in her book *Questions and Politeness* (1978). But it is Esther's perennial interest in how social interaction reflects and instantiates particular aspects of social structure that has always been our main point of contact with her, and she, in person and in writing, always reminds one to take one's nose out of the micro-details of interaction and ask what the social linkages and consequences of these patterns of interaction might be. In addition, Esther's work on parental roles and socialization practices has been an inspiration to me in my study of child language socialization in different societies.

The research reported here would have been impossible without the assistance of PB's Rossel consultant Anna Yidika, the transcribing and translating assistance of her late father Isodore Yidika, MC's Rossel data-collection assistant Taakême 'N:aamono, the linguistic and ethnographic expertise of Stephen Levinson, and the financial support of the Max Planck Institute for Psycholinguistics. We are grateful to them all. We are also profoundly grateful for the gracious welcome of the Rossel community and their support for our work; they have made Rossel Island our home away from home.

MC's work on this project was supported in part by a European Research Council Advanced Grant INTERACT (269484) awarded to Stephen Levinson, and a NWO Veni Innovational Research Scheme (275-89-033) awarded to MC.

Penelope Brown is a linguistic anthropologist with interdisciplinary interests ranging across linguistic pragmatics, conversation analysis, child development, and ethnography. She has worked for many years in two field sites: one (since 1971) with the Tzeltal Mayans of Chiapas, Mexico, and the other (since 2003) with the Rossel Islanders of Papua New Guinea, studying adult social interaction and child language and social development. She has recently retired from a long-term research position at the Max Planck Institute for Psycholinguistics in the Netherlands.

Marisa Casillas is assistant professor of comparative human development at the University of Chicago. She was a postdoctoral researcher in the Language Development Department at the Max Planck Institute for Psycholinguistics in Nijmegen, The Netherlands. She uses methods from developmental psycholinguistics to investigate the relationship between children's social interactions and their linguistic development. Since 2015 she has extended this work from Western populations only to include two non-Western communities: a Tzeltal Mayan village in the highlands of Chiapas, Mexico, and a remote island community in Papua New Guinea.

Notes

1. Papuan languages are non-Austronesian languages spoken in the Melanesian area.
2. Unlike on mainland PNG, English is the lingua franca in island PNG, not Pidgin.
3. The Jinjo area contrasts with the western end of the island, mostly Methodist dominated and with more contacts to the large island of Misima to the west.
4. In 2016, a doctor concerned about the high levels of maternal death in island PNG set up a base in Alotau, the mainland's nearest town, with a seaplane to provide airlifts for mothers in danger to the Alotau hospital.
5. If the baby does not drink its natural mother's milk but starts nursing with the new mother, it will belong to the new mother's clan. Otherwise, it retains the clan of its birth mother.
6. Children's ages are given in years and months, separated by a semicolon. Children's ages are for the most part accurately known, due to their birth in the local hospital and subsequent registration.
7. There are of course marital disputes, but these are very much frowned upon if displayed in public.
8. The first author has worked in this community for over forty years and has a large audio- and videotaped database of Tzeltal caregiver–child interaction; the second author has collected intensive film samples of Tenejapan babies, and she conducted psycholinguistic experiments with them in 2014 and 2015.

References

Armstrong, Wallace. 1928. *Rossel Island: An Ethnological Study*. Cambridge: Cambridge University Press.
Brown, Penelope. 2011. 'The Cultural Organization of Attention', in Alessandro Duranti, Elinor Ochs and Bambi B. Schieffelin (eds), *Handbook of Language Socialization*. Oxford: Blackwells, pp. 29–55.
Carstairs, G. Morris. 1958. *The Twice-Born: A Study of a Community of High-Caste Hindus*. Bloomington: Indiana University Press.
Cole, Michael, et al. 1971. *The Cultural Context of Learning and Thinking*. New York: Basil Books.
Demuth, Katherine. 1992. 'The Acquisition of Sesotho', in Dan I. Slobin (ed.), *The Crosslinguistic Study of Language Acquisition*, Vol. 3. Hillside, NJ: Erlbaoum, pp. 557–638.
——— . 2003. 'The Acquisition of Bantu Languages', in Derek Nurse and Gerard Philippson (eds), *The Bantu Languages*. Surrey, England: Curzon Press, pp. 209–22.
Goody, Esther N. 1972. '"Greeting", "Begging" and the Presentation of Respect', in Jean S. La Fontaine (ed.), *The Interpretation of Ritual: Essays in Honour of A.I. Richards*. London: Tavistock Press, pp. 39–72.
——— . 1973. *Contexts of Kinship: An Essay in the Family Sociology of the Gonja of Northern Ghana*. Cambridge Studies in Social Anthropology 7. Cambridge: Cambridge University Press.
——— . 1974. 'Parental Roles in Anthropological Perspective', in *The Family in Society: Dimensions of Parenthood*. Report of a seminar at All Souls College, Oxford, 10–13 April 1973. Department of Health and Social Security. London: HMSO, pp. 26–35.

———. 1975. 'Delegation of Parental Roles in West Africa and the West Indies', in Thomas R. Williams (ed.), *Socialization and Communication in Primary Groups*. The Hague: Mouton, pp. 447–84.

———. 1978. *Questions and Politeness: Strategies of Social Interaction*. Cambridge Papers in Social Anthropology 8. Cambridge: Cambridge University Press, pp. 17–43.

———. 1982. *Parenthood and Social Reproduction: Fostering and Occupational Roles in West Africa*. Cambridge Studies in Anthropology 35. Cambridge: Cambridge University Press.

———. 1991. 'The Learning of Prosocial Behaviour in Small-scale Egalitarian Societies: An Anthropological View', in Robert A. Hinde and Jo Groebbel (eds), *Cooperation and Prosocial Behaviour*. Cambridge: Cambridge University Press, pp. 106–28.

———. 2006. 'Dynamics of the Emergence of Sociocultural Institutional Practices', in David R. Olson and Mike Cole (eds), *Technology, Literacy and the Evolution of Society: Implications of the Work of Jack Goody*. New Jersey: Lawrence Erlbaum, pp. 241–64.

Kulick, Don. 1992. *Language Shift and Cultural Reproduction: Socialization, Self, and Syncretism in a Papua New Guinea Village*. Cambridge: Cambridge University Press.

Kulick, Don, and Bambi Schieffelin. 2004. 'Language Socialization', in Alessandro Duranti (ed.), *A Companion to Linguistic Anthropology*. Malden, MA: Blackwell, pp. 349–68.

LeVine, Robert A., S. Dixon, S. LeVine, A.L. Richman, P.H. Leiderman, C.H. Keefer and T.B. Brazelton. 1994. *Child Care and Culture: Lessons from Africa*. Cambridge: Cambridge University Press.

LeVine, Robert A., and Rebecca New (eds). 2008. *Anthropology and Child Development: A Cross-cultural Reader*. Malden, MA: Blackwell.

Levinson, Stephen C. 2006a. 'Matrilineal Clans and Kin Terms on Rossel Island'. *Anthropological Linguistics* 48: 1–43.

———. 2006b. 'On the Human "Interaction Engine"', in Nicolas Enfield and Stephen C. Levinson (eds), *Roots of Human Sociality: Culture, Cognition and Interaction*. Cambridge: Cambridge University Press, pp. 39–69.

———. 2022. *A Grammar of Yélî Dnye*. Berlin: Mouton.

Liep, John. 1983. 'Ranked Exchange in Yela (Rossel Island)', in Jerry W. Leach and Edmund Leach (eds), *The Kula*. Cambridge: Cambridge University Press, pp. 503–25.

———. 2009. *A Papuan Plutocracy: Ranked Exchange on Rossel Island*. Aarhus, Denmark: Aarhus University Press.

Malinowski, Bronislaw. 2008. 'Childhood in the Trobriand Islands, Melanesia', in Robert A. LeVine and Rebecca S. New (eds), *Anthropology and Child Development: A Cross-cultural Reader*. Malden, MA: Blackwell, pp. 28–33.

Mead, Margaret. 1928. *Coming of Age in Samoa*. New York: W. Morrow and Company.

———. 1930. *Growing Up in New Guinea*. New York: W. Morrow and Company.

Ochs, Elinor. 1982. 'Talking to Children in Western Samoa'. *Language in Society* 11: 77–104.

———. 1988. *Culture and Language Development: Language Acquisition and Language Socialization in a Samoan Village*. Cambridge: Cambridge University Press.

Ochs, Elinor, and Bambi Schieffelin. 1984. 'Language Acquisition and Socialization: Three Developmental Stories and their Implications', in Richard Shweder

and Robert LeVine (eds), *Culture Theory: Essays on Mind, Self and Emotion.* Cambridge: Cambridge University Press, pp. 276–320.
———. 2008. 'Language Socialization: An Historical Overview', in Patricia Duff and Nancy Hornberger (eds), *Language Socialization, Vol. 8: Encyclopedia of Language and Education*, 2nd edition. New York: Springer, pp. 3–15.
Rumsey, Alan. 2013. 'Intersubjectivity, Deception and the 'Opacity of Other Minds': Perspectives from Highland New Guinea and Beyond'. *Language and Communication* 33(3): 326–43.
———. 2015. 'Language, Affect and the Inculcation of Social Norms in the New Guinea Highlands and Beyond'. *The Australian Journal of Anthropology* 26(3): 349–64.
San Roque, Lila. 2018. 'Egophoric Patterns in Duna Verbal Morphology', in Simeon Floyd, Elisabeth Norcliffe and Lila San Roque (eds), *Egophoricity*: 405–36.
San Roque, Lila, and Bambi B. Schieffelin. 2018. 'Learning How to Know: Egophoricity and the Grammar of Kaluli', in Simeon Floyd, Elisabeth Norcliffe and Lila San Roque (eds), *Egophoricity*: 437–71.
Schieffelin, Bambi B. 1986a. 'The Acquisition of Kaluli', in Dan Slobin (ed.), *The Crosslinguistic Study of Language Acquisition: Volume 1, The Data.* Mahwah, NJ: Lawrence Erlbaum, pp. 525–93.
———. 1986b. 'Teasing and Shaming in Kaluli Children's Interactions', in Bambi B. Schieffelin and Elinor Ochs (eds), *Language Socialization Across Cultures.* New York: Cambridge University Press, pp. 165–81.
———. 1990. *The Give and Take of Everyday Life: Language Socialization of Kaluli Children.* Cambridge: Cambridge University Press.
Schieffelin, Bambi B., and Elinor Ochs. 1986a. 'Language Socialization'. *Annual Review of Anthropology* 15: 163–91.
——— (eds). 1986b. *Language Socialization Across Cultures.* Cambridge: Cambridge University Press.
Takada, Akira. 2005. 'Early Vocal Communication and Social Institution: Appellation and Infant Verse Addressing among the Central Kalahari San'. *Crossroads of Language, Interaction and Culture* 6: 80–108.
Weisner, Thomas S. 1982. 'Sibling Interdependence and Child Caretaking: A Cross-cultural View', in Michael Lamb and Brian Sutton-Smith (eds), *Sibling Relationships: Their Nature and Significance Across the Lifespan.* Hillsdale, NJ: LEA Press, pp. 305–27.
Weisner, Thomas S., and Ronald Gallimore. 1977. 'My Brother's Keeper: Child and Sibling Caretaking'. *Current Anthropology* 18: 169–90.
Whiting, Beatrice B., and John W.M. Whiting. 1975. *Children of Six Cultures: A Psycho-Cultural Analysis.* Cambridge, MA: Harvard University Press.

Conclusion

Felicia Kafui Etsey

'So will you be coming back?' I asked. 'I am not sure whether I will be back again because of my health. Now that the children are reading and writing very well in their own languages, we need to start thinking about how we can help them to improve in their comprehension and writing of small books for their own classrooms', said Esther in a solemn and passionate voice. Before she departed, she gave me copies of some of the short stories that the Bole children had written. In addition, she presented me with a reflective paper that she had written with the title 'Where Might GES Literacy Teaching Go After NALAP?' (Goody 2011).[1] She wanted me to consider working on the issues raised in her paper, especially with children who had learnt to read and write short stories in their own Ghanaian languages. She suggested that reading comprehension strategies should be intensified to help the students to improve in their reading and understanding of text.

Esther Goody lived in Ghana for long periods and worked mostly in northern Ghana from 1956 until 2011, when she left for the final time. She worked especially amongst the Gonja and Birifor ethnic groups and also learnt to speak their languages very fluently. While in Ghana, Esther wore many hats and conducted research in many fields. The chapters in this book pay homage to her, and bring into the limelight much of her research. Throughout her career, Esther Goody, as a distinguished social anthropologist and ethnographer working in Ghana, broke new ground in the fields of kinship, ritual, gender issues, social interaction and the role of language and learning in society. Many of these themes are well captured in this book.

In this concluding chapter, I would like to focus on part of Esther's late research in promoting mother-tongue literacy in primary schools, as it shows many of the qualities and interests of her life's work. Her diligence and passion were clearly displayed in how, even in her very advanced in years, she still dedicated so much attention to the field of language in society and to mother-tongue literacy instruction.

In the latter days of Esther Goody's life, she spent her strength, passion, efforts and 'pennies' ensuring that her belief in 'children reading in mother tongue first' reached some height before she left Ghana. In her innovative long-term research project in mother-tongue literacy, the Local Language Initial Literacy project (LLIL), Esther spent much of the 1990s, and up until 2011, conducting field research in northern Ghana among the Gonja, Birifor, Wala and Dagaari people. She trained teachers there to teach children in their own Ghanaian languages at the early stages of school, and documented its positive impact on the children's academic performance, and on their reading and writing (Goody and Bennett 2001).

At the beginning of the project Esther lived in Baale, and later moved to Bole, both in the Northern Region. Her major purpose and interest in introducing the LLIL project was to help average Ghanaian children in the public (i.e. state or government) schools, mostly children who were from the rural communities and struggling to learn to read and write. Esther's LLIL was grounded in second language research, which describes how important it is for children who are in a multilingual environment to learn in their mother tongue or native language before attempting to learn in a second language.

Overview of Benefits and Challenges of Initial Mother-Tongue Literacy Instruction Studies

Esther's mother-tongue language research confirmed the benefits children derive from instruction that encourages the use of mother tongue or primary languages (L1) to support the teaching and learning of English as a second language (L2), especially in the early grades of schooling (Thomas and Collier 1997; Freeman and Freeman [1994] 2001; Goody and Bennett 2001; UNESCO 2003). This is consistent with the widespread research-based knowledge that literacy skills acquired in L1 transfer across languages, particularly when the orthographies are the same. When multilingual children learn decoding, word level and reading comprehension skills in their own mother tongue, they are on the way to becoming successful readers and writers. Such children find it easier to learn the second language because they are able to transfer the skills learnt in their primary languages to the second languages. Conversely, learning the decoding, reading comprehension and writing skills in a foreign language first can be a difficult task for children (Etsey 2004).

Furthermore, as indicated in second-language research literature globally, conducting such initial mother-tongue literacy instruction research in multilingual and multicultural contexts is not an easy task, especially in countries where a colonial language has been adopted as a lingua franca or national language. Although there is a large body of research evidence, especially in African countries, to suggest that there are positive benefits of initial mother-tongue literacy as indicated above, there are a series of challenges that militate against such studies. In multilingual contexts, there are always a series of arguments and debates about what should be the language of initial literacy instruction. The challenging factors that hinder such sound pedagogical practice include the complex historical, political and psychological legacy of colonization in Africa (Lipson and Wixson 2003: 2). The initial mother-tongue research conducted by Esther Goody and all the series of similar follow-up interventions that were done in Ghana (see below), a typical multilingual and multicultural context, were not free of such effects.

Esther Goody, a strong and dedicated anthropologist and educator, built a supportive network with other international non-governmental organizations and local individuals working on mother-tongue literacy projects to enable her to fuel and build a capable team for the project. In particular, she collaborated with Kurt and Magdeleine Komarek at the German Agency for International Cooperation (GTZ), and she also worked closely with me at the University of Cape Coast.

Description of the Setting Up of the LLIL Project

The LLIL project was carried out in schools in the following communities: Mankuma, Bole, Baale and Gbogdaa in the Northern Region, and Nadowli, Cherekpong, Limanyiri, Sing and Loggu schools in the Upper West Region.

Esther's strategy of teacher training in the LLIL project was to identify interested people who had some level of proficiency in their own languages and train them to become the project teachers in the communities and schools where her projects were located. As part of our research network, we recruited excellent language experts who were graduates from the University of Cape Coast to become the master trainers. The selected project teachers who were trained went back to their communities to train other teachers, and also served as language teachers in the government schools. They taught the local languages and supported the students to read and write in their own languages.

The children were monitored throughout their primary school from the early years until Primary 6.[2] The results clearly indicated that if second-language learners are first taught to read in their own primary languages, they excel in their performance, and in understanding the content of lessons. They also find it easier to learn the target second language (Goody 2011: 3–4; Goody and Bennett 2001).[3]

Esther's research was groundbreaking because she worked with languages that have not been written down or accepted as part of the eleven official Ghanaian languages. The work with Birifor language was a typical example of how innovative Esther's research was, because this language is not one of the government's approved languages.

Legacies of Esther's LLIL Research Work in the Northern Region

Four different metaphors can be used to describe Esther's innovative research in mother-tongue literacy in northern Ghana. Her pioneering research in literacy instruction and language policy can be likened to *a farmer who clears a rocky ground for other farmers, a warrior in the front line of a battle, a mustard seed project and a foundation builder.* I will look at each in turn.

First of all, Esther's work in promoting mother-tongue literacy can be likened to *a farmer* who prepares a tough and rocky ground for other farmers to plant. Her contribution to literacy instruction in Ghana was outstanding, and provided the knowledge and information for other researchers, teachers and donors to build upon. Esther did her work in a very challenging situation and with lots of difficulty. However, she never lost hope or withdrew her commitment to this tough research. With limited financial support, and living among people who spoke a language she did not originally speak or understand, Esther was still able to achieve great success in her challenging research. She conducted her mother-tongue project in the remotest areas of northern Ghana, worked with people who were not familiar to her, and in a culture completely different from her own. In some of the areas where she worked at the initial stages, there was no electricity. She worked with languages that were not written down and not used for school teaching at the time she started her work.[4] It took a brave anthropologist like Esther to break those tough grounds, and she opened the door to many other researchers including PhD students who came from Canada, US, UK and Ghana to conduct their research work in northern Ghana. Esther, although very advanced in years, worked diligently, selflessly and tirelessly, and never feared for her life. She encountered challenges with some of the people she worked with but was able to resolve all her issues amicably, and lived at peace with all the people among whom she lived.

As a woman of substance, a mother, host and advisor, Esther supported many scholars, novices and student-researchers whose names are too many to mention here. These researchers attested to the fact that she supported and guided them in their research work, especially on topics related to her field of anthropology, language in society and mother-tongue literacy. Her support went beyond that of an 'academic advisor'; she was a mentor, a coach and a host to many novice researchers, read through their drafts, provided feedback and scaffolded them to publish their research findings. She was an avid reader who read through anything you gave her and was ready to provide feedback immediately. For example, Esther was able to critically read through my dissertation of over three hundred pages, and she provided me with detailed feedback and guidelines on how to publish it. In her work as a researcher, she established a close network with people who held similar interests to herself – a brave farmer who broke tough grounds indeed.

Secondly, Esther's pioneering work in mother-tongue literacy can be likened to *a front-line warrior* who plays a leading role on a battlefield against all forms of illiteracy. The first challenge or battle that Esther encountered in the field of education in Ghana, which moved her to start the LLIL project, was the issue of illiteracy in children's native languages and in the English language, as well as a lack of comprehension in learning in general. In two reports presented in 1994 and 2003 by Richard Kraft, an American educationist who evaluated the Ghanaian basic school education system for USAID and the Ghana Ministry of Education, he confirmed this problem of illiteracy in Ghanaian schools. These reports revealed a country where very few children finished their last year of primary school able to read with understanding. The documents described the illiteracy rates across the country as 'high, with serious regional and gender-based differences. Poor, rural children and adults are much less likely to be able to read and comprehend texts than urban or more affluent individuals. In addition, the gender gap is critical, with women lagging significantly behind their male counterparts' (Lipson and Wixson 2004: 1). These inequalities in educational opportunities, and linked problems such as lack of premises, teachers and teaching materials, were found to be especially acute in the north of the country and other 'deprived' areas, and were documented for example in Kraft et al., *A Tale of Two Ghanas: The View from the Classroom* (1995). This was a nationwide collaborative survey to which Esther Goody contributed the data on several of the regions in the north.[5] It showed 'great differences between schools in district capitals, urban centres and rural schools, not just in terms of quality but also in terms of community involvement and infrastructure (ibid.).

Kraft described this illiteracy problem in our Ghanaian schools in these words: 'Year after year, the school results show that there is a visible deficiency in pupils' performance in English at basic education levels. In the 2000s, the nationally administered Criterion Referenced Test (CRT), carried out annually since 1992, showed evidence that the vast majority of Ghanaian Primary 6 graduates remain functionally illiterate in English as well as in their own local Ghanaian languages (Ministry of Education, 2002a).'There is clear evidence that there is a deficiency in the instructional approaches that are being used in the teaching of the speaking, reading and writing of the second language. Failure to learn to read and in reading comprehension translates to the failure to learn other subjects' (Kraft 2003). The issue of illiteracy and the crisis in reading in Ghana is the topmost issue that Esther attempted to fight, and many other interventions continued this later.

This issue of illiteracy in Ghana might be related to other deep-rooted challenges in the country. A brief history of the language policy all the way back to the pre-colonial era of Ghana might explain these challenges, and why not much attention is paid to the teaching of the Ghanaian languages in Ghanaian schools. The two possible related factors that might contribute are the unstable nature of our language policy and the 'language wars' that have been going on since the pre-colonial era. As indicated earlier in the chapter, conducting initial mother-tongue literacy instruction projects and research in most multilingual and multicultural countries can be a very difficult and challenging task because of the complex effects of colonization.

The language policy, related to which is the language of instruction in the classroom, can be described as a political issue. In most cases, it is the government in power in a country that is most influential in this decision, especially in the lower levels of schooling. In Ghana, for instance, the instability and changes in government and changes of leadership from 1966 until 1981 seemed to contribute to the inconsistencies and fluctuation of the language policy as applied in schools and classrooms. Even though the situation has been better since 1985, the language policy issue still needs to be worked on and accepted as a stabilized document and practice in the country. The language policy that we can refer to as 'original' dates as far back as the pre-colonial years, when it was the result of a popular commission in the 1920s, the Phelps-Stokes Committee on Language in African Schools. This committee recommended a language policy that made 'teaching through the medium of the vernacular compulsory, at least in the lower classes of the primary school' (McWilliam 1959; Etsey 2004: 7). The policy was supported by the educational view that early education in the mother tongue would facilitate the learning of the second language, namely English (Sackey 1997).

Although Ghana, a multilingual and multicultural country, adopted English as the official language and the lingua franca of the country at Independence in 1957 because she was a former British colony, the government continued to implement the language policy of the colonial government. In the absence of a common indigenous language, English, the colonial master's language, was selected to serve both as a cohesive force internally binding the many tribes in Ghana (Boadi 1971) and as a common language for the multilingual groups in administration, the media and in schools. In Ghana, there are about one hundred linguistic and ethnic groups, speaking different indigenous languages in the country.[6] The government under the first president continued to recognize and promote the use of more Ghanaian languages – such as Akan, Ewe, Ga, Nzema, Dagbani – in the media and in schools. There were even discussions and attempts to select an indigenous language to make the country monolingual after Independence, but these attempts failed (Boadi 1971; Etsey 2004: 8). However, the language policy issue did not improve at government level until 1997, when the GTZ cooperated with the Ministry of Education on an official intervention, the Assistance to Teacher Education Pilot project (ASTEP), as described below.

Closely related to the language policy issue has been a deeply rooted psychological language battle taking place among the citizenry. In Ghana, as is common in countries that have adopted their colonial master's language, there are hidden language battles and arguments ongoing in the minds of the citizenry over which language to use in their homes and in the educational system. Since the colonial era, and all the way back to the coming of the missionaries into Ghana, there has been a raging debate about this between the elite, parents, politicians and educationists. In Ghana the issue is whether Ghanaian children should learn in their own native languages in schools during the early years – the 'mother tongue' position – or just learn by immersion in the English language from the beginning – the 'English-only' position. (English is the official language throughout later school and further education.) This battle is an extension from that in homes. In many elite homes, parents speak only English to their children, and so these children find it difficult to speak their own native languages. However, parents who do not speak English fluently, or believe in the acquisition of the mother tongue first, speak and train their children in their own native languages. The situation in northern Ghana where Esther worked was a critical one, as children there were fluent in their own languages but were not exposed to English and could not understand it; many parents still believed that immersion in English at school would give their children an advantage in life.

This sort of language battle, as Sackey (1997) indicated, could be traced again to the pre-colonial years, to the coming of three of the earliest missionary groups to the southern part of Gold Coast (now Ghana). Due to their religious agenda and working relationship with the people, they had significant impact on the citizenry and language groups among whom they worked. The language battle that emerged influenced the language policy development and the educational system of Ghana.[7] The effects of this, especially the English-only argument, can be clearly observed when any visitor enters some of our schools. Inscriptions such as 'Speak English Always' and 'Don't Speak Vernacular in the Classroom' welcome students to schools or classrooms that have been influenced by teachers who believe strongly in the English-only viewpoint. Other negative practices found in such classrooms were that the use of the local languages was treated as contentious behaviour, and children caught speaking their own local languages at school were sometimes penalized. The deep impact of these practices in our educational system is that many students therefore do not have any desire or interest to learn their own native languages. Even students who succeed in graduating from higher institutions or pre-service training institutions are literate only in English language and 'illiterate' in their own mother tongue. This is the influence of the 'English only' educators that often overshadows the mother tongue advocates, especially in the privately owned schools. No wonder Kraft (2003) found that many of our Ghanaian children graduate from primary school illiterate in both English and their own native language.

The effect of these two closely related issues of unstable language policy and the 'language wars' became a major contributing factor and challenge hindering mother-tongue literacy instruction interventions, especially in Ghana. This is an initial strong force that every mother-tongue literacy researcher has to fight against. Whenever there is an intervention or a programme to promote the teaching of mother-tongue literacy, this debate is brought up and most often quenches the initial enthusiasm of the project. Interestingly, the influence of the English-only belief can be felt in many schools throughout Ghana. The concern of finding trained teachers to teach local languages using sound pedagogies was one of the problems that the GTZ ASTEP programme tackled. GTZ came in to produce materials and to help to train pre-service teachers in the use of sound pedagogies in teaching first languages in Ghanaian classrooms. Unfortunately, due to the strong wind of a temporary change of the language policy in 2002, and subsequent policy confusions at both the national and local levels, the programme suffered and came to a halt. The support that was being given to Ghana in the training of teachers could not see the green light before it was nipped in the bud. The ASTEP materials that were designed for use right through the first three years of schooling (P1 to P3) in literacy, mathematics and science, to reflect the official policy on the language of instruction, could not be used as planned (Lipson and Wixson 2004: 7).

The discussion above outlines a challenge that can be likened to an influential ongoing language battlefield in Ghana. Esther Goody's Local Language Initial Literacy project was an initiative to fight this English-only perspective in a small corner of Ghana, and to prove that in fact when children are introduced to their own native languages early in school, the benefits are numerous. From the initial stages, her mother-tongue literacy intervention was criticized and sometimes condemned by the anti-mother-tongue supporters. It took Esther's brave steps as a great warrior to win the battle over these language policy conflicts. Despite all the local and national challenges, Esther continued with her foundational work and lobbying for mother-tongue instruction in schools. As a distinguished fighter, she adopted the right strategies by selecting people who were interested in learning their own languages, trained them, and used them in teaching the children in different communities. Despite the initial difficulties involved in Esther's LLIL project, she won the battle by getting her students literate in their own languages. The outstanding achievement of her project in the schools she worked with became the foundation of a much bigger and expanded mother-tongue literacy or first-language instruction in Ghana.

Thirdly, Esther's mother-tongue literacy project can be compared to a *mustard seed project* because of the limited funding she was working with. A mustard seed, although very small, can grow to become a big tree that caters for all kinds of birds, big and small. That is why the Holy Scriptures liken the mustard seed faith to a faith that can move mountains. Esther's confidence, strength and commitment to the LLIL programme is a big lesson that many more researchers have learnt from. She was never discouraged in her work, and was committed to it until late in her life. She never got tired of working until she became very frail. What an example for the younger researchers to follow. It seemed like a small project, but from her commitment to sharing and networking with other bigger NGOs and organizations, her small-sized mother-tongue literacy project has given birth, both directly and indirectly, to many bigger and similar projects in Ghana.

Fourthly, Esther's mother-tongue literacy instruction can be seen as a *foundation-building project* in Ghana. Building the foundation of any structure can be very difficult, but once in place, it is for others to continue. As a great researcher with the passion to improve literacy, Esther built a network with other government education ministries, NGOs and donors, and shared her work in northern Ghana with them. Esther's foundational project was followed by a series of other expanded forms of early-grade mother-tongue literacy interventions in Ghana, such as the Molteno project, NALAP and

EQUAL interventions, all with the purpose of improving the literacy situation in Ghana.

As rightly documented by Kraft, the intensive evaluation of the primary school system brought into the limelight the deep-rooted problem of illiteracy in the education system of Ghana. The situation is described in these words: 'There can be no question that the fundamental problem still facing the Ghanaian schools ... remains basic literacy skills in English [and] Ghanaian languages' (Kraft 2003: 3). The research report clearly indicated that there was a crisis of reading achievement in public schools in Ghana, and as Kraft clearly mentioned, English-only programmes could not solve this problem.

Kraft's 2003 report also caught the attention of the then Ministry of Education, Youth and Sports (MOEYS) and the Ghana Education Service (GES). The immediate response given to these findings by MOEYS and GES was to include learning of literacy and numeracy in Ghanaian languages and English as a key focus of their Education Strategic Plan (Ministry of Education 2002b). With a renewed interest in mother-tongue literacy and the deep desire to solve the nation's illiteracy problem and ensure that the majority of children who enter and complete primary school in Ghana learn to read with grade-level understanding, a series of pilot interventions were put in place to improve the literacy crisis in the country. Starting in the 2003/4 school year, these interventions overlapped with and extended Esther's mother-tongue project in the country.

The first major mother-tongue literacy instruction intervention put in place by MOEYS and GES in partnership with the United States Agency for International Aid (USAID, Ghana) was to contract the Molteno Project to pilot a reading programme from 2004 to 2006, similar to the Breakthrough to Literacy (BTL) approach run by them in South Africa. Molteno is a South Africa-based independent non-profit NGO. The Breakthrough to Literacy and Breakthrough to English pilots involved fifty primary schools in the Northern and Volta regions of Ghana, located in two districts of each of these regions (Ho and South Tongu districts in the Volta Region and Bole and West Gonja districts in the Northern Region). The programme was for Primary year 1 (P1) only, after which the language of instruction became English from Primary 2 (Lipson and Wixson 2004: 9).

The pilot school P1 teachers and head teachers received training and were actively engaged in the programme. The choice of Bole shows that Esther's foundational work was recognized in this pilot. The Molteno pilot programme used the regional local languages Ewe and Gonja to introduce the first-year pupils to literacy. As part of its methodology, pupils spent a significant amount of time composing their own sentences and reading them, similar to the Language Experience approach (Chatry-Komarek 2003: 76–77; Lipson and Wixson 2004: III).

The summary of the findings indicated that the BTL reading programme was successful in teaching children to read and write using their own languages; in general, they did better than pupils in the non-pilot schools. Other findings were that the attitudes and support of the stakeholders involved in the pilot programmes – district personnel, head teachers, P1 teachers, parents and community members – improved positively.

> All expressed enthusiasm for the pilot programs. They agreed that these programs were suitable and relevant, that they were far superior to the traditional approach, and that they should be expanded to include more Ghanaian languages and schools. Specific benefits noted included: improved teaching and learning of the Ghanaian language; attitudinal changes on the part of pupils and teachers in the form of punctuality, regular attendance and increased enrolment in P1; and more active participation of pupils in lessons. (Lipson and Wixson 2004: iv–v)

Many teachers also noted an increase in parents' interest in their children's schooling.

> Parents and community members asserted that the program was suitable because they liked the emphasis on the local language. At the same time, they acknowledged the importance of learning to read and write English, since it is an international/ national language used for examinations. (ibid.)

In general, although piloted on a small scale, the Molteno BTL programme made a mark on the learners and teachers in all the pilot schools, with 70 per cent of learners making good to excellent progress. The motivation level was high among both pupils and staff. My own experience with the BTL project showed that children were able to read and write by the end of Primary 1.

At the same time as the Molteno programme was being piloted, the Assistance to Teacher Education Project (ASTEP) local language literacy programme was also piloted in the Afram Plains area of the Eastern Region of Ghana. This pilot was based on the materials and training developed by GTZ. In their evaluation report, Lipson and Wixson reported that both BTL and ASTEP teachers said that, as a result of these intervention programmes, 'they enjoy teaching more, feel they are better teachers, teach differently than before, and that the children enjoy class more' (Lipson and Wixson 2004: v).

As a result of the success of these projects, the Ghana Education Service with the assistance of USAID made a bold decision in 2007 to develop, extend and scale up a quality mother-tongue and bilingual instruction at the national level, to all primary school learners starting from Kindergarten 1 to Primary 3. Following three years of comprehensive planning by a task force and materials development, the programme that was dubbed the National Literacy Accelerated Programme (NALAP) was initiated in Ghana in early 2010. This national (this is the term used in Ghana) literacy intervention was a comprehensive and well-structured programme that emphasized the teaching of mother-tongue literacy in eleven languages. The focus was to give a strong foundation to the children in their own first languages, and transition them gradually to an English component. Esther was very happy about this programme and always thought about how this intervention could be improved and made sustainable. The NALAP programme fully brought back the original national policy: that mother tongue should be used as the Language of Instruction (LOI) in the first three years of primary school (P1–P3), with English as a subject; and then, starting from P4, English would become the LOI and the Ghanaian languages would be studied as subjects.

After a year's intervention, the assessment of the programme showed that pupils' literacy in the local language was quite high and they were learning the contents of the lessons they were being taught. The NALAP intervention confirms the importance of mother-tongue literacy instruction and the appropriateness of the current language policy situation in which NALAP was embedded. The classroom observation data of the NALAP methodology, however, revealed that the majority of teachers spent significant amounts of time reading stories aloud to children, and then asking the pupils questions about the story. This improved the listening comprehension skills of children, but far less frequently were they taught reading comprehension or decoding skills.

Esther was fully involved in most of these follow-up mother-tongue literacy instruction projects that followed the establishment of her LLIL. This concern was documented in a paper she wrote in 2011 and distributed to many stakeholders with the question 'Where Might GES Literacy Teaching Go After NALAP?'

In 2014, the original NALAP methodology was revised and the name changed to An Integrated Approach to Literacy. The purpose of the revision was to holistically integrate the four skills of language – listening, speaking, reading and writing – in the thematic lessons and to align the themes in literacy to those in numeracy and environmental studies. This was not well developed in the original NALAP methodology, hence the need for the revision: 'This approach was consistent with the language policy which makes provision for the use of Ghanaian language as the medium of instruction from Kindergarten 1 and 2 and Primary 1 to 3 while introducing English gradually until Primary 3. From Primary 4, English becomes the medium of instruction' (Ministry of Education 2014: 1–2).

The success of the NALAP programme was followed by another reading intervention programme by USAID with the Ministry of Education dubbed 'Partnership for Education: Learning'. Introduced between 2015 and 2022, its aim was to improve the quality of early grade reading skills in Ghanaian public primary schools using a much more systematic phonics-based approach to the teaching of reading in the eleven approved Ghanaian languages and English. In the first year, the reading programme was prototyped in the town of Yendi (Northern Region), in the Dagbani language, as a precursor to the larger programme involving all eleven approved Ghanaian languages. Initial materials were developed in the Dagbani language, and the teaching of the key concepts was done in Dagbani, in Yendi schools. The process, feedback and lessons from the prototype helped in the development of a Teachers' Guide, pupils' books and other reading materials written in the other eleven languages, and in scaling up the programme to close to a hundred targeted districts in Ghana. For the last two years, in addition to the ongoing instruction in the Ghanaian languages, the programme was extended to include a Transition to English (TTE) programme, and materials for the pupils were developed in English language. The *Learning Programme* finally came to an end in 2022. The teaching and reading materials that had been developed were distributed to all the public schools in Ghana and the programme was handed over to the MOE and GES. The greatest challenge and concern for the educational system of Ghana, MOE and GES after all these wonderful interventions is the sustainability issue of how to ensure all these mother-tongue literacy programmes are continued in the schools to help to solve the literacy crisis, especially in the Ghanaian public basic schools.

In conclusion, Esther's research in social anthropology, language in society and mother-tongue literacy instruction broke new ground and became a foundation on which other such interventions have been built. One can only conclude that the little mustard seed that was sown by Esther over thirty years back has germinated, and grown.

Esther Goody in her mustard seed research in Ghana did everything possible to prove to policymakers that putting into practice the existing research on mother-tongue or primary language instruction could yield beneficial results in children who have been taken through it. The children in Esther's project schools developed writing skills in the earlier stages and became writers. Each language group produced a reading booklet in which they showed their writing skills in writing stories about some of the difficult topics that many children in other schools found hard to understand. The small texts written by the P4 to P6 children in Esther's project schools provide practical evidence of what can happen to children who go through effective early literacy intervention in their own primary languages.

An excerpt from one of the stories from the children's reading booklets, written in Birifor and translated by the project teachers, told a story that showed what Esther meant to the children in Baale. The title of the story was 'The History of Baale'. The child wrote:

> Mr John Kawuro was an opinion leader by then. ... When Mr John Kawuro Tiepar went to down south, he was converted to Christianity. He was the man who brought Methodist church to the community ... The pastor of the Methodist church told Mr Kawuro that he was going to bring school to the community ... Kawuro Kwesi David came ... to Dr Esther Goody and asked for some money to start the school building project. Dr Goody was so kind, and gave five hundred thousand cedis or fifty new Ghana cedis for the project. This money was a big amount of money at that time. Mr Kwesi went and hired a tipper truck to Baale, and it fetched ten trips of white sand.

Summary

In this story, the children captured one important characteristic of Esther that could not be left out when describing her contribution to Ghana. Esther was a philanthropist and a generous woman. She was very kind to the people among whom she lived. She was down to earth and shared her possessions with all types of people. As part of her educational work, she paid school fees for many of the children in the schools in Baale and Bole who came from disadvantaged homes. Gender issues were one of her favourite research topics apart from mother-tongue literacy. Because of this many women were drawn to her. Esther's contribution to Ghanaian women, schoolchildren, teachers and many other educators will remain a sweet-scented aroma that can never be forgotten. The significance of her mother-tongue research still continues today. This is the legacy of an original interdisciplinarian.

Felicia Kafui Etsey is a language, literacy and developmental reading expert, and has specialist knowledge in dealing with cross-cutting issues in the field of early childhood and elementary education. She received her PhD in 2004 from the University of Iowa in the USA in Language, Literacy and Culture. Her dissetation topic was on 'The Effects of Comprehension Strategy Instruction on Ghanaian English Language Learners'. She has been a consultant with the Ministry of Education and several non-government organizations on Ghanaian language policy. She worked closely with Esther Goody on mother-tongue language of instruction. She is a retired senior lecturer in the Department of Basic Education, University of Cape Coast.

Notes

1. GES is the acronym for the Government Education Service, and NALAP stands for 'National Literacy Accelerated Programme'. The latter will be discussed further on in this chapter.
2. Primary school in Ghana is from ages 6 to 11. Primary 6 in Ghana is thus equivalent to the last year of primary school (age 11) in both the UK and the USA.
3. Goody and Bennett carried out testing in 1996 and 1998, at the request of education officials, to provide tangible evidence of the effectiveness of mother-tongue teaching on initial literacy, and to support arguments for this policy at government level.
4. The following are the eleven approved languages that are used in schools: Akuapem Twi, Asante Twi, Dagaare, Dagbani, Dangme, Ewe, Mfantse, Ga, Gonja, Kasem and Nzema. Birifor language is still not part of these approved languages in 2023.
5. Editors' Note: Goody contributed substantially to Kraft's 1995 evaluation with her experience of the schools there since starting that phase of her research in 1992, anonymously writing a large part of it with the data she had collected. It represented a new level of the documentation of education in northern Ghana. See Kraft et al. 1995, especially Chapter 6.
6. See www.ghanaweb.com/GhanaHomePage/tribes/. Accessed 31 October 2024.
7. According to Sackey (1997), the Wesleyans tried to promote English supremacy in their churches and schools, but the Basel and Bremen missionaries who came from Switzerland and Germany respectively encouraged the speaking and teaching of the local indigenous languages in their churches, schools and the communities they worked in. The scholars among the Basel and Bremen missions developed the Twi and Ewe languages, and wrote many books. This situation gave birth to the two different scholarly views in the country: those who prefer to use the English language right from the early years of school with the belief that early learning will promote easier learning of the official language, and those who believe in the learning of the indigenous language.

References

Boadi, Lawrence A. 1971. 'Education and the Role of English in Ghana', in John Spencer (ed.), *The English Language in West Africa*. London: Longman, pp. 49–65.

Chatry-Komarek, Marie. 2003. *Literacy at Stake: Teaching Reading and Writing in African Schools*. Windhoek, Namibia: Gamsberg Macmillan.

Etsey, Felicia Kafui. 2004. *The Effects of Comprehension Strategy Instruction on Ghanaian English Language Learners: Comprehension Processes and Text Understanding*. PhD dissertation, University of Iowa.

Freeman, David E., and Yvonne S. Freeman. (1994) 2001. *Between Worlds: Access to Second Language Acquisition*. Portsmouth, NH: Heinemann.

Goody, Esther N. 2011. 'Where Might GES Literacy Teaching Go After NALAP?' Unpublished report. Esther N. Goody archive, Centre for African Studies, Cambridge University.

Goody, Esther N., and JoAnne Bennett. 2001. 'Literacy for Gonja and Birifor Children in Northern Ghana', in David R. Olson and Nancy Torrance (eds), *The Making of Literate Societies*. Oxford: Blackwell, pp. 178–200.

Kraft, Richard J. 2003. 'Primary Education in Ghana: A Report to USAID'. Accra, Ghana: USAID/Ghana and University of Colorado-Boulder.

Kraft, Richard J., et al. 1995. *A Tale of Two Ghanas: The View from the Classroom*. Accra, Ghana: Ministry of Education.

Lipson, Marjorie Y., and Karen K. Wixson. 2003. *Assessment and Instruction of Reading and Writing Difficulties*, 3rd edn. Boston: Allyn & Bacon.

———. 2004. 'Evaluation of the BTL and ASTEP Programs in the Northern, Eastern and Volta Regions of Ghana'. Report prepared for the Education Office and USAID Ghana. Retrieved 1 June 2024 from https://www.researchgate.net/publication/324132871.

McWilliams, Henry O.A. 1959. *The Development of Education in Ghana: An Outline*. London: William Clowes and Sons Limited.

Ministry of Education. 2002a. '2000 Report on the Administration of Primary 6 Criterion-Referenced Tests'. Accra, Ghana: Curriculum, Research and Development Division.

———. 2002b. 'Education Strategic Plan (2003–2015)'. Accra, Ghana: MOEYS.

———. 2014. *An Integrated Approach to Literacy: Teacher's Guide, KG 2*. Accra, Ghana: Ministry of Education / Ghana Education Service.

Molteno Project. 2004. *Breakthrough to Gonja, Grade 1 Teacher's Guide* (Trial Edition). South Africa: Maskew Miller Longman.

Sackey, John A. 1997. 'The English Language in Ghana: A Historical Perspective', in Mary E. Kropp Dakubu (ed.), *English in Ghana*. Accra: Black Mask Publishers, pp. 126–39.

Thomas, Wayne P., and Virginia P. Collier. 1997. *School Effectiveness for Language Minority Students*. Washington, DC: National Clearinghouse for Bilingual Education.

United Nations Educational, Scientific and Cultural Organization (UNESCO). 2003. 'Education in a Multilingual World'. Education Position Paper, Paris.

Afterword

John Keith Hart

In 1683, at the age of 51, John Locke was an unpublished Oxford academic – he hid his writings for fear of persecution – and the client of a discredited politician. During the exclusion crisis of the Catholic King James II's accession to the throne, he fled for his life to Holland and was sacked by his college. He returned to England six years later after William of Orange's establishment of a Protestant monarchy in the Glorious Revolution of 1688. He soon published his immortal *Two Treatises of Government* (1690), was appointed to the Board of Trade, and wrote influential pamphlets on money that helped to resolve the recoinage crisis of the next decade.

Before his death in 1704, Locke had become so famous that a correspondent could describe him without irony as 'the greatest man in the world'. The eighteenth-century Enlightenment was largely a response to Locke's work as an architect of the middle-class revolution. The Americans based their constitution on his ideas. Now he is often regarded as an apologist for capitalism and author of a narrow 'possessive individualism' on which economic orthodoxy is founded today. I do not find that story in the *Two Treatises*. Locke's Commonwealth was intended to preserve everyone's property in themselves and their possessions. Locke's preoccupation was with the political conditions of personal autonomy.

'The end of law is to preserve and enlarge freedom', he wrote. Freedom is 'a liberty to dispose and order, as he lists, his person, actions, possessions and his whole property within the allowance of those laws under which he is, and therein not to be subject to the arbitrary will of another, but freely follow his own'.

Both treatises are extended essays on parent–child relations. In the first, Locke denies the right of absolute monarchs to claim to be the father of their subjects. In the second, he allows only one exception to the rule of citizens' autonomy, childhood. He asks how we can protect children so that they will grow up to be independent. He was best known in eighteenth-century England for *Some Thoughts Concerning Education* (1703). Only a perverse reading would represent this far-sighted political project, so relevant in the present world crisis, as hiding the class dominance of capitalists behind a rhetoric of market democracy and natural rights.

Georg Simmel, in 'The Metropolis and Mental Life' (1903), pointed out that the early modern liberal revolutions were motivated by the need for freedom of movement. People needed to escape from the restrictions imposed on them by agrarian civilization. But by 1900 in Europe, liberalism had become existential: 'The deepest problems of modern life derive from the claim of the individual to preserve the autonomy and individuality of his existence in the face of overwhelming social forces...' Simmel asked how human personality and personal relations were being transformed by the increasingly impersonal society of large cities. People were drawn together physically in these huge agglomerations, and bombarded by multitudinous signs and sensations at high speed. As a result, they retreated into paying less attention to the individual qualities of others, and sought personal autonomy that was to some extent guaranteed by the anonymity of the crowd.

This new individualism was based more on the desire to distinguish oneself from others as a unique personality within a mass culture whose size and objective spirit were palpable. In small-scale pre-industrial societies, production and consumption were linked by exchanges between people who usually knew each other, and money was a marginal factor. Now mass production and consumption were linked in world markets, where most parties were unknown to each other, and money pervaded the economic process. The social psychology of metropolitans was thus dominated by detachment and by indifference to the qualities of people and things. Intellectual culture and money economy reproduced these attitudes separately and together, in both privilege abstract simplification and rational calculation, while neglecting those features of individuality that cannot be reduced to logic and numbers.

What struck me about the United States, when I taught there in the late 1970s and early 1980s, was that freedom is still more closely linked to movement than in Europe, even though identity politics now undermines the citizenship that emerged briefly during and after the Second World War. In the decades leading up to the First World War, 50 million Europeans left for the lands of temperate zone new settlement, three-quarters of them to the United States, especially to New York and the farmlands of the Midwest, with its great cities, Chicago and Detroit.

This raised a compelling question: 'How do we make society where there was none before and when we have so little in common?' All human beings are both individual and social. Society is not out there, like the national societies of modernity were supposed to be; we must all learn about society as we make it. In *The Souls of Black Folk* (1903), W.E.B. Du Bois claimed that America's most beautiful gift to the world – he said it was the only beautiful thing – was Black music, which he called 'the sorrow songs', a transcendence born of suffering. In my view, the United States' most distinctive intellectual gift to the rest of us has been social psychology, born in Chicago around 1900 and inspired by Simmel in the first modern age of globalization.

Its pioneers were G.H. Mead (symbolic interactionism) and W.I. Thomas (the cultural history of races, classes, and personality development), both at the University of Chicago, and Charles Cooley ('the looking glass self'), who spent his entire life in Ann Arbor, Michigan. They focused on child development, education and socialization. In the postwar period it became the study of 'how people's thoughts, feelings and behaviour are influenced by the actual, imagined, or implied presence of others' (Wikipedia). Human behaviour is to be explained through the interaction of mental states and social situations, as all human beings are individual subjects in objective social worlds. Social psychologists focused on how we become human as individuals and collectively.

In the 1970s I befriended John Dollard, a distinguished social psychologist who as a young man in the 1930s moved from Chicago with Edward Sapir to join the Yale anthropology department. His most famous monograph was *Caste and Class in a Southern Town* (1937), where he asked why poor Whites sided with their masters of the same race rather than the Blacks, as they were both exploited by the former. In 1973, when Huey Newton was on trial in New Haven, Connecticut, the Black Panthers issued a list of a hundred 'honkies' who would be spared in their revolution. John Dollard was on it. He told me that he had been excited to join anthropologists because they studied culture and must therefore be interested in how people get it. But they were not, and he had to teach a course there on acculturation himself, as 'Socialization'. Ever since, academic anthropologists have neglected social psychology and education, while the social psychologists still know nothing of the comparative study of kinship and marriage.

Ann Arbor likes to call itself 'the Athens of the Midwest'. The University of Michigan was the first American institution to introduce a democratic version of the German seminar teaching method, and today is a centre of excellence in a wide range of disciplines. Esther Goody absorbed the Midwestern tradition of social psychology literally with her mother's milk, as her father Ted Newcomb was one of its leaders then.

Almost accidentally, however, she found something to complement it in British social anthropology's preoccupation with kinship, a field founded by William Rivers, once president of the British associations for both anthropology and psychology. It was continued by A.R. Radcliffe-Brown and revived by Meyer Fortes with Jack Goody after 1945 – all of them, at least for a time, were at Cambridge University. She and Jack became a true partnership, making many field trips to northern Ghana, especially in the first decade of Ghana's independence. Their work together and separately culminated in their classical article on cross-cousin marriage. Then he took off into history and she launched her life work of synthesizing social anthropology and social psychology.

Apart from her fifty-five years of intermittent research in Gonja, northern Ghana, Esther also worked in England (London and Leicester) and India

(Gujarat). In her five books (two authored and three edited), she explored family sociology, parent–child relations, fostering, early commodity production and apprenticeship, sociolinguistic strategies of interaction, and the interactive sources of intelligence. Her last project in northern Ghana was on social variations affecting school performance, in particular the classical distinction between traditional states and stateless societies highlighted in Fortes and Evans-Pritchard's *African Political Systems* (1940). This work deserves to be made public, as it formed a suitable climax of her romance with the two disciplines to which she devoted her life.

Esther excelled as a teacher, unsurprisingly in small-scale social interaction. Her intelligence was sharp, tough and interrogative, but profoundly sympathetic. Everyone noted her remarkable ability to give herself to others without imposing herself on them. She did not excel in projecting her work to a wider audience, as Jack Goody did. But I believe her approach will find a growing reception in this century through the work of followers inspired by her. For our national societies are in disarray and, if humanity is to discover social forms conducive to our survival as a species, anthropologists must learn to merge an ethnographic tradition rooted in twentieth-century nationalism with a romantic methodology focusing on how human beings learn to live together on a world scale. Esther was a pioneer of that movement.

I should note Esther's secondary interest in economic anthropology, manifested especially in her two books published in 1982. This was a lively continuing topic of conversation between us. But her place in my world goes far beyond intellectual interests. I have lived in Cambridge for a quarter of my life and Esther was the kindest person I met there. Kindness and kinship share a linguistic root. In my darkest years, she gave me an unconditional refuge and self-effacing care when I needed them most. My love for her, like her reputation, can only grow in retrospect.

The Caribbean writer, C.L.R. James wrote, 'The distinctive feature of our age is that mankind as a whole is on the way to becoming fully conscious of itself'. We need a closer reading of Immanuel Kant's vision for an anthropology conceived of more as lifelong, practical and popular education than modern academic specialists have had any use for. Subjective individuals must learn how to combine personal experience with knowledge of an impersonal world in crisis. Emergent world society *is* the new human universal – not an idea, but the fact of our shared occupation of the planet crying out for new principles of association.

Previous universals (Catholic, White racist and bourgeois economics) were imposed by European expansion over five hundred years. They had no room for cultural particulars that are essential to human self-expression. Living in society must be personal and moral under laws made by democratic means. The early modern project (Humanism 1.0) is still mainly reflected in biographies that reduce our common human predicament to personal experience. Great literature and its digital successors lead individuals to discover their own versions of human truth through stories about specific personalities, relations, events and places.

Academic anthropology based on ethnographic fieldwork reflects this principle, but it was subverted in the last century by becoming a specialist compartment of universities dedicated to meeting the bureaucratic needs of national capitalism. Whatever happens to that system, anthropology for this century must become a lifelong self-learning tool for anyone who cares about making a world society fit for all humanity. Humanism 2.0 would require each of us to learn how to reconcile the personal and impersonal dimensions of our common human predicament. A neo-Kantian anthropology could be indispensable to this task.[1]

Kant conceived of anthropology as an empirical discipline, but also as a means of moral and cultural improvement. It was thus both an investigation into human nature and, more especially, into how to modify it, as a way of providing students with practical guidance and knowledge of the world. He intended his lectures to be popular and of value in later life. Above all, he wanted his *Anthropology from a Pragmatic Point of View* (1798), the first book to introduce anthropology as an academic discipline and a bestseller in its day, to contribute to the progressive political task of uniting world citizens by identifying the source of their 'cosmopolitan bonds'. It moves between vivid anecdotes and Kant's most sublime vision as a bridge from the everyday to horizon thinking.

If for Kant the main divisions of anthropology were physiological and pragmatic, he preferred to concentrate on the latter – 'what the human being as a free actor can and should make of himself'. This should be based primarily on observation, but it also involves the construction of moral rules. The book has two parts, the first and longer being on empirical psychology and divided into sections on cognition, aesthetics and ethics. The second part is concerned with the character of human beings at every level from the individual to the species, seen from both inside and outside. Anthropology is the practical arm of moral philosophy. It does not explain the metaphysics of morals, which are categorical and transcendent; but it is indispensable to any interaction involving human agents. It is thus 'pragmatic' in several senses: it is 'everything that pertains to the practical', popular (as opposed to academic), and moral in that it is concerned with what people should do, with their motives for action.

If we wish to make a personal connection with the world, we must try to engage with the human condition. This was supposed to be anthropology's purpose, but it is no longer. Being human is not something we inherit through our DNA. Becoming human is life, movement, and process. Whatever stops developing has become – it is a state, a dead thing. The last murderous century's project was to make an impersonal society ruled by capitalist markets, national bureaucracy, and scientific experts. Not surprisingly, most of its members found it hard to locate themselves in such a society. The most enduring legacy of the youth rebellion of the 1960s was the feminist movement. They taught us that the personal is also political. It is no coincidence that, of all the anthropologists I knew, Esther Goody inspired me to write my recent book, *Self in the World: Connecting Life's Extremes* (2022).

People have many sides, but I focus here on two. Each of us is a biological organism with a historical personality that together make us a unique individual. But we cannot live outside society, which shapes us in unfathomable ways. Human beings must learn to be self-reliant (not self-interested) in small and large ways: no one will brush your teeth for you or save you from being run over while crossing the street. We each must also learn to belong to others, merging personal identity in a plethora of social relations and categories. Modern ideology insists that being individual and mutual is problematic. Our culture anticipates a conflict between them, yet they are inseparable.

We embark on two life journeys – one out into the world, the other inward to the self. Society is mysterious to us because it dwells inside us, mostly inaccessible to thought. Writing brings the two into a mutual understanding that we can share. Lived society can become exposed to introspection in this way. Fragments of experience could then be combined into a whole, a world as singular as the self. There are as many worlds as individual journeys. If there is only one world out there, each of us changes it whenever we move.

John Keith Hart's research has been on economic anthropology, Africa, money and the internet. He contributed the concept of informal economy to development studies. His books include *The Memory Bank: Money in an Unequal World* (Profile, 2000), the edited volume *Money in a Human Economy* (Berghahn Books, 2017) and *Self in the World* (Berghahn Books, 2022). He has worked in five continents and co-founded the Human Economy Programme in Pretoria.

Note

1. See my essay in 5 parts, 'Anthropology as Humanist Education' from https://johnkeithhart.substack.com/p/anthropology-as-humanist-education-ee1. Contents: 'Kant's Anthropology from a Pragmatic Point of View (1798)'; 'The New Human Universal Is World Society'; 'Historical Origins of Our World's Current Impasse; Kant's Perpetual Peace (1795)'; 'The Relevance of Kant's Cosmopolitan Politics Today'; 'Renewing Kant's Vision in this Century'.

References

Dollard, John. 1989 (1937). *Caste and Class in a Southern Town*. Madison: University of Wisconsin Press.
Du Bois, William Edward Burghardt. 2008 (1903). *The Souls of Black Folk*. Oxford: Oxford University Press.
Fortes, Meyer, and Edward Evan Evans-Pritchard (eds). 2016 (1940). *African Political Systems*. London: Routledge.

Hart, Keith. 2022. *Self in the World: Connecting Life's Extremes*. Oxford and New York: Berghahn Books.

Kant, Immanuel. 2006 (1798). *Anthropology from a Pragmatic Point of View*. Cambridge: Cambridge University Press.

———. 2016 (1795). *To Perpetual Peace: A Philosophical Sketch*. Create space platform.

Locke, John. 1960 (1690). *Two Treatises of Politics*. Cambridge: Cambridge University Press.

———. 1703. *Some Thoughts Concerning Education*. Kindle.

Simmel, Georg. 1971 (1903). 'The Metropolis and Mental Life', in Levine, Donald. 1972. (ed.), *Georg Simmel on Individuality and Social Forms*. Chicago: Chicago University Press.

Appendix I

Esther N. Goody: Unpublished Notes

Editors' Note: These unpublished notes were made by Esther Goody in October 2014 with a view to prefacing a collection of her papers. It provides a lovely account in Esther's own voice of how she remembered her many intellectual trajectories, and provides more 'back story' than we were able to include in the Introduction. From her notes to herself regarding sections to be amplified and material to be inserted, it is clear that although she was writing this with publication in mind it was very much still a work in progress. The notes become less tightly organized towards the end as she addresses ideas she is currently working on. At the end of the appendix, the editors have added a bibliography of the works she cites; for her own publications, we refer readers to the fuller bibliography in Appendix V.

Thoughts on Links between Ideas and Research

(Draft of possible preface for book of my republished essays – from chapters in books and journals. This will need editing.)

Typically, a new project happens when I am immersed in a local situation that puzzles me.

For instance:
Fieldwork for my PhD dissertation was to be on kinship in central Gonja. We were living in the old town of Gbuipe, where the founder of the Gonja kingdom, NdeWura Jackpa, is buried. As I began to get a sense of compounds and family life, two things in particular struck me as different from rural communities at home. First was the fluidity of movement between households. In the evening, cooked meals were sent between compounds; within a compound men ate together, women ate in small groups with the children. Far more curious, gradually it was clear that the children were not only from Gbuipe.

Many had been sent from, or brought from, other Gonja communities. Gradually I realized that some siblings born in a household lived elsewhere. What was this mobility of children all about? The dissertation, and later the book *Contexts of Kinship*, analysing this material tried to understand how bilateral descent, and rearing each other's children in fostering, had come about in this society. Much of the analysis was based on numerical material that expressed patterns of marriage, divorce, residence across distances, and of fostering.

However, having laid out these patterns, the picture still seemed two-dimensional. I realized there was another kind of pattern cutting across everyday activities. Two were strongly positive, binding folk together: the regular, and elaborate exchanging of cooked food at ceremonies; and greeting (and begging) within and across communities. Two of these patterns expressed and managed danger and hostility: one was the existence and threat of ancestral supernatural power; and the other, complex beliefs and behaviour about witchcraft. These sociocultural patterns I called 'relational idioms'. These relational idioms have led to later papers that explore them as new puzzles. (See below.)

Other Puzzles

Questions

In 1974 I had a chance for another stretch of fieldwork in northern Ghana. Gonja weaving had always intrigued me, and the work on fostering implied the question as to how weaving skills were transmitted across generations. Daboya, across the White Volta River in central Gonja, was known as the centre of weaving, so I arranged for one of their best weavers to let me become his apprentice. For three months I sat at 'my' loom as part of the weaving area.

Immediately I had a problem. The loom and how to use it were strange. My instinct was to ask my 'master' questions. Yet none of my fellow apprentices asked any questions. (Actually they sometimes played guessing games among themselves during the long day, but for amusement.) At first I sat silent all day. Later I realized I could ask for help from fellow apprentices. But this was not about questions, but about what to do for broken threads, or poor loom tension.

Then something happened that suddenly made me think again about questions. My master's new wife had a baby, so after a week, I went to greet her and see the baby. Sitting with them in her small, dim room, I watched as she conducted a conversation with the infant, based on questions: 'Why are you crying, I have just fed you? Shhh'; 'This is your father's apprentice, she has come to meet you. If you cry, she will run away and tell your father'.

Pondering this fascinating 'conversation', I began to see that similar 'exchanges' were common between mothers and their infants in Daboya. The paper I did looking at kinds of questioning and its relationship to power and status became the Malinowski Lecture of 1975, published in *Questions and Politeness* (1978).

Witchcraft: Gender and Power

On first working with the Gonja, witchcraft was not one of my interests. During the excellent Cambridge preparation for fieldwork, reading several detailed studies of witchcraft left me thinking – Well, that's one thing I won't have to deal with.

Unfortunately, no one explained this to the Gonja... Once in Gonja, being around during everyday activities meant hearing comments on, concern about, and occasional attributions of witchcraft. On one routine Friday morning greeting of the Bunsunu Divisional chief, I found his small hall in the midst of a trial of a woman for killing three of her family. For some time afterwards, I participated in such local discussions in the community. However, work on dissertation topics inevitably took most attention.

Several years later, Mary Douglas organized the annual social anthropology conference around the topic of witchcraft. This seemed an opportunity to revisit my Gonja notebooks to look at the material on witchcraft. (I remember welcoming the chance to set aside for a time working on overdue final ESRC grant reports for the fostering work.)

By this time I had returned for two more periods of fieldwork in northern Ghana, one in Kpembe (eastern Gonja), and one in Bole (western Gonja). In Bole, for several weeks I spent mornings sitting in on medical divining sessions by an elderly woman. During this time with her, I found that mothers brought children to her for diagnosis and treatment. With them she seemed both skilled and wise. However she told me that this was dangerous, since the children sometimes died. Then there might be talk of witchcraft. On returning to Bole some twenty years later, I learned that my friend had died (apparently peacefully in old age), but she had not been properly buried in the town graveyard, but taken out into the forest and left, naked, for animals, 'Because people knew she was a witch'.

As I brought together and reviewed these very different aspects of witchcraft in Gonja, two contrasting patterns were clear.

For ruling and Muslim men, witchcraft powers were sought for as signs of legitimate importance. A successful chief has to have stronger mystical powers than those he must compete with. Chiefs expect to be attacked by other chiefs' witchcraft. Indeed, there is no search for the cause of death when a chief dies, since it is known it was due to a rival's stronger witchcraft.

For women, assertions of witchcraft are actually dangerous. Before the British took over Gonja, one of the main responsibilities of chiefs was to control women witches. Since chiefs were known to themselves have strong witchcraft powers, when there were many, or strange, deaths, local folk demanded that the chief deal with the witch responsible. Every court had some warriors known to have mystical strength necessary to deal with witches. Such a man would take a woman witch into the forest to kill her there. The British could not permit this. Now people still joke about it, but in fact even now an accused witch usually runs away.

Writing the paper for Mary Douglas's conference I found it was about the puzzle: What is going on in Gonja society so that a threat of death from witch-craft by a man is seen as part of his legitimate role. Yet when a woman seems to threaten a community by witchcraft, the necessary response is for the chief to control her – in whatever way is necessary. Hence the paper's title, 'Legitimate and Illegitimate Aggression in a West African State'.

I spent 12 years as an anthropological consultant to the Ministry of Health and Social Welfare in London. Among other things, we commissioned research on domestic violence, and then held a conference bringing together people working with women's shelters, doctors, social workers and the police. Later, I was asked to contribute a paper to a Max Plank conference on *Herrschaft*. Since *Herrschaft* literally means 'man's power', I could not resist doing one about this domestic violence material: 'Why Must Might be Right? Observations on Sexual Herrschaft'.

The fate of this paper turns out to also be instructive about social anthropo-logical views on gender and power at that time.

As things worked out, although I had sent the paper ahead, end of term obligations in Cambridge made it impossible for me to read it there myself. Someone read it for me, and I was sent notes on the discussion. Apparently comments were heated. People were shocked that it described a pattern, repeated several times in unrelated societies, in which women were 'known' to be bad, and thus it was men's duty to control them; severe constraints were sometimes thought necessary. This does happen in Christian belief, which I mentioned but did not emphasize. (Apparently one person said I had got even the Bible wrong.) However more interesting were cases from Australia and Latin America where there was no Christian influence. No answer was offered about why this pattern of 'naturally' bad women should be common.

Bemused, I sent a copy to an old friend, Sherry Ortner, asking for com-ments. After some time, she did answer, saying that this paper was very harmful to the feminist cause; it must not be published. I left it in the *Herrschaft* confer-ence volume, thinking no one would read it anyway. Some seven or eight years later one of the conference participants was at a meeting in Japan. She was very hostile!

In fact, this paper was eventually published in the American Journal *Mind, Culture and Activity*. Later it was included in a collection of papers from this journal (Goody [1986,] 1987, 1997).

Later, when Harvard wanted a woman as professor for women's studies, Prof. Tambiah asked me if I would consider it. However it seemed to me that having struggled once with feminist complications, to risk this again would not fit with the kind of research I wanted to do.

Greeting and Begging

Puzzles can appear when doing basic ethnography, for instance observing court, community and domestic life in Kpembe (eastern Gonja), the elaborateness, indeed elegance, of greeting activities demanded detailed recording. Once this was laid out, several patterns appeared. It seemed these were linked to seeking several kinds of support, ranging from assistance with farming, to a wife, to chiefship.

[Add brief description of greeting gestures: junior actor must come to senior.]

When a chief or elder is passing: I watched a woman set down a heavy water pot, and crouch in greeting; a youth on a bicycle stopped, got off his bicycle and partially crouched in greeting; children greeting parent must lie down and greet verbally, rising when permitted; when greeting the chief in his hall, different postures are appropriate for men and women, for members of ruling estate, for Muslims, and for different commoner groups.

Children must greet both parents in early morning and in evening – all their lives. Kin and senior townspeople should greet the chief every Friday and every Monday, morning and evening.

[Add dialogue as key to 'doing' greeting and begging activities.]

Joking Relations: The Emergence of Roles and Rules

When I was asked in 1995 to do the Radcliffe-Brown memorial lecture, I agreed without knowing just what to write about. The main part of the research in northern Ghana on effects of formal authority on learning was underway. This involved comparison of two sets of acephalous and centralized societies. I really enjoyed working for the first time in acephalous societies. In one of these, joking relations were vague and occasional. In the Gonja kingdom, however, joking was quite elaborate. For the lecture I read again Radcliffe-Brown's papers on joking relations. These turned out to lead in an unanticipated direction: The emergence of roles and rules.

In his final book, *The Theory of Social Structure* (1957), Nadel highlights the striking importance for the anthropologist of patterns. Where do these patterns come from? With a detailed, empirically grounded analysis, he shows that daily interaction between individuals in social roles results in patterns: father–son; priest–supplicant; teacher–pupil. Nadel wants to understand how individuals become basic for societies. Thus it is important that links between individual actions work specifically at the level of the local community. Repetition leads to routines, to expectations of reasonable/legitimate behaviour, in effect to roles, and to rules.

But how does this work? What is the process by which roles and rules emerge? If we take joking relations as an example, sociocultural frames lead to role dialogues. In South African patrilineal societies, mother's brothers joke with their sister's sons; sister's sons must respond in joking mode.

Radcliffe-Brown's 1952 account starts by pointing out that in these patrilineal societies, jural authority is vested in male agnates. It is determined by generation. Sons are under their fathers' authority; obedience is absolute. However, members of a patrilineage cannot marry each other. Wives must belong to different patrilineages from their husbands. They are under the authority of their fathers. People say about sisters, that if they had been boys, they would have had the same rights – to property and to authority – as their brothers. Because of this, sister's sons have implied claims to their mother's lineage. So when a sister's son seizes property from his mother's brother, the uncle cannot and does not object.

This ambiguity leads to anger and hostility between the mother's brother, who is supposed to support and assist his sister and her children, and the nephew, who feels he has not received what is due to him. (This account seems to be based on Radcliffe-Brown listening to what people say; and his observations of the effect of confrontations.) Drawing on my observations in northern Ghana, empirically what one meets is formulaic challenges and formulaic responses between two joking partners: in South Africa and northern Ghana between grandparents and grandchildren, between mother's brothers and sister's sons, between cross-cousins, and often between dyads identified as members of competing ethnic groups.

These dynamics are enacted verbally, through dialogues that often resemble games. Through familiar role routines, potentially aggressive interactions come to be enjoyed, even delighted in. The Radcliffe-Brown paper includes accounts of a woman training her granddaughter to laugh instead of crying when pinched; and of bystanders using exaggerated joking to prevent joking partners from coming to blows.

[Quote from R-B paper on gradual duplication across role dyads that become recognized roles and their rules: pp. 140ff]

Dynamics of the Emergence of Sociocultural Institutional Practices

This paper was conceived and written when I had a chance to contribute to the festschrift being put together for Jack Goody (2006). It responds to an apparent contradiction between the many patterned responses he described, where kinship adapts to new technologies. These analyses do not support the current anthropological truism that every society is unique.

How can these patterned regularities of institutional practice be reconciled with this manifest local variation? At one level this is a problem of the transience of theoretical fashions. Yet this apparent contradiction of the regular patterned effects of specific tools on social forms, on the one hand, and the essential uniqueness of each society on the other, deserves attention. If uniqueness is a core characteristic of individual societies, this begs the question of how that uniqueness contributes to the emergence of the regular patterns of adaptation to technical innovations.

There are two terms to this proposition: the social and cultural dynamics of daily life, of which the uniqueness of individual societies is the result; and the patterns that emerge locally and come to be similar across societies. Although distinct, these are closely interdependent. To explore these relations, we need to move down to the level of accounts of particular societies. Then we can focus on those features around which a particular social and cultural world is shaped.

In asking how to understand the relation of individuals to social structure, Nadel says there are two basic factors. One is the patterns of interaction between actors in key roles. The other is the centrality of these patterns to emergent social structures.

How do role dyads lead to patterns? In simple societies roles tend to link close kin: mother/child, father/child, husband/wife, brother/brother... Bateson's 1936 account in Naven shows siblingship is a strong bond, and when used in classificatory mode, can link members of different kin groups. Nadel develops this account of roles by arguing that empirically they always extend through time. With experience, role-partners come to have expectations of each other. This is reinforced as individuals occupy many roles over time. In this way, role rights and expectations come to be shared within the community.

Here we see a source of specifically local patterns of roles and rules:

Since resources, constraints, cultural meanings etc. also differ across local communities, we also see how and why neighbouring communities, and thus neighbouring societies, differ from each other.

Sociocultural Stable Strategies

Within each society at any given time, individuals make plans and choices that have to work in their community. For instance, for men in the Birifor village of Baale, effective farming is very important, not only to have enough food, but as a matter of pride as a household head. One man married an older widow so he could draw on her skills in planting and harvesting to extend the size of his farm. People commented openly that of course he would not want her as a wife, but he needed another woman to plant and harvest for him. The widow was clearly pleased; she would not have to struggle to find food to eat. Among the neighbouring Gonja, men avoid having to farm themselves. (It is still felt to really be work for slaves.) Nor do Gonja women farm – 'They don't know how; they would spoil my farm'.

Although their communities are interspersed, the sociocultural world in which Birifor and Gonja men and women make plans and choices is very different.

How do the local plans and choices come to have stable patterns? These decisions have to work on several levels. First, alternatives have to be 'conceivable' in the literal sense. People have to think of them as natural. For instance, Birifor women define themselves and are seen by others as farmers. So the separation of conjugality into sexual and labour components is perfectly sensible.

It would be 'unthinkable' in Gonja to marry a woman for her farming skills (see above), and this does not happen.

Adaptations to these factors in the organization of farm labour have to mesh with existing constraints and affordances. A man cannot meet all his needs with his sons' labour if they also have to farm for fathers-in-law. Nor can he use his sons for tasks considered appropriate for women. When many individuals adapt to the same economic/cultural/social constraints and affordances, in solving the same problems, their choices and decisions are likely to form recurrent patterns. Over time these similar strategies tend to become shared strategies. If they are effective, they may become socioculturally stable strategies,[1] what may be called institutionalized strategies.

Dynamics of the emergence of socioculturally stable strategies (SCSS) at the local level may be metaphorically analogous to the evolution of biologically stable strategies (BSS) described by Maynard Smith (1988: 118–19). These are genetically stable strategies such as the lookout role of male deer, while others, especially females and children, graze. Of course socioculturally stable strategies are normative and not genetic. For socioculturally stable strategies it seems that where a replicated individual strategy turns out to be the most effective way to respond to shared constraints and affordances in order to meet key goals, it may turn out to be unavoidable.

At first such SSCS are perceived as individual strategies that work particularly well. Their persistence is pragmatic, depending on their continued effectiveness. If the balance of constraints and affordances alters, the strategies will change. Later, as individuals continue to follow similar strategies, these may come to be recognized by 'others as the best or correct strategy', thereby gaining normative force. They may come to have names, be endowed with moral force; and finally be enforced by sanctions.

At this point they have become socioculturally stable strategies, institutionalized SCSS.

How Might Local Emergent Patterns, SCSS, Come to Be Similar
Across Societies?

The emergence of socioculturally stable strategies as a general dynamic of local communities and societies is, of course, theoretical. Because this emergence occurs over time, it cannot be directly observed. One way to evaluate such a postulated process is to see whether it is analytically useful. Field observations are full of strategic actions of individuals. But how are we to observe the manner in which some of these individual strategies become stable and shared, and institutionalized?

The puzzle is easier once we see that at least three levels of process are involved.

The first, 'lowest' level comes from the fact that all adult human social interaction involves spoken language.[2] This is the daily informal dialogue written about by conversation analysts like John Gumpertz and Paul Drew.

A second level of processes linking individual interactions with local patterned relationships is grounded in role interactions (as powerfully analysed in Nadel's 1957 magnum opus). Because roles are dyadic, interaction involves dialogue. A frequent feature of role dialogues is replicated patterns. For instance politeness, which is the subject of the classic study by Brown and Levinson (1978, 1987). Other studies of dyadic role dialogues are my work on greeting and begging (1972), questions (1978), joking relationships (1998), and prayer (1995), and David Zeitlyn's 1995 account of divination as dialogue.

[Explain how this shapes both individual plans and decisions, and social forms.]

Empirically, reading unrelated ethnographies from different continents, recurrence of similar patterns of greeting, politeness, joking relations, etc. is striking.

Area specialists can identify a third level of recurrent patterns within regions like New Guinea, Australia, Amazonia, South Africa and West Africa. The kind of patterns and institutions involved differ by region. The study, *Parenthood and Social Reproduction*, considers sub-Saharan West Africa. Here we find modes of parenting and transmission of adult role skills vary across societies with levels of sociopolitical complexity (Goody 1982).

How to Summarize?

Dialogue – the Current Puzzle

The current puzzle is understanding the importance and nature of dialogue.

This will be a new book. For the present I think of it as The Dialogue Book ... Sections will include:

The One Real Difference between Apes and Homo Sapiens is that Only
We Humans Have Spoken Language

However, accounts of the transition from lower primates to modern humans
virtually ignore spoken language. See for instance *Machiavellian Intelligence I*,
eds Byrne and Whiten, 1988.

This gap leads us to wonder how the emergence of spoken language might
have occurred. An awkward question, since of course we will never know;
orality leaves no artefacts. However, the primate scholar Robin Dunbar (1996)
has made thoughtful suggestions. These link grooming among close kin with
emergence of orality. He terms this primate early communication 'gossip', as a
way of saying it is not mainly about meaning. The social anthropologist must
also wonder how using early language shaped social relations, not only among
close kin, but more widely within groups. Here, in studying current communities, 'dialogue' is more useful, since shared meaning is involved.

These issues are explored in my chapter from *Machiavellian Intelligence II*,
'Social Intelligence and Language: Another Rubicon' (1997). Also, in brief published Comments in the JRAI, and a book review there (Goody 2010, 2012).

The Study of Socioculturally Framed Routinized Dialogue Modes: Politeness,
Greeting and Begging, Questions, Joking Relations, Divination, and Prayer

What kind of work does a dialogue mode do for Nadel's patterns of
interaction?

In general terms, dialogue modes predetermine what role partners say to
each other. Also hand and body movements are specified in some religions, and
often with those in power.

In several modes the dialogue and posture routines enact the power/hierar-
chy aspect of role relations. This is particularly clear in Gonja greetings between
chief and commoner and supplicant. However the same formal deference is
required, and evident, in greetings between kin. Wives show deference to husbands (and of course husband's parents, brothers and older sisters); sons and
daughters defer to parents and grandparents.

Because each dialogue mode has its particular relationship 'work' to do, it is
useful to include in this book summaries of the original papers for each dialogue mode.

A Fundamental Aspect of Understanding Dialogue is Based on the Fact That
Each Newly Born Human Has to Learn How to Speak

This is explored in at least two of Jerome Bruner's studies. In Oxford he
observed, over several months, mothers with infants approaching one year. He
found mothers engaged their babies in conversation, also playing verbal games
with them. The infants of course did not yet quite know the meanings of sounds
being used. In effect these games were laying down grammatical patterns that

mothers made into play (Bruner and Sherwood 1976). In Bruner's later study with mothers and slightly older babies, mothers modelled, using actions while talking, how to solve simple construction problems. Over the observation period, mothers first carried out the task, then led the baby to do more and more of it him/herself. The process Bruner found here has come to be called scaffolding (Bruner 1977).

There are of course classic cases in which children never learned to speak. Such children were reared by animals, or by disturbed parents who never spoke to them. It is clear then, that pace Chomsky, whatever kind of mind we inherit, the mind alone is not sufficient for being able to use speech. Each new human has to learn to use language. Bruner says this is made possible due to humans being provided with what he terms the language acquisition support system (LASS). This is not principally linguistic, but ways in which adults pass on the culture of which language is both instrument and creator. Elements of LASS vary from the special kind of reciprocal attention between mother and infant studied by Trevarthen (1979), to oral language formats, to games, to readiness to see patterns and rules.

An anthropologist looking in detail at transition across life stages in many societies must be struck by how varied are the ways in which this transition is successful. Assuming that Bruner is right that children everywhere learn to speak their mother tongue (this term is especially appropriate since it is usually mothers who de facto ensure that infants learn to use language), it would be interesting to look at what are the consistencies in ways in which language learning is supported in various societies.

Of course societies where language learning was not effectively supported, would not be there to study.

Probably the last section of the 'Dialogue Book' will return to the problem of exploring Nadel's puzzle about how individual relationships link to social structure.

To be continued later.

Notes

1. Editors' note: This is Goody's own term.
2. This comment was slightly bemusing to the editors as Esther herself worked on non-linguistic communication. See also, e.g., James Woodburn on silent trade. In fact, Goody at one point drafted notes for a possible edited volume on *Silence*, including Woodburn and others, on how both speech and silence are interwoven in varying ways in communication by different peoples (in the Esther Newcomb Goody Archive at the Centre of African Studies, Cambridge University).

References

Bateson, Gregory. 1936. *Naven: A Survey of the Problems Suggested by a Composite Picture of the Culture of a New Guinea Tribe Drawn from Three Points of View.* Cambridge: Cambridge University Press.

Brown, Penelope, and Stephen C. Levinson. 1978. 'Universals in Language Usage: Politeness Phenomena', in Esther N. Goody (ed.), *Questions and Politeness.* Cambridge: Cambridge University Press, pp. 56–289.

———. 1987. *Politeness: Some Universals in Language Usage.* Cambridge: Cambridge University Press.

Bruner, Jerome S., and Virginia Sherwood. 1976. 'Early Rule Structure: The Case of Peekaboo', in Jerome S. Bruner, Alison Jolly and Kathy Sylva (eds), *Play: Its Role in Development and Evolution.* Harmondsworth: Penguin Books.

Bruner, Jerome S. 1977. 'Early Social Interaction and Language Acquisition', in H.R. Schaffer (ed.), *Studies in Mother-infant Interaction.* London: Academic Press, pp. 271–89.

Byrne, Richard, and Andrew Whiten (eds). 1988. *Machiavellian Intelligence: Social Expertise and the Evolution of Intellect in Monkeys, Apes, and Humans.* Oxford: Clarendon Press.

Dunbar, Robin I.M. 1996. *Grooming, Gossip and the Evolution of Language.* London: Faber & Faber.

Maynard Smith, John. 1988. 'Origins of Social Behaviour', in A.C. Fabian (ed.), *Origins: The Darwin College Lectures.* Cambridge: Cambridge University Press.

Nadel, S.F. 1957. *The Theory of Social Structure.* London: Cohen & West.

Radcliffe-Brown, Alfred R. 1952. *Structure and Function in Primitive Society: Essays and Addresses.* Glencoe, IL: The Free Press.

Trevarthen, Colwyn B. 1979. 'Communication and Cooperation in Early Infancy: A Description of Primary Intersubjectivity', in M. Bullowa (ed.), *Before Speech.* Cambridge: Cambridge University Press.

Zeitlyn, David. 1995. 'Divination as Dialogue: Negotiation of Meaning with Random Responses', in Esther N. Goody (ed.), *Social Intelligence and Interaction: Expressions and Implications of the Social Bias in Human Intelligence.* Cambridge: Cambridge University Press, pp. 189–205.

Appendix II

Jean La Fontaine: A Memory of Esther Goody

Editors' Note: Jean La Fontaine produced this evocative memory of Esther Goody in response to questions sent to her by Mary Goody. It shows, we feel, a personal side to Esther not available in the Introduction. La Fontaine did her doctorate at Cambridge (1953–57), and in retirement is Professor Emeritus in social anthropology at the London School of Economics.

Esther's husband, Jack Goody, was my supervisor in my second year as a Cambridge undergraduate. He had not long returned from fieldwork and was living alone in Maids Causeway, where we undergraduates used to go for our supervision. When I was in Uganda doing the research for my PhD he married again, but I did not meet Esther Newcomb Goody when I returned to Cambridge as Jack and Esther had gone to Ghana. I met her when they came back, but I did not see much of her during the hard last year of writing my PhD. When I finished it, I left for the United States where I had a fellowship, and on my return married John Sackur (a former student in the department). He joined the Foreign Office and we were almost immediately posted abroad, so I had little contact with the Goodys for some time.

My real friendship with Esther dates from much later. I returned to an academic career when my marriage did not last, eventually getting some teaching in Cambridge. While there I learned that Jack and Esther had two daughters about the same age as my two; we were invited to spend a weekend with them in their lovely big house in Adams Road. The four girls immediately became close friends, and the two holidays we shared in France cemented their friendship and ours.

During the teenage years of our girls, Esther and I used the odd moments together when they were preoccupied to discuss all we had in common – our interests in Africa, our anthropological field research there, the problems of combining work and motherhood – and, I expect, to share gossip about our colleagues in Cambridge (for her) and London (for me). For both of us it seemed an outlet for any difficulties that either of us experienced, to talk to a fellow anthropologist with similar maternal responsibilities but different academic attachments. I was immensely impressed by Esther's deep involvement in her work during our times in France. I was much lazier and considered it 'time off', while both Goodys worked. Then, as always, Esther appeared a retiring soul, very modest and quiet, in contrast to her rumbustious husband.

Esther and I were both products of Meyer Fortes' view of anthropology and, in those early days, we had similar professional interests and approaches to our subjects. Our contributions to his Cambridge volume *Marriage in Tribal Societies* (1962) show the strong African focus he established in the department. My supervisor while I was in the field was Audrey Richards, who shared with Meyer the emphasis on ethnography that, presumably, they had both learned as students of Malinowski at the London School of Economics. Passed down to Esther and me, this acceptance of the vital importance of a most careful collection of data as the only sound basis for theoretical analysis was something we shared. We both began our work in Africa and on kinship and domestic organization – debts we owed to Meyer. Until the arrival of Edmund Leach, Meyer's view of society, and his approach to comparison as the best way to understand it, was established as the foundation of Cambridge social anthropology. Taking this for granted, Esther and I had much in common then.

It was hard work being a female academic, and no doubt Esther also suffered from it. There was considerable prejudice to counter (in my interview for the readership at the London School of Economics I was asked whether my children would stop me writing, and was asked the question twice more when I answered 'No'). While the department will have benefitted from the combined ability of the Goodys' fieldwork and their specializations, each in their own gender, Jack's character and seniority made his work more acceptable and accepted in the department. Esther's rather different approach was not recognized and did not receive the notice it should have done.

However, the department was shaken by the difference of academic approach introduced by Edmund Leach. Its effect was not felt so much at undergraduate level, but emerged in the weekly fieldwork seminar where arguments could become very heated. I found Leach's work very interesting but guessed, rightly, that Jack and Esther would remain loyal to Fortes. Had I stayed in the department that might have affected my relations with them, but as it was, I did not spend much time in Cambridge until the differences between its two most senior members had been accepted as given. Their major disagreement never interfered with my friendship with Jack and Esther.

My work was influenced by Audrey Richards' book on girls' initiation (Richards 1956), and my contribution to her Festschrift was intended to display this (La Fontaine 1972). I do not remember the detail of my talk with Esther about her contribution but I do remember thinking how different it was from our rather more conventional pieces. From a later perspective – and, of course, if I had considered the title of her article in the ASA volume on witchcraft, 'Legitimate and Illegitimate Aggression' (1970) – I should have understood that her view was both psychological and anthropological; her later work showed this clearly. Doubtless her father, the well-known American social psychologist, had influenced her thinking.

Esther's development of a position in which she could demonstrate the social element in what most anthropologists ignored as individual behaviour, tended to distance her from my interests in ritual and symbolism, but if our academic interests parted company we still argued as friends – when we had time. I am happy to discover that conversations we had in our earlier days of talk, when I was working on the traditional beliefs and practices of the Gisu in Uganda, were useful to her in thinking about witchcraft in northern Ghana (La Fontaine 1963; Goody 1970).

I am sure that her work on adoption and the composition of households lay behind my insistence to Sandra Wallman much later that it was important to distinguish 'family' from 'household'. The West African practice that Esther described of 'lending' one's children to kin as a means of cementing relationships with them made it clear that household organization could be constructed from a number of links that were different from the ties between members of a family, or more distant links of kinship, that might all be conceptualized differently. Adoption and the understanding of inter-individual behaviour are two important aspects of Esther's work that have been both neglected and underestimated.

Alas, I saw little of Esther in our later years – London and Cambridge seemed to grow further and further apart – but she remains a warm, intelligent presence in my memory.

References

Fortes, Meyer (ed.). 1962. *Marriage in Tribal Societies*. Cambridge: Cambridge University Press.

Goody, Esther N. 1970. 'Legitimate and Illegitimate Aggression in a West African State', in Mary Douglas (ed.), *Witchcraft: Confessions and Accusations*. ASA Monographs 9. London: Tavistock Publications.

La Fontaine, Jean S. 1963. 'Witchcraft in Bugisu', in John Middleton and E.H. Winter (eds), *Witchcraft and Sorcery in East Africa*. London: Routledge & Kegan Paul.

———. (ed., with introduction). 1972. *The Interpretation of Ritual: Essays in Honour of A.I. Richards*. London: Tavistock Publications.

Richards, Audrey I. 1956. *Chisungu: A Girl's Initiation Ceremony among the Bemba of Zambia*. London: Faber & Faber.

Appendix III

Interview with Suzanne Hoelgaard,
1 November and 3 November 2018

Suzanne Hoelgaard was a doctoral student in social anthropology at Cambridge University from 1977 to 1983. Supervised by Esther Goody, she was part of the early cohort of Cambridge PhD students to conduct anthropological fieldwork in the UK. She and Barbara Bodenhorn (who is the prime interviewer here) overlapped between 1977 and 1978, not only as Esther's students, but also as members of Wolfson College, where they met. Alicia Fentiman recorded and Mary Goody transcribed the interview.

BB: How did you first meet Esther Goody?

SH: Somebody mentioned – because I was so interested in doing a study of something to do with child development and child welfare – there is someone in Cambridge, Dr Esther Goody.

So then I went to the department, found out where Esther's office was, and I just knocked on her door, brazenly, no previous appointment, no nothing. And she came out with a big smile, and I said 'I'm so and so, I've just come up from Oxford, I've just finished my MPhil, and I really would like to work on something to do with adoption, child welfare, family policy and the care and socialization of children'. So I went in there and we talked, and she told me that she'd been working a lot on fostering.

Well, after about ten minutes she said 'Sure'. So she took me on. Then and there. No preliminaries. And I was just so shocked, because I thought I'd have to write some formal proposal, and I'd have to come up with a very specific project. Nope. She said 'Sure!' I was so pleased. I thought she was so charming, she was so straightforward, and she was so kind of informal, you know, she just took me in there, sat me down, probably gave me a cup of tea or something. Of course later I realized she was at the time working on a collaboration with the local Social Services. One of, I think, her key priorities was to try and apply anthropology to practice, and that was where I could fit in, because she wanted to look and find out something about the way foster care operates in *this* country, which is a completely different system, a completely different function from the West African context.

BB: When I first got to Cambridge, there was that 'Anthropology and the Community' seminar group happening with Esther and Pat Owens. Had it been established when you were starting out, or did it come later?

SH: It came later. Esther's interests were in exploring the British social services on the ground from a holistic anthropological angle. Esther and Gilbert Lewis were supervising David Anderson, who was on leave for nine months from his position as a local authority social services officer, and was given a desk in the department. Esther and David established the seminar together in 1981.[1]

It really landed me in at the deep end, because she wanted me to do a study of the entire *system*, you know, so it wasn't just a matter of looking at how children develop or don't, and what their relationships are and who plays what role. No! I had to look at the entire legal system, the bureaucracy involved, the mediating social worker, you know, the relationships between the [birth and foster] families. ... It was very interdisciplinary: ... I had to read Etzioni [1969] and Mary Douglas [1966] about all the legal and administrative framework and the policy changes over time, as well as the comparative settings, e.g. Esther's work and Meyer Fortes' on kinship fostering ... plus psychology, plus John Bowlby [1953] and Rutter's [1972] work on children and separation anxiety.

I was particularly keen to get the children's perspective, and that turned out to be a real stumbling block, because the social workers were very protective, and quite closed. At that time there had been several deaths of children while in state care [see e.g. Howells 1974], and so they were of course very sensitive: about what I wanted to do, regarding who I wanted to talk to. Talking to the children was ultra-sensitive... And so to get access to the fieldwork site, informants and files proved very difficult ... and negotiation with social services, even with Esther's backing, went on for six months, and then it came to a complete halt. Luckily, I was introduced to a former Social Services director who was concerned about my situation and liaised with the head of a Social Service department, who took me on. This officer was very open-minded and approved my project because I was going to talk to social workers, team leaders, and the families, and so he saw I could get some information that might be helpful to them. That's how I got in, just by chance, by luck.

This is all part of Esther's huge contribution I think – that she was one of the few people, certainly in the department, to think about doing anthropology in the home counties and elsewhere in Britain. So there was Judith Okely [1984] and Esther herself. Not just doing anthropology there, but having a practical impact. And she wrote that article in the journal *RAIN*, 'Can Anthropology Contribute to Social Policy?' in which she refers to Pat Owen's and my PhD studies [Goody 1984a]. It was a short article, but it was one of the first. Loads of sociologists had already been doing research on kinship networks and shared care of children in the UK, and I had to read all that too: Madeline Kerr's *The People of Ship Street* [1958], Elizabeth Bott's *Family and Social Network* [1957], Raymond Firth's *Two Studies of Kinship in London* [1956]... Firth was an anthropologist of course, but there were very few people [in the discipline] at that time who were actually going out there, *here*, so to speak.

So [in the early 1980s] Esther asked Pat Owens and me to do some of the 'Anthropology and the Community' seminars: Pat did the 'Health' aspect, and I did the 'Family Policy and Child Welfare', but our initial input was very limited due to our other commitments [see postscript below]. Eventually through these joint sessions with the academics and practitioners – which included social workers and, later, some heads of nursing from Addenbrooke's Hospital – Pat and I ended up not just giving seminars to graduate students, but teaching anthropology to nurses and paramedics. This is going on a tangent a bit, but it's all relevant to Esther's practical kind of bent. I had the idea that we could expand our focus towards international development, because I thought it was very relevant. My feeling was, after my fieldwork in Colombia, that development starts with the children, it starts with the whole infant care, socialization, education, healthcare, all of that, nutrition and so on; if they don't get that right, they won't have the resources to move forward.[2] That was sort of my starting point – or my kind of end point if you like.

AF: So what was your [postdoctoral] Colombia project about?

SH: The project, sponsored by the Overseas Development Administration, was on family and child welfare and substitute care of children. I worked with the Colombian Institute of Family Welfare, ICBF, and had two assistants, a lawyer and an anthropologist. My field research included a parallel study commissioned by the World Health Organisation [Hoelgaard 1988b], which was archival and based on case files detailing placement practices and outcomes, and the legal decisions made through the courts.

BB: This was before you started working on international adoption?

SH: Well no, it was not, it was all related... that was the thing that fascinated me most, almost, because in Colombia, foster care is only used for pre-adoption placements. It's not used at all for childcare. They have institutions of varying descriptions, and some of them are really awful and some of them are very good, and the five private adoption agencies, who are registered with the ICBF, which has its own adoption service, but they run their own show. Those were the ones I was interested in, because they're all run by daughters of presidents and other upper-class women. And 50 per cent of all those kids are sent abroad. Why? Because they think with the Colombian political situation, which is very problematic, and the poverty there, that abroad the kids are going to get an education, and a swimming pool – in America or Europe – with well-to-do adoptive parents. This is all in my adoption report and my articles; it's about the kind of cultural influences on policy and practice [See Hoelgaard 1988a, 1988b, 1998].

BB: But it also links up quite directly with Esther's work about students in London.

SH: Yes, it links up absolutely... but it's not straightforward, as the situation is the reverse. Whereas the West African parents were confronted with Western ways of doing things, so very different from their practices at home, the Colombians had adopted Western ways of doing things in their childcare and protection legislation, and had emulated Western adoption provisions, which in the meantime had been revised in the UK, US and elsewhere. The country, like some of its neighbours, has long-standing traditions of private fostering and informal adoption of children, but practitioners were ignoring their own local resources in favour of sending children to foreign homes. A lot of these foster carers, who were recruited to provide a temporary, pre-adoption service for infants and young children, were very keen to adopt their foster children, even without any pay or anything and even if it was going to involve some more hardship for them; they wanted to keep those kids. This applied even for some of the slightly older children, not just the infants. Because in Colombia the courts are involved in the whole adoption process; the social workers who place the children are all lawyers, for instance. And, I found, they hadn't got the broader psychological perspective...

I gave talks to Colombian decision-makers and social workers about these issues, and outlined new developments in policy and practice in the UK, US and elsewhere based on detailed studies of the outcomes of foster and adopted children's adjustment according to their age, characteristics and nature of the placements. I pointed out the spontaneous attachments that infants and young children tend to form with their 'de facto' parents and the separation anxiety of severing these bonds, which I observed in several cases, which can lead to long-term mental health problems [see John Bowlby's pioneering WHO study of 1951]. These problems are likely to be exacerbated in intercountry adoptions, and ethnic mixing of adoptees and children in the Colombian case. I had been encouraged to give these talks by the Institute of Family Welfare officers, and was asked to send them my final report [Hoelgaard 1998], but the interesting thing is, when I last looked at the statistics a couple of years ago, nothing has changed – half of Colombian adoptees are still being sent abroad, and at least four of the private adoption agencies I researched are still operating.

When I went to Colombia, Esther was very supportive. This was at a time when suddenly a lot of organizations were taking on anthropologists as advisors, as consultants. ... Well that happened thanks to people like Esther, because she had been involved with the NHS, and with some of the social services in

London, and had been writing about these sorts of things. I think really she was very much one of the first people to do this.

BB: I wanted to ask you about those cohorts of early students of Esther's who were encouraged to do anthopological work in England. Marilyn Strathern of course was one of them, and you were one of them.

AF: Who else was there?

SH: Pat Owens was also there. Her work was on Social Housing Policy in Cambridgeshire, and she did detailed case studies of interventions with families on housing estates. She was a great help in integrating me, as I arrived in the Lent Term and did not know anyone.

AF: In my first-year cohort [1982] was Tanya Luhrmann; she worked on witchcraft in East Anglia, but she was supervised by Jack Goody and Ernest Gellner. There was also Mark Graham who worked among the West Indians in Brixton, so that was very interesting.

SH: Like Sue Benson! She was also in New Hall [now Murray Edwards], first as a student, when Esther was her Director of Studies, and then as a Fellow.[3] Sue Benson's ethnography is of course extremely relevant to Esther's work, because Esther was more concerned with cultural translation than with racial identity. That kind of dynamic Esther analysed very well; her ideas about cultural *mis*-translation were extremely useful to me.

***

SH: She had this very open and very friendly benign smiling American style, and then there were all these layers of strategic thinking, theoretical thinking... but there was this human quality that she had, which was unique...

AF: Susan Drucker Brown's brief comment at the funeral was quite interesting because there was another side of Esther; not only was she a great scholar and doing lots of very interesting things in anthropology and with other disciplines, but [as Jean la Fontaine also notes] also raising a family and entertaining people every weekend or sometimes almost every night with Jack.

SH: I don't know how she did it... She had huge amounts of energy.

AF: Because Susan Drucker Brown can remember going over to Shelly Row, when they had the two little terraced houses there, and how Jack loved to have a party and have friends over, and discussions and all that, and there's Esther with the two children, trying to put them to bed and get them ready for school and then entertaining.[4]

Even up until very recently, when I last saw her probably last November, despite their divorce [in 1999], she always talked about the impact Jack's work had had... even up to her most recent writing, still acknowledging that.

BB: There was a great intellectual generosity there, with Esther. And I think it's important to recognize some of their joint publications; the most recent one is Goody and Goody (1996).[5]

SH: Jack's work on adoption, "On Nanas and Nannies" [1962] – which is excellent, I think it's really very insightful – but I have a feeling that his interest in children and child socialization came from Esther... He led her to Ghana I suppose, she followed him to Ghana and what did she find, she found her own niche, right then and there, nobody had ever done that before... And what I feel a little bit sad about is that I have read more recent works by various people working in that area, and her work is not necessarily included in references or acknowledged. And I find that really sad, because *she* is the one, *I* think, who really pushed that, who introduced that whole area. I mean, loads of sociologists, psychologists, historians and so on have written about all of this, what adoption was for, and whether it was crisis or tradition or whatever, what people did in the past, such as sharing childcare among kin and relations [e.g. Bott 1957, Kerr 1958, Stack 1974]. But Esther's take on it and that very detailed way in which she did it, looking at whole systems and all the implications in terms of family relations and networks, and the socio-economic kind of framework in which this takes place, and so on, all of that was really novel and I wish somebody would pick it up. I always tell my students, if I have anybody working on that I say go read Esther's work...

***

BB: When I first got here, the notion in the department that you'd be interested in *applied anything* was so anathema... So my feeling is that Esther was able more or less to hold her own. You had this very strong pressure from this department to move theory forward and to make your intellectual contribution that way. But her response was 'Yes fine, but we need to be thinking about how it is that we can be engaging people on the ground'. So what I'd like to know a little bit more about is whether this engagement with policy and applied aspects of socialization, as it's working its way through in England, was that for a *period* of her life, or was that during the *entire* period of time that you knew her?... As her interests are changing, is her commitment to the kinds of anthropological engagement with policy in the UK changing... does that also go through shifting?

SH: Well that's a really hard question... I think it goes through shifting... I'd have to look up her publications and her reports to see.[6] Because there are all these unpublished reports... When I was working on Esther's annotated bibliography, we – Kusum Gopal and I – went and talked to Aidan Baker, the head librarian in charge of the archives at the Haddon Library, and he was very helpful. He showed us various things held in the archival section, and a list of her reports that have not been published.

***

SH: I would have liked to write something [for the seminar day in Esther's honour] about identity, because that really was the mainstay of my interest... Because Esther's work on fostering is about family networks and social identity in that sense, of how you belong to a wider network, how you can move from your nuclear family into the extended family, and all the *compadrazgo* [godparenting] sorts of parallels there, but you retain your identity throughout... And of course in state-managed, or agency-managed adoption in the UK, US and Western countries generally, it was all confidential – you changed your identity completely, certainly until a couple of decades ago. And in the Colombian case you change not just your name and your formal legal status, but you change your culture, your language, your citizenship, you change everything; it was a total transformation. I did want to write about that, and I wanted to write about how a lot of these adoptees now are trying to reverse that, they are going back, like many transnational Korean adoptees [see e.g. Eleana Kim 2010].[7]

Postscript

Looking through my diaries soon after we met at Pembroke, I managed to establish a more precise timeline for Esther's initiatives to introduce a more applied approach in the Department and how to engage with local realities, including my own involvement in this.

In 1978, when I was preparing for doing fieldwork 'at home', Esther was already liaising with Cambridgeshire Social Services and one of their officers, David Anderson, who was given a desk in the Department. She wanted to explore how anthropological approaches might be applied to contemporary social problems. To this end she organized some joint workshops with social work and health practitioners, and called in some of her students doing local research, including Pat Owens and myself. She wanted us to exchange ideas across conventional barriers between theory and practice, and see what we might learn from each other.

She continued to pursue this effort in her subsequent seminar series on 'Anthropology and the Community' in the 1980s with David Anderson. When she was leaving for fieldwork in Africa, she asked Pat to help with the seminars, but as Pat was in a full-time post at the London School of Economics she could only make a limited contribution. After submitting my PhD in 1983 I added some sessions on family policy and child welfare. Our initial seminars coincided with Esther's publications [e.g. Goody 1983, 1984b] which reflect her interest in applying anthropology to problems in our own backyard. I took time out from these seminars between 1986 and 1991, during my Colombian research. Pat and I resumed our seminars on health and child welfare in the Department, but the uptake of students proved to be modest, so we joined David Sneath's option 'Anthropology and Development', organized with Development Studies. To fit in with this, we widened our horizon towards international policies and provisions on health, family welfare, children's rights, education, child labour, and such like. As these interdisciplinary seminars attracted many more students from both departments, we carried on with them, on and off, into the late 2000s. We also gave a course at Homerton for paramedics on anthropological theory and methodology.

For my part, since relocating to the Centre for Development Studies a decade ago, I have continued to teach on these themes, in addition to mentoring students on a wide range of development issues and advising them on academic writing. Being a committed applied anthropologist, more interested in research methods and practicalities than the finer points of theory (except, that is, for structuralism!), I feel extremely fortunate to have been among Esther's cohort of students who have shared in her early initiatives to make anthropology more relevant to pressing concerns in our own society. Throughout my research and teaching I have been inspired by her vision and sought to pass it on to students coming my way, so it is very encouraging that many of them have ended up in NGOs and other jobs where they are helping to make our crazy world better.

David Anderson: The Genesis of the 'Anthropology and the Community' Seminars

Editors' Note: The following is a recollection contributed by David Anderson, dated 15 February 2023.

'After twenty years of working in social work I felt the need to stop and think, and was offered a nine-month fellowship from the Central Council for Education and Training in Social Work. Pat Owens had introduced me to Mary Douglas and the concept of Anomaly, and I went to see Jack Goody, to ask if the Department of Social Anthropology had interests in local communities. He offered me a desk in that department, and arranged for me to have some informal supervision from Esther Goody and Gilbert Lewis. This was enormously valuable to me. In exchange, Esther and I established a fortnightly seminar called 'Anthropology and the Community', at which either a practising social worker or an anthropology researcher would present a short paper, and there would be discussion. Fifty people were on the mailing list, and twenty or so came each time. The seminar ran from 1981 until 1987, and was a rich experience for us all. I was based in the Anthropology Department for a year, and eventually produced a report: 'Anomaly: Themes from Social Anthropology in Social Work', thanks to the help and encouragement of Esther and Gilbert. It was a rich time for me, and I hope it opened doors for social workers wanting to think about their work, and for young anthropologists wanting to enter the field of social research and action.'

Notes

1. *Editors' Note:* This information is from Anderson's recollections of the time, sent to the Editors by Suzanne Hoelgaard in February 2023, and reproduced in full at the end of this appendix (above). Anderson explains that he and Goody ran these seminars, with other contributors, from 1981 to 1987.

2. *Editors' Note:* Hoelgaard's fieldwork in Colombia, from late 1986 to January 1988, was sponsored by the Overseas Development Administration (later known as the Department for International Development or DFID) and the World Health Organisation, and linked to a research Fellowship at Wolfson.

3. *Editors' Note:* Sue Benson worked on race and gender in Brixton. Her PhD was published as *Ambiguous Ethnicity: Interracial Families in London* (Cambridge University Press, 1981).

4. Excerpt of contribution read at Esther Goody's funeral, 7 February 2018, by Susan Drucker Brown: "In the winter of 1962 I arrived in Cambridge having been accepted as a PhD student in the Faculty of Archaeology and Anthropology. In my first visit to Professor Meyer Fortes, he recommended that I introduce myself to Jack and Esther Goody. Esther, he said, was an American like me, and she had come here as a graduate student and married her supervisor. I was not, he said, to follow her example in that respect. I did go to see the Goodys, who were living in a tiny house on Shelly Row. I think that during my first year in Cambridge, though I was officially living in Newnham, in fact I spent more time in Shelly Row. Jack was a charismatic person. Shelly Row was the scene of an almost permanent party of students and faculty invited by Jack. How Esther managed two small children (Mary around three and Rachel a year old), and a demanding job teaching anthropology, as well as a house full of partying guests, I cannot imagine. The household was warmly welcoming and it was an informal refuge from the elaborate formalities of Cambridge in the 1960s."

5. *Editors' Note:* We have found five such articles: Goody and Goody 1966, 1967, 1992, 1995, 1996. (Note: Esther is first named author on the 1992 and 1996 papers, while Jack is for the others.)

6. Mary Goody notes that her interest, if not direct involvement with UK policy, continued. Her late grant report for the Spencer Foundation in 2009 talks about her proto-findings for her northern Ghana Authority and Learning project as potentially relevant to the learning situation of minority group children in the UK. Her interest in affecting policy (internationally) was clear right up to the end of her life in her commitment to influencing programme planning for local language literacy teaching in northern Ghana (see Goody 1996).

7. Colombia is now party to the 1993 Hague Convention on Protection of Children and Co-operation in Respect of Intercountry Adoption, and adoptees can apply to the ICBF for access to their birth records. Moves to open adoption records first emerged in the 1950s in the United States following pressure from adoptees, and later birth mothers wanted to locate their children (Paton 1954; Fisher 1973; Triseliotis 1973), which led to changes in the law in some US states and in the UK (Howe, Sawbridge and Hinings

1992). In recent decades this has prompted numerous 'search and reunion' studies (see e.g. Kim 2010 on returning Korean adoptees) and television documentaries (e.g. the BBC series 'Long Lost Family').

References

Benson, Sue. 1981. *Ambiguous Ethnicity: Interracial Families in London*. Cambridge: Cambridge University Press.

Bott, Elizabeth. 1957. *Family and Social Network*. London: Tavistock.

Bowlby, John. 1951. *Maternal Care and Mental Health*. Geneva: World Health Organization.

_____. 1953. *Child Care and the Growth of Love*. Harmondsworth: Penguin Books.

Douglas, Mary. 1966. *Purity and Danger: An Analysis of Concepts of Pollution and Taboo*. London: Routledge & Kegan Paul.

Etzioni, Amitai (ed.). 1969. *The Semiprofessions and their Organization*. New York: The Free Press.

Firth, Raymond (ed.). 1956. *Two Studies of Kinship in London*. London: University of London, Athlone Press.

Fisher, Florence. 1973. *The Search for Anna Fisher*. New York: Arthur Field.

Goody, Esther N. 1983. 'Family Policy in a Multi-culture Society', in Alfred White Franklin (ed.), *Family Matters: Perspectives on the Family and Social Policy*. Oxford: Pergamon Press, pp. 43–48.

_____. 1984a. 'Can Anthropology Contribute to Social Policy?' *RAIN* 63: 2–6.

_____. 1984b. 'Marriage of Close Kin in Ethnic Minorities in the United Kingdom'. (Evidence submitted to commission on revision of laws concerning close marriage.)

_____. 1996. 'Authority and Learning in Northern Ghana'. End of Award Report for Economic and Social Research Council, UK. See Esther Newcomb Goody Archive, Centre of African Studies, Cambridge University.

_____. 2009. 'The Role of Dialogue in Building Understanding in the Classroom' (Grant number 200700080). Unpublished End of Award Report for the Spencer Foundation, Chicago, IL. See Esther Newcomb Goody Archive, Centre of African Studies, Cambridge University.

Goody, Esther N., and Jack Goody. 1996. 'The Naked and the Clothed', in John Hunwick and Nancy Lawler (eds), *The Cloth of Many Coloured Silks: Papers on History and Society, Ghanaian and Islamic, in Honour of Ivor Wilks*. Evanston, IL: Northwestern University Press, pp. 67–89.

Hoelgaard, Suzanne. 1988a. 'Adoption Law, Policy and Practice in Colombia'. Report for Overseas Development Administration. Department of Social Anthropology, University of Cambridge.

_____. 1988b. 'Child Protection Laws and Practice in Colombia'. Report for the World Health Organization. Department of Social Anthropology, University of Cambridge.

_____. 1998. 'Cultural Determinants of Adoption Policy: A Colombian Case Study'. *International Journal of Law, Policy and the Family* 12: 202–24.

Howe, David, Phillida Sawbridge and Diana Hinings. 1992. *Half a Million Women: Mothers Who Lose Their Children by Adoption*. London: Penguin.

Howells, John G. 1974. *Remember Maria*. London: Butterworths.

Kerr, Madeline. 1958. *The People of Ship Street*. London: Routledge & Keegan Paul.

Kim, Eleana. 2010. *Adopted Territory: Transnational Korean Adoptees and the Politics of Belonging*. Durham, NC: Duke University Press.

Okely, Judith. 1984. 'Fieldwork in the Home Counties'. *RAIN* 61: 4–6.

Paton, Jean M. 1954. *The Adopted Break Silence: The Experiences and Views of Forty Adults Who Were Once Adopted Children*. Life History Study Center, University of California.

Rutter, Michael. 1972. *Maternal Deprivation Reassessed*. Harmondsworth: Penguin Education.

Stack, Carol. 1974. *All Our Kin: Strategies for Survival in a Black Community*. New York: McGraw Hill.

Triseliotis, John. 1973. *In Search of Origins: The Experiences of Adopted People*. London: Routledge & Keegan Paul.

Appendix IV

Selected Tributes

What follows is a cross section of messages from colleagues and students from across the world, that we have included to show the range of people whose lives Esther touched. Some are more personal letters to family, while others are written for public reception.

Ziba Mir-Hosseini, Professorial Research Associate, Centre for Islamic and Middle Eastern Law, SOAS, University of London

Context: Contribution to tributes on the website of the Department of Social Anthropology, Cambridge University, January 2018.

Honouring Esther Goody

In 1975, armed with my BA in Sociology from Tehran University, I came to Cambridge hoping to pursue a PhD. I had no clue what I wanted to do apart from the fact that I was interested in studying women and the family. A friend who was teaching Persian at what was then the Faculty of Oriental Studies suggested that I should talk to Dr Esther Goody, and made an appointment for me. I went to Adams Road, with my PhD proposal in hand. I'll never forget my first meeting with Esther. I said I was interested to study changing family patterns in Iran, but I added (as many new graduate students coming from very different academic cultures such as that of Iran still do), 'I will do research on whatever you want me to'. Esther said something to the effect that, 'There's no need to apologize for your interest, you should do what you want to do'. Somehow, I must have convinced her that I was 'PhD material', capable of carrying out an independent research project. She took me under her wing at a time when I was quite lost. She gave me books to read and assigned essays for me to write. After that, I came back to Adams Road every month to see her. In this way, Esther began teaching me Anthropology and guided me for a year before my formal enrolment as her PhD student. This was what Esther was as a teacher – immensely kind and generous; she went out of her way to support her students and enable them to develop their potential.

In 1984, five years after the Iranian revolution, I returned to Cambridge. As I began looking for a place to rent, Esther invited me to stay at Adams Road, telling me – 'Ziba, stay here; if you go, Jack will bring another student, and I'd rather have you here than anyone else'. But she knew my situation. I ended up staying with Esther and Jack for six years. They both made me feel at home, but it was Esther's support and mentoring that enabled me to continue my post-doc research and set me on the path I have followed ever since. She continued guiding me in my new areas of research ... I treasure the memories of so many ad hoc conversations over dinner and in the kitchen while cooking. Although we never shared a research interest in West Africa, I learned a great deal from her comments on my work in both Iran and Morocco.

I feel so privileged to have known Esther. She gave me a home when I needed it most; she introduced me to Social Anthropology, and was an important influence on my ideas, showing me new ways of seeing things. She was not only a supervisor, but a mentor and a friend.

Ziba Mir-Hosseini, January 2018

Lynne Brydon, Honorary Senior Research Fellow, Department of African Studies and Anthropology, University of Birmingham

Context: sent October 2014 for the seminar in honour of Esther N. Goody held at the Department of Social Anthropology, Cambridge University, 1 November 2014.

Reminiscences and (probably mis-) memories!

Scanning through the list of names on the email [about the seminar] I thought that perhaps I might be the only one of us who benefited from Esther's help and support both at undergraduate and postgraduate levels. I was an interloper into part II Soc Anth in 1969, having been a Natural Scientist for my first year. Esther was Director of Studies, and welcomed me into her group of, I think, four New Hall undergraduates going into second year. I'd been nervous about moving from sciences to humanities, so she'd helped me organize a couple of supervisions during the previous long vacation with Sandy Robertson... thus beginning my initiation into Anthropology and my encounter with West Africa. Sandy at that time had just come back from Ghana and was producing the book with John Dunn. When term began Esther sent us to Keith Hart for supervisions, continuing the West Africa connection. And when we saw Esther for Director of Studies meetings I was amazed how 'normal' she seemed... when meetings finished exactly on time because she had to pick up the girls from

Brownies. She had a life; she was the first person I met, I think, to make me realize that you could have a successful professional life and still do the other things that women were supposed to do (in the 1960s).

As we progressed into the third year, we became more and more familiar with Esther, who now supervised us too, and loved to be invited to Adams Rd for supervisions... much more informal, either inside or out... or for the occasional party.

I began postgraduate work in 1972, after a year's VSO teaching in Ghana as a scientist. My first supervisor was Meyer, who had the most meticulous understanding of fieldwork and could not overemphasize its importance in anthropological research, but he retired more or less as I went to do fieldwork, and Esther took over. These were the days before any communications revolution so letters were the order of the day... a telegram in an emergency perhaps! But, about half way through my fieldwork, in late 1973, I think, Esther came to visit me in the hills of the Togo Ranges. This caused at least small panic: what to give Esther to eat? What to drink? Where to sleep? There was no problem in what to do if Esther were willing to be paraded around at least one village nodding and greeting and smiling at people... many of whom did, in fact, speak some English.

To get to Amedzofe then (and still now, to some extent), meant a scramble for a seat on the market day open-sided Bedford truck going back from Ho. RK, the driver, always said that there was no point in trying to drive the roads sober... an untarred corkscrew up the mountains. But Esther did not balk at the trip and arrived. I managed to feed her with tinned fish, and the next day she bought me a chicken... all eaten with rice. I had hired a couple of rooms in a swish house in the Christian section of the village and there was a space for a bucket shower and a pit latrine... so what more could we need? What I particularly remember from Esther's visit and subsequently was her amazement that so many people – but in particular, girls – went to school in Amedzofe... and that obvious amazement and statement of the abnormality of Amedzofe, in that sense, really grounded me in terms of subsequent work that I've done.

Esther's support after the return to Cambridge, the patience and good sense, not to mention the fabulous comparative information she brought from other parts of Ghana, really underpinned the fact that I wrote up/ analysed and so on in two years. It was the very early days of computers and I'd done surveys and censuses, and it took almost a year to code and make them fit to be mechanically analysed. But Esther was always ready to point out that analysing data with computers was just that – a mechanical process – it's what we do with what comes out of the computer... and what we do about establishing context and history that's really important.

I studied with Esther for almost seven years... and I think myself extremely lucky, both in terms of the intellectual support she gave, and the moral and human example she showed in her dealings with us, as students, at whatever stage. And since then, of course – her continued work has been an inspiration to us all.

Lynne Brydon, October 2014

Francesca Bray and A.F. (Sandy) Robertson, Professors Emeriti of Social Anthropology, University of Edinburgh

Context: Correspondence to family, 1 February 2018.

Dear Mary and Rachel,
We send our heartfelt sympathies for your loss. We had just heard yesterday, via the anthropology grapevine (ASA newsletter). We can't unfortunately attend the funeral (as in Paris) but will certainly be thinking of Esther on that day. Each of us has so many fond memories of Esther, and will greatly miss her.
   For myself, Esther was the person who taught me (in the little kitchen corner in Lacapelle) how to smash garlic cloves so the skin comes off easily – which means I think of her every time I smash garlic, that is to say at least three nights a week! She was also the quiet but inexorable voice of feminist anthropology, influencing me forever in her insights into who works at what, at what age, and into the learning of material skills, in cooking, weaving and other crafts, and how apprenticeship and play entwine. I have recommended her work to countless students and colleagues over the years, and always reflected her work in my own work on technology and gender. So there's the garlic, and the politics of scholarship, and in addition Esther's generous hospitality and her wry sense of humour. All engrained in me, none ever to be forgotten.
   So please think of us thinking of Esther ... and do keep in touch, we'd love to see either or both of you in Edinburgh.

With much love,
Francesca

PS Am copying Vicky, currently stuck in Florida, but I expect you've written to her separately.
1 February 2018

Magdeleine (Marie) Chatry-Komarek, International Consultant on Language Education (retired) and LLIL Collaborator

Context: Correspondence to family, 21 January 2018.

Dear Mary, Dear Rachel,
Your mother was an impressive person – and she was both a mentor to me, and a very dear friend. We met in Accra some fifteen years ago, and worked after that in cooperation. Together with my husband we were preparing textbooks in local languages – and Esther joined us. She said she was learning a lot with us – but I am sure I learnt a lot from her and I know how much I owe her. The last time we worked together was 2008: we met in Anamabo and loved the time together. And of course, she invited us both to Cambridge two years ago and we stayed at her place for a few days.

I am with you in your sorrow.
Magdeleine (Marie Chatry-Komarek)
21 January 2018

Stephen Levinson and Penelope Brown, Emeriti Members of the Language and Cognition Department, Max Planck Institute for Psycholinguistics, Nijmegen, Netherlands

Context: Contribution to tributes on the website of the Department of Social Anthropology, Cambridge University, February 2018.

My (Steve's) first contacts with Esther must actually be earlier than I remember, when I was an undergraduate in Cambridge Arch and Anth Tripos. There I remember Meyer Fortes rubbishing Erving Goffman and the American inter-actionists as 'pin-pong ball sociology'. Into this not necessarily friendly environment came Esther, daughter of the famous social psychologist Theodore Newcomb, and with interests in the conduct of social interaction. When we (my wife Penelope Brown and myself) moved to Cambridge in 1975, we must have seemed like kindred spirits, coming fresh from UC Berkeley with PhDs focusing on social interaction in ethnographic settings (Mayan Mexico and Tamil India, respectively). We developed jointly a theory of politeness expressed in language which claimed to have general application, and Esther was enthusiastic enough about it to arrange publication in a collection she was editing (*Questions and Politeness*). We remember vividly the Friday evening seminars, followed by evening hospitality at the Goody's house in Adams Road, where Esther would have hurried back to rapidly produce bangers and mash for distinguished visiting anthropologists. It was a level of hospitality we always aspired to emulate but never succeeded. There we met Godelier, Barth, Sperber, Woodburn, Turner, and scores of other famous names. Busy Cambridge lives precluded substantial collaboration, but in 1989 we found ourselves together again in Berlin, where Esther was at the Wissenschaftskolleg for the year. In discussion with us, she organized a groundbreaking meeting that crystallized in her book *Social Intelligence and Interaction*, which argues for the centrality of social interaction in the human constitution. We went on to mature careers in the Netherlands, following lines of work very congenial to Esther's preoccupations with dialogue as a tool with which sociocultural worlds – e.g. roles and associated norms – are actually constructed. We didn't actually overlap in space and time all that often, but Esther came several times to our institute to engage in intense discussions on her ideas about dialogue. Her work on parental roles and socialization practices has also been an inspiration to me (Penny) in my study of child language socialization in different societies.

Stephen Levinson and Penelope Brown, February 2018

Michael Cole (Emeritus Professor of Psychology, University of California Santa Barbara), Sheila Cole (Author) and Jennifer Cole (Professor of Anthropology, University of Chicago)

Context: Correspondence to family, for funeral 7 February 2018.

Dear Mary, Rachel, and fellow mourners,
It is difficult for us to describe the many ways in which we cherished Esther, or the important role that she played in our lives. First, there is the professional side of our relationship. For Mike, Esther was an anthropologically sophisticated colleague seeking to combine the methods and theories of psychology and anthropology, a position that is rarer than you might think. They were exchanging ideas and discussing their shared interest in the origins of language and culture when emails from Esther came to an end. For Sheila, Esther provided an important role model for how to have a career and a family at the same time. Esther was also Jenny's mentor at Cambridge. She, together with Gilbert Lewis, helped make Jenny an anthropologist, deeply indebted to the British tradition of Social Anthropology. Jenny didn't LOVE kinship while learning kinship charts, but several years later while riding in a canoe on the Mangoro River in Eastern Madagascar she overheard her co-voyagers joking with one another about how they were going to drown the other person in the river so that the crayfish could eat their eyes out. The penny dropped there and then: Esther had not been making up that strange thing called the joking relationship when she'd taught Radcliffe-Brown all those years ago. The lessons Esther taught Jenny are still with her and very much evident in her research practices and writing to this day.

We all feel lucky that Esther and Jack took Jenny into their home, and put up with her badly behaved, furniture-consuming border collie puppies as if they were members of the family. Our warm memories of gatherings on Adams Road, picking red currants or having Sunday night dinner and watching mystery shows, will not be forgotten.

Our deepest sympathy at your loss. It is shared in varying degrees and many ways by countless people across the globe.

The Cole Family
6 February 2018

David R. Olson, Professor Emeritus of Cognitive Developmental Psychology, Ontario Institute for Studies in Education, University of Toronto

Context: Correspondence to family, 20 January 2018.

Dear Mary and Rachel,
I share your sorrow in the loss of Esther. She was a lovely and generous person. But beyond that she made at least two great advances in the social sciences. First, in *Questions and Politeness* she showed that a seemingly innocent difference between grammatical structure (imperatives and interrogatives) hid an important social function, namely, social control. And second, she was the first to show how change in political/social structure was reflected in the structure and organization of education, broadly conceived.

So in losing Esther, our discipline also loses one of its leaders.

Sincerely,
David Olson
20 January 2018

Dr Leslie Casely-Hayford, Social Development Consultant, Associates for Change (AfC)

Context: Correspondence to family, 4 February 2018.

Dear Mary,
Hope you are well amidst all this... please find a short reflection on your mother's wonderful life and how she touched so many of us.

I knew Esther Goody since arrival in Ghana in the mid-1990s. Through her important ethnographic works, I first went to visit her in Cambridge when I started my DPhil at Sussex and remained a 'Ghana' friend whenever she would visit Accra. She was very influential in my decision to conduct an educational ethnography among the Dagomba peoples of Northern Ghana. Esther's frank and open nature towards learning meant she never stopped continuing to assist minority languages and diverse groups throughout Ghana to have a voice. Her work was influential in demonstrating the importance of assisting children to learn their mother-tongue language as a foundation for literacy. Her works among the Gonja and later among the Birifor peoples are pivotal to ethnographic researchers the world over. Most importantly, she will be remembered in her home in Bole District, where for the last fifteen years of her life in Ghana she was a true Ghanaian, living among the people, standing up for the values and assisting the rest of us in learning the value of culture, language and identity. We will miss her dearly and remember her in our hearts and on our journeys to northern Ghana.

With loving greetings,
Dr Leslie Casely-Hayford
4 February 2018

Fati Mumuni, Friend and Research Interpreter in Bole, Northern Region, Ghana

Context: Correspondence to family, 3 February 2018.

TRIBUTE TO DR ESTHER NEWCOMB GOODY
A faithful friend is a sturdy shelter, he/she that finds one finds a treasure.
A faithful friend is beyond price; no sum can balance his/her worth.
Sirah 6: 14–15 (Catholic Bible)
    I met Dr Esther Newcomb Goody through her husband Emeritus Professor Jack Goody in 1986 while I was a teacher in Damongo Secondary School, and we have been friends until she died on that fateful 18th January, 2018.
    Esther was a mother, friend and mentor. I assisted her in her research as an interpreter and companion in the Gonja traditional area. Esther was generosity itself. She impacted very much the people of Bole traditional area when she came back to help with the teaching of mother tongue to schoolchildren from primary 1 to 3. This was to improve on learning, reading and understanding of the English language.
    Apart from her educational project, she identified women who were into yarn making, and helped them financially in local cloth making (she was in Daboya in the Gonja district to understudy the weaving of the local cloth some-time back). She gave soft loans to her workers to enable them to educate their children, build houses and pay hospital bills. In fact she helped those near her accomplish their pressing needs financially. Esther was a mentor to many in Bole. Dr Esther Goody is missed and will be missed dearly by all who came close to her.
    Personally, I miss her so much because she was not only a mentor but a mother and friend. How can I forget Nteri, my friend, as I called her? Whenever I referred to her as 'Kabroniche', White woman, she wasn't happy because she said it was racist, but in Gonja we always address people by reference and description.
    My dearest Nteri, how can I forget you when you surprised me with a gift of a house with all in it? You were so selfless that you only took an almost empty suitcase out of the house. And the best of it all was when you asked me to sleep in your room and on your bed! What a generous woman you were! You gave me what my parents couldn't give me. You gave me what the chief of Bole and the District chief executive coveted! How can I ever forget you? How can I forget you when all I do is to read the novels you left me? How? How? How?

Your house is still identified as Esther Goody's Residence. Its name will never change. Never, for I call it yours! I call it 'Kabroniche pe', White woman's home. You will forever be remembered by me and the people of Bole. Even though I know what you thought, rest in the bosom of the Good Lord. Amen.

May You Rest in Perfect Peace. Amen.
Fati Mumuni
3 February 2018

Paola Filippucci, Senior Lecturer in Anthropology, Murray Edwards College, Cambridge University

Context: College Blog, Murray Edwards College Website ('In Remembrance of Dr Esther Goody'), 1 February 2018.

Esther Goody, who died on 18 January 2018, was a Fellow of New Hall from 1966 until she became an Emeritus Fellow in 1999. During this lifelong association with the College, Esther was a College Lecturer in Social Anthropology; she was also the Director of Studies in Archaeology & Anthropology (1966–72), the Director of Studies in Social & Political Sciences (1966–71) and the Director of Studies in Part II Social Anthropology (1975–82); and a Tutor (1975–78). Several generations of New Hall Arch and Anth and SPS alumnae will remember Esther's enthusiasm for Anthropology, her intellectual fierceness and love for debate, her constant encouragement to challenge assumptions and think outside the box, but also her ability to make difficult concepts accessible, to use her formidable ethnographic knowledge to give life and relevance to abstract ideas, always reminding students that at the core of Anthropology are real, live people who can and deserve to be understood. Esther also taught those of us who went on to become anthropologists to approach both theory and ethnography with empathy, imagination and care for the people we worked with, and that nothing is uninteresting about people and their lives. All of us will also remember Esther's personal warmth, her informality and directness, and her extraordinary commitment to supporting and encouraging students at all stages in their career, often tangibly by helping to find funds for research students to realize their projects. Esther's commitment to the College did not end with her retirement: as a Fellow Emerita she continued to attend College events and join discussions about College matters; in particular she was always willing to meet students and Fellows in Arch and Anth, SPS/PPS and HSPS, keen to hear from us about new ideas and debates, and about changing aspects of the course.

Esther's inspirational teaching also took place in the Department of Social Anthropology, where she was a Lecturer and later Reader. Esther lectured for many years on a wide range of topics, but in particular on one of the core areas of Anthropology, kinship; she was also one of the women who pioneered teaching on gender, an emergent and innovative area of the discipline from the early 1970s. Esther also broke new ground by introducing and running for many years a paper combining Psychology and Social Anthropology, that was shared between Social Anthropology and Social and Political Sciences, and was an early precursor of the interdisciplinary teaching that now forms the core of the Human, Social and Political Sciences Tripos.

Esther's teaching was fuelled by a very distinguished research career that was ethnographically centred on Africa, Ghana in particular, but theoretically spanned a wide range of themes and issues broadly connected with human intelligence and the interplay between its social and psychological aspects. Her influential published works concerned, among others, the role of language in society and social encounters, social intelligence and interaction, learning in the context of labour and apprenticeship, parenthood and parental strategies, and the relationship between interest and emotion in kinship, in each case grounding 'big' ideas and abstract theorizing in wonderfully detailed, sensitive and evocative ethnographic case studies. These works broke new ground in Anthropology and have stood the test of time, foreshadowing themes that have become centrally relevant in today's Anthropology such as the ethics of kinship, the relationship between Anthropology and Psychology, and the contribution of Anthropology to the study of intelligence and cognition. In recent years Esther was excited by the new approaches to 'her' themes and keen to continue to contribute to the debate. Even after retirement she continued to carry out research, conducting a study in Ghanaian primary schools about the role of dialogue in learning and about modes of teacher–pupil communication in the classroom. Characteristically, when she recently presented the findings of this research at a student-led Departmental seminar, she concluded her abstract by stating that 'all this needs discussion, challenge, and debate'. These words encapsulate Esther's continuing and lifelong passion for intellectual enquiry, debate and exchange, which were at the heart of what made her such an outstanding and valued anthropologist, teacher and colleague. She will be greatly missed by all who knew her.

Paola Filippucci, 1 February 2018

Chris Hann, Director Emeritus, Max Planck Institute for Social Anthropology, Halle, Germany

Context: Cambridge University Social Anthropology department website tributes February 2018; read at Esther Goody's Memorial at Murray Edwards College, 9 June 2019.

My knowledge of the Goody family always had a male bias, since Jack was the supervisor of my PhD in the 1970s. Yet it is to Esther that I owe my first exposure to undergraduates in a Cambridge lecture room. She and Jerry Leach invited me to give a guest lecture in a series they organized. I think it was the Lent term 1978, and it probably had to do with non-industrial labour organization. I prepared carefully for a week, and threw in tons of field data. My performance was feeble in every respect but Esther tried to salvage what she could by asking a few gentle questions, in order to draw out some links to the main themes of that series.

In the early 1980s when I was a Research Fellow, Esther and Jack invited my wife and me to supper on numerous occasions at their house, 8 Adams Road. Ildikó was new to Britain and found relaxed conversations with Esther a welcome tonic after the stuffiness she experienced in other quarters of Cambridge. It seemed to us that, in addition to the seminar room in Free School Lane and the student bar at King's College, the living room and kitchen at Adams Road were a third vital locus for the exchange of anthropological ideas in those years.

I joined the Department as an Assistant Lecturer in 1984. Esther was an established member by then and we were colleagues until 1992. (Jack spent little time in Cambridge in this period.) She taught mainly kinship, cross-cultural Psychology, and of course West African ethnography. Since our topics barely overlapped, we had relatively little to do with each other directly. I recall her dedication to students at every level, her quiet professionalism at meetings (including examiners' meetings), and of course her unswerving commitment to Ghana and continuous cooperation with scholars there, including many former students.

Only much later, when returning to Cambridge to examine a PhD in the Faculty of Economics in 1997, did the magnitude of Esther's achievement as an ethnographer of domestic organization become clear to me. Her data were so good that Renata Serra could use them to build and test her formal models of adoption and fostering. Esther generously provided ethnographic advice and inspired the career of this young development economist. Her pioneering work has been internationally influential; for example, in Germany her work on adoption has been continued and extended above all by Erdmute Alber, and in the US by Cati Coe. Work on family and household in northern Ghana is continued to the present day in Germany by anthropologists such as Carola Lentz and Andrea Behrends.

Esther spent the year 1989/90 at the Institute for Advanced Study in Berlin and developed her concept of 'sexual *Herrschaft*' during this sojourn. By this time the range of her publications was extraordinary. My personal favourite (though it is hardly representative) is the collection she edited for the Cambridge Papers in Social Anthropology series in 1982. *From Craft to Industry: The Ethnography of Proto-industrial Cloth Production* was one of the last volumes of its kind. To my mind its combination of general theory and ethnographic studies, written by senior staff as well as junior researchers, exemplified the spirit of the series. Esther contributed both the Introduction and an ethnographic chapter on Daboya weavers. The Cambridge Papers were highly influential in establishing the global reputation of the Department in the era of Meyer Fortes and Jack Goody. But which young scholar nowadays can afford to submit her work to an edited volume, let alone a collection confined to the precincts of a single department? The creative synergies of the more intimate collegiality of that era are impossible in the climate of today's audit culture and saturation publishing.

In the winter following Jack's passing in July 2015, I visited Esther at Adams Road. The ostensible purpose was to check some details for the memoir I was writing about him, but it was time finally to overcome this patriarchal bias. It was wonderful to enter the big house again, and to appreciate a stream of her reminiscences. Before I left she printed out the draft of a new text and pressed it into my hands, implying that I should digest it on the way home and offer comments. It was about language and cognition, but after reading it I felt just as inadequate as I had on the occasion of that first university lecture forty years ago. I concluded that Esther's curiosity and sharp intellect were alive and well. Now that she is no longer with us, the Department will celebrate her many original scholarly contributions, notably at the interfaces between Social Anthropology, language and Behavioural Psychology. We shall also remember the generous support and hospitality she extended to so many colleagues and students over decades.

Chris Hann, February 2018

Marilyn Strathern, Emeritus Professor of Social Anthropology, University of Cambridge

Context: Read at Esther Goody's funeral, 7 February 2018.

We have known Esther Goody in many different ways. But what a privilege that has been!

I always knew that Esther attached importance to her middle name, Newcomb, her father being a founding figure in Social Psychology; I didn't know that when he was at the Tavistock, London, the teenage Esther sat in on Social Anthropology lectures at UCL – her first taste of the subject that was so much her life and work.

But before life and work, what about herself? 'An adventurous, questioning spirit; a stickler for rigorous research methods but not allowing herself to be restricted by academic convention' – these are her daughters' words, summoning Esther's boundless energy, the more effective for the mildness with which she pointed to what mattered. Sidestepping convention applied to things non-academic as well. For her, family had always been part of it all. I recall Mary and Rachel – toddler and baby – in undergraduate supervisions. At the same time, I shall never forget the electrifying impact of my first one. Esther set me an essay topic, all about rigour and method, and I practically ran to the University Library filled with eye-opening exhilaration about getting to work (later I became a PhD student).

Kinship and friendship were woven through her research and scholarship. Yet, in her quiet Midwestern way, it was a quality of care less performed – showing one's feelings – than enacted.

***

Born in 1932 to Theodore and Mary Newcomb, in Cleveland, Ohio, Esther was the eldest of three, followed by Suzanne and Tim. Two childhood experiences may have shaped her sense of household: the family's mobility before settling in Michigan (Ann Arbor); the many intellectual and sociable gatherings at the parental home.

Esther obtained her BA in Sociology and Psychology at Antioch College, not yet twenty-two, despite the interruption in London. Fired by that taste of Social Anthropology, she audited some Cultural Anthropology classes at home, but they weren't the same! Having tracked down Meyer Fortes, briefly in Chicago, she obtained a year-abroad grant to visit Cambridge. Meyer sent her to Jack Goody for supervision, and their forty-year collaboration began. It was during her doctoral fieldwork in northern Ghana (1956–57) that they married.

Completing her PhD in 1961, Esther taught at Newnham (1961–63), before returning to Ghana for two years' fieldwork when Mary and Rachel were aged four and two. The children recall going up north with her, staying with an au pair in Accra, being flown out during the 1966 coup. Esther returned to a college fellowship at Murray Edwards, New Hall as was. The scene was set for that remarkable period when she simultaneously continued first hand research, with six years of grants for work in the UK; supervised and lectured, being appointed to University Lecturer in 1972; and kept the family going, throwing her energies into house-hunting 8 Adams Road so they could move out of the Shelly Row cottages. Esther and Jack's house became a second home both for Jack's first family and for generations of graduate students. Not to speak of the publication of her book, *Contexts of Kinship* (1973). No wonder the children were lulled to sleep by the sound of typewriters.

The initial Lectureship was short lived. In her words, the appointment of her husband to the William Wyse Professorship necessitated resignation. However, she reapplied when a vacancy arose; later was made Reader. Much of her life was lived away from Cambridge: visiting fellowships in Stanford, Berlin, Stockholm; annual summers in France; above all her love of northern Ghana and the Gonja people gave her a second home there.

Interspersed with work in London and Leicester, and in India (Gujarat), research ideas took her time and again to Gonja, where, after retirement (in 1999) she was in residence for nine months of the year. A major programme on authority and learning lasted in fact until 2009. An unexpectedly negative reaction to her findings, namely the dramatic difference it made to rural children learning to read if they began in the vernacular, both dismayed her and aroused her curiosity as to its cause: that was a circumstance open to empirical enquiry.

A long-standing concern with policy process – Esther worked with the UK Department of Social Security on transmitted deprivation, and was Scientific Advisor on social services – informed her postgraduate teaching. She encouraged attention to community issues otherwise submerged in the curriculum, and to ethnographic study in Europe. Unrestricted by academic convention, indeed. As to method and rigour, she was a fierce champion of – and initiated – pre-fieldwork PhD training in the Department. A paper on apprentices concludes with penetrating questions about how anthropologists learn to study learning.

***

Esther was a pioneer. The following was written after a colloquium in her honour in 2014 [abbreviated].

> A woman before her time, Esther exemplified interdisciplinarity long before the concept became aspirational across the social sciences. She produced, without fanfare, against-the-grain accounts of Gonja parenthood and then drew out its implications for Ghanaian parents studying in England. She took the linguistic turn before the term was invented. Her attention to learning and literacy accompanied an on-the-ground commitment to children's education. Her research lived and breathed 'engaged anthropology'.

There was more. Interest in socialization, cognition, fostering and occupational roles came together in a pair of books: *From Craft to Industry*, and the prize-winning *Parenthood and Social Reproduction*. Yet she had also (she said in retrospect) been teased for years by a line of thinking that linked studies of social dynamics to fundamental questions of human evolution. Her 1975 Malinowski Lecture, innocently titled 'On Asking Questions', presaged the acclaimed *Questions and Politeness* (1978). Twenty years later, the collection *Social Intelligence and Interaction* (1995) led to a public lecture at the British Academy (1997) on the emergence of roles and rules.

What is described of her as a person – vitality, openness and wit – is as true of her writing. Out of her method came brilliance; out of brilliance, making things matter; and out of that, empathy.

***

To end. That first essay of mine. Think of Esther's dedication to learning about learning. My task was to understand Durkheim's method of demonstration, not outlining what he advocated but *using his method* to work through an imagined example. What illuminating pragmatism! She seemed to like the result, although her comments also said clearly: Try harder! Could do better!

True too today. I wish I could have captured the many expressions of love and respect that have come from those not present this afternoon. But, then, as she spoke so eloquently of interchange at the heart of language, for those who are here, I know that whatever is said you will be augmenting with your own thoughts.

As for Esther on this sad occasion, people talk of gentle guidance, of quiet professionalism, and, in the phrase of a 1970s research student, a sense of calm and confidence-imbuing purpose. I leave us with an image that this particular student still holds. A group of them were trying to make up for lack of formal doctoral training. 'In order for our meetings to be legitimate', she writes, 'Esther came and presided, NOT (in capitals) to interfere, but she came with her mending box and nodded appropriately from time to time, and occasionally interjected a comment'. It was enough that she had been there.

Marilyn Strathern, 7 February 2018

Appendix V

Esther N. Goody: Bibliography

Published Work

1962. 'Conjugal Separation and Divorce among the Gonja of Northern Ghana', in Meyer Fortes (ed.), *Marriage in Tribal Societies*. Cambridge Papers in Social Anthropology No. 3. Cambridge: Cambridge University Press, pp. 14–54.

1966. 'Fostering of Children in Ghana: A Preliminary Report'. *Ghana Journal of Sociology* 2(1): 26–33.

1970. 'Kinship Fostering in Gonja: Deprivation or Advantage?' in Philip Mayer (ed.), *Socialization: The Approach from Social Anthropology*. ASA Monographs 8. London: Tavistock Publications, pp. 51–74.
Also see 1982. In Esther N. Goody. *Parenthood and Social Reproduction: Fostering and Occupational Roles in West Africa*. Cambridge Studies in Anthropology 35. Cambridge: Cambridge University Press, pp. 37–54.

1970. 'Legitimate and Illegitimate Aggression in a West African State', in Mary Douglas (ed.), *Witchcraft: Confessions and Accusations*. ASA Monographs 9. London: Tavistock Publications, pp. 207–44.

1971. 'Forms of Pro-parenthood: The Sharing and Substitution of Parental Roles', in Jack Goody (ed.), *Kinship: Selected Readings*. Harmondsworth: Penguin Readings in Sociology, pp. 331–45.

1971. 'Varieties of Fostering'. *New Society* 5: 237–39.

1972. '"Greeting", "Begging" and the Presentation of Respect', in Jean S. La Fontaine (ed.), *The Interpretation of Ritual: Essays in Honour of A.I. Richards*. London: Tavistock Press, pp. 39–72.

1973. *Contexts of Kinship: An Essay in the Family Sociology of the Gonja of Northern Ghana*. Cambridge Studies in Social Anthropology 7. Cambridge: Cambridge University Press.

1974. 'Parental Roles in Anthropological Perspective', in *The Family in Society: Dimensions of Parenthood*. Report of a seminar held at All Souls College, Oxford, 10–13 April 1973. Department of Health and Social Security. London: HMSO, pp. 26–35.

1974. 'Introduction', in Diana Gladys Azu, *The Ga Family and Social Change*. Cambridge: African Studies Centre.

1975. 'Delegation of Parental Roles in West Africa and the West Indies', in Thomas R. Williams (ed.), *Socialization and Communication in Primary Groups*. The Hague: Mouton, pp. 447–84.

Also see 1975. In Jack Goody (ed.), *Changing Social Structure in Ghana*. London: International African Institute, pp. 137–66.

Also see 1978. In Demitri B. Shimkin, Edith M. Shimkin and Dennis A. Frate (eds), *The Extended Family in Black Societies*. The Hague: Mouton.

1978. Esther N. Goody (ed.). *Questions and Politeness: Strategies in Social Interaction*. Cambridge Papers in Social Anthropology 8. Cambridge: Cambridge University Press.

1978. 'Towards a Theory of Questions', in Esther N. Goody (ed.), *Questions and Politeness: Strategies in Social Interaction*. Cambridge: Cambridge University Press, pp. 17–43.

1978. 'Some Theoretical and Empirical Aspects of Parenthood in West Africa', in Christine Oppong et al. (eds), *Marriage, Fertility and Parenthood in West Africa*. Changing African Family Monographs No. 4. Canberra: Australian National University Press, pp. 227–72.

1982. *Parenthood and Social Reproduction: Fostering and Occupational Roles in West Africa*. Cambridge Studies in Anthropology 35. Cambridge: Cambridge University Press.

1982. 'Daboya Weavers: Relations of Production, Dependency and Reciprocity', in Esther N. Goody (ed.), *From Craft to Industry: The Ethnography of Proto-industrial Cloth Production*. Cambridge Papers in Social Anthropology 10. Cambridge: Cambridge University Press, pp. 50–84.

1982. Esther N. Goody (ed.). *From Craft to Industry: The Ethnography of Proto-industrial Cloth Production*. Cambridge Papers in Social Anthropology 10. Cambridge: Cambridge University Press.

1983. 'Family Policy in a Multi-culture Society', in Alfred White Franklin (ed.), *Family Matters: Perspectives on the Family and Social Policy*. Proceedings of the symposium on 'Priority for the Family' held at the Royal Society of Medicine, London, November 1981. Oxford: Pergamon Press, pp. 43–48.

1984. 'Parental Strategies: Calculation or Sentiment?: Fostering Practices among West Africans', in Hans Medick and David W. Sabean (eds), *Interest and Emotion: Essays on the Study of Family and Kinship*. Cambridge: Cambridge University Press and Paris: Editions de la Maison des Sciences de l'Homme, pp. 266–77.

Also see 1984. In translation in *Emotionen und Materielle Interessen*, Veröffentlichungen des Max-Planck-Instituts für Geschichte 75. Göttingen: Vandenhoeck & Ruprecht.

1984. 'Can Anthropology Contribute to Social Policy?' *RAIN* 63: 2–6.

1984. 'Introduction: The Persistence of Care Roles across Space and Time', in Lisa Gilad and Deidre Meintel (eds), *Female Migrants and the Work Force: Domestic Repercussions*. *Anthropologica* 26(2): 123–34. Toronto: University of Toronto Press for Canadian Anthropological Society.

1986. 'Why Must Might be Right? Observations on Sexual Herrschaft'. *Cambridge Journal of Anthropology* 11(3): 1–34.

Also see 1987. *Newsletter for the Laboratory of Comparative Human Cognition* 9(2): 55–75.

Also see 1991. 'Warum die Macht rechthaben muß: Bemerkungen zur Herrschaft eines Geschlechts über das andere', in Alf Lüdtke (ed.), *Herrschaft als Soziale Praxis: Historische und sozial-anthropologische Studien*. Veröffentlichungen des Max-Planck-Instituts für Geschichte 91. Göttingen: Vandenhoeck & Ruprecht.

Also see 1997. In Michael Cole, Yrjo Engeström and Olga Vasquez (eds), *Mind, Culture, and Activity: Seminal Papers from the Laboratory of Comparative Human Cognition*. Cambridge: Cambridge University Press, pp. 432–72.

1989. 'Learning, Apprenticeship and the Division of Labour', in Michael W. Coy (ed.), *Apprenticeship: From Theory to Method and Back Again.* Albany: State University of New York Press, pp. 233–56.

1991. 'The Learning of Prosocial Behaviour in Small-Scale Egalitarian Societies: An Anthropological View', in Robert A. Hinde and Jo Groebbel (eds), *Cooperation and Prosocial Behaviour.* Cambridge: Cambridge University Press, pp. 106–28.

1991. 'Rural Diversification in Africa: Comments on the FAO Conference on Population, Agriculture and Rural Development, Rome 1987.' *Cambridge Journal of Anthropology* 15(3): 53–62.

1993. 'Informal Learning of Adult Roles in Baale', in Michèle Fiéloux and Jacques Lombard (eds), with Jeanne-Marie Kambou-Ferrand, *Images d'Afrique et Sciences Sociales: Les Pays Lobi, Birifor et Dagara (Burkina Faso, Côte d'Ivoire et Ghana).* Paris: Karthala-Orstom, pp. 482–91.

1995. Esther N. Goody (ed.). *Social Intelligence and Interaction: Expressions and Implications of the Social Bias in Human Intelligence.* Cambridge: Cambridge University Press.

1995. Study team contributor in Richard Kraft et al., *A Tale of Two Ghanas: The View from the Classroom.* Accra, Ghana: Ministry of Education.

1995. 'Social Intelligence and Prayer as Dialogue', in Esther N. Goody (ed.), *Social Intelligence and Interaction: Expressions and Implications of the Social Bias in Human Intelligence.* Cambridge: Cambridge University Press, pp. 206–20.

1997. 'Social Intelligence and Language: Another Rubicon?', in Andrew Whiten and Richard W. Byrne (eds), *Machiavellian Intelligence II: Extensions and Evaluations.* Cambridge: Cambridge University Press, pp. 364–96.

1998. 'Social Intelligence and the Emergence of Roles and Rules'. Radcliffe-Brown Lecture in Social Anthropology. *Proceedings of the British Academy 97.* London: The British Academy, pp. 119–47. Retrieved 20 October 2024 from https://www.thebritishacademy.ac.uk/documents/2460/97p119.pdf.

1999. 'Sharing and Transferring Components of Parenthood: The West African Case', in Mireille Corbier (ed.), *Adoption et Fosterage.* Collection De L'Archéologie à L'Histoire. Paris: De Boccard, pp. 370–88.

2001. 'The Social Anthropology of Craft Production', in Neil J. Smelser and Paul B. Baltes (eds), *International Encyclopedia of Social and Behavioral Sciences.* Amsterdam: Elsevier, pp. 2883–88.

2002. 'The Roles of Knowledge and Policy in Contributions of Research on Education to Development: Observations on Social Anthropological Research for the 21st Century.' Keynote address to 1997 Pan-African Association of Anthropologists. *Cambridge Journal of Anthropology* 23(1): 1–19.

2003. 'Foreword', in Marie Chatry-Komarek, *Literacy at Stake: Teaching Reading and Writing in African Schools.* Windhoek, Namibia: Gamsberg Macmillan.

2006. 'Dynamics of the Emergence of Sociocultural Institutional Practices', in David R. Olson and Michael Cole (eds), *Technology, Literacy and the Evolution of Society: Implications of the Work of Jack Goody.* Mahwah, NJ: Laurence Erlbaum, pp. 241–64.

2010. 'On Mechanisms of the Emergence of Systematic Sociocultural Variation: Some Comments on Nettle's "Beyond Nature versus Culture"'. Comment Article. *Journal of the Royal Anthropological Institute* 16(1): 155–57.

2012. 'Co-operation and the Origins of Spoken Language'. Review Article. *Journal of the Royal Anthropological Institute* 18(2): 461–65.

2013. 'A Framework for the Analysis of Parent Roles', in Erdmute Alber, Jeanett Martin and Catrien Notermans (eds), *Child Fostering in West Africa: New Perspectives on Theory and Practices*. Leiden and Boston: Brill, pp. 23–60.

2019. 'About the Curious Power of Dialogue', in David Shankland (ed.), *Dunbar's Number*. Occasional Paper No. 45 of the Royal Anthropological Institute. London: Sean Kingston Publishing, pp. 125–35.

Goody, Esther N., and JoAnne Bennett. 2001. 'Literacy for Gonja and Birifor Children in Northern Ghana', in David R. Olson and Nancy Torrance (eds), *The Making of Literate Societies*. Oxford: Blackwell Publishers Ltd, pp. 178–200.

Goody, Esther N., and Jack Goody. 1992. 'Creating a Text: Alternative Interpretations of Gonja Drum History'. *Africa* 62(2): 266–70.

Goody, Esther N., and Jack Goody. 1996. 'The Naked and the Clothed', in John Hunwick and Nancy Lawler (eds), *The Cloth of Many Coloured Silks: Papers on History and Society, Ghanaian and Islamic, in honour of Ivor Wilks*. Evanston, IL: Northwestern University Press, pp. 67–89.

Goody, Esther N., and Christine Muir Groothues. 1977. 'The West Africans: The Quest for Education', in James L. Watson (ed.), *Between Two Cultures: Migrants and Minorities in Britain*. Oxford: Basil Blackwell, pp. 151–80.

Also see 1982. In Esther N. Goody, *Parenthood and Social Reproduction: Fostering and Occupational Roles in West Africa*. Cambridge Studies in Anthropology 35. Cambridge: Cambridge University Press, pp. 217–33.

Goody, Esther N., and Christine Muir Groothues. 1979. 'Stress in Marriage: West African Couples in London', in Verity Saifullah Khan (ed.), *Minority Families in Britain: Support and Stress*. Studies in Ethnicity No. 2. London: Macmillan, pp. 59–88.

Goody, Jack, and Esther N. Goody. 1966. 'Cross-Cousin Marriage in Northern Ghana'. *Man* 1(3): 343–55.

Also see 1969. In Jack Goody (ed.), *Comparative Studies of Kinship*. Stanford, CA: Stanford University Press, pp. 216–34.

Goody, Jack, and Esther N. Goody. 1967. 'The Circulation of Women and Children in Northern Ghana'. *Man* 2(2): 226–48.

Also see 1969. In Jack Goody (ed.), *Comparative Studies of Kinship*. Stanford, CA: Stanford University Press, pp. 184–215.

Also see 1982. In Esther N. Goody, *Parenthood and Social Reproduction: Fostering and Occupational Roles in West Africa*. Cambridge Studies in Anthropology 35. Cambridge: Cambridge University Press, pp. 91–109.

Goody, Jack, and Esther N. Goody. 1990. 'Marriage and the Family in Gujarat', in Jack Goody, *The Oriental, the Ancient and the Primitive: Systems of Marriage and the Family in the Pre-industrial Societies of Eurasia*. Cambridge: Cambridge University Press, pp. 160–78.

Goody, Jack, and Esther N. Goody. 1995. 'Food and Identities: Changing Patterns of Consumption in Ghana'. *Cambridge Journal of Anthropology* 18(3): 1–14.

Muir Christine L., and Esther N. Goody. 1972. 'Student Parents: West African Families in London'. *Race* 13: 329–36.

Unpublished Work

1961. 'Kinship, Marriage and the Developmental Cycle among the Gonja of Northern Ghana'. PhD thesis, University of Cambridge. Archived at Cambridge University Library.

1970. 'The Kpembe Study: A Comparison of Fostered and Non-fostered Children in Eastern Gonja'. Manuscript report. Archived at Social Science Research Council Archives, London; The Haddon Library, University of Cambridge; Esther Newcomb Goody Archive, Centre of African Studies, Cambridge University.

1971. 'Education Without Schools: The Fostering of Children in West Africa'. Haddon Library, Cambridge University.

1975. 'On Asking Questions'. Malinowski Memorial Lecture at the London School of Economics and Political Science, delivered 4 March 1975.

1976. 'Why is "Black is Beautiful"?'. Commissioned paper for the DHSS/SSRC Joint Working Party on Transmitted Deprivation.

1981. 'Time, the Division of Labour, and the Composition of the Production Unit in West Africa'. The Haddon Library, Cambridge University: Xerox.

1984. 'Marriage of Close Kin in Ethnic Minorities in the United Kingdom'. Evidence submitted to commission on revision of laws concerning close marriage.

1992. 'Modelling, Work and Play in the Situational Scaffolding of Adult Role Skills in Northern Ghana'. *Apprenticeship* symposium. American Anthropological Association, San Francisco. Esther Newcomb Goody Archive, Centre of African Studies, Cambridge University.

1994. 'Authority and Learning in Northern Ghana. Phase II: Authority and Learning in Primary Schools. Report on First Year (July 1993–June 1994)'. Report for Economic and Social Research Council, UK. Esther Newcomb Goody Archive, Centre of African Studies, Cambridge University.

1996. 'Authority and Learning in Northern Ghana'. End of Award Report for Economic and Social Research Council, UK. Esther Newcomb Goody Archive, Centre of African Studies, Cambridge University.

1996. 'Modelling, Play and Responsible Practice: The Learning of Adult Role Skills in Baale'. Conference on *Culture and the Uses of the Body*. Fyssen Foundation, Paris.

1997. 'Authority and Effective Learning in Northern Ghana, Spencer Foundation First Annual Report: October 1996–September 1997'. Esther Newcomb Goody Archive, Centre of African Studies, Cambridge University.

1998. 'Authority and Effective Learning in Northern Ghana, Spencer Foundation Second Annual Report: October 1997–September 1998'. Esther Newcomb Goody Archive, Centre of African Studies, Cambridge University.

1998. 'English Reading Comprehension in Primary Class 3: Factors in Effective Learning in Northern Ghana'. Report to Deputy Director General of Education, Government Education Service, Accra, Ghana.

1998. 'Improving English Reading Comprehension by First Learning to Read in Ghanaian Language: Gender and Urban/Rural Variables'. Report to Director General of Education, Government Education Service, Accra, Ghana.

Ca. 2005. Draft Report, Grant number R000239984. Penultimate Year of Award Report to the Economic and Social Research Council, UK. Esther Newcomb Goody Archive, Centre of African Studies, Cambridge University.

2006. 'Effects of Hierarchical and Egalitarian Modes of Teaching and Learning in Northern Ghana'. Grant number R000239984. End of Award Report to the

Economic and Social Research Council, UK. Esther Newcomb Goody Archive, Centre of African Studies, Cambridge University.

2009. 'The Role of Dialogue in Building Understanding in the Classroom'. Grant number 200700080. End of Award Report for the Spencer Foundation, Chicago, USA. Esther Newcomb Goody Archive, Centre of African Studies, Cambridge University.

2010. 'Memorandum from Dr Esther Goody, "Local Languages Initial Literacy" Research'. Bole, Northern Region, 18 April 2010. Esther Newcomb Goody Archive, Centre of African Studies, Cambridge University.

2011. 'Where Might GES Literacy Teaching Go After NALAP?' Unpublished report. Esther Newcomb Goody Archive, Centre of African Studies, Cambridge University.

Goody, Esther N., and Christine L. Muir. 1972. 'Report on SSRC-funded Study of West African Families in London'. Manuscript report. Social Science Research Council Archives. London: Mimeo.

Muir Christine L., and Esther N. Goody. ca. 1971. 'Preliminary Report of a Survey of West African Families in London'. Manuscript report. Social Science Research Council Archives, London: Mimeo.

Muir Christine L., and Esther N. Goody. 1972. 'Factors Related to the Delegation of Parental Roles among West Africans in London'. Manuscript report. Social Science Research Council Archives, London: Mimeo.

Index

A

abstraction
  in maths learning, 165
  levels of, 163
accountability (ethnomethodology), 196
accusations, of injury, Gonja, 54
acephalous
  Birifor, 28, 133
  Konkomba, 130
adoption
  Iñupiaq, 71
  Ottoman, 81–2
aggression, legitimate and illegitimate, 53, 54, 62
Aizley, Harlyn, 70–2
Akan, Ghanaian language, 227
Alaska
  Division of Youth Services, 39 n. 13, 40 n. 24
  See also Iñupiaq, Iñupiat
algorithm, algorithmic, 142, 157–8, 162, 164
Amedzofe, Ghana, 104–8, 110, 113
angel babies, 72
anthropology in the community, 14, 27–8, 282
apostasy, 84–5, 87
apprentice weavers, Gonja, 123
apprenticeship
  'apprentice fosterage', 15
  changing patterns, 15
  continuity and change in a migrant community, 23
  fluid family dynamics, 15
  institutionalized fostering, 14–5

learning to weave, 15–18
milking chores as, 140–1, 160
'school fosterage', 20
  See also questions
archive, the, 74
ARTs. See Assisted Reproductive Technologies
Assisted Reproductive Technologies, 71
Austen, Jane, 59
autotelic, school maths, 159
Avatime, Ghana, 104–11, 113–4
  childcare arrangements, 9
  globalized kinship relations, 9, 37

B

Baale, Birifor village, Ghana, 133–6, 223–4, 233–4
baamsi, musicians at court, Mamprusi, 172, 182–4
Baer, Mark David, 86
Bennett, JoAnne, 29
Berlin workshop. See Implications of a Social Origin of Human Intelligence workshop
bilateral kinship structure, 8, 55, 244
biology vs. 'biology', 71
Birifor, Ghana, 28–9, 43 n. 60, 122–3, 126, 133, 136, 222–4, 233–4
  acephalous, 28
Bodenhorn, Barbara, 9, 11, 36, 39 n. 13
Bole district, Ghana, 222–4, 230, 234, 230
  Damba festival, 6–7, 21
Brown, Penelope, 25, 29, 33, 38, 197
Bruner, Jerome S., 18, 253

Brydon, Lynne, 37
BTL, Breakthrough to Literacy programme, 230
'Burying SM' case, 191
Byrne, Richard W., 26

C
Cambridge University
    Centre for Family Research, 67
    Department of Social Anthropology, 67
    Esther Newcomb Goody Archive, 43 n. 67
Carrithers, Michael, 25
Casillas, Marisa, 29, 33, 38
Chatry-Komarek, Magdeleine (Marie), 42 n. 55, 58 and 59, 224
child labour, cocoa industry, 112–3
child play
    division of labour, Konkomba, 131–3
    rituals, Konkomba, 133
    See also informal transmission of knowledge
'child-levy', Ottoman, 9, 37. *See also* devshirme
child-rearing practices and beliefs, Rossel Island, 204–5
childcare, communal nature, Rossel Island, 206–7
circulation in time and space, 5–9
    circulation, hierch vs aceph, 8
    circulation of women, Gonja, 5–8
    fluid childcare arrangements, Avatime (*see* L. Brydon, this volume)
    fragmentable nature of parenthood and childhood (*see* B. Bodenhorn, this volume) mobile kinship strategies, 8
    See also P. Sant Cassia, this volume
classroom
    classroom materials in different language, 34
    dynamics, reflection of larger social ethos, 32
    interaction, 'egalitarian' communities, 32
    interaction hierarchical communities, 32
    learning, relation to modes of authority, 34
Climbié, Victoria, 113
closeness and distance, English ideas of, 56–8
cohesiveness, types of, 161–2
Cole, Michael, 124. *See also* zone of proximal development

collection
    as commemorative practice, 72
    memorialization, 73
Colombia. *See* San Juan, El Cauca, Colombia, 140–1, 144, 149, 159, 163
communication
    role of speech in relation to human sociality, 36
    as a social process, 24–6
    See also drumming, evolution, non-speech modes (prayer, song), social intelligence, speech
competence and performance in Vygotsky, 124
conception, intimate, 70–1
conjugal relations
    England, 58–9, 61–2
    Gonja, 51, 54–6
consumption, 70
Cooley, Charles, 238
Cortés, Hernán, 68
Craven, Anna, 10
Crete, 81, 83, 85, 89–90, 92, 95–6, 98
CRT. *See* Criterion Referenced Test, 226
'crypto-Christianity', 90, 92–3
curriculum
    domestically-based and school-based, 140
    milking, 160
CWCNG. *See* E.N. Goody, 'The Circulation of Women and Children in Northern Ghana'
Cyprus, 81, 85–7, 89–93, 97–8

D
Daboya, Ghana, 15–6, 19
    strip-woven cloth, 19
    weaving industry, 15, 23
Dagaari, Ghanaian language, 223
Dagbani, Ghanaian language, 227, 232, 234
Damma ritual, Mamprusi, 177–8, 180–2, 184
    asuba morning performance, 177–8
    greetings, 178–9
    night-time performance, 182
    noon performance, 179–80
    twilight performance, 180–2
Davidoff, Leonore, 60, 64 n. 13, 15–6 and 19
desire, natural vs. 'natural', 71
devshirme, 80, 82, 85, 93

DHSS, Department of Health and Social
  Security, UK, 14, 40 n. 26
divorce
  Gonja, 54–5
divorce, Ottoman, 81, 84, 86–91, 95, 97–8
  and remarriage, 81, 87–8, 90, 95
Dollard, John, 238
domestic roles, Gonja, 52, 54
domestic violence against women, 23
Douglas, Mary, 265
Drucker Brown, Susan, 37, 262
drum, drummers
  'deep' history, Gonja, 20
  as form of communication, 20
  Mamprusi, 20, 37
drummers, Mamprusi
  advice and praise to the king, 173
  core narrative, 171
  court occasions, 173
  paid, 173
  translation from drumbeats to names, 171–2
  See also lunaba, lunga, lungsi, naamyuya
Du Bois, W.E.B., 237
Dunbar, Robin, 252
Durkheim, Émile, 197

E
Esch, Edith, 25, 41 n. 41
Etsey, Felicia Kafui, 3, 30, 32, 38, 42 n. 58 and
  59
Evans-Pritchard, Edward E., 239
evolution
  dialogue and evolutionary cognitive shifts,
    34, 36, 252
  emergence of 'roles and rules', 26
  See also intelligence, language
Ewe (Ga), lingua franca, Ghana and Togo,
    111, 227, 230, 234

F
family relations
  generated through assisted reproductive
    technologies, 71
  ghostly fathers, 71
  modern vs. traditional model, challenged, 9
  See also siblings
female conversions, Ottoman, 88, 90, 92,
    95–8
feminist critiques, 51
Fentiman, Alicia, 29, 37

Filippucci, Paola, 39 n. 3
Firth, Raymond, 57–8, 64 n. 12
Foley, William
  influence on E.N. Goody, 27
  See also Conversational Analysis
Fortes, Meyer, 3, 104, 189, 238–9, 256
  archive, 170
  commitment to accurate ethnography and
    documentation, 5, 37
  developmental cycle of domestic groups, 5
  female-headed households, 5
  influence on E.N. Goody, 26
  social analysis and recognition of flux, 14
fostering, fosterage
  Christian missionaries, by, 109
  Ghanaian children, by British families, 111
  Gonja, 52
  as good parenting, 13
  instrumental, Avatime, 108
  Iñupiaq, 66
  kin, Amedzofe, 106
  older women, by, Amedzofe, 108
  Ottoman, 80–4, 91–5, 97
  psychological consequences for children
    (*see* Kpembe Study purposive, Gonja,
    12)
  and reciprocity, 12
  for school, 20
  See also apprenticeship, Gonja,
    performativity of parenting, West
    Africa, West Indian
FPP. *See* E.N. Goody, 'Forms of Pro-
  Parenthood'
fragments, fragmentation
  of intimate knowledge, 67–8, 75
  of maths learning, 150
  of milking learning, 158
Freud, Sigmund, 199
Fukushima Daichii, 67
funerals, Mambila
  dancing (*see suàgà* songs)
  tensions, linguistic expression, 195–7
  tensions, traditional vs. Christian and
    Muslim, 192–3
  traditional, 191–3

G
Galton, Francis, 64 n. 10
Gellner, Ernest, 262
gender identity, 62

GES, Ghana Education Service, 222, 230,
    232–3
gesture, human, 25, 252
Gonja, Ghana, 122, 123, 137, 222–3, 230
    drum history, 20
    fluidity of kinship residence patterns, 5–8
    fostered and non-fostered children, 9
    greeting rituals, 25
    hierarchical, 28
    informal learning, 28–9
    kinship, 8
    purposive fosterage, 12
    transmission of weaving skills, 15
Good, David, 25, 26
Goody, Esther Newcomb, 80–84, 87, 93, 98
    'About the Curious Power of Dialogue', 36
    anthropology and social policy, 9, 14
    anthropology in the community, 14
    app. I, emergence of roles and rules, 247–9
    app. I, emergence of sociocultural
        institutional practices, 248–51
    app. I, on dialogue, 252–3
    app. I, on puzzles and research, 243–4,
        246–7, 252
    app. I, on questions, 244–6
    app. I, on witchcraft, 245–6
    app. I, sociocultural stable strategies,
        249–51
    'Authority and Learning in Northern
        Ghana' project, 122
    biography, 1–3
    Cambridge colleges affiliation, 3, 39 n. 3
    'Can Anthropology Contribute to Social
        Policy?', 14
    on children, social roles, and language, 200
    Contexts of Kinship, 5
    'Creating a Text: Alternative
        Interpretations of Gonja Drum History',
        with J. Goody, 20
    'Delegation of Parental Roles in West
        Africa and the West Indies', 12–3, 39 n.
        17, 40 n. 24
    doctoral dissertation, 5
    economic anthropology, 239
    Esther Newcomb Goody Archive, 43 n. 67
    fieldwork, Gujarati, India and Leicester,
        UK, 23
    'Forms of Pro-Parenthood', 11, 66, 80–1
    From Craft to Industry, 23

'Herrschaft and Social Praxis', 23
    ‘ Legitimate and illegitimate aggression in a
        West African state', 53, 256
    Malinowski Memorial Lecture, 18–20, 245
    Marriage in Tribal Societies, 256
    member of government organizations, 40
        n. 26
    on mystical power, 62
    on negative relations, 52
    'On Asking Questions', 18
    Parenthood and Social Reproduction, 10,
        23, 39 n. 12, 41 n. 36
    'Parenthood in Africa after E.N. Goody'
        conference, 14, 40 n. 25
    performativity of kinship, 5–8
    pro-sociality processes, 216
    promoting mother-tongue literacy, 222
    Questions and Politeness, 217
    Radcliffe-Brown Lecture, 26
    Reader in Social Cognition, 3
    relational idioms, relationship of, 54, 244
    research methods, 5, 11, 14
    Social Intelligence and Interaction, 25
    Spencer Foundation report, 33
    supervisor of L. Brydon, A. Fentiman, M.
        Strathern, 114, 137, 63
    'The Circulation of Women and Children
        in Northern Ghana', with J. Goody, 8,
        79, 84, 104
    The Making of Literate Societies, 123
    'The Quest for Education', with C. Muir
        Groothues, 13
    'The Roles of Knowledge and Policy in
        Contributions of Research on Education
        to Development', 27
    'Towards a Theory of Questions', 123, 171,
        189, 197
    Tributes, 269–83
    'Where Might GES Literacy Teaching Go
        after NALAP?', 32, 222
    See also interdisciplinarity
Goody, Jack, 80, 84, 87, 238, 262–3, 265
    co-authored works. *See under* Esther
        Newcomb Goody
    E.N. Goody married to, 3
    E.N. Goody's supervisor, 3
GTZ, German Agency for International
    Cooperation, 224, 227–8, 231
Groothues, Christine. *See* Muir, Christine

Gujarati, Leicester, UK, 22–3, 41 n. 34 and 35
Gumperz, John, 41 n. 42

H
Hart, John Keith, 38
historical pawnage, Ghana, 109
Ho district, Ghana, 230
Hoelgaard, Suzanne, 258–65
Holocaust, commemorating, 37, 66, 73, 74, 75
households, moving between, Gonja, 52
Howell, Signe, 82
Humphrey, Nicholas, 25
husbands and wives. *See* wives
Hymes, Dell, 41 n. 42

I
Ilyagiit (additions, kin), 71
Implications of a Social Origin of Human Intelligence workshop, Berlin, 24–5
incest, in English kinship, 61
informal transmission of knowledge hierarchy and authority, 122
intelligence
    dialogic negotiations of meaning, 26
    'Machiavellian intelligence', 26
    See also social intelligence
interaction with children, Rossel Island
    autonomy, 209–13
    child-centred vs. situation-centred, 217
    interactional engine, 217
    small delicts, 213–6
    style, 205–6
interaction with children, Tzeltal Maya, Tenejapa, Mexico, 217
interdisciplinarity, 27
    E.N. Goody´s work with sociolinguists, developmental psychologists, and educators, 1 sociolinguistics, 5, 11
    use of social and cognitive psychology, 5, 11
    See also Berlin workshop
intimacy, intimacies, intimate, 58–61
    animated, 70, 72, 75
    as an analytic, 68
    conception, 70–1
    at a distance, 75
    as a function of network, 69
    immanent dependencies, Povinelli's, 69

intimus, 68
    and kinship, 67
    obligation, 70, 72
    techno-, 70
    unwanted, 67, 72
    vulnerability, 70, 72
irony, Tzeltal women, 25

J
James, C.L.R., 239
Janissaries, 83–5, 90, 94, 96

K
Kant, Immanuel, 239–40
kepin. See kiambin kiambin, 91, 98
king's installation, Mamprusi, 182–4
    Baamyo, leading singer, 171, 182
    text interpretation, 183–4
    text transcription, 186–7
kinned, feeling, 67
kinship, 67, 71, 74
    English, 56–7
    fragmenting and reassembling, 67–8
    Gonja, 52, 55–6
    and intimacy, 67
    Iñupiat, 77 n. 18
    systems, 51, 53
knowledge
    made visible, 67
    partial nature of, 68
    transmission, 14–23
    transmission, formal and informal methods, 28–9
    See also apprenticeship, learning, questions, teaching
Komarek, Kurt, 42 n. 55 and 59, 224
Komarek, Magdeleine (Marie). *See* Chantry-Komarek
Konkomba, Ghana, 8, 23, 28–9, 37, 43 n. 60, 122–6, 130–3, 135–7
    Acephalous, 28
    children and young adults carrying sand, photograph, 127
    women and children peeling cassava, photograph, 129
    See also A. Fentiman, this volume
Kraft national survey, Ghana, 29
Kraft, Richard, 29–30, 225–6, 228, 230
Kuper, Adam, 58–9, 61, 64 n. 9–11

L
La Fontaine, Jean, 39 n. 6
language
    dependent on, and producer of social
        interaction, 25
    'language wars', 30, 38
    proto-language as tool for cooperation, 26
    role of language in human evolution, 25
    See also Berlin workshop, F.K. Etsey this
        volume, social intelligence
language socialization, 199–200
    cultural variation, 200
    and developmental and cognitive
        psychology, psychological anthropology,
        and psycholinguistics, 200
Laserna, Catalina, 29, 33, 37
Lave, Jean, 23
Layne, Linda, 67, 70–2, 74–5, 77 n. 14, 15
    and 17
Leach, Edmund, 256
learning
    in acephalous communities, 28–9
    adult roles skills in a small preliterate
        society, 133
    to become a woman, Konkomba, 131
    to become a woman, San Juan, 144
    craft skills, Gujarat, India, 23
    egalitarian setting advantage over
        hierarchical, 32
    in hierarchical communities, 29
    to hoe, boy, Birifor, 133–5
    informal (*see* A. Fentiman this volume)
    informal and formal, 142
    informal and formal (*see* C. Laserna this
        volume)
    informal 'no fail' vs. formal 'most fail', 33
    in a mother tongue, 30, 33, 34
    numeracy, informal vs. formal, 33
    prosocial skills (*see* P. Brown and M.
        Casillas, this volume)
    same-script vs. assembly-line, 143
    skills, Konkomba, 130
    as a social process, 24
    Vygotskian, 142
    See also classroom, F.K. Etsey, this volume
Leicester, 23, 41 n. 35
Levinson, Stephen C., 25, 197, 201, 217
Lewis, Gilbert, 265–6

LLIL, Local Languages Initial Literacy
    project, 30, 32, 223–5, 229, 232
Locke, John, 236
LOI, Language of Instruction, 232
LoWiili, Ghana, 8, 63
Luckmann, Thomas, 25
lunaba, chief drummer, Mamprusi, 171
lunga, lungsi, drums and drummers,
    Mamprusi, 171
collective memory, 185

M
Magilow, David, 72–4
male conversions, Ottoman, 81, 85–98
Malinowski Memorial Lecture, 18–20
Malinowski, Bronislaw, 199, 256
Malintzin (also Malinche), 68
Mambila, Cameroon and Nigeria, 20, 37, 190
Mamprusi, 20, 37
    drummers performances and genealogy,
        171, 184–6
    performer, musician and drummer,
        photograph, 178
    royal succession, 176
    See also ayiiri, naam, solima, yuri, yuya
marriage
    close, England, 62–3, 64 n. 16
    as a contract, Gonja, 52
    repeated, Gonja, 55
materiality
    thing/person boundary, 67–8, 75
Mead, G.H., 238
Mead, Margaret, 199
milking
    boy helps mother make cheese,
        photograph, 144
    and maths, differences, 162–7
    and maths, similarities, 142
    undivided social space, 144–5
minga, community labour, San Juan,
    photograph, 149
mixed marriages and intermarriages,
    Ottoman, 80–1, 85, 87–97, 98
Moctezuma, 68
MOEYS, Ministry of Education, Youth and
    Sports, Ghana, 230
Molteno Project, 229–31
mother-tongue literacy instruction, 30–32, 42
    n. 55, 223–4. *See also* LLIL

Muir, Christine, also Christine Muir
Groothues, 6, 12, 13

N
Na Gbewa, founding king, Mamprusi, 171,
177, 181, 183
naam, trascendental element, Mamprusi, 171
naamyuya, performance, Mamprusi, 173
Nadel, S.F., 247, 249, 251–3
Nahua, 68
NALAP, National Literacy Accelerated
Programme, 32, 42 n. 58 and 59, 222,
229, 231–2
names, Iñupiaq, 74–5
Nayiiri, king, Mamprusi, 171
court, by S. Drucker Brown, etching, 185
Newcomb, Mary (née Shipherd), 1
Newcomb, Theodore, 1, 238
Newton, Huey, 238
Nzema, Ghanaian language, 227, 234

O
Ochs, Elinor, 199
Olson, David R., 24
Osages, 69
Overseas Development Administration, 34

P
Paper Clips
video documentary, 66, 73
paperclips
as agentive and productive, 74
as controversial tool, 73–4
as symbol, 73
See also Paper Clips
parenthood, parenting, 9–14, 39, 40 n. 25, 41,
70, 77
fracturability, of, 11–12
as cluster of responsibilities, 77 n. 17
Patel, Geeta, 70
peer-role playing, 28–9. *See also* A. Fentiman,
this volume
Peirce, Leslie, 82–3
performativity of kinship. *See* circulation
in time and space, performativity of
parenting. *See also* M. Strathern, this
volume
performativity of parenting, 9–14
equal achievements, fostered and non-
fostered children, 11

fostering strategies, Ghana, 10
Kpembe Study, 9–11, 14
Perry, Ruth, 61, 64 n. 17
persons, personhood
partible, 67
partible, Iñupiaq, 74–5
Piaget, Jean, 199
play-cooking, girls, Birifor, 134–6
PNG, Papua New Guinea
politeness, 20, 25, 37, 41
theory, 197
Pontali wura (chief), 19
Povinelli, Elizabeth, 69, 72
power, mystical, Gonja, 55
prayer, 93, 179, 191–3, 195–6
pro-parenthood, 66, 80, 82–84, 100
property settlement, England, 58
prosociality, Rossel Island, 29

Q
questions
avoidance, 18
claim to authority, 18
as 'control valence', 18
in maths lessons, 152, 155
meaning, relative status of participants,
123
and power, 141
and social relations, 18
See also teaching

R
Radcliffe-Brown, A.R., 238
joking relations, influence on E.N. Goody,
26, 247–8
lecture, 26
reassembly, reassembling, 67, 71
reincarnation, Iñupiaq, 75
relations, relational
kinsfolk and social, England, 57
positive and negative, 52–6
positive tenor of, 53
positivism, 57
relationship
involving rupture and alliance, 76 n. 4
relationship fashioning, 68
relationship-making, 67
Richards, Audrey, 256
Rivers, William, 238

Rosaldo, Michelle, 36
Rossel Island, Papua New Guinea, 29, 33, 201–4
  Church and other institutions, 202
  demographics, 203–4
  gender-differentiated roles, 203
  kinship, 201

S
Sahlins, Marshall, 53, 63 n. 3
Sant Cassia, Paul, 37
scaffolding, 18, 29, 142–3
  Konkomba and Birifor, 136
  maths learning, 151
  See also P. Brown and M. Casillas, and C. Laserna, this volume
Schieffelin, Bambi B., 199
sentiment, England, 58–9
separation, Gonja, 54, 55, 57
sharia, 87–8, 91, 98
siblings
  England, 59–62
  Gonja, 52, 54, 56, 58
Simmel, Georg, 237
Sioux, 69
sisters and brothers. *See* siblings
skull cult of the chief, Mambila, 193–4
social intelligence
  AIP, anticipatory interactive planning, 25–6
  language, both cognitive and social, 24
  social contexts enable human intelligence, 25
  as a social process, 24
  See also evolution, language and communication Social Science Research Council, UK, 9
solima, proverbial names, Mamprusi, 175
Somié, Cameroon, 190
  religious composition, 190
song, 133, 171, 175, 203, 212–3, 237. *See also sùàgà* songs South Tongu district, Ghana, 230
speech, 25, 36–7, 75, 141, 170–2, 195
  LASS, language acquisition support system, 253
  patterns of continuous mutual coordination, 25

See also Implications of a Social Origin of Human Intelligence workshop
sperm, 70, 71
  donor, 71, 75
  ghostly, 67
Strathern, Marilyn, 8, 9, 36, 39 n. 3, 40 n. 27, 262
surveyability, 160
sùàgà songs, funeral dancing, Mambila, 191–6

T
tabula rasa fallacy, 167–8
Tallensi, Ghana, 8
TATs, Thematic Apperception Tests, 11
  test figure, drawing, 10
  See also interdisciplinary teaching
  formal education, Ghana, 29–30
  implicit vs. explicit, 18
  language barrier, Ghana, 30
  politics in decision making, 30, 32
  See also classroom, learning
technology, technologies, 67–8, 70–1
temporary marriages, Ottoman. *See kiambin*
termination of marriage. *See* divorce
theory of interaction, 36
Thomas, W.I., 238
Togo, Togolese, 111
TTE, Transition to English programme, 233

U
uncanny, the, 70–1
UNESCO, 223
University of Michigan, Ann Arbor, 3, 238
USAID, US Agency for International Development, 43 n. 64, 226, 230–2

V
video
  as research tool, 28–9, 32, 126, 137, 200
  See Paper Clips
Volta, region and river, 104, 106, 109
Vygotsky, Lev, 18, 29, 124
  zone of proximal development, 18

W
Wala, Ghana, 28, 223
  hierarchical, 28
  informal learning, 29

West Africa, West African
  kinned relationships, 15
  parents fostering, London, 12–3
  situated learning, 23
West Gonja district, Ghana, 230
West Indies, 13
  fostering, 40 n. 21
Weston, Kath, 67, 70, 72–3, 76
Whiten, Andrew, 26
Whitwell, Tennessee, US, 73, 74, 75
witchcraft, Gonja, 53–55, 257
wives
  Gonja, 54–6

residence of, at marriage, 52
  from, to sisters, 51
World Bank, 34

Y
yuri, yuya, names of kings and royal chiefs,
  Mamprusi, 171, 173–4
Yélî Dnye, Papuan language, 201, 203

Z
Zeitlyn, David, 20, 37
zone of proximal development, 18, 41 n.30,
  124, 161

www.ingramcontent.com/pod-product-compliance
Lightning Source LLC
LaVergne TN
LVHW021602060925

820435LV00004B/54